International Organisation

International Organisation

A Conceptual Approach

edited by
Paul Taylor and A. J. R. Groom

Frances Pinter Ltd. London
Nichols Publishing Company, New York

Copyright © Paul Taylor, A.J.R. Groom 1978

First Published in Great Britain in 1978 by
Frances Pinter (Publishers) Limited
161 West End Lane London NW6 2LG

Printed in Great Britain by
A. Wheaton & Co. Ltd., Exeter

ISBN 0 903804 22 0

Published in the U.S.A. in 1978 by
Nichols Publishing Company
Post Office Box 96
New York, N.Y. 10024

International Organisation

Bibliography: p
includes index.
1. International agencies.   1. Taylor, Paul Graham.
2. Groom, A.J.R.
JX1995.154   341.2   77-13731
ISBN 0-89397-025-5

CONTENTS

PREFACE

This volume is intended to cover the range of concepts and ideas about international organisation which are prominent in the 1970s. The editors, both teachers of international organisation in the University of London, have been impressed by the difficulty of finding a single volume which brought together most of these concepts and which arranged them in a coherent and accessible form. Although the following chapters do not cover all aspects of contemporary international organisation theory, they describe the broad features of the terrain, and attempt to convey an impression of the overall picture. In the second part an attempt has been made to sketch an overall typology, which is explained in the first chapter of that section and which covers various aspects of international organisation and international integration.

The first and third sections form a prelude and an epilogue to this typology. They include an account of the evolution, and a description of the range of international organisation, a consideration of international institutions as actors, and, in part three, a number of essays on perspectives of international organisation. Each chapter is complete in itself, the first chapters in Parts One and Two are intended to provide a framework for the subsequent chapters. The final chapter attempts to point to new perspectives.

We are most grateful to our contributors for the splendid co-operation which they have given us. We are also grateful to Mrs. E. Mitrany for allowing us to dedicate this volume as a tribute to the life and work of her husband Professor David Mitrany, who contributed so much to the study of international organisation. Finally we should like to thank Mrs. Muriel Walker, Mrs. Diane Austin, Miss Hilary Parker and Miss Angela Kaufman, for their unstinting secretarial assistance.

London September 1977   P.G.T.
                                                           A.J.R.G.

PART ONE

CHAPTER ONE

THE ADVENT OF INTERNATIONAL INSTITUTIONS
A.J.R. Groom

The focus of this book is on modes of organisation and not on particular institutions. The approach is conceptual rather than empirical. However, this chapter will touch upon the historical and philosophical background of attempts to organise European and, later, world society and the bodies to which such attempts have given rise. It will concentrate more on the embryonic period of organisation than on its contemporary maturity since that, after all, is the subject of the rest of the volume.

The Study of International Organisation and Institutions
Why should international organisation be studied? Students of social science are committed to the quest for an empirical theory of behaviour. They assume that behaviour is patterned and that hypotheses can be formulated and tested against the data in such a way that behavioural regularities can be identified. Probabilities can be assigned to the regularities and the propositions can then be offered as grist to the decision-maker's mill — whether for good or for ill. However, social scientists are, at present, far from being able to offer even a paradigm of an empirical theory of behaviour. Any avenue of research towards such a theory is, therefore, worthy of consideration and the study of international organisation has, *prime facie*, much to recommend it.

Any patterned interaction between actors is likely to give rise to some form or degree of organisation. The organisational form is thus the indicator of a system of transactions. Of course, the institutional form may be very incomplete in its reflection of what actually happens and of what is important; nevertheless, it is a starting point. It is a sign post to activity. But an organisational form may be more than this. It can also be the forum for decision-making and thus a nodal point in a network of transactions. Since the study of decision-making — that is, the process by which demands are made, goals are determined, roles are allocated, means are devised and feedback is assessed — is crucial in any attempt to describe and explain behaviour, the institutional aspects of organisation become of great interest and relevance.

A patterned interaction between actors or a set of transactions can be analysed on the basis of the actions of its constituent parts. But the whole may be greater than the sum of the parts. There may be a systemic input arising from the interaction of the parts over time in an organisational framework which can best be captured through study of the activities taking place in and about its institutional form. There are those who would reject the notion of a systemic input and content themselves with the summing of the parts. They rightly point to the difficulties involved in the empirical identification of a systemic input — difficulties so great, in their view, as to deny its existence. Yet the careful observation of simulations, and the more intuitive analyses of the real world, suggest that the systemic input is both real and important and that it should be given attention in this instance through the analysis of institutions.

In this volume there is a special interest in institutions as well as in the general problems of organisation. While organisation refers to the fact that there is a system, that behaviour is not random and that it has an element of repetition which creates additional systemic inputs, institutions refer to the structures within, by and through which the systemic functions are performed. Talcott Parsons' version of structural functionalism with its four-fold framework of pattern maintenance, integration, goal attainment and adaptation for the examination of organisation has been much used in several branches of social science. It has also been rightly criticised as static since it stresses pattern maintenance rather than envisioning creative change towards an open future. Nevertheless, the four functions are a useful conceptual framework in themselves (when disassociated from Parsons' conception of polity), as institutional forms can be related to each of them. Such forms are important not only because they relate to functions performed, that is the fact of organisation, which is, of course, evidence of behaviour, the understanding of which is the ultimate goal, but also because they influence behaviour. Institutions are a framework within which transactions may be facilitated, co-ordinated and even stimulated. In none of these roles is the influence of the institutional framework entirely absent. Structural variables always have some influence on behaviour. Thus institutions are both evidence,of, and actors in, systems of transactions.

These reasons for the study of organisation and institutions apply at any systems level or in any functional dimension. The concern of this volume is with world society and in particular with 'international' organisation and institutions. The academic study of International Relations has been characterised by the use of the state as the basic unit of analysis and the dominant school of thought for the last three decades or more has been the power or 'realist' school. However, this paradigm has been under challenge for some time in both its principal aspects — the state as unit of analysis and power as the dominant characteristic of relationships. The use of systems analysis and a greater emphasis given to legitimised relationships does not imply that state actors and power politics are unimportant, but merely that they are not axiomatic. Nevertheless, the choice of unit of analysis is crucial, since it influences the questions asked, the organisation of the data and the findings. There is a need, therefore, to know what unit of analysis is appropriate for which cases. The tremendous range of international institutions which taps the real world in so many of its facets may provide evidence that will help to clarify the appropriateness of competing paradigms. These, then, are some of the reasons why international organisation and institutions should be studied. Are they also the reasons why they are in fact studied?

Presumably even if international institutions and organisation were of no conceivable interest to social scientists there would still be a statistical distribution of people who would be interested in them for their own sake in the same way that there are people who collect milk bottle tops. Their interest would be relatively pure, idiosyncratic and unsullied by notions of general utility. The second reason why scholars study international organisation and institutions is rather more important: the study of international relations grew out of the study of international organisation and institutions and has been greatly influenced by it. Along with the diplomatic historian, the international lawyer, with a penchant for institutions, and the progressive rationalist social engineer and institution builder of the late nineteenth and early twentieth centuries were the progenitors of International Relations as it emerged as an academic subject after the First World War. Courses on international institutions or international organisation have been the staple diet of students ever since — often to their chagrin. However, the study of international organisation has changed. While old-style legal and historical analyses still exist and do, indeed, still have a place, the study of international organisation has entered the main stream of the behavioural approach. Evidence of this can be found in the changing type, subject matter and methodology of articles in *International Organisation* — the leading journal in the field.

It is a sad fact that the study of international organisation and institutions is in a serious imbalance. First, there is very little to be found in the (Western) literature on the notion of organisation *per se* as applied to world society. Yet anthropologists and sociologists (not to mention social anthropologists!) have for long been active in this area. While their findings may not be automatically transferable to a different systems framework, their paradigms are, to say the least, of great heuristic value. Structural functionalism suitably amended and the frameworks used by Almond and others in comparative politics have not been exploited in more than a few cases. The literature on bureaucracy is burgeoning, yet it has made relatively little impact on the study of secretariats. A central concern of social science as a whole is decision-making, but the functional elements in the decision-making process such as the articulation of demands, recognition of demands and so on have not been used often as a framework for comparative analysis. Instead there is a plethora of general works of a descriptive, historical or legal bent on the United Nations or the League of Nations and a growing body of case studies of aspects of those bodies and certain alliances and common markets often of considerable methodological sophistication. To this can be added a monograph or two on each of the major Specialised Agencies and regional organisations but very little on non-governmental organisations with the exceptions of the International Committee of the Red Cross and the League of Red Cross Societies. This, of course, is to be expected in that the state-centric power paradigm of International Relations has been the dominant one, but if the cobweb model or multi-centric transactions model of world society is to be given empirical validity then the focus will have to shift to transnational NGOs. Here is a fertile area for aspirant doctoral candidates (and others) and their labours might add greatly to the choice of appropriate paradigms and the posing of relevant questions.

If what has been studied is but a part of the whole, has there been an equal degree of complacency in research methods? The response to this question is somewhat more encouraging. The greater epistemological awareness, the increasing sophistication in research techniques, the growing meticulousness in the observation, collection and analysis of data that have characterised the study of international relations generally in the last two decades have not been without their effect on research on international organisation and institutions. Again, the empirical evidence for this can be found in the pages of *International Organisation*, *World Politics* and the *Journal of Common Market Studies*. For example, the analysis of records is no longer confined to an historical interpretation of resolutions and speeches. Analyses of voting behaviour that would have been virtually unthinkable by hand can now be undertaken using a computer. But voting and speech-making may tell little, or even be misleading, about who was the principal lobbyist for a resolution and the intensity of commitment to it, so techniques of field investigation and participant observation have been developed. Moreover, simulation offers the possibility of experiment through manipulation and replication and, while problems of validation of findings with the real world are considerable, such research has proved useful. The thousands of international institutions also provide scope for aggregate data analysis.

There is no empirical evidence to suggest that there is any methodological 'royal road' in the study of international organisation and institutions and it would, therefore, be wise, in its absence, to adopt an open-minded attitude. Just as research using traditional methods can be second-rate, misconceived or badly executed, so can research using more scientific methods. The study of international organisations and institutions is, therefore, useful but fraught with difficulties as well as being too frequently devoted to areas which do not always reflect developments in the real world.

The Emergence of International Institutions

International institutions are a recent phenomenon. If we restrict ourselves to the modern period and to 'western' types of international organisation and institutions then our period of interest begins in 1815 and comes to maturity in another great burst of 'peacemaking' and systems organisation a little over a century later. Since then there has been almost continuous expansion in variety, numbers and functional dimension of institutions with the exception of the period of the Second World War. This tremendous growth is the outcome of two major events which left their mark on nineteenth century Europe — the birthplace and still the centre of the international institutions

15

world – and, more recently, on much of the rest of the world. These two events were the industrial revolution and the French revolution.

Prior to the industrial revolution trade had been relatively limited in Europe, since there was no mass production, exceedingly bad and dangerous communications and small markets. The industrial revolution changed all that. The flow of goods, services and people increased many-fold both within Europe and between Europe and other continents. The world became a more integrated place as a Euro-centric, but quasi-global, economy came into being. Of course, it was not an equal development and much of it took place within the boundaries of particular political units which sometimes defended themselves against transnational systems with devices such as tariffs, yet the contrast with the previous state of affairs was clear enough. However, the French Revolution and the activities of Napoleon accentuated a trend in the opposite direction.

The French Revolution was many things, but not least it was a great harbinger of nationalism in Europe. The emerging middle class in France, seeking to carve out for themselves a place in a society which was dominated by a dynastic regime presiding over a 'feudal' structure of aristocrat and peasant, helped to create a revolutionary situation which boiled over in 1789. No longer would a family, such as the Bourbons, define the political unit, rather it would be defined by the nation under the aegis of, and in many ways thanks to, the middle class. In the nineteenth century the middle class waged a nationalistic struggle against aristocratic universalism and proletarian internationalism and won. In this they were given a good start by the French Revolutionary and Napoleonic armies which, while often welcomed as liberators, outstayed their welcome by becoming imperial reorganisers. They evoked a nationalist response from Spain to Russia, yet their institutional reorganisation gave a fillip to nationalism in Italy and elsewhere. Whereas in the war at the beginning of the nineteenth century it was possible for a group of gentlemen-scholars from London to travel to Paris to confer with their counterparts there, in the war at the beginning of the twentieth century it would have been in-conceivable for them to have travelled between London and Berlin. State boundaries were no longer permeable and loyalty to nation displaced loyalty to class or to interest in the event of a clash of loyalties.

While the industrial revolution tended to promote transnational ties and functional integration on a largely anational and aterritorial basis, the growth of nationalism and the creation of nation-states served to give state authorities a gatekeeper role in the movement of goods, services, people and ideas. Both freedom of movement and control were desired: were they incompatible? In absolute terms they were, but in practical terms international institutions provided a means by which an acceptable balance could be achieved. The purpose of international organisation was to promote freedom of movement under a set of rules which were negotiated by governments, governmental bodies or national branches. The effects of the French and industrial revolutions were reconciled by the development of international institutions to bring about controlled integration. As the Euro-centric world became both more integrated and more nationalistic international organisation became more evident.

The development of international institutions was slow, with only a handful of IGOs and INGOs in the first half of the nineteenth century, but by the last quarter of the century it was gathering momentum. It has grown apace since both in numbers, in variety of form and in functional dimensions. At some point the rate of growth in the number of IGOs may slacken but this is not an immediate prospect. Nor is there likely to be any limitation on the number of INGOs. The threat to their growth lies more with a governmental backlash in an attempt to exert control or gate-keeping functions. Nevertheless, barring a catastrophe in the world system such as a nuclear war, it is not unreasonable to expect a continued rapid growth in international organisation and institutions and, moreover, for this growth to be in numbers, variety of form, and in functional dimensions. International institutions, as we are considering them, developed out of a Euro-centric world society and are to be found in greatest abundance within the Western developed world. International institutions may in the future develop more fully within and between the socialist and developing worlds. Moreover, the birth rate of institutions greatly exceeds the death rate. The student of international organisation, it seems, need have little fear of un-employment.

The Philosophical Spirit of the Times

International organisation and institutions are also an indicator of modernity. Both the French and industrial revolutions — and sub-sequent events — were powerful indicators that men were not prepared to accept either their social or physical environments as given. Such environments were manipulatable, albeit clumsily and with little effective control. The possibility of change conceived and initiated by man was evident and in many instances it required some

17

form of international organisation. It is no coincidence that the 'take-off' period for international institutions was also marked by a great flowering of rationalist and progressive thought. Western European elites were, as the nineteenth century progressed, growing increasingly confident of their ability to control their physical environment through the application of science. The rational, scientific approach which appeared to be vindicating itself in science might, therefore, also be applied to social problems. Hence the original 'functional' institutions.

There also developed among the major Powers a self-confidence in their ability to define, elaborate and impose upon international society a code of acceptable behaviour. Such a code was, of course, primarily designed to facilitate great Power relations and to promote their interests. A general spirit of optimism can also be seen in the procedural innovations in international institutions, in attempts to civilise the conduct of war, in the opprobrium poured on secret alliances and in the efforts to improve standards in such areas as conditions of work or the control of the traffic of drugs or of women.

The general atmosphere of exhilaration, achievement and the prospect of further success gave rise to a belief in progress. Progress was to be based on reason and its achievement would lead mankind to unity. It was assumed that what was reasonable was self-evident to any fair-minded man or group and that such values were shared values, at least in the civilised world. To the extent that reasonable behaviour was not forthcoming, it was due to a lack of civilisation, an autocratic system of government or to deviancy. If the cause was lack of civilisation the British were prepared to shoulder the 'white man's burden', the Americans to accept their 'manifest destiny' and the French embark upon a *'mission civilisatrice'*. There was no room for pluralism: rationality was defined by white, Christian, imperialist Capitalists who sought to impose their conception of it upon the rest of the world. The imposition of European rationality and civilisation provided an ideology for colonialism, if it was not its only motive. Should the 'cause' of non-rational behaviour, so defined, be an undemocratic form of government then the situation was more delicate. The notions of liberty, equality and fraternity were far from being universally accepted throughout Europe. Indeed, it was not until the Western democracies had defeated the more autocratic Central Powers and lost their Eastern ally in 1918 that Woodrow Wilson was able to state his ideas at full force. Even then he was constrained by foot-dragging on the part of Clemenceau and Lloyd George, among others. The argument ran that man would behave rationally if he was allowed to do so and that he would pursue his individual interests in a reasonable manner from the point of view of the collectivity. A democratic structure would therefore allow public opinion to influence governments and to ensure their good behaviour. But democracy could only flourish in homogeneous nation-states so that in order to make the world safe for democracy it was necessary to make it national. In the event that the government of a democratic, national state transgressed the norms of reasonable behaviour then it would be rightfully treated like the autocratic, revolutionary and colonial states and subject to sanctions until it reverted to non-deviant behaviour.

The doctrine of nationalism was the reason why no great desire was evinced for a universal state. Sanctions were to be the preserve of a league of separate nation-states, a specifically international institution, not of a world Leviathan. Schiffer points to a further reason why this was so from the progressive point of view as 'Unity achieved among free peoples by the community of natural interests and by the general recognition of common standards of reason and justice seemed to be superior in dignity to unity effected by a powerful world government. The ideal situation which progress was expected to bring about could satisfy men's desire for living in separate independent groups, as well as their longing for a sphere of reason, liberty and justice beyond the states'.[1] It is in man's insistence upon the state and yet his anxiety about adjusting the circumstances of its existence in international society that we find a further reason for the growth of international organisation and institutions. How in fact, did they set about trying to achieve this?

A Hundred Years of Organisation

The modern state system is often said to have finally crystalised about the time of the Congress of Westphalia in 1648. However, it was not until an equally famous postwar Congress, that of Vienna in 1815, that international institutions of a modern type emerged. The institutions of the next century can be categorised as high or low politics institutions. The prime high politics system was the Congress system, as later modified by the Hague conferences. At the same time a network of low politics institutions began to spread. The trends began then are still with us and it is with this in mind that there follows a survey of the nineteenth century system.

The meetings of the Congress system were relatively frequent with only 36 years of the century ending without meetings.[2] But the system remained relatively unorganised and there was in no sense a legal obligation to hold meetings or to attend them. Nor was there a set pattern to the form of the meetings or to the type of decisions taken and their execution. It was an extremely pragmatic system, but the great Powers certainly regarded it as an institutional mechanism and it was used as such. It was hierarchically organised, being conceived by and for the benefit of the great Powers, as a class, for the discussion of matters of general interest for the European system. It was the forum within which they could regulate their own problems and impose their will upon the small Powers. In so doing the great Powers tacitly acknowledged that each would submit its own policy to the scrutiny of its peers and respond to their judgement in a satisfactory manner. The process was a reactive one: a Congress would be called if one or more Powers held their interests or that of the system as a whole to be threatened by the policy of another Power or by internal developments within a state. The Power invoking it could not claim any special advantage for itself. But the whole process was effective only when the plaintiff was upheld by the other members. In such a case there was an overwhelming alliance in face of which it was deemed prudent by the offending Power to back down. Smaller Powers were invited to play a role if the great Powers thought that the matter at hand warrented it, but for the most part the small Powers were the objects of the Congress system rather than participants in it. More generally so far as high politics was concerned the Congress system was, in Sir Alfred Zimmern's worlds, 'the medicine of Europe rather than its daily bread'.[3]

Thus worked a classical balance of power system. It was founded upon the inability of any one actor to overthrow the system and a clear recognition on the part of all that submission to rules that were far from onerous was better than the risk of attempts at hegemony or anarchy. Power politics were the mores of the system, both between the great Powers individually and between them collectively and other actors. It worked because there existed a certain common rationality, trusted information, common perceptions and, until towards the end of the period, a high degree of tactical flexibility. It was also firmly rooted in an environment — political, social, economic and physical — which changed rather slowly. When the change became sufficiently great — particularly in regard to nationalism in the multi-national Empires of Eastern and Southern Europe and industrialisation in the United States and Japan — no amount of tactical flexibility could do more than stave off collapse.

20

The balance of power system has no notion of systemic adaptation other than collapse: there is no creative path to an open future. This collapse of 1914–18, in the progressive-rationalist climate of the early twentieth century, gave an added impetus to other notions which had already surfaced in the Hague system.

The Hague system was an attempt to modify and potentially to transform the Congress system. The power politics basis of the Congress system could not be abolished overnight but, given the progressive-rationalist assumptions of the time, the balance of power system to which it had given rise could be made safer. In fact, the Hague Conferences of 1899 and 1907 were exercises in arms control, that is, they sought to make a system of power politics safer in the context of the developing technology of war. Some, at least, had a conception of changing the nature of war through incremental reforms. The means used in the Hague system to achieve this end involved measures to contain the arms race, the codification and amelioration of the law and conduct of war (along with the Red Cross) and procedures for the consideration of political questions. In contrast to the Congress system, the Hague conferences included the small Powers not only of Europe but also of Latin America as a matter of right.[4] Thus, substantively, the Conferences initiated a concern — arms control broadly defined — that has remained with us to this day as well as establishing an institutional form, since the Conferences may be taken as the beginning of a general assembly of the independent governments of the world to consider political questions of mutual concern — a function continued in the Assembly of the League of Nations and the General Assembly of the United Nations. If the Congress system was, with its successors, the League's Council (and Conference of Ambassadors) and the UN's Security Council, the institution of the great Powers, the Hague Conferences, and its successors, were that of the small Powers. The relationship between the two was not, and is not, always easy.

The successor institutions to the Hague Conferences developed a general competence for all matters of political interest and are not merely bodies which respond to a high politics crisis as and when it arises. Such a competence was first mooted in the Hague meetings. They gave rise to the expression of an embryonic will to provide a permanent order for the rational promotion of good relations between states as well as the peaceful settlement of disputes. The social engineers and the lawyers set about drafting an institutional framework and code to enshrine the liberal-progressive-rational

21

principles to which all reasonable men would adhere. They did not progress far in the two Hague Conferences, but they started the foundations on which, to no small degree, the League of Nations was built. In this work the growing network of functional institutions was an inspiration, example and guide.

The functional institutions of the nineteenth century have been classified into three categories by Paul Reuter[5] :— International River Commissions, temporary quasi-colonial organisations and administrative unions. Moreover, they existed both in Europe and the Americas. The Central Commission of the Navigation of the Rhine is perhaps the oldest international body in continuous existence.[6] It is an example of Reuter's first category which was envisioned in Article 5 of the Treaty of Paris (30.v.1814) and Articles 108—116 of the Final Act of the Treaty of Vienna of 1815. It is a classic example of a functional institution in that the convenience of all demanded that the great multi-national rivers of Europe be given a single regime. The second category contained arrangements whereby a group of European states undertook jointly to provide or supervise services that non-European authorities were unwilling or unable to provide, such as in public health or finance, in areas such as the Ottoman Empire, its successor states and China. They were on the whole short-lived, although in part they seem to be the precursors of the League's mandates and the UN's trust territories and temporary administrations such as in West Irian and de facto in the ex-Belgian Congo. Of far greater importance are the administrative unions dealing with such matters as telegraph, posts, rail transport, economic, scientific and social affairs. Many of these bodies still exist, after a suitable metamorphosis to take account of the changing environment. Their significance is collective, cumulative and continuous. Moreover, they were and are supplemented by an even greater network of international non-governmental organisations.

A similar process is evident in Latin America where the first rather abortive efforts at international organisation occurred at the Congress of Panama in 1826. However, while in Europe no single Power had a preponderant role in the process of organisation, the United States aspired to such a role in the Americas to the chagrin of some Latin American governments. From 1889 Conferences of American States were held regularly, which gave rise to numerous conventions, not all of which were implemented. By 1901 a Commercial Bureau had emerged which, in 1910, became the Panamerican Union, dealing with cultural, administrative, technical and political matters. With the Monroe Doctrine concerned with high politics, the Panamerican system combined elements of the Hague system with administrative unions. It was thereby a direct forerunner of the League and Americans, both North and Latin, had a major role to play in the philosophy behind and in the actual drafting of the Covenant. The extent to which non-governmental organisation grew in the Americas is more difficult to discern.

The essential features of nineteenth century international governmental institutions have been summarised by Plano and Riggs in the following manner: [7]

'1. Membership was usually, though not always, limited to sovereign states. Unless regional in scope, such organisations typically were universal in the sense that membership was open to all qualified states without political or moral conditions,

2. The organization was created by a multilateral treaty. The treaty served as a constitution which specified the obligations of its members, created the institutional structure, and proclaimed the objectives of the organization and the means by which they would be pursued.

3. A conference or congress was usually established as the basic policy-making organ. The conference was comprised of all members of the organization and would meet infrequently typically once every five years.

4. Decision-making was based on the principle of equalitarianism, with each member having an equal vote and decisions reached by adherence to the principle of unanimity. In time this gave way somewhat to the principle of majoritarianism, especially in voting on procedural questions.

5. A council or other decision-making organ of an executive nature was often created to implement policies between meetings of the general conference. It typically had a limited membership and was established by the conference. Its primary responsibility was to administer the broad policy decisions laid down by the general conference.

6. A secretariat was also established to carry out the policies of the conference and council and conduct the routine functions of the organization. The secretariat was headed by a secretary-general or director-general, a professional civil servant with an international reputation.

7. Some organizations, like the river commissions, exercised judicial or quasi-judicial powers. Some created special international courts to decide controversies arising out of their administrative

operations.

8.   Some were endowed with a legal personality enabling them to own property, to sue and be sued in specified areas, and, in some cases, to enjoy a measure of diplomatic immunity.

9.   Financial support was based on contributions from member governments. The organization established a formula for contributions based on a principle such as 'ability to pay', 'benefits derived', 'equality', or a combination of these.

10. Competence of the organization was usually limited to a functional or specialised problem area as set out in its constitution. Organizations of general competence in political, economic, and social areas were not established until the twentieth century.

11. Decision-making was carried on in two ways: (1) by drafting international treaties and submitting them to member governments for ratification; and (2) by adopting resolutions recommending action by member governments. A few possessed administrative and minor policy-making powers independent of the governments that had created them'.

By the time of the First World War a recognisable system of organisation and its attendant institutions had emerged. It encompassed both Europe and the Americas, high and low politics, governmental and nongovernmental activity. In terms of felt need, ideological conviction and experience the prerequisites for expansion were present and the building of a new world after the Great War was the pretext.

The Beginning of Twentieth Century Institutions

The First World War resulted in a marked decrease in the Eurocentricity of the international organisation and institutions system. The effect was not felt immediatly due to the isolation of the United States, the exclusion of the Soviet Union and the slow growth of nationalism in the colonial world. The mondial nature of the new system was not predicated upon the First World War, since the growth of the United States and the decline of colonialism were independent factors leading to the decrease in Eurocentricity. Nevertheless, there was a new globalisation in intent and, to a lesser extent, in activity. The institutions of the League were universal in aspiration and centralised in structure (unlike the UN which stresses coordination, decentralisation and regionalism). The League mechanisms strove to promote economic and social welfare throughout the world and to provide a means to settle disputes. Indeed, as it failed in the latter it endeavoured, through the Bruce reform proposals, to strengthen the former in a vain attempt both to find a new role and to stave off the Second World War.

The collapse of the European system in the First World War was interpreted by the rationalist-progressives as a vindication of their analysis. While their belief in the automaticity of progress could not be other than shaken by the carnage of 1914–18, they argued that the war was due to the failure to apply rationalist principles to political problems. Autocratic polities pursuing their private interest were to blame. Democracy, national self-determination and institutional mechanisms for the peaceful resolution of disputes based on procedures acceptable to all men of reason and goodwill were the remedy. War no longer served a social purpose at an acceptable cost: the mechanisms of the League were both to obviate it and to act as its functional equivalent. They would obviate it by replacing power politics with the development of economic and social programmes designed to increase the welfare of all through cooperation. A network of co-operative relationships would thus give rise first to interest in common and, eventually, to common interests, so that power politics – the pursuance of selfish interest with no regard for and to the detriment of the interests of others – would become a thing of the past and democratic world opinion would ensure that this would so remain. The mechanisms of the League would also act as the functional equivalent of war in that there were elaborate procedures to handle disputes in a manner any reasonable man would accept as satisfactory – and sanctions to enforce them in cases of non-compliance.

The rationalist-progressive belief in the essentially co-operative nature of human relations is well-founded theoretically in that objective conflict exists only in cases in which an actor has a single value or goal.[8] In practice, however, parties to a conflict may see their relationship in objective terms, and experience has shown that it may take much more than institutional tinkering to induce them to accept the subjective and erroneous nature of their view. Institutionalised mechanisms for the settlement and resolution of disputes are, of course, important, but only if they are legitimised by the actors in the system. The dreams of the well-meaning international lawyer and the hopes of the progressive-rationalists gave rise to the League of Nations Covenant in which such dreams and hopes were tempered, both in the drafting and in later practice, by the wiles and ways of old-style political practitioners. In short, the League system was too out of touch with political reality seriously to be able to influence it in the peaceful processing of demands for change. It was seen too frequently as the instrument of the victors and it sought to preserve their values against any potential threat from the defeated or revolutionary states. The institution of colonialism was woven into its very fabric. It was an instrument with which conflict could be waged rather than resolved; it was a weapon of the victors and the *status quo* Powers, yet outside the sphere of high politics it met a felt need and its social and economic activities thrived and prospered.

Whatever the successes and failures of the League and the UN there can be no doubting the tremendous growth in type and numbers of institutions. Organisation has proceeded apace with some 300 IGOs, 3000 INGOs and a similar number of BINGOs (Business International Non-Government Organisations!). These institutions can be categorised in many ways, although the categorisations do not always eliminate overlapping. The most common rubrics are governmental and non-governmental, general and specialised, regional and universal, and, forum and service. Institutions can also be classified by the dominant mode of decision-making and its relation to structure and this is the *raison d'être* of this volume. In this instance, the interest is not in particular institutions, but in different approaches to organisation, from attempts at highly structured supranationality to informal nodes in rapidly changing networks of transactions. But in order to put these approaches into a proper context there is a need to be cogniscent not only of the reasons for the growth of international organisations and the increase in numbers and diversity of international institutions, but also the range of functions that they perform.

Eugene Skolnikoff[5] has produced a useful typology notwithstanding the caveats that such a typology is arbitrary and that some functions can be listed under more than one category. Although Skolnikoff was primarily concerned with IGOs, nevertheless, his framework can also be applied to INGOs. Four primary functions are identified: general assistance, regulation, operation and settlement of disputes. The first function is concerned for the most part with the provision of information and knowledge and the facilitation of exchange. Regulation is concerned with formal or informal law-making, the attribution of roles and the guardianship of the rules of the system. Operation deals with the actual implementation of programmes by the international institution itself (as opposed to its members), while the settlement of disputes is a function which arises whenever any of the previous functions are not fulfilled to the satisfaction of members. Clearly each institution and organisational approach will fulfill these functions in a different manner but Skolnikoff's typology, along with that of Parsons and Almond, does have the virtue of putting some order into thinking and of providing a basis for comparison. These typologies together with this survey of the advent of international organisation and institutions enable the contemporary world of international institutions to be broached.

Notes

1. W. Schiffer: *The Legal Community of Mankind*, New York, Columbia University Press, 1954, p. 155.
2. See Stanley Hoffmann: *Organisations Internationales et Pouvoirs Politiques des Etats*, Paris, Colin, 1954.
3. Sir Alfred Zimmern: *The League of Nations and the Rule of Law, 1918–1935*, London, Macmillan, 1936, p. 78.
4. Inis L. Claude: *Swords into Plowshares*, New York, Random House, 3rd edition revised, 1964, p. 25 *et seq.*
5. Paul Reuter: *International Institutions*, London, George Allen and Unwin, 1958, p. 207 *et seq.*
6. However, it was reduced to two members while Alsace-Lorraine was under German control from 1871–1918 and therefore does not qualify under the Union of International Associations Yearbooks' coding rules.
7. J.C. Plano and R.E. Riggs: *Forging World Order*, London, Collier-Macmillan, 1967, pp. 12–13.
8. See A.J.R. Groom: *Strategy in the Modern World* (forthcoming).
9. E.B. Skolnikoff: *The International Imperatives of Technology*, Geneva, Carnegie Endowment Study Group on International Organisation, 1970, pp. 95 *et seq.*

Selected Reading

Inis L. Claude: *Swords into Plowshares*, New York, Random House, 3rd edition revised, 1964.

Charles Dubois: *Le Droit des Gens et les Rapports des Grandes Puissances avec les autres États avant le Pacte de la SDN*, Paris, Plon, 1921.

Stanley Hoffmann: *Organisations internationales et pouvoirs politiques des états,* Paris, Colin, 1954.

J.C. Plano and R.E. Riggs: *Forging World Order*, London, Collier-Macmillan, 1967.

CHAPTER TWO

INTERNATIONAL INSTITUTIONS: DIVERSITY, BORDERLINE CASES, FUNCTIONAL SUBSTITUTES AND POSSIBLE ALTERNATIVES

Anthony J.N. Judge

Introduction

This chapter reviews the complete range of international organisations. The conventional categories used are first examined and then various ways of distinguishing between the many kinds of organisation and degrees of 'internationality' are considered. The problem of borderline cases is discussed, together with non-organisational substitutes for organisations and possible alternative forms of organisation. Quantitative information on the growth of international institutions and indicative data on regional organisations are also presented.

A major difficulty in obtaining some understanding of international organisations is the variety of organisational forms which need to be considered. Abstract classification schemes, particularly when simplified for convenience, tend to conceal the existence of well-developed groups of organisations with distinct features. The approach employed here has been to use several different ways of breaking up the range of organisations and to cite several examples of organisations of any particular type.

The intent is not to put forward a new systematic classification of international organisations but rather to facilitate an appreciation of the variety of bodies which could be incorporated into any such scheme. A comment on the three conventional categories used (intergovernmental, international nongovernmental nonprofit, and multinational corporation) is thus a valid point of departure. The second breakdown of international organisations is developed on the basis of the terminology used in the actual title of the body. The intent here is to show the limitations of this obvious, but somewhat superficial, approach, as well as its value in distinguishing between some kinds of organisation. The scheme developed is based on the relationship between such bodies and the meetings by which they were created.

Another categorisation used is based on the structural peculiarities of some kinds of organisation. Bodies are distinguished in terms of their hybrid character, dependent character, semi-autonomous character, relationship to leadership, regional orientation, functional orientation, heterogeneity of membership, structural complexity, or minimal structure.

Some international organisations may also be usefully characterized by the special emphasis they give to a particular mode of action. Others may be distinguished by the specialized nature of their preoccupation (as contrasted with any more conventional classification by subject). A significant number of bodies called 'international' can also be usefully distinguished in terms of peculiarities in their geographic orientation or distribution of membership.

In addition to the above rubrics, there are a number of groups of organisations with other special characteristics such as commemoration of individuals, focus on charismatic personalities, special patronage bodies, alumni associations, retrogressive bodies, and hyper-progressive bodies.

Each of the dimensions mentioned brings out different aspects of the range and variety of international bodies. Several examples of organisations in any such group are cited to give a better grasp of the kinds of bodies which exist. Each named body is described in the *Yearbook of International Organizations*[1] and the number in parenthesis following each name is the permanent reference number in that *Yearbook*. It should be stressed that a particular body could well exemplify several of the special characteristics discussed, although it may only have been cited because of the apparent dominant nature of a particular characteristic. The term 'apparent' is deliberately used because the characteristic in question may not necessarily be of great importance in determining the actual functioning of the organisation (e.g. the *Howard* League for Penal Reform could *perhaps* just as well be called the *International* League for Penal Reform).

It should also be stressed that in the main the dimensions and characteristics discussed attempt to draw attention to the many exceptional cases rather than to distinguish between organisations lacking any of the characteristics noted. It could be argued that there is a central core of international organisations which can only usefully be classified in terms of aims, internal structure, control, activities and membership. Unfortunately, it is these same bodies which tend to be multifunctional and therefore to be difficult to capture adequately and meaningfully in the schemes which have been proposed to date. Given the preponderance of organisations possessing characteristics distinguishing them, to a greater or lesser degree, from a model international organisation, it is appropriate to attempt a descriptive review on this basis − in anticipation of a more adequate and comprehensive scheme.

Conventional Categories

It is usual to distinguish between three main types of 'international organisation', namely: intergovernmental organisations, internationall nongovernmental organisations, and multinational enterprises.

1. INTERGOVERNMENTAL ORGANISATIONS

The *Yearbook of International Organizations*, which aims to identify and list all intergovernmental organisations, defines such bodies as:

(a) being based on a formal instrument of agreement between the governments of nation states;

(b) including three or more nation states as parties to the agreement;

(c) possessing a permanent secretariat performing ongoing tasks.

A detailed re-examination of this matter by Singer and Wallace questioned this conventional definition. In particular they argue: 'It may be objected, of course, that *bilateral* organisations should not be included on the grounds that they are not 'really' IGOs, as we usually conceive of them because they result from 'contractual' rather than 'law-making' treaties. There are two points to be made here: One, this objection is met by us in that mere treaties or pacts are excluded by other criteria; we only urge that an organisation's bilateral character cannot of itself be grounds for exclusion. Further, such exclusion would not only leave out such important organisations as the North American Air Defense Command (NORAD) but would also force us to drop such *multilateral* organisations as the Rhine River Commission when historical circumstances temporarily reduced the membership to two.'[2]

Singer and Wallace also consider the distinction between IGOs and NGOs in the case of 'mixed' organisations, some of whose delegations are appointed by governmental agencies or ministries and some by private bodies such as corporations. They conclude that 'it would be unreasonable to exclude organisations simply because a number of their members were not national states. Instead we adopted the criterion employed by the UN Economic and Social Council (ECOSOC): whether or not the organisation was created by a formal instrument of agreement between the governments of national states.'[2] There appears to be some conflict here with the ECOSOC definition of a nongovernmental organisation, namely: 'Any international organisation which is not established by intergovernmental agreement shall be considered as a nongovernmental organisation for the purpose of these arrangements, including organisations which accept members designated by government authorities, provided that such membership does not interfere with the free expression of views of the organisation.'[3]

They also object to the inclusion of associations or confederations of IGOs as constituting additional IGOs on the grounds that such bodies are not independent. They exclude treaties or agreements administered by another international organisation (such as the various special unions of the International Union for the Protection of Industrial Property). Finally, in cases where two separate IGOs claim jurisdiction over the same domain (e.g. the Commission européenne du régime du Danube, Rome and the Danube Commission, Budapest), only the organisation 'with evident de facto control over the domain' is included.

2. INTERNATIONAL NONGOVERNMENTAL ORGANISATIONS
A clear and unambiguous theoretically acceptable definition of international NGOs remains to be formulated. Much research on these bodies is based on those described in the *Yearbook of International Organizations*. The criterion for inclusion in that publication is based on the ECOSOC definition of NGOs (noted in the previous section) which however fails to define the meaning to be given to 'international organisation'. The editors of the *Yearbook* have therefore developed a set of seven rules designed to identify an international NGO in terms of aims, members, structure, officers, finance, autonomy, and activities. The intent has been to include only those bodies oriented to three or more countries.

Skjelsbaek in reviewing the growth of NGOs using the above definition regrets the use of 'a legalistic criterion to distinguish between intergovernmental organisations (IGOs) and international nongovernmental organisations (NGOs). This criterion defines IGOs as organisations established by intergovernmental treaty, as specified in the United Nations Economic and Social Council (ECOSOC) resolution of 1950, regardless of the character of their membership. Most but not all IGOs

31

include only governmental members, and in practice many NGOs have both governmental and nongovernmental members.'[4] He concludes that the *Yearbook* list of NGOs is somewhat different from and more restrictive than a list of organizations compiled according to minimum criteria for '*trans*nationality' which he puts forward, namely: 'At least two different countries must be represented in the organisation and one of the representatives must not be an agent of a government.'[4] The editors of the *Yearbook* have responded in part to these and other pressures (see comment below) in the 1977 edition by splitting the range of international organisations into two groups, the first based on the original criteria and the second on looser criteria discussed below. They still exclude pure bilateral bodies (e.g. a 'Franco-German' association).

3. MULTINATIONAL ENTERPRISES

As with IGOs and NGOs, there is no clear definition of multinational or transnational corporations. A study by the United Nations Secretariat lists many proposed definitions.[5] Much data is available about the several hundred most economically powerful corporations likely to constitute the basis for any list. The editors of the *Yearbook of International Organizations* have published the results of their surveys to determine probable numbers in term of different criteria based on the distribution of subsidiaries between countries[6] and more recently have published such information as one section of their experimental *Yearbook of World Problems and Human Potential*.[7]

The controversy, discussed below, over the term to be applied to such bodies goes beyond the issue of whether the one or other word is more appropriate for designated entities. Sahlgren notes that 'Even among those using the terms "transnational corporations" or "multinational enterprises", for instance, there is still a wide margin of disagreement as to which entities are or are not included . . . some would like to see partly or wholly-state owned enterprises excluded from the scope of the term "transnational corporations". . . . others have argued that such enterprises display characteristics and motivations that are essentially identical with those of privately-owned enterprises.'[8]

4. COMMENT ON ORGANISATIONAL 'EXISTENCE'

Identification of 'international organisations' raises problems concerning what is meant by the 'existence' of an organisation in terms of different perspectives.

a. *Legal.* International nongovernmental organisations have no existence in international law. They are organisational 'outlaws'. One legal study of international organisation notes: 'Des associations revêtant les formes d'une organisation internationale peuvent aussi être créées par des personnes de droit privé ou de droit non étatique . . . Mais, n'étant pas formees par des Etats, ce ne sont pas là des organisations internationales au sens stricte des termes'.[9] Those NGOs recognized by the United Nations under Article 71 of the Charter acquire a measure of legal significance. It is important to note however that NGOs which are recognized as existing by one IGO are not necessarily recognized as existing by another even if both IGOs form part of the UN system. There have also been attempts to extend the interpretation of the status of private persons in international law to cover collectivities.[10] It is interesting to note that multinational corporations are 'nongovernmental organisations' having no existence in international law despite efforts within the framework of the European Economic Community. This creates an embarrassing situation for the United Nations which for political reasons is obliged to examine 'international' entities whose legal existence it cannot recognize. (The practical consequence is that the UN unit studying such bodies cannot send a questionnaire to them.) Ironically since the UN Charter does not distinguish between profit-making and non-profit making bodies, the only way that the UN Commission on Transnational Corporations may be able to relate to such bodies is under Article 71 governing relations with NGOs.[11]

   b. *Political*. Organisations with a so-called 'universal' membership, such as the United Nations, have considerable difficulty in recognizing the existence of 'regional' bodies such as the Council of Europe, the OAS, or the OECD and in establishing any working contract with them.[12] This has been due to suspicion within the universal bodies that the regional bodies could only reflect a partisan political viewpoint which would disturb the delicate balance of power amongst the universal body's membership. Such political reasoning may also be used to reinforce legal arguments concerning NGOs when the suspect organisation does not have members from all the countries represented in the universal body.

   A UNESCO/UNITAR International expert meeting on the study of the role of international organisations in the contemporary world (Geneva, 1976) reluctantly concluded that NGOs were also international organizations but for political reasons could only acknowledge that multinational corporations 'engaged in activities which affected international organisations' and therefore such *relations* could not be neglected, although the *corporations* could not be considered as a phenomenon in their own right. (The main purpose of the meeting was to specify the contents of a series of textbooks for widespread use.)

c. *Impact.* Presumably because of a desire to simplify the international system to a point at which it becomes comprehensible and quantifiable, there is a tendency to use a measure of political or economic impact as a means of determining whether to give attention to an organisation or organisational category. A body therefore exists to the extent that it has impact. Since many international bodies do not act to have an impact in a manner which would be considered significant to an economist or to a political scientist, they are frequently ignored in studies from such perspectives. For example, Keohane and Nye note that the impact of inter-societal interactions and transnational actors in international affairs has often been ignored both in policy-oriented writings and in more theoretical works, and that when they have been recognized they have often been consigned to the environment of interstate politics, and relatively little attention has been paid to them in their own right or to their connections with the interstate system.[13] Singer and Wallace, for example, are quite explicit about exclusion of NGOs from their analysis: 'our interests (and, we suspect, those of most of our colleagues) are more concerned with IGOs than with non-governmental organisations . . . as an *in*dependent variable, one can hardly urge that the amount of NGO is likely to be important in accounting for many of the theoretically interesting phenomena, which occurred in the system of the past century or so.'[2] Proof of impact is therefore required before scholarly attention can be given to the existence of the organisational phenomenon giving rise to that impact. Ironically research and debate on international organisations and their political impact may well be conducted under the auspices of bodies excluded from the categories of the discussion as being without impact. (This leads to an effort on the part of some impact-conscious organisations, such as the Club of Rome, to define themselves as being '*non*-nongovernmental' in order to distinguish themselves from NGOs.)

A counter-trend has however been stimulated with the publication edited by Keohane and Nye[13] which focuses on a wide variety of transnational interactions, including nongovernmental associations, multinational business enterprises, revolutionary movements, cartels, scientific networks, and the like.

5. COMMENT ON 'TRANSNATIONAL' VERSUS 'INTERNATIONAL' It is still common practice to blur the meaning to be attached to 'international organisation'. It is frequently taken to mean inter-

governmental organisation only, although in other cases it may include NGOs but not multinational corporations. Attempts have been made to use 'transnational' to clarify the situation. Thus for Keohane and Nye 'transnational interactions' describe the movement of tangible or intangible items across state boundaries when at least one actor is not an agent of a government or an intergovernmental organisation.[13] They therefore consider that both NGOs and multinational corporations are transnational organizations together with some contemporary revolutionary organisations, and bodies such as the Roman Catholic Church and the Ford Foundation.

In discussing NGOs, Skjelsbaek states that 'For an organization to be "transnational" two minimal requirements must be met: At least two different countries must be represented in the organisation and one of the representatives must not be an agent of a government. In practice it would probably be wise to specify that at least one-half of the members of the multilateral organization should not act in a governmental capacity.'[4] Judge and Skjelsbaek have attempted to encourage use of 'transnational associations' as a substitute for 'international NGOs' to distinguish them from other types of transnational organisations.[14] The Union of International Associations, following a symposium on transnationality in relation to nongovernmental organisations in Geneva in 1976[15] changed the name of its periodical in 1977 from *International Associations* to *Transnational Associations.*

The situation has however been confused by debate within the United Nations on 'multinational corporations' as originally termed by the Secretariat and the business community. The Group of Eminent Persons invited to study their role noted the 'strong feeling that transnational would better convey the notion that these firms operate from their home bases across national borders' transcending all forms of individual state control. In arguing in support of a Latin American draft resolution to ECOSOC for a UN focus on 'transnational' as opposed to 'multinational' corporations the point was made that:

'The term "multinational corporation" had been applied both to enterprises operating in all parts of the world without a home base and to those which had a main office in one country and branches in other countries, for which the term "transnational corporations" was more descriptive. In Latin America enterprises had been established whose concerns were different from those of multinational corporations, as normally understood, but whose structures were similar. . . It would clearly be desirable to use the term "transnational corporations" for enterprises operating from their home bases across national borders and reserve the term "multinational corporations" for those established by agreement between a number of countries and operating in accordance with prescribed conditions.'

This debate subsequently led to the establishment by ECOSOC of a 'Centre on Transnational Corporations'.[8] 'Transnational', for the inter-state community, must now bear the many negative connotations originally associated with 'multinational' which appears to have been 'laundered'. The attempt to switch from the existing descriptor for NGOs, which contains a logical negative (with negative connotations in some circumstances[16]), to 'transnational' should be assessed with caution now that the latter is acquiring some negative connotations. These are not relieved by the choice of the other term of the descriptor because of problems of translation (e.g. 'corporation' is translated into French as 'société', which is used in the titles of many NGOs).

Classification Categories

ORGANISATION TERMINOLOGY

International organisations, whether governmental or nongovernmental, use any of an extensive range of terms in their official titles. These may include terms such as union, association, office, agency, centre, or alliance. There is a great deal of confusion associated with the meanings to be attached to such terms in practice. It is therefore not usual to attempt to classify an organisation on the basis of whether it is a 'union', a 'confederation', a 'committee', or a 'league', for example. A 'centre' may in fact resemble an 'association' more than it resembles most other 'centres'; equally an 'association' can be more like what is commonly understood to be a 'centre'. The range of terms can be use-fully ordered by relating the organisations in question to the meetings by which they were established or through which they work. This brings out the strengths and limitations of this seemingly obvious approach to classifying organisations. The numbers in parenthesis following the *names of organisations* cited as examples, identify the reference number of the description of the organisation in the 16th edition of the *Yearbook of International Organizations*.

0. GENERAL

The greatest confusion lies in the use of terms such as

association	fellowship(*)	foundation
federation	academy(*)	club
society	college(*)	league
confederation	brotherhood(*)	movement
organisation	solidarity(*)	brigade(*)
union	guild(*)	chamber (*)
alliance	order(*)	

In each case this may mean an organisation of individuals, an organis-
ation of national organisations, or any possible variation on these.
Intergovernmental bodies only use those terms without an asterisk.
Examples of use of these terms include:

International Chamber of Shipping (A1492)
Association of South East Asian Nations (A0165)
Alliance for Progress (A1062)
International College of Surgeons (A1513)
World Assembly of Youth (A3456)
Brotherhood of Asian Trade Unionists (A0200)
Rosicrucian Order (A3163)
European Broadcasting Union (A0598)
Confederation of Asian Chambers of Commerce and Industry (B0390)
Society for International Development (A3228)
League of Arab States (A2903)

An important variant in the case of some intergovernmental bodies
stresses the domain for which the body is responsible.

West African Economic Community (A3424)
East Caribbean Common Market (A4346)

Other interesting variants are illustrated by the following:

Bahal International Community (A0180)
Boys Brigade (A0195)
Salvation Army (A3172)
Apostleship of the Sea (B0066)
Church of Christ Scientist (A0275)
World Citizen Party (B0365)
Mondcivitan Republic (A3668)
International Rehabilitation — Special Education Network
European Parliament (A0667)

1. TREATY-RELATED

Intergovernmental organisations are, by definition, centred on an international treaty or agreement. In some cases the name of the treaty may be embodied into the name of the organisation.

General Agreement on Tariffs and Trade (A0985)
North Atlantic Treaty Organisation (A3005)

Another group intimately linked to international legal questions is that of *courts and tribunals*:

International Court of Justice (A3379)
European Court of Human Rights (A0438)
Permanent Court of Arbitration (A3107)
Nuclear Energy Tribunal (B4644)

A final group, specially governed by treaty provision, is that of *military and control* authorities:

Allied Control Authority for Germany (B0042)
Security Council (B3376)
International Authority for the Ruhr (B1385)
East Caribbean Currency Authority (A0477)
International Supervisory and Control Commission for Cambodia, Laos and Vietnam

2. CONFERENCE

There are many bodies which take their names from the principal (statutory) meeting in which their members participate.

conference	congress
assembly	forum

A fully representative and sovereign body may thus meet periodically and take decisions defining the policy of the organisation which binds its subsidiary organs. The procedure and composition of such a meeting may be defined by the constitution of the body or the original treaty.

Standing Conference of Rectors and Vice-Chancellors of
    European Universities (A3288)
European Conference of Ministers of Transport (A0695)
Conference for the Regions of North West Europe (A0398)
World Assembly of Youth (A3456)
European Atomic Forum (A0590)

Conference Commissions

Such general conferences when they occur may give rise to commissions of the conference which meet in the intervening months or years between sessions of the conference and possibly during it. In practice such commissions are either given or acquire a fair degree of autonomy. It may therefore happen that although the (periodic) conference does not constitute an organisation in its own right, the commission may take on a more or less permanent organisational form. The number of members is generally limited and their selection is made according to rules established by the conference (or body) by which it was created and to which it reports. In some cases the commission may be created by a conference which is not held again.

> International Commission for Bee Botany (A1522)
> International Commission for Northwest Atlantic Fisheries (A1537)
> Standing Commission for International Congresses on the History
> of Religion (B3787)
> Permanent Commission of International Congresses of Home
> Hygiene (B3094)

Conference Committees

A general conference may establish working bodies charged with examination of certain points on the agenda during sessions. Such *ad hoc* bodies, by definition, would not constitute permanent organisations. The confusion of terminology may be such that 'committee' may replace 'commission' in the previous case.

Joint Bodies

A general conference may establish a joint body with some external body.

> Joint FAO/WHO Codex Alimentarius Commission

Regional and Specialized Bodies

Each of the above types of body may also be created regionally, or in terms of some special concern, by the general conference or as a specialized regional body by a regional conference.

3. COUNCIL

A general conference may elect or appoint a

> council
> governing council

governing body

This is a body which tends to be large (relative to the executive body) because it is fairly representative of the general conference and is able to exercise certain of its powers. Again the conference itself may or may not be held periodically or constitute a permanent organisation.

World Council of Churches (A3501)
Council of Europe (A0435)
Council for Mutual Economic Assistance (A0432)
Consultative Council of Jewish Organisations (A0413)
International Social Science Council (A2466)
Economic and Social Council of the United Nations (B3377)

In complex organisations, the council may create its own commissions, committees, and joint bodies with external organisations. This may also occur regionally, or in terms of some special concern of the council. There is some confusion between the use of 'council' and 'commission' or 'committee' as defined in the previous and following sections. The limitations of this approach are illustrated by the presence of the Council of Europe and COMECON in the examples cited.

4. EXECUTIVE COMMITTEE

A conference may elect an executive body of comparatively restricted membership (or it may be appointed by the council) with such names as

executive committee
steering committee
administrative council
administrative board
standing committee
permanent committee

Even though the conference may not constitute an organisation in its own right, such bodies may take on permanent organisational form.

Executive Committee of Nongovernmental Organizations associated with the United Nations Office of Public Information (B4757)
Standing Committee of the International Embryological Conference (A3278)
Executive Committee for the Common Market of the European Brushware Federation (B0915)

40

Again, as the last example indicates, regional, specialized and joint bodies of this kind may be created.

5. SECRETARIAT

The permanent body may take on a name derived from an operational rather than a policy-making or decision-making unit.

Commonwealth Secretariat (A0376)
European Space Agency (A0868)
International Bureau for Declarations of Death (B1412)
Secretariat for Tourism Integration in Central America (B0061)
International Labour Office (A2183)

Again, regional, specialized and joint bodies may be created.

6. DEPARTMENT

Departments of an organisation do not, by definition, constitute autonomous organisations in the sense of interest here, although some bodies of this type may acquire special significance as international actors.

Specialized Section on Fruit and Vegetables of the Committee of Agricultural Organizations of the EEC (B3267)

A section of a large organisation may, however, participate in interdepartmental bodies involving several agencies.

United Nations Inter-Agency Working Group on Indexing and Documentation

Such bodies are, however, difficult to distinguish from those discussed in the following section.

7. TERMS WHICH REFER TO TYPES OF ACTIVITY

A (periodic) conference, or even a conventional organisation, may establish one or more activities which themselves take on permanent autonomous organisational form, whatever the continuing status of the body by which they were established. The emphasis given to a particular mode of action may even be reflected in the actual name of the organisation, thus distinguishing it from conventional organisations (possibly to the point of raising the question as to whether it really should be considered as an organization). Three groups may be usefully distinguished: meeting-type events, programmes/projects, and organisations.

41

Meeting-type events

A single meeting held under the auspices of an international body tends (if it is especially large) to take on the form of an organisation. Since the duration of such 'organisations' is never more than 1 to 5 years, depending on the preparatory and follow-up period required, it is not usual to consider such bodies as organisations in their own right, although from a social, political, budgetary and legal point of view this could well be hard to establish. Even a meeting of (rather than 'under the auspices of') an organisation can be considered an independent organisation.

'Certain people do not agree that a Congress is an independent entity existing only for the duration of the Congress. They consider that a Congress is more often an organ or an activity of a permanent international organisation. Nevertheless, it is necessary to bear in mind the legal question – the problem of the responsibility of the promoters of the congress in case of accident, fire and liability for damages. In order to clearly define the limits of responsibility as regards the meeting-place, the time and those in charge, both locally and internationally, *it seems necessary to consider a congress as an independent legal entity which exists for a determined length of time.*'[17]

Events of this type include

meetings	exhibitions
shows	contests, games
trade fairs	events

Examples worth considering are

World Youth Forum (organised as an activity of the United Nations)
Olympic Games
International trade fairs

and their relation, in some cases, to such bodies as

Commonwealth Games Federation (A0198)
International Olympic Committee (A2303)
World Ploughing Organisation (A3573) and contests
Federation of International Music Competitions (A0948)
European Association of Music Festivals (A0572)
International Exhibition Bureau (A1819)
Union of International Fairs (A3354)

42

Programmes/Projects

There are many examples of organizations which can be considered as programme-bound in some way, possibly because of special political or funding problems. These can be grouped as follows:

Programme:	World Food Programme (B3543)
	United Nations Development Programme (B3382)
	United Nations Environment Programme (B1161)
	Special Committee for the International Biological Programme (B3262)
	Colombo Plan Council for Technical Cooperation in S. and S.E. Asia (A0287)
Campaign	Freedom from Hunger Campaign (FAO)
	Campaign for A World Constituent Assembly (A0806)
	International Committee of Crusade of the Blind (B0291)
Project	OECD High Temperature (Dragon) Reactor Project
	OECD (Halden) Reactor Project
	Project Concern (B0567)
	Joint European Torus Project
Survey	World Fertility Survey (B3067)
	Association of African Geological Surveys (A0116)
Fund	International Monetary Fund (A2266)
	United Nations Childrens Fund (B3380)
	International Defence and Aid Fund for Southern Africa (A4333)
	World Wildlife Fund (A3608)
Emblem	Association for International Cotton Emblem (B0101)
Register	International Registry of World Citizens (A2409)
	International Association for the Rhine Ships Register (A1231)
Prize	International Lenin Peace Prize Committee (B2819)
	International Commission for the Eriksson Prize Fund (B1531)
	Standing Committee for Nobel Prize Winners' Congresses (B3275)
System	Suez Canal Users Association (B3302)
	Taurus Express Conference (B3308)

Honeywell Large Systems Users Association (Europe) (B4420)
World Science Information System (B4668)
Southern European Pipeline Company (B4619)
Intelstat (A2627), Intersputnik (B0760)
Eurovision (A0590), Intervision (B0755)

Periodical   International Ursigram World Days Service (A0930)
International Union for the Publication of Customs
Tariffs (A2674)

Exchange   European Commodities Exchange (B3612)
European Association for the Exchange of Technical
Literature in the Field of Ferrous Metallurgy (A0558)

Stocks   Commonwealth Collection of Micro-organisms (B3022)
International Eye Bank
International Board for Plant Genetic Resources (B3151)

Organisation

A large organisation may create bodies to undertake specific activities.
The political, legal, and financial circumstances under which such bodies
are established may render them relatively autonomous even though
links to the parent body are maintained. Typical activities include:

information centre	training college
library	laboratory
advisory service	research institute
museum	educational academy

Other bodies, with the same level of preoccupation, may be created
under a variety of circumstances such that the relation to the creating
body or bodies becomes tenuous or of limited significance. Such
organisations, particularly when active at one physical location only,
differ somewhat (especially in terms of the status of membership)
from conventional international bodies.

Information   International Tsunami Information Centre (A2646)
International Time Bureau (B4062)
International Food Information Service (B2731)
Commonwealth Legal Advisory Service (B0097)
Afro-Asian Employment Service
International Scientific Film Library (A2437)

Research	International Rice Research Institute (A2417)
	European Southern Observatory (B3947)
	Asian Conservation Laboratory (B1663)
	Jungfraujoch Scientific Station (B2852)
	International Centre for Theoretical Physics (B2724)
	International Computation Centre (A1645)
Education	Asian Trade Union College (B4149)
	International Centre for Advanced Technical and Vocational Training (A2186)
	International Diplomatic Academy (A1793)
	European University Institute (B3293)
	College of Europe

STRUCTURAL CHARACTERISTICS

A number of international bodies may be usefully characterized by peculiarities in their structure. These may be grouped as follows. (The sub-headings indicate broad classes of structural peculiarity).

A. HYBRID CHARACTER:

This group is distinguished by the manner in which conventional international organisation categories (IGO, INGO, multinational) are blurred in some way. Although not uncommon, little attention has been given to them.

1. *Intergovernmental profit-making corporations.* Such bodies are created by international convention

European Company for the Chemical Processing of Irradiated Fuels (A0682)
European Company for the Financing of Railway Rolling Stock (A0683)

Some international financial bodies are of this kind

Asian Development Bank (A0077)
International Finance Corporation (A2057)

2. *International profit-making corporations with governmental shareholders.* Other shareholders may include intergovernmental financial bodies

Andean Development Corporation (B0409)

45

Sifida Investment Company (B0558)
Hotel Company for the Development of Tourism in Africa (B4599)

Many of the regional development corporations are of this kind. Non-governmental institutional investors may also be shareholders in some of these bodies, particularly in the case of regional airlines:

Air Afrique (B2886)
Scandinavian Airlines System (B2723)

Another interesting example, owned by the Governments of the U.K., Australia and New Zealand is the British Phosphate Commission.

3. *International profit-making corporations linked to intergovernmental organisations.* Some corporations may be part of an intergovernmental system:

East African Airways Corporation (A4214), one of four corporations of the East African Community
European Investment Bank (A0670), under a provision of the Treaty of Rome

Others may be created by an intergovernmental body.

Arab Livestock Development Corporation (B4915)
Arab Chemical and Pharmaceutical Corporation (B3621)

as was proposed by the Council of Arab Economic Unity.

A body like the World Bank may find it useful to stimulate the creation of *ad hoc* consortia of governmental and private enterprises to undertake or finance certain projects.

4. *Multinational corporations with major governmental shareholders.* A conventional multinational enterprise may well have extensive participation by one or more governments as shareholders:

British Petroleum
FIAT
Royal Dutch Shell

In some cases the multinational corporation may be completely state-owned.

5. *Multinational corporations operating as non-profit organisations.* A unit of a multinational enterprise, incorporated under the law of one

country, may operate on a non-profit basis for tax reasons. Funds are provided as transfers from other units of the same enterprise.

Esso Research Laboratories, engaged in 'research' but not sales.
ITT Europe, engaged in 'administration' but not sales.

6. *Not-for-profit corporations.* Some research-oriented international bodies operate on a non-profit basis, although in other respects they may resemble multinational enterprises.

Battelle Memorial Institute (B0187)
Stanford Research Institute (B0211)

7. *Multinational enterprises created by non-profit bodies.* For operational or tax reasons, one or more international non-profit organisations may create a multinational enterprise

Cercle Graphique Européen (B2547) created by bodies including the European Cultural Foundation.

8. *International non-profit body created by multinational enterprises.* A trend in this direction may already be seen in the creation of international trade or employer associations by enterprises, some of which could be called multinational. The limiting case of cartels or price-fixing rings may be considered non-profit bodies since the cartel is usually designed to increase the profit-making capacity of its members rather than to make a profit itself. This is also the case of the numerous freight and shipping conferences. There also exist bodies like the

Business and Industry Advisory Committee to OECD (A0204)

created by industry federations of OECD member countries. Although there do not yet seem to be any clear examples of this form, it is probable that it will at some stage be in the interest of one or more multinational enterprises to create more conventional international non-profit organisations. Such bodies could range from personnel associations through social welfare and collective security bodies to specialist pools. Perhaps an early example is the

International Centre for Industry and the Environment (B4921)

created to represent industry views on the environment, mainly to the United Nations Environment Programme.

Another interesting example is the

International Frisbee Association (B2770)

Frisbee is the registered trade mark of the Wham-O Manufacturing Company for Flying Saucers used in sports games. The company undoubtedly derives considerable benefit from its interest in the association.

A 'user association' may be established on the initiative of concerned clients rather than by a multinational enterprise.

Honeywell Large Systems Users Association (Europe) (B4420)

9. *International non-profit bodies created as operational fronts.* It may be in the interest of a governmental (or intergovernmental) group to stimulate the creation of a conventional non-governmental body, and ensure its financial viability, in order to promote some particular political or other viewpoint. Examples of this sort emerged as a result of disclosure of indirect C.I.A. financing of bodies such as the

Coordinating Secretariat of National Unions of Students (B2594)

Many argue that a significant number of conventional INGOs based in the Eastern bloc countries fall into this category.

Clearly some INGOs with commercial or industrial groups as members could be considered as operational fronts to provide the impression of non-partisan support for a particular position.

There is also the possibility that some INGO-type organization could in fact become a front or vehicle for some form of international criminal activity as has been the case at the national level (e.g. those labour unions in the USA alleged to be 'mob-run' or with strong 'mob-connections' — many with 'international' in their title).

10. *International non-profit bodies created by intergovernmental organisations.* It is occasionally in the interest of an intergovernmental body to stimulate the creation of a conventional INGO. This may be done as a method of decentralizing an activity which the IGO would otherwise be obliged to support. It is also a means of ensuring the existence of a supportive constituency. The clearest examples are the groups of INGOs created 'under UNESCO auspices':

International Music Council (A2277)
International Political Science Association (A2369)
International Social Science Council (A2466)

Council for International Organizations of Medical Sciences (A0431)
International Council for Philosophy and Humanistic Studies (A1728)

Some of these bodies may in fact receive subsidies from UNESCO, have their offices in the UNESCO Secretariat, or even have some of their secretarial services performed by UNESCO. An interesting example of this is the

Conference of INGOs Approved for Consultative Arrangements (A and B) with UNESCO (A0407)

Although this body is not given the usual consultative status recognition by UNESCO, its offices are in the Secretariat, its meetings are provided with considerable UNESCO support (rooms, interpreters, etc.), and revision of its Constitution is conducted with the approval of UNESCO. Its resolutions are very supportive of UNESCO programmes.

11. *International non-profit bodies created with government support.*
Particularly in those developing countries where there is little independent organisational activity, a government may be intimately involved in the creation of a conventional INGO and the provision of support for its ongoing activities. The INGO may be created and supported partly for prestige reasons linked to the promotion of certain political viewpoints. This is often the case with regional INGOs in Africa which for this reason are usually rather fragile. Examples are the many short-lived efforts at establishing regional trade unions, student organizations or professional bodies (e.g. journalists). Another characteristic of such bodies is that the national member organisations are often closely linked to the dominant political party.

The special support of one government is not confined to regional bodies. It occurs particularly with institute-based organisations.

International Commission for Small Scale Vegetation Maps (A1529)

12. *Secret groups* (other than orders). The need for secrecy in criminal groups, politically subversive groups, or groups engaged in industrial or conventional espionage (or counter-espionage) may be such as to erode and blur the attribution they might otherwise have as governmental, commercial or associational activities. For example, a terrorist group has been described as functioning rather like a multinational corporation: 'An operation would be planned in West Germany by Palestine Arabs, executed in Israel by terrorists recruited in

49

Japan with weapons acquired in Italy but manufactured in Russia, supplied by an Algerian diplomat, and financed with Libyan money.'[18] The international network of terrorism, based on transnational links between governmental bodies sponsoring and supporting terrorism, has been reviewed by Yonah Alexander.[19]

13. *Intergovernmental organisations with a special relationship to one government.* For Historical, financial or other reasons a government may have a special relationship (possibly extending to effective control) with an otherwise conventional intergovernmental body.

> International Children's Centre (A1496) which has an 'Administrative Council of 17, 6 being appointed conjointly by the French Minister of Foreign Affairs and the Ministry of Public Health and Population, and 11 being coopted by the first 6.'
> Italian-Latin American Institute (B2837)

14. *International nongovernmental organisations with government-related membership.* There is a range of organisations whose members are strongly linked to governments either as government agencies, nationalized industries or with government funds. The distinction between governmental and nongovernmental then becomes rather fine, particularly since some bodies of this kind have been subsequently transformed into intergovernmental organisations..

> International (Railway) Carriage and Van Union (A1445)
> Inter-Parliamentary Union (A2832)
> Association of Secretaries-General of Parliaments (A0160)
> Commonwealth Parliamentary Association (A0372)
> Interpol – International Criminal Police Organisation (A1775)
> International Union of Official Travel Organisations (A2745)

The last example has recently been transformed into the inter-governmental body:

> World Tourism Organisation.

15. *International nongovernmental bodies with special status in international law.* There are a few organisations in this group.

> International Committee of the Red Cross (A1623), recognized by the Geneva Conventions of 1929 and 1949
> Sovereign Military Order of Malta (B4374), has a legal position

similar to that of the Holy See after the end of the Pontifical States in 1870 and before the creation of the Vatican State in 1929; has plenipotentiary ministers accredited to, and recognized by, a number of countries.

Bodies such as

International Union for the Conservation of Nature and Natural
    Resources (A2654)
International Council of Scientific Unions (A1752)

may acquire special status by being cited in legal instruments establishing programmes of the United Nations, such as the United Nations Environment Programme.

The Roman Catholic Church is centred on the Holy See which is recognized on a par with governments by some countries and as such has a special status in international law.[20] Ivan Vallier notes that the 'notion of the Roman Catholic Church as a transnational actor is both intriguing and elusive. Its global empire, and thus its transnationality, ties it to many situations, no two of which are exactly alike.'[21]

16. *Revolutionary movements.* Such movements are more or less loosely linked into transnational organisations of national parties. Such world revolutionary movements, with or without a formal secretariat, generally recognize Peking, Moscow or Havana as the first among equals

Organisation of Afro-Asian Latin American Peoples Solidarity
    (A3029)

Universal ideologies that have not secured a power-base in the form of a liberated nation-state, such as the Anarchists or the Fourth (Trotskyite) International have escaped centralization but at the cost of coherence and the benefits of secure sanctuary. There is a great variety of host society/revolutionary movement relationships, ranging from total support to total opposition. 'The major curiosity is that every revolutionary organisation aspires to eliminate the necessity for most "revolutionary" transnational contacts as rapidly as possible and to begin acting as a normal, if militant, government no longer dependent on the mesh of world revolutionary society or the uncertain world of illicit agreements, minisummits, and secret conferences.'[22]

17. *Political parties.* Such bodies naturally have a special relationship

51

to government, but are linked as NGOs through such bodies as

Socialist International (A3220)
European Christian Democratic Union (A0620)

B. DEPENDENT CHARACTER:

This group is distinguished by various kinds of dependence on another organisations such that in a particular case if the other ceased to exist there would be no further reason for the dependent body to continue.

1. *Supporting bodies.* Some organisations, usually INGOs, only exist to stimulate public support for other bodies, usually IGOs.

International Student Movement for the United Nations (A2597)
World Federation of United Nations Associations (A3539)
International Union of League of Nations Associations (B2733)

2. *Personnel associations.* Large intergovernmental agencies tend to give rise to personnel or staff associations. These may be for general purposes (e.g. salary negotiations) as for example, the case of those linked to ILO, WHO, FAO and UN. (Some of these have links between agencies which are more extensive than the permissible formal relationships. Such cross-cutting memberships can lead to secretariat work stoppages in several agencies as occurred in 1975 and 1976 during salary and pension negotiations. They are all members of the Federation of International Civil Servants Associations.) Some of the associations may be for specific purposes as is the case with the so-called United Nations Sports Commission which is not a commission of the United Nations, but of its personnel. Slightly different is the case of the United Nations Womens Guild which includes staff members and women (or wives of delegates) in national delegations to the United Nations or its Agencies and tends to act in support of UN programmes.

The multinational corporations are giving rise to a new kind of dependent body, namely trade unions of employees of specific multinationals (e.g. Nestlé).

3. *Consultative bodies.* A number of INGO bodies have been created specifically for purposes of facilitating consultation with intergovernmental agencies.

Conference of Nongovernmental Organisations in Consultative Status with the UN Economic and Social Council (A0409)

Conference of International Nongovernmental Organisations
approved for Consultative Arrangements (A and B) with UNESCO
(A0407)

4. *Pressure groups.* Somewhat similar to the consultative bodies are the several hundred commercial, industrial and professional groups created to clarify and express their positions with respect to the many regulations formulated within an emerging economic community

Association of EEC Glucose Manufacturers (B0125)
Consultative Committee of Bar Associations of EEC Member
Countries (B0412)
Union of EEC Advertisers Associations (B0498)

5. *Opposition bodies.* Just as there are supporting bodies, so it could perhaps be argued that some groups are in fact created to oppose the activities of other bodies.

World Anti-Communist League (A3454)
Organization of Afro-Asian Latin-American Peoples Solidarity
(A3029) against imperialism and colonialism
Anti-Monopoly Committee of Petroleum Workers of the
Mediterranean, Black Sea and Middle East (B0581)

6. *System dependent bodies.* Some bodies are created in response to the existence of a technological system as user organisations.

Honeywell Large Systems Users Association (B4420)
Suez Canal Users Association (B3302)

Of a somewhat different kind are such bodies as the

United Nations Press Correspondents Association (B4662)

C. SEMI-AUTONOMOUS CHARACTER:

In contrast to the dependence stressed in connection with the previous group, this one is characterised by some degree of autonomy despite close links to a particular intergovernmental body. As such it is more typical of some intergovernmental bodies.

World Food Programme (B3543)
World Food Council (B3430)
International Rice Commission (A2416)

International Poplar Commission (A2371), which is one of several
  bodies established by FAO conventions and agreements
International Book Committee (B4845)
Intergovernmental Copyright Committee (A1115)
Intergovernmental Oceanographic Commission (A1118)

A somewhat different case is that of a body like the

Joint Inspection Unit

set up with an independent status by the UN General Assembly to
examine finance-related matters of the United Nations and its
Specialized Agencies. Mention should also be made here of the semi-
autonomous nature of some regionally or functionally specialized
bodies of larger organisations. (These are considered separately below.)

D. RELATIONSHIP TO LEADERSHIP:

This group is characterized by the special nature of the leadership and
the less-than-democratic control it is presumably in a position to
exercise over the policies of the organisations. In effect the membership
of such bodies exchange democratic procedures for some other
ordering mechanism in which they have greater confidence.

1. *Chartered bodies.* Some organizations receive a special patent or
charter (or other form of patronage), often from a religious authority
such as the Pope.

Apostleship of the Sea (B4961)
International Association of the Children of Mary (B4326)
Caritas Internationalis (A0216)
Consilium de Laicis (B0442)
Movement for a Better World (B0160)
Motamar, World Muslim Congress (A3561)
Rabetata al-Alam al-Islami, Muslim World League (A4378)

In the case of the United Kingdom, the Crown authorizes many
'royal societies' with Commonwealth-wide membership.

Royal Agricultural Society of the Commonwealth (B4139)
Royal Commonwealth Society for the Blind (B3167)
Royal Commonwealth Society (B0100)

Although organisations of this kind may be democratically structured
in all other respects, it is clear that any such charter may be revoked and

this possibility would tend to ensure a special sensitivity to the wishes and interests of the Pope and the Crown respectively. In practice this may lead to the appointment within the organisation of 'advisory' councils largely made up of people with the desired sensitivity.

2. *Orders.* There are orders of various kinds where the leadership is believed to possess greater knowledge or wisdom than the general membership, such that the degrees of such insight are supposed to determine the levels within the order.

Rosicrucian Order (A3163)
International Supreme Council of World Masons (A2610)
Sovereign Military Order of Malta (B4374)
Sufi Order (B3745)

Aside from the reasonably visible orders cited above, the many secret societies also belong to this type although because they are secret it is not usual to take them into consideration as varieties of INGOs.

Orders of chivalry are of special interest because of their historical importance as an early form of nongovernmental actor (for example the Europe-wide role of the Order of Knights Templar and its network of commanderies prior to its dissolution in the 14th century) and their intimate relationship to monarchies and nobility, religious or military hierarchies, or other powerful and well-connected groups — even at the present time. Boalt et al.[23] have examined the European orders as organisations from a sociological perspective. A register of genuine orders of chivalry has been produced by the International Commission for Orders of Chivalry[24] whose secretary-general has reviewed the problems of distinguishing between such orders, although without considering non-chivalric orders such as the freemasons which he notes as having been allegedly created following the suppression of some of the early orders of chivalry.[25]

3. *Military Structures.* A military system of ranking may be preferred to clarify the distinction between different levels of ability.

Salvation Army (A3172)
Boys' Brigade (B0195)
Sovereign Military Order to Malta (B4374)

4. *Charismatic leadership.* Where the organisation has in effect been created as a vehicle for the communication of the views of one

individual, the formal structure (however it is arrived at) does not have the same significance as in conventional bodies.

Divine Light Movement
Holy Spirit Association for the Unification of Christianity (B3092)
International Meditation Society (A4546)

E. REGIONAL (SUB) GROUPINGS:
Some well developed international bodies with membership in several continents may give rise to regroupings of the membership at the regional level. It is not always clear whether such regional groupings are deliberate creations of the international body (and thus a form of sub-grouping) or whether they are independent bodies which may establish (or break) formal links to the international body.

Asian Football Confederation (A0079)
African Table Tennis Federation (A0024)
Inter-American Regional Organisation of Workers of the ICFTU (B1096)

F. FUNCTIONAL (SUB) GROUPINGS:
As with the regional regrouping discussed above, some international bodies may give rise to regroupings of the membership around specific topics or activities. Again it is not always clear whether such functional groupings are deliberate creations of the international body or whether they are independent bodies which may establish (or break) formal links to the international body.

International Commission for the Nomenclature of Cultivated Plants (B1536)
International Society of Developmental Biologists (A2539)

Both the above are part of the International Union of Biological Sciences (A2698).

G. HETEROGENEOUS MEMBERSHIP:
The organisations in this group have members which may constitute a mixture of governmental, nongovernmental, or business organisations and be international or national. The membership may also include individuals.

International Institute of Administrative Sciences (A2138)

includes: governments, national and international sections,
corporate bodies and individuals.
International Council of Scientific Unions (A1752)
includes: scientific academies, national research councils,
associations of institutions, governments and international
scientific unions.
Consultative Group on International Agricultural Research (A4468)
includes: African, Asian and Inter-American-Development Banks;
the Commission of the European Communities; the Ford,
Rockefeller and Kellogg Foundations; the International Development Research Center; 13 governments.

H. COMPLEX CHARACTER:
This group is distinguished by the structural complexity which results
from conventional INGOs or IGOs becoming members of an INGO
or of an intergovernmental body, respectively.
Clear examples in the case of IGOs are:

Conference of International Catholic Organisations (A0406)
Council for International Organizations of Medical Sciences (A0431)
Conference of World Organisations interested in the Handicapped
(A0458)

Some of these may in their turn become members of such bodies as the:

Conference of NGOs in Consultative Status with UN ECOSOC
(A0409)
Conference of INGOs approved for Consultative Arrangements with
UNESCO (A0407)

An equally complex situation occurs with the various independent
international scientific unions (some with other international scientific
bodies as members) which are themselves members of the International
Council of Scientific Unions. In addition these members may group
together in various combinations (with the encouragement of ICSU) to
form inter-union commissions on special topics.
In the case of the IGOs, examples are:

Protein-Calorie Advisory Group of the United Nations System
(B0824)
Consultative Group on International Agricultural Research (A4468)
Inter-American Committee for Agricultural Development (A1059)
with five IGO members.

I. MINIMAL STRUCTURE:

This group of bodies is characterized by an explicit awareness of the weaknesses of the structural options open to international bodies and a deliberate attempt to work (or experiment) with some minimal structure.

> Q International Movement (B0700)
> Club of Rome (A4013)
> UNISIST, World Science Information System (B4668)
> United Nations University (B2488)
> Mankind 2000 (A2943)

Such 'organisations' when contacted will often vigorously deny that they are organisations and will particularly insist that they do not belong to the same class as conventional IGOs or INGOs, which they may well perceive as ineffective.

J. MULTI-NATIONAL STRUCTURE:

Related to the previous group are those 'non-organisations' which avoid any formal international structure. More or less formal organisations within a number of countries simply recognize each others' existence and engage in informal exchanges, possibly leading to a harmonization of policies or various forms of joint action. At one extreme this merely constitutes a normal stage prior to the formation of any conventional international body (or any substitute for it), but of more interest is the deliberate use of this approach as a means of avoiding the international formalization of a well-developed multi-national relationship, as is the case with various movements: guru-based, alternative-technology, alternative-lifestyle, radical or revolutionary politics, etc. This is also a characteristic of invisible colleges and some scholarly networks which do not need to be encumbered with any formal organisation because of the frequency of contact between those involved.[26]

CHARACTERISTIC MODES OF ACTION

Many international organisations may be usefully characterized by the emphasis they give to a particular mode of action. The emphasis may even be reflected in the actual name of the organisation, thus distinguishing it from the majority of organisations (possibly to the point of raising the question as to whether it really should be considered as an organisation).

The modes of action concerned are listed below. In each case

examples of international bodies are given. In most cases the names of
the bodies provide sufficient clue to the manner in which the organisation is oriented by the mode in question. The list has here
been split into two parts. The first part, grouping the cases where the
mode of action constitutes a social artefact in its own right (e.g. a
meeting-type event, project, or campaign) embodied in the name of
the organisation, forms part of the 'activity sub-group' of the
tentative classification on the basis of organisation terminology
(see above). The second part, listed below, groups other characteristic
modes of action.

Treaty

Warsaw Treaty Organisation (A3422)
Atlantic Treaty Association (A0179)
Agency for the Prohibition of Nuclear Weapons in Latin America
(A0031) which administers the Treaty for the Prohibition of
Nuclear Weapons in Latin America
Central Treaty Organisation (A0254)

Agreement Administration

General Agreement on Tariffs and Trade (A0985)
International Tin Council (A2632)
International Wheat Council (A2812)
International Whaling Commission (A2811)

Some of the commodity arrangements renewable after one or more
years result in the dissolution of the administering body at the end of
each such period and its continuation under the new agreement.

Arbitration

Permanent Court of Arbitration (A3107)
International Centre for Settlement of Investment Disputes (A1476)

Clearing

Asian Clearing Union (A4644)
Bank for International Settlements (A0184)
West Africa Clearing House (B4799)

Negotiation

Group of 77 (B0728)
Group of 10 (B1004)

Nomenclature

International Commission for the Nomenclature of Cultivated Plants (B1536)
International Commission on Zoological Nomenclature (A1573)
International Building Classification Committee (A1411)

Standardization

International Organisation for Standardization (A2314)
International Bureau of Weights and Measures (A1440)

Travel

World Expeditionary Association (B0136)

The major activity of this body is to facilitate low-cost air travel for members.

Examination

International Baccalaureate Office (A1389)

Field Action

International Secretariat for Volunteer Service (A2441)
Oxford Committee for Famine Relief (B3041)

Personal Contact

Experiment in International Living (A0917)
International Business Contact Club (B4548)

Commemoration

International Committee for World Refugee Year (A1762)
World Association for Celebrating the Year 2000 (A3460)
International Auschwitz Committee (B1384)
International Gustav Mahler Society (B2624)

Computation

International Computation Centre (A1645)

Language

International Association of French-Language Sociologists (A1286)
English-Speaking Union (A0529)
Universal Esperanto Association (A3399)

Preoccupational Character

It is interesting to split off from the complete range of international organisations those bodies which can usefully be grouped in terms of some general preoccupation (as contrasted with a more conventional classification by subject).

Defence and National Security

This is a well-defined group of bodies

Warsaw Treaty Organisation (A3422)
South-East Asia Treaty Organisation (A3256)
Anzus Council (A0059)

Commodity

Again this is a well-defined group of bodies. [27]

International Sugar Organisation (A2606)
Organisation of the Petroleum Exporting Countries (A3038)

Product

This is a less clearly defined group when the concern is with a specific product rather than with the relevant manufacturing industry or trade.

European Centre for Carbon Black (A0608)
European Cement Association (A0606)
International Frisbee Association (B2770)

Industrial Economic Process

There are numerous organisations related to manufacturing or extractive industries.

International Group of National Pesticide Manufacturers' Associations (A2090)
International Wallpaper Manufacturers Association (As806)

These are often closely related to trade associations.

International Federation of Meat Traders Association (A1954)
International Cocoa Trades Federation (A1508)

There is also a group concerned with services and delivery of skills.

European Federation of Productivity Services (A0906)
International Association of Mutual Insurance Companies (A1319)

International Foodservice Distributors Association (B0290)

Finally there is a further group of employer organisations, possibly associated with particular industries

International Organization of Employers (A2322)

Occupation

Directly related to many of the industrial or economic processes noted in the previous section there are trade unions and professional organisations.

International Federation of Petroleum and Chemical Workers (A1975)
Trades Union International of Workers in the Metal Industries (A3327)
International Bar Association (A1396)
International Banker Association (A1394)

In addition to economic occupations there are organisations associated with social and recreational activities.

International Senior Citizens Association (A2454)
International Amateur Rugby Federation (A1160)

Technique

Some occupations and processes have distinct techniques or methods associated with them which may be the preoccupation of an international organisation.

International Committee on High-Speed Photography (A1631)
International Waterproofing Association (A2808)

Research

Many international organisations are concerned with general or specific areas of research or study, whether in science and technology or in art and culture.

International Astronomical Union (A1382)
International Union for the Study of Social Insects (A4256)
International Association for the Study of Ancient Mosaics (A1235)
International Federation for Theatre Research (A1842)

Social Amelioration

Some international organisations have always been preoccupied with improving society, whether through social welfare in developed societies, general development and aid programmes in the less developed countries, or in the form of crisis relief.

> International Council on Social Welfare (A1770)
> International Council of Voluntary Agencies (A1762)
> League of Red Cross Societies (A2907)

Value or Belief Propagation

Many international organisations are primarily concerned with the widespread propagation of particular values or beliefs.

> International League for the Rights of Man (A2205)
> Christian Peace Conference (A0272)
> Salvation Army (A3172)
> World Council of Churches (A3501)

GEOGRAPHIC CHARACTERISTICS

A number of bodies which may be called 'international' can be usefully characterized by peculiarities in their geographic orientation or distribution of membership. These may be grouped as follows:

A. GEOGRAPHICALLY FOCUSSED

This group is distinguished by mention of a specific, and generally small, geographic feature in the name of the organisation.

1. *Region.* In this case a region is named, generally an area where three frontiers meet.

> European Group for the Ardennes and the Eifel (A0776)
> Liptako-Gourma Region Integrated Development Authority (A4474)

2. *Lake.* This is similar to the previous case.

> Lake Chad Basin Commission (A4496)
> International Commission for the Protection of Lake Constance
>   (A4500)

3. *River.* There are a number of examples of organisations concerned with rivers flowing between two or more countries.

Danube Commission (A0464)
Central Commission for the Navigation of the Rhine (A0241)
Organization for the Development of the Senegal River (A3036)

4. *Place*. A number of bodies are concerned with specifically named locations.

International Auschwitz Committee (B1384)
International Action Committee for Safeguarding the Nubian Monuments
International Association for the Schweitzer Hospital at Lambaréné (B0193)
Jungfraujoch Scientific Station (B2852)
International Association for Fundamental Research on the Furnace at Ougrée (B3913)

5. *Territory*. In some cases a whole territory is named.

Committee for the Control of the International Zone of Tangier (B0307)
Charles Darwin Foundation for the Galapagos Islands (B0260)
Allied Commission for Austria (B0041)
Agudath Israel World Organisation (A0032)

A special case occurs where there is some intent to inhibit activity in the territory, such as by boycott.

(Arab) Bureau for Boycotting Israel CHINCOM (Embargo on strategic goods for China)
Consultative Group Cooperation Committee (B4582) for the embargo on export of strategic goods to the Eastern bloc
International Defence and Aid Fund for Southern Africa (A4333)

B. GEOGRAPHICALLY DISPLACED

This group includes those bodies which have some unusual combination of geographic features.

Association of American Chambers of Commerce in Latin America (B0786)
World Association of Estonians (B0027)
World Federation of Hungarian Jews (B4767)
European Branch Association of Commonwealth Language and Literature Studies (B4590) with secretariat in Denmark

This also includes exile organisations.

Assembly of Captive European Nations (A0097)
Christian Democratic Union of Central Europe (A0265)

C. REGIONAL ORGANISATIONS WITH EXTRA-REGIONAL MEMBERSHIP

Some bodies whose names appear to limit the distribution of membership in fact have members from other regions with equal voting rights.

Asian Development Bank (A0077)
Scandinavian Society for Plant Physiology (A3198)

D. SECRETARIAT-LOCATION ORGANISATIONS

In those countries with a long tradition of international activity an umbrella type of body may be created.

Federation of International Associations established in Belgium (B0945)
Federation of Semi-Official and Private International Institutions established in Geneva (B0956)
Liaison Committee of International Nongovernmental Organisations established in France

E. GEOGRAPHICALLY FRAGMENTED MEMBERSHIP

A number of bodies, which may be termed 'regional', in fact have a dispersed membership.

Organisation for Economic Cooperation and Development (A3023)
Coordinating Bureau for Non-aligned Countries (B2507)

Other examples, which have not yet given rise to permanent international bodies, may be found associated with land-locked countries and arid, tropical or mountainous regions.

F. PLACE-NAMED ORGANISATIONS

This group is distinguished by the presence of a city name in the title or acronym of the organization. The city may be either that of (1) the secretariat and regular meeting point, (2) the place of signature of a relevant treaty (which may also be the secretariat or place of the first meeting) or (3) the place of the first meeting (which may also be the location of the secretariat).

(1)   The Hague Conference on Private International Law (A1006)
Rehovot Conference on Science in the Advancement of New
States (B3155)
Oxford Committee for Famine Relief (B3041)

(2)   Paris Union — International Union for the Protection of
Industrial Property (A2669)
Berne Union — International Union for the Protection of
Literary and Artistic Property (A2670)
Warsaw Treaty Organisation (A3422)

(3)   Colombo Plan for Technical Cooperation in South and
South-East Asia (A0281)
Pugwash Conference on Science and World Affairs (A3148)
The Club of Rome (A4013)

G. INTERNATIONALLY-OPERATING NATIONAL ORGANISATIONS

There are many organisations which are primarily national but which
nevertheless are mainly concerned with operational programmes (usually
aid or relief) in other countries.

American Council of Voluntary Agencies for Foreign Service (B0457)
Cooperative American Relief Everywhere (B0420)
UK Standing Conference for the Second Development Decade
(B4254)

Such bodies may in fact acquire consultative status with the United
Nations Economic and Social Council on a par with conventional INGOs.
An older variation on this form is the missionary society, although
increasingly such societies despatch missionaries from several base
countries.

Council for World Mission (B4835)

H. INTERNATIONALLY-FOCUSSED NATIONAL ORGANISATIONS

Whilst usually without operational programmes in other countries, there
is a range of national organisations which is primarily interested in
international relations and world affairs. The preoccupation is
generally academic but may include an attempt to educate a selected
group (e.g. policy makers) or the public.

International Peace Research Institute, Oslo
Pakistan Institute of International Affairs
Institute for World Order, New York

66

I. NATIONALLY-SUPPORTED INTERNATIONAL ORGANISATIONS

Some otherwise quite conventional international bodies are mainly supported (e.g. funding, services or office facilities) by one national body, possibly a government agency.

Stockholm International Peace Research Institute (A3944)
International Children's Centre (A1496)

J. MINIMALLY-INTERNATIONAL ORGANISATIONS

There is a tendency for some national organisations to attempt to stimulate their development into international bodies by adopting a name which creates the impression that such a development has been accomplished. This may be for prestige reasons but it may also be based on an honest but very simple, interpretation of the meaning of 'international'. Thus there is a whole range of organisations based in the United States, with a small proportion of membership in other countries (often only Canada or Mexico, if any), which are named 'International . . . ' This is especially true of labour unions and trade associations.

International Longshoremans and Warehousemens Union (B1348)
International Brotherhood of Electrical Workers (B4454)
International Oxygen Manufacturers Association (B4912)

It is useful to note here that federated states may legitimately give rise to a wide range of 'intergovernmental' organisations at the federal level with names having a form indistinguishable from that of conventional intergovernmental bodies.

K. BILATERAL AND SIMILAR BODIES

The well-established bilateral form of organisation is not usually considered as belonging to the general range of international organisations. There is however a development of this form in which one of the partners is a continental grouping but in which each member is of equal status.

Italian-Latin American Institute (B2837)
Association Europe-Japan (B2117)
Federation of European American Organisations (A0935)

The last example is in fact a federation of bilateral organisations.

OTHER SPECIAL CHARACTERISTICS

COMMEMORATIVE ORGANISATIONS

Some international bodies are specifically conceived to commemorate or celebrate past or future events.

International Auschwitz Committee
World Association for Celebrating Year 2000 (A3460)

Others give recognition to a major worker or leader in their special field when an organisation is formed to develop that or related work

Howard League for Penal Reform (B1012)
Nansen International Office for Refugees (B2968)
Stefan Banach International Mathematical Centre for Raising Research Qualifications (B0656)
Bernoulli Society for Mathematical Statistics and Probability (A1209)
International Rorschach Society (A2422)
International Gutenberg Society (B2093)
International Grotius Foundation for the Propagation of the Law of Nations (B2086)
Von Karman Institute for Fluid Dynamics (B3420)
International Heinrich Schutz Society (B2100)

INDIVIDUAL WORK FOCUS

Distinct from the previous group is one in which the concern is not so much with acknowledging an early leader as with limiting attention to the collective work, approach or ideas of that leader.

International Margaret Morris Movement (B0643)
International Montessori Association (B2267)
International Gustav Mahler Society (B2624), and other composer societies
International Dostoevsky Society (B3222), and other author societies
Amis de Robert Schuman (B4316)

An interesting variation on this is a body whose membership is restricted to former students of an individual and (more recently) to students of the original students.

Bockus International Society of Gastro-enterology (B4870)

Another well-developed variation of this group is the religious order inspired by the work and rules of a particular individual.

Tiers ordre franciscain (B4831)
Tiers ordre dominicain (B4565)

CHARISMATIC PERSONALITY FOCUS

Organisations in this group (which are often exceptionally well-endowed financially due to the number and enthusiasm of members) are each centred on the activities of one charismatic individual. The identity of the individual may not necessarily be present in the organisation name.

International Meditation Society (B4546) and several others such as the Maharishi European Research University (B3384) centred on the Maharishi Mahesh Yogi

Holy Spirit Association for the Unification of World Christianity (B3092) centred on Sun Myung Moon

Hubbard Association of Scientologists (B1013) and other bodies centred on L. Ron Hubbard

Divine Light Movement centred on the family members of the Mahariji-ji

Bodies of this kind which operate internationally are a relatively recent phenomena although their number is now increasing rapidly.

SPECIAL PATRONAGE

It is appropriate to mention here the group of organisations which have a special form of patronage, namely certain Catholic organisations which receive a charter from the Pope, and royal societies with Commonwealth-wide membership which receive a charter from the Crown. (These are discussed under Structural Characteristics.)

INDIVIDUAL ACTIVIST

It is useful to note that a number of smaller organisations depend for the continuation of their activities on the dynamism of one individual. Whilst presenting all the characteristics of a conventional organisation (and few of the charismatic variety noted above), such bodies may thus be nurtured through to non-dependence on the individual although such a presence may be essential during the early growth stages. Clearly if the organisation does not 'take wing', such bodies may then be perpetuated as shells until the person ceases to animate it.

ALUMNI

There are a number of organisations of former students of international educational bodies.

Association of Attenders and Alumni of The Hague Academy of International Law (B0119)
Association of Former Students of the College of Europe, Bruges (B0133)
World Union of Marist Old Boys (B0840)
World Organization of Former Students of Catholic Teaching (A4159)
Association of Former Students of the Cité Internationale of the University of Paris (B4220)
World Confederation of Former Students of Don Bosco (B4114)

Another small group, similar to the above, is that of organisations of winners of a particular international prize.

Standing Committee for Nobel Prize Winners' Congresses (B3275)

MILITARY UNIONS

There is a movement among the western democracies to secure representation of the human rights of military personnel, in terms of material benefits and working conditions, through membership in trade or public employee unions. This has been explored in the case of the European armed forces by Ezr Krendle,[28] where the potential impact on NATO forces is of obvious importance.

RELIGIOUS BODIES

Many religious bodies use conventional organisational forms for their international activity.

World Methodist Council (A3557)
World Federation of Islamic Missions (B4536)
World Fellowship of Buddhists (A3541)
World Christian Congress (A3561)
Watch Tower Bible and Tract Society (B3423)
International Federation of Mazdaznan Women (A1953)

In some cases, however, the conventional terminology is replaced by a religious form, without affecting the conventional character of the organisation.

Church of Christ, Scientist (A0275)

This is only possible where there is a minimal religious hierarchy as is characteristic of some sects.

A further group is created, however, when the religious hierarchy supplants any member-determined organisational structure. This is the case typified by the Roman Catholic Church with the range of papal commissions and religious orders, but also in such bodies as

International Society for Krishna Consciousness (B2247)

SEMI-HUMOROUS

There is a small group of organisations which have been created for fun, or at least somewhat with tongue-in-cheek.

Association for the Promotion of Humor in International Affairs (B3896)
International Association of the Bald-Heads (A1357)
Worldwide Fairplay for Frogs Committee (B3541)

This group may also be considered to include organisations of collectors of somewhat unexpected objects. Clearly this group includes organisations of little significance. However, this does raise the important questions of where the cut-off point should be located, why, in whose interest, and at whose expense.

RETROGRESSIVE BODIES

There is a group of bodies with concerns which would tend to be considered retrogressive by most of the international community.

International Flat Earth Research Society (B0371)
West European Federation of National Socialists (B2519)

A variation on this group would include the organisations which might be evaluated as pseudo-scientific or, in another variant, as pseudo-religious. This would, however, raise the questions of how and why the evaluation is to be performed, and again, in whose interest and at whose expense.

HYPER-PROGRESSIVE BODIES

In contrast to the previous group, there are organisations with concerns whose occurrence would tend to be considered of low-probability or only of possible significance in the long-term future.

Contact International (A0416), concerned with UFOs

International Committee for a New Planet (B4639)
Institute of Parascience (A4454)
Mondcivitan Republic (A3668)
International Commission for the protection of Planets against
    Microbes from Earth (B2419)
Planetary Citizens (B3023)
Psywar Society (A4314)

Some would argue that the various bodies promoting world government should be included here. It is interesting, however, to note the reception accorded the International Astronautical Federation when it was founded in 1950. One intergovernmental agency rated such a pre-occupation as the domain of 'lunatics' (the editors of the *Yearbook of International Organizations* at that time were also forced to reassess their own policies on such cases).

SHIPPING CONFERENCES

These are groups of shipping lines operating on usually well-defined routes, with basic agreements to charge uniform rates. The word 'conference' denotes no single system but is a generic term covering a wide range of common services and common obligations undertaken by shipowners serving particular trades. Broadly speaking, the term denotes a meeting of lines serving any particular route, aimed at agreement on uniform and stable rates of freight and the provision of services, under stated working conditions in the trade. A conference ranges from a very informal association to a well developed organisation with a permanent secretariat behind it. In 1965 there were about 360 conferences operating in the various trades of the world.[29] Their manner of operation is of concern in terms of its potential for exploitation and unfair competition.[30]

CARTELS

It is also appropriate to make special mention of cartels (of which shipping conferences may be one variety). These may take the form of import cartels, export cartels and agreements on standards. They may only involve private corporations or may have the implicit or explicit support of government, or some direct form of government participation.[31]

Problems of Classifying International Organisations

A. BORDERLINE CATEGORIES

As was noted in a cautionary remark concerning the specific examples cited in the previous sections, the organisations are included there to show that a body could be 'international' according to some characteristics. Some of the bodies, however, would tend not to be identified as presenting a sufficient degree of 'internationality' at this time — for reasons other than those for which they were cited as examples.

This is a very real problem which has pre-occupied the editors of the *Yearbook of International Organizations* — a reference book designed to provide descriptive listings of all 'international' governmental and nongovernmental bodies. Over the years they have developed an empirical set of criteria for deciding whether an organisation should be included or not. With the latest edition, however, they are obliged to note that:

'With the increase in the number and the variety of bodies called 'international', it has become more and more difficult to limit a *Yearbook of International Organizations* only to those organisations corresponding to the selection criteria used for previous editions, even though those criteria remain valid as a definition of 'minimal internationality'. Consider the following examples:

— the practice of the United Nations Economic and Social Council to give consultative status to an increasing number of 'national' nongovernmental organisations on the same basis as for international nongovernmental organizations. Previously this was only done in exceptional cases. (By agreement with the United Nations, all organisations acquiring consultative status are described in this Yearbook.)

— the creation of three hundred nongovernmental committees to coordinate commercial and industrial activities within the European Economic Community countries. Such bodies therefore acquire a special 'federal' (rather than international) character within the Community.

— the creation of a large number of semi-autonomous regional or functional bodies of governmental or nongovernmental organisations, making it difficult to determine satisfactorily the degree of autonomy justifying their inclusion as separate entries.

— the emergence of a variety of new kinds of organisation which

raise unresolved questions as to whether such bodies should be considered as 'international' or not, although they clearly represent a mutation which it is important to reflect in this Yearbook.
In recent editions these difficulties have been met either by excluding the body (and merely mentioning it in the entry on the organisation to which it had some dependent relationship), giving it a 'short entry', or (particularly in the case of intergovernmental bodies) giving it a separate full entry.'

The new procedure adopted in the 16th edition has been to extract from the original numbered sequence of organisations (now called Section A) all those organisations which do not appear to conform to the editors' unchanged criteria of an active, independent international organisation. These organisations, together with many others included for the first time, form a new numbered sequence (called Section B). This section therefore includes any other organisation which may be perceived as 'international' according to broader criteria. (It also includes international bodies in process of formation as well as dormant or defunct organisations.)
This procedure has the effect of clarifying the nature of the bodies satisfying the minimum criteria of 'genuine' internationality. But loosening the criteria for the second section results in the inclusion of a wide range of bodies which raise the question of exactly what can usefully be called 'international' or 'transnational'. Whilst it is clear that some of these bodies present characteristics which it would be difficult to justify as 'international', others possess a blend of characteristics which place them in a borderline zone. Earlier paragraphs help to clarify the ways in which bodies may be perceived as lying within this zone, but further work is required to determine exactly what can be meant by an 'international' or 'transnational' body.

B. ORGANISATIONAL SUBSTITUTES
Functions performed by conventional international bodies may also be performed by substitutes for such bodies under certain circumstances as was implied in an earlier section.
One example of how a need satisfied by a conventional organisation may be satisfied by a functional equivalent is the case of a subscribership. In one setting it may be necessary to have interaction between members via an 'organisation', while in another the need for such interaction

74

may be satisfied by a journal to which individuals can subscribe. Another example is the case of an 'agreement' which may be considered an hyperformal organisation. In one setting a written or even verbal agreement may satisfactorily regulate relations between members, in another an equivalent agreement may have to be administered by a secretariat via an organisation. Where formal agreement is not possible, an 'organisation' may perform the necessary mediating or negotiating functions between its members. A final example is the case of a meeting, and particularly large periodic meetings, in a series. In terms of activity, this may be more significant than a small normally constituted organisation.

Of particular interest at this time is the increasing importance of various kinds of international information and data networks (possibly based on telex or real-time computer links), by whatever bodies they may be operated or ultimately controlled, if any. One important variety is associated with the movement of bibliographical information (UNISIST, AGRIS, INIS, DEVSIS, and the like). Another is associated with movement of quantitative scientific data (weather, earthquakes, astronomical phenomena, etc.). Yet another is concerned with movement of financial data within networks of major banks, governments and financial institutions. Few of these have received scholarly attention, one recent exception being international (news) wire services.[32] The more sophisticated varieties, with fewer but more powerful users, are available through computer networks. One example is TECHNOTEC which is a technology exchange data base service offered by the Control Data Corporation to facilitate worldwide technology transfer through the CYBERNET/KRONOS timesharing networks. (A special problem is associated with such services, for although few constraints are placed upon users their regular use of such services may effectively bind them into dependence on them making the user vulnerable to unilateral decisions on the part of the institutions or country in which the processing power or files are located — which, for example, may be especially serious where complex national economic computations of low technology countries can only be switched onto computers based in high technology countries. What organisation or country could risk dependence on a United Nations computer system when its files and access could be frozen by a General Assembly majority decision?)

One consequence of focusing on conventional organisations only is that functional equivalents, particularly in non-Western cultures, are excluded from the analysis, thus introducing cultural bias and jeopardizing comparative studies. Another consequence is that even within a certain culture an 'organisational analysis' will exclude many styles of organisation performing functions which mesh with those of the organisations we are trying to isolate for closer scrutiny, thus rendering the analysis incomplete.

A further complicating feature is that a conventional organisation may, for example, perform functions for a 'membership' but at the same time produce a periodical which serves as a focal point for a 'subscribership' which is neither identical nor coterminous with the membership. A further complicating feature derives from the dynamics of a social system in that the growth or decay of a particular organisation form may be accompanied by transference of functions to another organisation form, for instance due to change in technology. The ability to accomplish this transference may be hindered by inertial features, such as vested interests identified with particular patterns of organisation. Because we are trapped within our categorical straitjackets we are unable to appreciate fully the complex and subtle ways in which the various forms of organisation share and switch the burden of particular social functions between them. Proposals for social change therefore tend to be based on a rather myopic vision of the functions currently performed by a limited number of conventional organisations, rather than on a panoramic view of the rich and complex organisational ecosystem in which many species flourish and interact.

C. ALTERNATIVE CATEGORIES

In addition to the organisational substitutes discussed above, it is appropriate to draw attention to what may be called alternative styles of organisation.

It is a frequent complaint of those dissatisfied with international NGOs (and IGOs to a much lesser extent) that most of these bodies are based on a Western model or concept of organisation. As such it is claimed that they do not reflect the style, practice or tradition of organisation in non-Western societies. This said however the regional organisations in such societies tend to differ very little organisationally from the Western model, except perhaps in the degree of direct or indirect government influence on their activities. The only non-Western bodies which the author has been able to locate which could be said to represent the beginning of an alternative approach to organisation at the international level are the Waqf in the Arab culture and associations between widely dispersed Chinese populations based on the family name or the ancestral province. Whether organisational forms currently emerging from the Chinese social experiment could be employed at the international level is a matter for attention (particularly regarding the manner of participation of nation states), but there seems to be no evidence of any use of such a distinct form.

As was mentioned earlier, deliberate efforts have been made in some cases to create minimally structured organisations which blur into informal networks of individuals, groups or institutions. Where these bear a recognized name, they may presumably be considered as semi-formal bodies. Others are purely informal (e.g. the commune network).

The pattern of links between organisations across national boundaries may be such that the resultant network effectively constitutes an organisation in its own right but at a different level. Such 'organisations' emerge without being deliberately designed and created. (It would be useful to know how this process could be facilitated.)

The relations between members in an organisation are conventionally governed by statutory and procedural provisions detailed in appropriate documents. With the advent of computer data networks linking widely dispersed terminals, a new form of organisation is emerging. The rules governing the interaction between the members are precisely embodied in the computer software by which the member users interact through the data network. This technique, known as computer conferencing, has given rise to what are being called 'on-line intellectual networks'.[33] Some of these already cross national boundaries, linking many institutions. Clearly the rules governing the participation of member-users can be modified to include most of those which are essential to the functioning of a normal organisation.

The increased use of the technique noted in the above paragraph could also be accompanied by sophisticated modifications to control procedures in organisations. The current range of organisations is limited because of the need for simple voting and control procedures and easily understandable membership groups. The calculating and dis-play power of the computer permits the use of complex weighted voting techniques to allow for a considerable variety of possible distinctions and means of safeguarding against abuse. For example, one member might be allocated 10 votes on one issue range and 70 on another, with the total votes from particular voting blocs being weighted in terms of a complex index, itself governed by a weight changing at an agreed rate over the life of the organisation. This would permit a much more subtle make-up of organisation membership, reflecting more closely the relative interests, capabilities and qualifications of members. The variety of organisational structures would therefore increase. Organisations could be successfully created from combinations of members which would currently be considered improbable or unstable.

The above techniques make possible the existence of organisations which only 'cohere' and 'exist' on particular issues, or which might have a wide voting membership on one issue, but a very limited voting membership on another. This takes us to a point where the concept of an organisation as a distinct and well-defined structure (other than in computer terms) is replaced by an emphasis on the potential components of a structural pattern at any one time and the stimulus necessary to call each of them into play. This formalization of organisation dynamics is foreign to conventional thinking about formal organisation but is close to the normal intuitive understanding of the operation of small groups, informal organisations and pressure groups.

Clearly the above trends would encourage the emergence of issue-oriented organisations, presenting all the characteristics of a permanent formal organisation except that they would be designed to terminate after a period of days, weeks or months. Such bodies might even be rapidly 'created' by computer from a pool of members who have registered interest in participating in any such bodies activated by a sufficient number of requests in response to an urgent issue. The whole procedure of informing members, registering statutes, obtaining funds and initiating action would be handled through data networks. A situation might emerge in which considerably more temporary organisations of this kind existed than those of a more permanent conventional nature. This would have many implications which cannot be explored here.[34]

D. QUANTITATIVE DATA

The growth and development of international organizations has been analyzed quantitatively by many authors[2, 4, 35]. Many of these analyses have been based on the bodies identified in successive editions of the *Yearbook of International Organizations* and its predecessors.

A summary of the growth of international organisations by sector is given in Table 1. The Table also shows how the data on organisations in the new Sections A and B of the 1977 edition of the *Yearbook* relate to the original series on which earlier studies have been based. Clearly the number of bodies in Section B and the reasons for which they are there emphasize the importance of clarifying the meaning of 'international organisation'. A summary of the results of Wallace and Singer's study of intergovernmental organisations is included as Table 2 for comparison.

The differences in criteria should be borne in mind as discussed earlier.

The organisations coded on computer files for Section A were subjected to a preliminary analysis of their members, where this information was available. (This analysis will be performed as a regular feature of future editions together with supplementary analysis of the output tapes once appropriate computer programmes have been developed). One part of the analysis is summarized by Table 3 which indicates by country the number of international organisations (whether IGO or NGO) in which that country is represented.

Conclusion

This chapter in many ways raises more questions than it answers. The confusion over the nature and quantity of international/transnational organisation is at the moment only partially clarified by simplistic definitions of the entities which are thus selected for study. In some ways the contentment with the distinction 'IGO, NGO, multinational' resembles the situation of zoologists prior to the classification of 'omnivores, herbivores and carnivores' into a multiplicity of animal species interrelated to different degrees. It is perhaps abusing the metaphor to suggest that the widespread preference for 'big game' impedes the development of understanding of the communication networks in the organisational ecosystem as a whole and of the role of the many smaller or less numerous species. Despite the lack of conceptual clarity, the variety of organisational forms functioning in some way transnationally continues to increase. At some stage it will presumably be possible to trace the manner in which these forms increase, decrease and evolve in response to the opportunities open to them.

Notes

1. *Yearbook of International Organizations*, Brussels, Union of International Associations, 1977, 16th edition.
2. Michael Wallace and J. David Singer, 'Intergovernmental organization in the global system, 1815–1964; a quantitative description', *International Organization*, 24, 2, Spring 1970, pp. 239–287.
3. UN/ECOSOC Resolution 1296 (XLIV), June 1968.
4. Kjell Skjelsback, 'The growth of international nongovernmental organization in the twentieth century', *International Organization*, 25, 3, Summer 1971, pp. 420–442.
5. United Nations, *Multinational Corporations in World Development*, New York, 1973, ST/ECA/190.
6. *Yearbook of International Organizations*, Brussels, Union of International Associations, 1968–1969, pp. 1189–1214 (including tables of aggregate data on 7000 multinational business enterprises), partially revised in following edition 1970–1971, pp. 1028–1046.
7. *Yearbook of World Problems and Human Potential*, Brussels, Union of International Associations and Mankind 2000, 1976, (Section M).

I.O.— F

8. Klaus A. Sahlgren, 'Transnational Corporations; terminology', *International Associations*, 28, 12, 1976, pp. 577–578.
9. W.J. Ganshof van der Meersch, *Organisations Europeennes*, Bruxelles, Bruylant, 1966, pp. 33–34.
10. Universite Catholique de Louvain, Premier Colloque du Department des Droits de l'Homme, 24 octobre 1969; *Les Droits de l'Homme et les Personnes Morales*, Bruxelles, Bruylant, 1970.
11. See comment on activities of the ECOSOC Commission on Multinational Corporations in *International Associations*, 26, 1974, 10, pp. 464–467.
12. Sir Peter Smithers, *Governmental Control; a prerequisite for effective relations between the United Nations and non-UN regional organizations*, New York, United Nations Institute for Training and Research, 1972.
13. Robert O. Keohane and J.S. Nye, Jr. (eds.), 'Transnational Relations and World Politics', *International Organization*, 25, 3, Summer 1971.
14. A.J.N. Judge and K. Skelsbaek, 'Transnational associations and their functions', in: A.J.R. Groom and Paul Taylor (eds.), *Functionalism; Theory and Practice in International Relations*, University of London Press, 1975, pp. 190–224.
15. Documents published in *International Associations*, 28, 1976, 12; *Transnational Associations*, 29, 1976, 1–2 and 6. See also: *The Future of Transnational Associations from the Standpoint of a New World Order; Report of a Symposium*, Brussels, Union of International Associations, 1977, p. 211.
16. A.J.N. Judge, 'Conceptual distortions from negative descriptors; the possibility that "nongovernmental" may be comprehended as "antigovernmental" in some languages', *International Associations*, 26, 1974, 3, pp. 150–155.
17. G.P. Speeckaert, *The Various Types of International Meetings*, Brussels, Union of International Associations, 1967, p. 8.
18. Walter Laqueur, *Guerrilla*, Boston, Little, Brown, 1977.
19. Yohan Alexander, 'International network of terrorism'. (Paper presented to a panel on international terrorism at the 18th Convention of the International Studies Association, 1977, St. Louis.)
20. H.E. Cardinale, *The Holy See and the International Order*, Gerrards Cross, Colin Smythe, 1976.
21. Ivan Vallier, 'The Roman Catholic Church; a transnational actor', *International Organization*, 25, 3, Summer 1971, pp. 479–502.
22. J. Bowyer Bell, 'Contemporary revolutionary organizations', *International Organization*, 25, 3, Summer 1971, pp. 503–518.
23. Gunner Boalt et al., *The European Orders of Chivalry; a sociological perspective*, Stockholm, Norstedt, 1971, p. 151.
24. International Commission for Orders of Chivalry, *Register of Orders of Chivalry*, Edinburgh. The Armorial, 1970 (Report of the Commission 1960–1963), p. 12.
25. Lt. Col. Gayre of Gayre and Nigg, *The Knightly Twilight; a glimpse at the chivalric and nobiliary underworld*, Valetta (Malta), Lochore Enterprises, 1973, p. 172.
26. Diana Crane, 'Transnational networks in basic science', *International Organization*, 25, 3, Summer 1971, pp. 585–601.
27. International Peace Research Institute, 'Producer Associations; cooperation among developing countries in export pricing and marketing of primary commodities'. (Paper prepared at the request of the UNCTAD Secretariat.) Oslo, PRIO, 1975, p. 92 (PRIO 22–45).
28. Ezra S. Krendle, 'Group representation in European Armed Forces'. (Paper presented to a panel on military unionism in the western democracies at the 18th Convention of the International Studies Association, 1977, St. Louis.)
29. *Croner's World Directory of Freight Conferences*, 'The Liner Conference System; report by the UNCTAD Secretariat', New York, United Nations, 1970 (E.70.II.D.9).
30. United Nations Conference on Trade and Development, 'The Liner Conference System; report by the UNCTAD Secretariat', New York, United Nations, 1970 (E.70.II.D.9).
31. Material on cartels is available within studies by UNCTAD on restrictive business practices.
32. Mary Emery and J.C. Pollock, 'Wireservices in the global network'. (Paper

presented at the 18th Annual Convention of the International Studies Association, St. Louis, 1977.)

33. See collection of articles in *Transnational Associations*, 29, October 1977; also: 'Operation trials of electronic information exchange for small research communities', (US National Science Foundation, Division of Science Information, Access Improvement Program, Washington DC, 1976, NSF 76–45).
34. See also A.J.N. Judge, 'Communication and international organizations', *International Associations*, 22, 1970, 2, pp. 57–79.
35. Chadwick F. Alger and David Hoovler, 'The feudal structure of systems of international organizations', *Proceedings of the International Peace Research Association Conference*, (Varanasi, February 1974), 1975.

TABLE 1   *International Organisations by Category (1909–1972)*

Column grouping: "IGOs" covers the Intergovernmental organisations column; "International Nongovernmental Organisations (NGOs)" covers all remaining columns.

Year	Intergovernmental organisations	Bibliography, documentation, press	Religion, ethics	Social sciences, humanistic studies	International relations	Politics	Law, administration	Social welfare	Professions, employers	Trade Unions	Economics, finance	Commerce, industry	Agriculture	Transport, travel	Technology	Science	Health, medicine	Education, youth	Arts, literature, radio, cinema, TV	Sport, recreation	Sub-total I A-Section NGOs	EEC/EFTA NGOs	Nat. NGOs with UN consultative status	Sub-Total II: NGOs	Short entries	Defunct/Dormant	Sub-total III B-Section IGOs/NGOs	Total IGOs/NGOs
1909	37	19	21	10	12	3	13	10	2	1	3	5	5	5	8	21	16	10	6	6	176	–	–	176	–	–	–	213
1951	123	–	–	–	–	–	–	–	–	–	–	–	–	–	–	–	–	–	–	–	832	–	–	832	–	–	–	955
1954	118	29	79	38	83	12	31	52	56	49	14	116	32	28	34	81	101	54	41	67	997	–	11	1008	–	–	–	1126
1956	132	26	70	57	61	13	28	52	67	48	15	123	27	40	36	69	100	56	34	51	973	–	12	985	–	–	–	1117
1958	149	33	79	55	71	14	30	53	67	49	16	134	34	43	50	77	104	62	34	55	1060	–	13	1073	–	–	–	1222
1960	154	34	87	57	92	17	37	56	73	54	26	163	46	57	60	83	123	68	57	65	1253	–	13	1268	–	–	–	1422
1962	163	41	86	57	99	15	42	64	76	54	30	160	55	57	63	92	133	71	57	72	1324	216	12	1552	–	–	–	1715
1964	279	54	87	67	106	14	45	70	78	59	33	168	64	63	70	118	150	83	65	76	1570	233	15	1718	–	–	–	1897
1966	199	58	93	80	111	15	48	76	93	63	35	211	76	72	83	137	173	91	70	90	1675	245	15	1935	188	707	1155	3029
1968	229	69	103	90	125	22	54	88	105	70	40	233	83	76	102	152	214	105	75	93	1899	273	16	2188	398	741	1419	3547
1970	242	63	109	95	127	22	54	95	112	70	45	239	83	82	113	174	225	106	80	99	1993	288	15	2296	341	742	1386	3621
1972	280	72	112	104	144	27	58	104	119	70	47	251	88	89	133	184	256	116	80	110	2173	283	14	2470	325	938	1560	4013
1976 *	308	77	129	133	132	30	65	120	132	67	56	273	105	93	147	190	306	134	93	119	2401	–	–	–	–	1067	3720	6474
(**)	–	(39)	(53)	(57)	(129)	(22)	(74)	(75)	(72)	(10)	(72)	(107)	(62)	(64)	(104)	(87)	(92)	(103)	(40)	(27)								

* Criteria broadened to permit inclusion of many new borderline cases in a new Section B. Criteria maintained for a Section A, but some existing borderline cases reallocated from Section A to Section B.

** Secondary allocations of Section A organisations (IGOs *and* NGOs) to other subject headings.

Information based on a table included in the 15th edition of the *Yearbook of International Organizations* and amended from date in the 16th (1977) edition.

TABLE 2 *Growth of intergovernmental organizations (1815–1964)*

Period	No. of IGOs	No. of memberships	Mean no. nations per IGO	Mean no. IGO per nation	Mean percentage universality	Mean no. shared memberships	No. of nations
1815–19	1	6	6.1	0.3	26.1		23
1820–24	1	6	6.1	0.3	26.1		23
1825–29	1	6	6.1	0.3	24.0		25
1830–34	1	6	6.1	0.2	21.4		28
1835–39	2	18	9.0	0.6	29.0		31
1840–44	2	18	9.0	0.5	25.7		35
1845–49	2	18	9.0	0.5	23.7		38
1850–54	2	18	9.0	0.5	22.5		40
1855–59	3	24	8.0	0.6	19.0		42
1860–64	3	21	7.0	0.5	15.9		44
1865–69	6	54	9.0	1.4	23.1	0.5	39
1870–74	7	65	9.3	1.9	27.3	0.8	34
1875–79	9	106	11.8	3.1	34.6	1.4	34
1880–84	11	136	12.4	3.9	35.3	1.8	35
1885–89	17	203	11.0	5.3	31.4	2.6	38
1890–94	21	267	12.7	7.0	33.5	3.1	38
1895–99	23	299	13.0	7.3	31.7	3.4	41
1900–04	30	412	13.7	9.6	31.9	4.0	43
1905–09	44	639	14.5	14.2	32.3	6.8	45
1910–14	49	753	15.4	16.7	34.1	7.9	45
1915–19	53	826	15.6	16.2	30.1	7.6	51
1920–24	72	1336	18.6	21.2	29.5	9.4	63
1925–29	83	1528	18.4	23.5	26.3	10.2	65
1930–34	87	1639	18.8	24.6	28.5	10.5	66
1935–39	86	1697	19.7	25.3	29.5	11.0	67
1940–44	82	1560	19.0	24.0	29.3	10.9	65
1945–49	123	2284	18.6	30.5	24.8	13.0	75
1950–54	144	2684	18.6	32.7	22.7	14.2	82
1955–59	168	3338	19.9	37.1	22.1	15.7	90
1960–64	195	4436	22.7	36.4	18.6	14.3	122

Table 2 is composed of columns from various tables in Wallace and Singer's publications: David J. Singer and Michael Wallace, 'Intergovernmental Organization and the Preservation of Peace, 1816–1964: Some Bivariate Relationships', *International Organization*, XXIV, No. 3 (1970); and Michael Wallace and David J. Singer, 'Intergovernmental Organization in the Global System, 1815–1964: A Quantitative Description', *International Organization*, XXIV, No. 2 (1970); and from Skjelsbaek, Kjell, 'Development of the Systems of International Organizations: A Diachronic Study', *Proceedings of the International Peace Research Association Third General Conference*, Vol. II: *The International System,* IPRA Studies in Peace Research No. 4. Assen, Netherlands: van Gorcum & Comp. N.V., (1970). There were unfortunately some minor printing errors in the earlier presentations of Singer and Wallace's data and Skjelebaek used a preliminary and uncleaned version of the same. Corrected figures reproduced from: Skjelebaek, Kjell, 'Shared Memberships in intergovernmental Organizations and dyadic war, 1815–1954', in: Edwin H. Fedder (ed.). *The United Nations: problems and prospects,* St. Louis, Center for International Studies, University of Missouri, 1971, pp. 31–61. (Differences from total sin other tables are due to minor differences in criteria and inclusion of bilateral organizations).

TABLE 3 *Number of International Organisations (IGO and INGO) in which countries are represented*

Africa	1960	1976	Australasia/Pacific	1960	1976
South Africa	367	602	Australia	424	870
Egypt	288	463	New Zealand	285	590
Nigeria	84	426	Fiji		107
Morocco	187	347	Other	84	260
Tunisia	139	341			
Kenya	73	316		793	1827
Ghana	126	307			
Other	1003	5239	Europe	1960	1976
			France	976	1574
	2267	8041	German Fed. Rep.	911	1480
			UK	818	1473
America	1960	1976	Belgium	913	1428
USA	671	1190	Italy	884	1402
Canada	535	1046	Netherlands	909	1384
Argentina	430	815	Switzerland	796	1317
Brazil	458	807	Sweden	705	1228
Mexico	379	720	Denmark	672	1179
Venezuela	277	590	Austria	708	1142
Chile	337	567	Spain	593	1136
Other	2787	6358	Norway	602	1053
			Finland	548	1017
	5874	12091	Other	4384	8771
				14419	25584
Asia	1960	1976			
Japan	454	949			
India	432	801	TOTAL (all)	27260	56442
Israel	402	778			
Philippines	220	454			
Iran	186	406			
Korea South	121	400			
Lebanon	187	399			
Other	1905	4712			
	3907	8899			

1960: Based on an analysis of data in the *Yearbook of International Organizations* (1960–1961), 8th edition.
Number of organisations 1165. The IGO participation component of the above totals is: Africa 273, America 817, Asia 557, Pacific 73, Europe. 1396.
1976: Based on an analysis of the location of members of 2075 international organizations (but excluding EEC-oriented commercial and professional groups). In the case of 175 organizations, two groups of countries represented were present (due to two distinct membership categories). This would result in some countries being counted twice for one organisation.
The data was derived from the information held on computer tape for the *Yearbook of International Organizations* (1977), 16th ed. which was collected early in 1976.

CHAPTER THREE

ORGANISATION THEORY AND INTERNATIONAL ORGANISATION

Leon Gordenker and Paul R. Saunders

The very term, international organisation, suggests that intergovernmental institutions and related bodies might be understood by means of theory and research applying to organisations generally. Much study of international organisation includes a value-laden, teleological tone. The concept of international organisation relates closely to reformist and normative notions of great variety. Furthermore, governments pretend to use their participation in international institutions to further normative purposes of their own. In such a setting, a wider concept of organisation has an attractively neutral tone. Furthermore, it has a generality of application that promises insights into structures with a variety of purposes and into the activities of participants who seek rather different ends.

If international organisation constitutes a category which fits into existing organisation theory and research, then the latter concepts could usefully be applied without difficulty. If international organisation can only partially be placed in the framework of organisation theory, this could be adapted to seek answers of relevance in the international context. Or if instead international organisations fall outside of the concepts of organisation, then at least any attempt to assimilate two different approaches could be abandoned.

International organisation has special characteristics, which induce some scholars to treat it as unique among political phenomena. Whether international organisation be treated as an existential situation or as a process, it nevertheless involves governments as participants and, formally, states as members of institutions. States exist only formally and theoretically; they represent an abstraction of vital activities and real persons in a given context. Governments have a more concrete existence, incorporating authorized persons who at least formally concert their action to gain specific ends on behalf of all subjects of the state. In international institutions governments formally act on behalf of states members. The shift of analytic levels from concrete governments to clusters of concerted activities along presumably agreed lines gives a certain abstract quality to international institutions. Furthermore, the wider the scope of an institution, the greater the tendency to view its activities in abstract terms. The United Nations, for instance, has a general programme of economic cooperation related to concepts of the new international economic order; with a whole world of particularities to subsume under a single doctrine, an abstract statement of purpose and process hardly could be avoided.

If international organisation is primarily concerned with processes, if it involves the creation of new values or redistribution of old ones and the making of decisions about these values, it nevertheless operates on individual persons only in exceptional circumstances. In this respect it is quite unlike governments, especially where the administration of programmes is involved. It is also unlike most familiar administrative or economic bodies, which do involve the treatment of individual conduct.

Finally, the instruments of compulsion and discipline in international organization have a thin, underdeveloped and unreliable character. Governmental agencies usually have an ultimately coercive capacity of some sort to deal with aggravated dissent. Social institutions employ value systems to which members conform and various devices to use against those who do not. Economic bodies have the possibility of offering direct material incentives for good performance and deprivation for poor work. International organisation uses much less direct means for coping with antisocial behaviour on the part of its governmental participants. When it can use coercion, the occasions are highly restricted and contingent on complex decision-making in other contexts, such as national capitals and diplomatic networks.

Accepting the possibility that international organization has little in common with organisation theory as it is usually understood, this chapter aims at determining the degree to which such theory can be used in analysing what has become a vast network of organised international relations. This network includes elaborate international institutions, created with some pain and a great deal of constitutional

85

apparatus. The experience of such bodies spans several generations and has produced a great body of factual information about their functioning. In addition, a great many more varieties of organised international relations rely on deliberately created formal structures which, however, have only partial governmental participation. Some of these bodies in fact are largely private. The very richness of this subject matter calls out for theoretical treatment as a means of simplification. At the same time, the variety may give some advantages in finding analogues or direct applications from organisation theory and research, which has somewhat similar variety.

In trying to establish the relevance to international organisation of organisation theory, its vast writings can conventiently be divided into three related categories. The first of these involves personal behaviour within organisational structures. The second deals with the structures and functions themselves. And the third concentrates on the relationship of organisations to their environments. It probably would be generally accepted that the conception of organisations covers deliberately created or maintained relationships among individuals (who also conduct activities aside from those in question) for the purpose of attaining a specific goal. Studies of organisations which involve the allocation of tasks to individuals on a rational, or at least deliberate, pattern and the exercise of authority have to do with bureaucracy, a mode of framing work that has special relevance to government and large-scale economic enterprises.

Max Weber[1] pioneered modern analysis of rational allocation of tasks as a means of organising work. His careful exploration of bureaucracy impelled two generations of researchers to try to understand the relationship of individuals in a formal hierarchy. His research has special relevance to governmental administration. It came, of course, before international organisation was a significant concern of social scientists and therefore involved no treatment of such bodies. His successors and critics called attention to the political role of governmental bureaucracies and also to the difficulties of actually inducing behaviour among individuals in accordance with the formal pattern.

Such criticism led increasingly to the study of the behaviour of individuals and interpersonal relationships within bureaucracy. Such writers as Chester Barnard[2] and Phillip Selznick[3] considered leadership as a principal problem of organization. At the same time, problems of managements in industry resulted in the sponsorship of studies of

86

factory conditions, where formally constructed, hierarchic, bureaucratic modes of organisation had reached to the limits of rationalization. Much recent research in fact concentrates on personal and group performance in specific industrial or institutional settings: it emphasizes relationships between workers and supervisors, among workers and between organisational representatives and their clients.

Studies focussing on interpersonal relationships often include the efforts of managers, industrial psychologists, or others interested in making modern industrial work both less frustrating to the workers and more productive. Such aims encourage bias, favouring schema to achieve harmony and efficiency in the course of productive work over understanding of organisations as such. Because of this bias, such studies address themselves principally to those empowered to make reforms. The narrow focus on industry, which is by no means implicit in the study of leadership and interpersonal relations in organisations, limits their relevance to broader questions raised by sociologists and political scientists.

Research emphasizing interpersonal relationships and managerial efficiency tend to open the Pandora's box of the psychology of personality and leadership. Its frightening disorder encourages many non-specialists to hold the lid tightly down. At the same time, its quality of digressing from questions most often raised by students of politics and society probably heightens the academic reaction represented by the structural stream of research. Like the venerable formal-legal school of political interpretation, the structuralists emphasize the abstract forms which shape organisations and let the individual fade into the background. But they seek explanation in behavioural studies instead of in by-laws.

A novel theme developed by March and Simon[4] and by Crozier[5] springs from the recognition that the question of what actors will do when confronted by complex challenges emanating from an ever-changing environment puzzles not only observers but the actors themselves. The actors are tied into a web of personalities linked by formal and informal rules, constrained by social norms and powered by diverse motives. In dealing with such a situation, three things are at a premium: facts about the environment, ideas about appropriate responses, and certitude about one's facts and theories. Considerable power then accrues to those who can extract facts from the environment, promulgate ideas which can serve as a basis for coherent planning and action, and 'absorb uncertainty' by selectively paring away the world's native complexity. These activities define the cognitive environment in which others work.

March and Simon and their successors emphasize the communicational structure which creates for every individual a mental box in which to think and work. Their assumption that people behave more or less rationally within these constraints allows them to leap over the morass of personal psychology in which much of the leadership literature lies. Thus accounted for, the actors fade into the background of the controlling structure. In international relations, as we shall see, structuralism has generated a highly abstract approach from which the individual has disappeared entirely.

A recent emphasis on extrinsic or environmental factors as determinants of organisational behaviour derives from Talcott Parsons'[6] general systems theory. Parsons observed that survival is the first precondition for attaining a goal. Organisations do seem to act as if self-preservation is imperative as it is for individuals. To survive, an organisation must satisfy the demands of the body. Since the conditions for survival seldom remain constant for long, a successful organisation must devote a significant portion of its planning and resources to adapting to a changing environment. When Easton[7], Apter[8], Almond[9], and others introduced a version of Parson's approach in political science, the emphasis on adaptation travelled along. Their schemes of analysis spotlight clients' demands upon organisations: their kind, number, consistency, rate of change, and the like.

The clients' demands and the organisational goals may coincide for a business firm whose goal is to keep the customers satisfied. For an international organisation trying to influence governments which insist on viewing it as a servant rather than a counselor, the two can conflict. Then the road to success may narrow to a tightrope – or worse. But within this conflict may lie a hidden opportunity. Ernst B. Haas has made much of the creative possibilities inherent in goal conflict, as we shall shortly show.

An organisation's environment often consists of other organisations such as its clientele, suppliers and competitors. A trickle of work on interorganisational relations has run during the last two decades from the wellsprings of this fact. William M. Evan[10] recently gathered many of the relevant papers into an anthology. Many of these, as a glance at the titles will show, address themselves to specific questions concerning business and government. Of the studies which address the subject as a whole, Evan's own article, 'An Organisation-Set Model Of Interorganisational Relations', contains the most generally useful perspective, one which other authors have used to orient their own studies.

(e.g. P.M. Hirsch, 'An Organisation — Set Analysis Of Cultural Industry Systems, ibid.)

Evan's method of analysis requires the selection of a 'focal organisation' around which to centre the study. One then identifies other organizations with which it interacts, and classifies these as 'input organisations' or 'output organisations' according to their functions with respect to the focus. The resulting interactional map, Evan suggests, can usefully be described in three terms: its size, or the number of organisations in it; its diversity, or the degree to which the organisations replicate or fail to replicate each others' functions; and its shape, or the graph-theoretic classification into which it falls (chain, tree, wheel, etc.).

Evan then notes that in order to study the effects of an organisation upon the others, one must step down from the organisational level of abstraction to the actor level in order to examine the ways in which the interorganisational effects operate. In practice, this means examining the roles of the actors who form the boundary between organisations. Evan suggests four dimensions along which these roles can be analysed: according to whether they perform input or output *functions* with respect to the focus, the degree of formal education or expertise they require, their position in the organisational hierarchies, and the normative reference-group orientation (i.e. toward the focal organisation, environmental organisations, or toward a profession). He sets forth a number of hypotheses relating these variables, and suggests that this model could explicate organisational changes caused by the reciprocal effects of the focal organisations' internal structure and its external relations.

This promising beginning parallels the thrust in political science toward a 'transnational' theory of world politics which conceives it as the direct interaction of organisations at all levels, rather than just the interaction of states with international organizations and each other.[11] But in order for Evan's theory to help the transnationalists, its perspective must bend in the political direction so that the parallels can meet. Following Parsons, Evan employs the sociological concepts of structure and function, which bear no clear relation to the political concepts of power and authority, despite the efforts of the Functionalists to make them do so. Also, as we will show in the concluding section of this article, international organisation has evolved special forms which differ from organizations as they are normally conceived. These forms may make the analysis of transnational relations in terms of 'organisations' difficult without further clarification.

Ernst B. Haas devotes a chapter of *Beyond the Nation-State* to the development of a theory of organisation which can identify the interaction and mingling that obscures 'the boundaries between the system of international organisations and the environment provided by the nation-state members'.[12] Although the chapter marshalls many perceptive observations by Haas and others on the behaviour of organisations, and international organisations in particular, it remains vague at key points, and displays a curious ambivalence between a structuralist and a leadership approach. Initially, Haas declares himself interested only in the structural aspect of organisation; yet he gives the greatest weight to the effects of creative leadership, which is eminently a personal matter. Moreover, he writes within the context of an exploration of integration of existing states, a distinct but not necessarily usual form of international organisation.

Haas initially observes that most previous writings on the theory of organisations pass silently by his main concern: the capacity of an organisation to transform its environment. The issue does not lack importance. Implicitly or explicitly, transformation of the state system forms a major goal of the United Nations family of organisations. Functionalists of various kinds believe that such capacity exists and that its exercise will determine the future of world politics. Still, Haas found no earlier effort to tackle the question. The classic Weberian model of horizontally structured bureaucracy looked very little like the vertical ordering of international society, where hierarchic control was at a minimum. The human-relations school centred on harmony and efficiency. But the harmony within an international organisation was simply irrelevant to the issue of transformation, and its efficiency could not be rated in the absence of a consensus on how to evaluate its performance. International society clearly lacked such a consensus. Finally, those writers who focused on organisational capacity for survival and adaptation — the systems theorists — generally equated viability with an organisation's ability to perform functions necessary to the system as a whole. This perspective, Haas argues, binds transformational capacity to the clients' perceptions of their needs: it ignores the posibility that an organisation might actively shape those perceptions instead of passively responding to them.

In order to shape clients' perceptions, Haas maintains, leadership must be political, not technical. In the inertial and partly hostile environment of the state system, an international organisation can rarely pursue its goals in a straightforward fashion under the administration of experts. The systemic transformation will arise out of a creative tension between the goals of the organisation and the demands of its clientele — a tension which must be managed by a creative leadership so that the organisation does not on the one hand expire for lack of support, or on the other hand become an adjunct to the existing order. To work with this tension, leadership needs a certain vagueness in its objectives and programmes so that it may cater to a shifting consensus, and not give its enemies anything too specific to attack. But the vagueness must not extend so far as to confuse the staff about its ultimate purposes, or to suggest no direction to governments. Leadership may consciously manipulate this tension for its transforming effect but often in an unplanned and instinctive fashion to meet the common-sense exigencies of the moment.

To effect transformation, an organisation must do four things.

Firstly, it must function with special sensitivity to its environment. Leadership must keep one eye on the shifting pattern of consensus within its clientele and adjust its goals and programmes in order to keep the tension at its optimal level.

Secondly, it must practice methods of conflict resolution which not only promote compromise btween hostile positions but also transform the combatant's objectives by upgrading them. Haas uses the work of J.D. Thompson and A. Tuden to identify four modes of making decisions with four corresponding structures which perform them:

1) Computation performed in a bureaucratic structure.

2) Compromise performed through bargaining in a representative structure.

3) Judgement performed through voting in a collegial structure.

4) Inspiration caused by the use of charisma in an anomic structure.[14]

Of these four modes of conflict resolution, Haas dismisses computation and inspiration as the least likely to produce integration. Within bargaining and judgement, he identifies three patterns of decision: deciding on the basis of the least common denominator of acceptability to the participants (which is the basis of classical diplomatic negotiations); splitting the difference (when there is a difference to be split); and transforming the conflict by upgrading the participant's demands, that is discovering a higher level in which all parties are on agreement. The last type of decision-making most strongly favours integration, for it expands the scope of consensus among — and presumably broadens — the administrative scope of the organisation as a result.

Should governments become aware that this process forms the wind and water which erodes their sovereignty, would they not simply refuse to bargain in that style, regardless of the short-term benefits? Haas replies that governments may indeed awake to the effects of upgrading, but by then they will be engaged in the daily administration of international programmes, which will make a psychic irritant of doubt. Rather than doubt the value of their daily work, government workers will cast the doubt out of their beliefs in accord with the effect known as 'cognitive dissonance'. Haas' argument equates governments with their administrative bureaucracies and ignores individual leaders entirely. Almost as if to test whether the leaders still had an influence, Charles De Gaulle was to express his doubts about the effect of the European Economic Community upon France's sovereignty. He dragged the integrative process to a temporary standstill which has still-felt effects.

Thirdly, the organization must develop a programme which is dynamic in order to assure itself of support. To exert its transforming effect upon a resisting world society, it must not merely survive, but grow in scope. At the same time, its programme must fit within the 'jaws of the ideological vise that is provided by the heterogeneous environment.' [15] This calls for canny political programming in order to maintain the critical tension mentioned above.

Finally, in order to generate demands for a wider jurisdiction, the organizational output must please the clients and inspire them to ask for more. In Haas' terms, there must be feedback. This critical effect provides the motor which moves integration forward.

Haas' ideas opened new theoretical territory. Heretofore, he had discussed only the pro-integrational effects of international organisations and how these might be increased. The way these effects operate upon target organisations was ignored. This made welfare-oriented international organization resemble a catalyst which, if injected into world affairs, would transform the state system into a more stable form. By all rights this discussion, which encompasses half of the integration process, should receive half of the attention. But here the discussion becomes perfunctory. Haas wonders if the oligarchic nature of the principal targets of integration — governments, parties, and interest groups — will hinder their capacity to adapt themselves to seize the benefits offered by integration. He asserts that it will not, because such oligarchies have adapted to changed surroundings in the past.[16] He then considers three groups of target organisations: pluralistic states, totalitarian states, and states with tradition-based societies. The former, he argues, will readily seize the benefits offered by integration, and having bitten the apple, will demand more. The totalitarian state will reject many integrationist programmes on ideological grounds; yet some of the programmes, especially if technical, will be to its liking, and it, too, will have bitten the apple. The state with the traditional society is the hardest to tempt, for its organisations will carefully avoid outside influence as a matter of principle.

In 1967, after de Gaulle's government forced the EEC to put aside indefinitely the majority decision-making of Transitional Stage III of the Treaty of Rome, Haas and his associates[17] proposed revised theories which to some degree took the nature of the target state into account. The revised theories unfortunately did not seize the chance to consider integration as the action of one organisation upon another. In *Beyond The Nation-State*, Haas had qualified traditional Functionalism by showing that integration was not fully automatic but hinged upon the organisational qualities of the transforming organisation. The post-1967 studies sought to qualify Neo-functionalism by showing that integration also depended on the properties of its targets. But instead of examining the mechanisms of integration within the state as Haas had done within the ILC as a transforming organisation, these writings took a more abstract, speculative cast.

Haas[18] began by seeking to fill De Gaulle's dent in a fashion that has been rightly criticised as *ad hoc* and indeed contradictory.[19] Haas divided leadership styles into political-dramatic and economic-incremental types, and theorized that political-dramatic national leadership could make the course of integration erratic but not halt it. The meaning of these styles is far from clear — could not political leadership be incremental, or economic leadership dramatic? — and along the way Haas also seems to argue both sides of certain issues at once.[20]

Phillipe C. Schmitter, in a series of articles[21] and Lindberg and Scheingold in *Europe's Would-Be Polity*[22] developed sophisticated and elegant models which permitted the possibility of at least temporary dis-integration. Lindberg and Scheingold give noteworthy attention to the structure and activities of the target states. Even so, the penetration into the state is scant in terms of theory and data alike. Most of the variables which Schmitter advances to express the effect of the target — size, transaction rate and density, elite complementarily, similarity of social structure — compare states to each other, for he postulates that integration thrives on a homogeneous clientele. Using Apter's systems terminology, Lindberg and Scheingold speak of the 'support' a political system receives. This term summarizes the states' effects upon the organisation without disclosing their actual mechanisms. The way in which states work their effects lies hidden within the broad generality of 'support'. Neither of these authors do what they hope international organisation will do: deeply penetrate the state's sovereign hide.

A related body of writing assumes that the potential for integrating states can be studied through the nature of mass and elite attitudes toward the issue. It can be linked to the traditional Functionalist notion that integration will spread as people learn of its benefits. There seems to be a tacit assumption that all that is necessary for integration is that enough people favour it. This assumption is just too simple. Group behaviour does not equal the sum of the members' inclinations. To give an extreme example, a majority of elites and masses in a country may favour integration, but swayed by an unfavourable press, each person believes himself in the minority and never takes the trouble to organise (irrational!) for a losing cause.

Functionalism includes a history of treating organisations as akin to rational monoliths. Graham Allison has shown that this is not necessarily the most productive way of treating governments for foreign policy studies. Treating governments as organisations could, according to Allison, provide new insights to relieve the intellectual stagnation. (See footnote 36 below.) Integration studies could perhaps also benefit from the infusion of fresh data and ideas which would come from considering the interaction of organisations.

Robert W. Cox took a step toward such a theory in his article entitled 'The Executive Head: An Essay on Leadership in International Organisation'.[23] Cox begins with the provocative statement: 'The quality of executive leadership may prove to be the most critical single determinant of the growth in scope and authority of international organisations.'[23] He examines the relationships between the executive head on the one hand, and his organisation and its environment on the other. He finds the executive head in control of the relationships within certain limits. The limits are of three kinds: those which result from the limited malleability of the staff, of the member states, and of the international system itself (that is from the difficulties of dealing with many states simultaneously).

The first set of constraints arises from the executive head's need simultaneously to hold a certain loyalty among his staff, maintain a geographic balance and retard the formation of empires and special-interest groups within the bureaucracy. These goals can interfere with each other.

In an environment of homogenous states, Cox suggests, these goals can be met through a system of secondment, in which the bureaucracy is built of personnel on loan from member governments. Since the environment is homogeous, most loaned officials are likely to support the organisation and hence offer their loyalty to its head. The loan procedure and indeed the organisation itself could probably not exist in an environment which uniformly opposed it. The loan system facilitates building a balanced staff, and the rapid turnover discourages the formation of empires and special interests. In addition, this system helps familiarize government officials with the organisation and its work, which will help promote its 'spillover' into increased responsibility and more tasks. This strategy has the disadvantage of creating double loyalties. While the staff may favour the organisation, the brevity of its tenure means that its primary indebtedness is still to its government, on which its long-term employ depends. In the days of the League of Nations, Cox contends, double loyalties caused dramatic problems. But in the Europe of today, little friction will be felt.

Global international organisations, such as the ILO, however, do not enjoy a homogeneous, supportive environment. For them, Cox favours a policy of gradually developing a full-time staff. This will give the staff time to develop *esprit d'corps*, although it may tie the executive's hands somewhat on the question of geographic balance. Cox believes that a long stint of service is a better guarantor of closed ranks than ideological homogeneity.

'The relatively strong sense of unity within the early postwar staff of ILO (which was working in a world of sharp ideological divisions, especially prominent among the labour movements with which it had to deal) contrasts with the internal divisions present now within the secretariats of the European Communities, divisions which follow national, political party and pressure group lines. The narrower range of ideological divergency within the six seems to have encouraged a franker policy of representation of interests within the secretariat with a consequently greater measure of diversity than exists where an established tradition exercises its formative power in the education of newcomers in conformity.'[24]

The problem of double loyalty is curtailed by this policy. Personnel are not likely to abandon all contacts with their member governments and any interest groups with which they are affiliated, but to continue discoursing with them. This practice creates a two-way leak of information through the bureaucracy as a side-effect.

Whatever the benefits of this policy, it does encourage *immobilisme*. Cliques of specialists devoted to sub-goals and abetted by certain elements of the clientele may develop. The executive head must neutralize the drag these can exert on policy in order to protect the flexibility which Haas found essential. The executive head can rarely confront dissident specialists because of internal and external political repercussions. At best, he can give other sectors of the organisation his support and hope the dissident ones will die of old age — an expensive process that accounts, according to Cox, for the high percentage of deadwood in international organizations.

The executive can, however, retard the formation of empires based on entrenched interests by manipulating his staff. For this, Cox suggests three strategies:

1) The executive head keeps control by delegating as little as possible.

2) The executive head presides over a cabinet of top officials. The cabinet has shown itself to be a poor instrument of decision-making; however, it can encourage staff to take a less parochial attitude by seeing what is occuring in each others' jurisdictions. It can also bring to light internal conflicts in which the executive may need to intervene.

3) The executive head delegates some of his functions but retains control over a 'reserved' area. These reserved functions are those which Haas claims are key to organisational growth, for example, goal definition, creation of organisational ideology, and the maintenance of clientele support. For these, the executive head relies on a staff responsible only to himself, which he can use as advisors, a sounding board and a source of intelligence.

The autonomy of the member states provides a second source of constraints. In order to loosen them, Cox would have the executive head seek clients who are also clients of member governments. Albert Thomas, the ILC's first Director-General, used his affiliations with the Socialist Party and several union organizations (the International Federation of Trade Union Workers (IFTU), the Section Française de l'Internationale Ouvrière (SFIO), and the Confédération Générale du Travail (CGT)) to bring pressure to bear on the French government in a controversy which was brought before the Permanent Court of

International Justice. His successor, Harold Butler, lacked such contacts and was forced into resignation in a later controversy with France. John Winant, the next Director-General, found that Franklin Roosevelt's high regards were not enough to obtain governmental permission to move the organisation to the United States. David Morse, the Director-General until 1970, surmounted several crises successfully by using his influence among certain liberal businessmen, Catholic groups, and the AFL-CIC.

The executive head must come into office with such contacts, Cox notes. Merely holding the office will not give them to him. In order to use his network successfully, the executive head needs access to senstiive intelligence. A successful head will somehow acquire this.

In dealing with governments, the executive must sometimes compromise his goals. However, he must not compromise his credibility as a spokesman for the organisation's ideals. This demands a certain political and rhetorical finesse which the executive head should bring to his office.

The executive must be sensitive to how much initiative the current configuration of the international system will allow him to take. If the system permits only mediation and 'quiet diplomacy', the executive must simultaneously:

1) acquire and maintain the confidence of all major segments of opinion;

2) be identified with a definite, though to some extent flexible, ideology representing a consensus within the organization, i.e. his suggestions must be seen as conforming with the aims and purposes of the organisation and not as seeking merely agreement for its own sake and at any price; and

3) have adequate intelligence at his disposal so that he can make constructive suggestions and avoid pitfalls.[25]

Cox notes that items one and two potentially conflict; and the executive must bring item three to the job.

The taking of political initiative requires even greater discretion. Governments may allow the executive to mediate their conflicts when these become too costly. But if governments believe that the deadlock is worth the price, initiative-taking can be political suicide. Using Hammarskjold's famour Congo initiative as an example, Cox points out that '(An) initiative-taking Secretary-General cannot become a substitute for a Security Council that does not work because no consensus exists.'[26]

The alignment of states also limits the role an international organisation can play. In Cox's view, international organisations in tight bipolar systems are likely to lose autonomy and gain the appearance of strength by aligning with one pole. In a looser system, such organisations may try to mobilize independent states but within the limits of tolerance of the major powers. Within a genuinely multipolar system, a brokerage role becomes possible.

Having made these stipulations about the backgrounds, talents, and choices of successful executive heads, Cox examines the system-transforming potential of international organisation. He tentatively concludes that the executive head's ability to bring pressure to bear on governmental policy depends on his ability to influence governmental clients, to reach below the government into the society which supports it. He finds three requisites for this:

1) access to domestic groups having influence;

2) adequate intelligence concerning their goals and perceptions; and

3) ability to manipulate international action so that these groups can perceive an identity of interest with it.[27]

All of these requisites imply a pluralist polity. Cox concludes: 'The prospects of system change through the agency of international organis-ations and their executive heads would seem to be linked with the progress of pluralism in politics.'[28] Following David Apter's reasoning, Cox suggests that the most likely points of penetration of non-competitive or ideological polities are the scientific elites, who are apt to be impatient with orthodoxy and to demand free access to information abroad in the pursuit of their work. But Cox finds little hope for the successful penetration of such polities by international organisations in the near future – and little hope for influencing the policies of such governments should the penetration occur.

This discussion takes us a step further towards an organisational theory of integration. Cox focused on leadership in international organisation as the most significant single factor in integration, and showed how leadership penetrates the state in order to accomplish its job. The sharper focus on the mechanism of integration netted Cox a substantive new result: a new precondition for integration which generates a much gloomier picture of integration' prospects than Haas's original view.

If Cox is correct in his belief that the executive head, and not the organisation itself, activates the transforming effect upon the state system, then the critical interactions occur between an individual and the organisation. Instead of a theory of interacting organisations, a theory of the interaction of organisations and individual leaders will be needed. With the leadership literature in disrepair, this goal seems distant.

Still, Laitin and Lustick[29] recently made a promising start towards incorporating the notion of process into a theory of leadership. They factored skill into five components, and postulated a decision-making cycle into which these components enter at various stages. As the authors point out, their work lacks a method of evaluating the skill components other than by the success or failure of the leader's strategies (which is what they would like to predict).

Any operationalisation of this scheme must also be hampered by the difficulty of finding sources to document perceptual and cognitive skills. If speeches, memoranda, *aides-memoires*, and similar documents offer any clue to these, perhaps the recent work of Axelrod[30] will help extract the information. This technique uses a highly reliable coding scheme to produce a 'cognitive map', the inner world or concepts and relationships in which the individual thinks. Such a map is of course static, but current work on the types and rates of changes in such maps could yield measures for several of Laitin and Lustick's skills, such as scope and imagination.

Ernst B. Haas[31] recently set forth a neo-neo-Functionalist theory of integration. Its component of organisation theory looks much more like the purely structural approach promised in *Beyond The Nation-State* than like the leadership-based approaches which have dominated the field so far. He argues that previous theories of integration assumed an incremental style of decision-making in which governments make a series of disconnected *ad hoc* decisions, trying at each moment to improve their lot. Groping about for an answer to the problem of the moment, leaders would think back to the successes of international cooperation in this or other sectors, and opt for more of the same. But a new style of decision-making is competing with incrementalism in Europe, disengaging this motor of integration. European leaders are puzzled by the complexity of perceptions and motives they see around them. They can be overwhelmed by the intricate interrelatedness fostered by modern politics and technology, which makes the various geographic and policy areas hard to separate since decisions seem to work so many unexpected results in remote sectors and far places. They are turning to a style of decision for coping with a world too complex to be tinkered with in an *ad hoc* fashion and too complex to be understood in its wholeness.

This style, which Haas calls 'fragmented issue linkage', involves tactics of delay, keeping options open as long as possible, and a constant building up and tearing down of theories about how various issues interact. International organisations will reflect this style, Haas claims, by developing a structural 'sloppiness'. Instead of the classical bureaucratic hierarchy where each individual or unit is controlled by one, and only one, superordinate, control may come from several superordinates, or even from the same level of organisation — a structure which graph theorists call a *semi-lattice*.

Structuralism in international relations, of which Haas' theory is an instance, has taken on a very abstract and formal cast recently, with much borrowing from the mathematical theory of graphs.[32] There is a good reason for this. If Haas is correct and the world is a rapidly changing muddle, then we had best become students of comparative muddles. Theories based on ideal types suffer when nothing stays ideal for long. Graph theory spurns typologies. Instead, it offers a way of encoding complex relations between a large number of variables, just the way they are, and for deriving a number of suggestive numbers from this network.

The waning approach of linear systems theory (models based on systems of linear equations) also offered a way of representing complexity. However, the model demanded that the representations be more specific than the data would allow. To tell much about the properties of the system, the coefficients in the equations must be evaluated. This means knowing with what weight each variable influences each other. Graph theory, on the other hand, can derive precise results about the system only knowing if the relationship between variables is positive or negative (increase or decrease, like or dislike, etc.). For this reason, graph-theoretic structuralism may become a growing concern in international relations for a while.

The application of organisation theory to international relations has been slight, confined to one field of inquiry — integration — and to a handful of authors. Knowing this, one cannot help but ask: is organisation theory really relevant to international studies? Because international relations consists of interacting organisations, the answer must be 'yes'. Yet if the corpus of organisation theory now available can throw new light on the subject, why are applications so rare? One would expect that as scholars engaged in 'fragmented issue linkage', they would try such a germane way to link the fragments. Could it be that international relations and international organisation in particular employ peculiar forms and processes which the available literature does not discuss? We believe that this is the case.

100

Firstly, the literature of organisation theory has little to say about the interaction of organisations, which is the stuff of which much of international relations is made. As Evan[33] notes in his introduction, the subject is in its infancy. Evan's own work is perhaps the first model capable of organising the subject as a whole. His introductory article has not yet been elaborated with relevant research.

Organisation theory seemssto focus on four ideal types of organisation: the classical bureau, the small group, leadership (as an organisational sub-unit of one) and voting bodies. This reflects an emphasis on business and government.

International organisations certainly contain these types, and there is a theoretical literature devoted to each. Yet it would be wrong to say that we understand an international organisation because we understand each of its parts in isolation. One can claim, like Cox, that for a certain purpose we need to focus on only one part of the organisation (the leadership, in his case). But the behaviour of a part cannot be understood apart from the whole. In order to discuss leadership in the ILO, Cox found it necessary to delve into the dynamics of the bureaucracy and of the organisations which formed the environment. Without some knowledge of *how the parts interact*, one cannot understand the behaviour of an organisation, or its effects upon its organisational environment.

In theory, one can decompose most contemporary politics and economics into a global network of the four ideal types of organisation. For convenience, one can cluster these bodies into groups which seem especially interdependent and call them general organisations. These groupings may or may not agree with those understood by the actors, who also use the term for purposes of their own. Nevertheless, clustering can simplify analysis by reducing the number of units under consideration. One could say that Cox studied the dynamics of an 'organisation' consisting of the Director-General of the ILO, the International Labour Office, and various governments and interest groups. For his purposes, he did not find it necessary to introduce the Governing Body or Conference. Thus,he defined out of his 'organisation' units which the actors, at least formally, consider linked together and part of the environment. Having isolated the relevant sub-units, Cox had to proceed without the aid of organisation theory to elucidate their reciprocal effects. Whether constructing such an 'organisation' for analytic purposes or remaining with the organisations the actors see, one needs a theory of how the basic types behave when connected in various configurations or general organisations. The literature lacks this.

Secondly, while most organisations apparently can be decomposed into sub-units which belong to the four basic types, there are at least two kinds of international organisation for which this cannot be done: the patchwork organisation, or para-organisation; and the organisation of organisations, or meta-organisation. Even equipped with a theory of how the four types interact, the international organisation specialist would still encounter at least two confounding structures.

Consider first the classical bureau, of which the army is the archetype. Anthony Downs[34] defines four properties of a bureau:

1) It is large. Generally, any organisation in which the highest-ranking members know less than one half of all other members can be considered a bureau.

Largeness insures that members cannot base all of their interaction on personal knowledge of each other, as in a small group, but must interact through organisational rules.

2) A majority of its members are full-time workers who depend upon their employment in the organisation for their income.

The rules and procedures of the bureau form a game which members play for their benefit. It is the members' desires to win that patterns organisational behaviour, according to Downs. If the members derive their income from other sources, the link between structure and behaviour is weakened.

3) The initial hiring of personnel, their promotion within the bureau, and their retention therein are based at least in part on some type of assessment of the way in which they have performed or can be expected to perform their organisational roles. They do not depend solely upon either ascribed characteristics . . . or periodic election to office by some constituency outside the bureau.

For the bureau to be classical, there must be a rule-based ecology of games.

4) The major portion of its output is not directly or indirectly evaluated in any market external to the organisation by means of voluntary *quid pro quo* transactions.

This property distinguishes a bureau from many other forms of organization which share the first three properties.

Now consider UN peacekeeping forces, a form of international armed force. Do they satisfy Downs' criteria? Indisputably, they meet the first and the last points. But what of the dependence on organisational rewards and performance evaluations which supposedly motivate and

and constrain individual behaviour? The anomalous structure of peace-keeping organisations to date has vested this control in many hands. The Secretary-General, although the nominal leader, has had a lamb's share of it.

The Secretary-General has created these organisations by pasting together segments of others to suit the political exigencies of the moment. Typically, the farrago includes national brigades of varied provenance, military commanders and their staffs borrowed from expedient sources, locally hired assistance, professional diplomats on leave, officials of several international secretariats, representatives of force-contributing nations, representatives of the host states, the governments supplying logistics (typically the United States or Britain), the Security Council or a political committee representing the General Assembly, and of course the Secretary-General himself and his personal advisors, who organise and coordinate the activities of these diverse elements.

The Secretary-General's control over many of these individuals suffers from two severe limitations. Many of the borrowed individuals come as units — as brigades, bureaus, and the like. The Secretary-General cannot reach inside these to discipline individual members. He can only acquire and discharge the unit as a whole. More importantly, these individuals owe their continuing sustenance not to the peace-keeping force but to their parent organisation. The organisation, if we may call it such, has to a great extent a reward structure created either by other organisations for extraneous purposes, or by individuals bent on the advancement of careers in any of a multitude of organisations.

Peace-keeping organisations have also been so evanescent that little institutionalization has had time to appear. Neither the valuation of traditional procedures for themselves, which Selznick discusses; nor the organizational language for the absorption of uncertainty, which March and Simon describe; nor Haas' core of dedicated and loyal staff; nor even standard operating procedures apart from those with which the borrowed units come have had time to develop. Such long-term developments as entrenched specialists and *immobilisme* are out of the question. Terminated early in their life-cycle, peacekeeping organisations have never formed the characteristic features of the bureau.

If Haas' new propositions predicting organisational untidiness are correct, this kind of patchwork (which we call a para-organisation) may become increasingly common. Surely this structure is no bureau, but a separate form of organisation deserving its own rubric and body of literature. Here is a case where scholars of international organisation must adapt and develop organisation theory to their own special ends.

International voting bodies also diverge from classical counterparts. The classical voting body consists of rational individuals with ordered lists of preferences each of whom tries to secure a collective decision which favours him to whatever degree the situation will permit.[35] But in an international voting body, the voters do not formally represent their own interests but those of an organisation. Actually, the voters probably act on a combination of organisational and personal interests, depending on the strictness of their instructions and their loyalties to careers and causes. In the international setting, the 'voter' often appears to be an organisation rather than an individual, because the votes cast represent foreign policy decisions taken by a foreign office. Only if the foreign office is treated as a person can classical voting theory apply. Graham Allison[36] (*passim*) has shown that to treat an organisation as if it were a rational individual is not necessarily the most fruitful way to understand its behaviour. The theory of voting bodies has much to say about such matters as how rational individuals will coalesce or trade votes in order to win their objectives. But it discloses nothing about how organisations will perform in a legislative setting.

Like the peacekeeping organisation, the international voting body incorporates a structure to which organisation theory has not heretofore been applied. Its formal members are not individuals but other organisations. This structure, which we call a meta-organisation, neutralizes many of the forces which are thought to elicit organisational behaviour from individuals. To be sure, the member organizations are composed of individuals, but they do not directly depend on the meta-organisation for their salary or advancement. Many of these individuals will never directly communicate with members of other member organisations, making it difficult to speak of an organisational language or socialisation into organisational norms. Reflecting the horizontality of authority in the current state system, they may not consider communications from their 'superordinates' in the meta-organisation authoritative or binding in any way.

By way of further divergence from the usual approach of organisation theory, delegates may have influence in each others' foreign offices, and even in the interest groups which form the constituencies of the various governments represented. If so, it becomes more difficult to treat the 'voters' as distinct entities. Instead, there exists an overlapping network of individuals and organisations which makes delegates, foreign offices, and interest groups alike seem an integral part of the decision-making process.

Two main factors now limit the applicability of organisation theory to international organisation:

1) Theories about interacting organisations — a major concern in the international arena — are just beginning to develop.

2) International organisation can take on forms with which organisation theory has yet to come to grips, probably because of its emphasis on governments and business firms.

Neither of these factors prohibits the use of the organisation-theoretic appraoch, emphasizing the effects of organizational structure on organisational behaviour. They simply mean that scholars of international relations should not dismiss the approach because the sociologists whose province it has been have not developed fully applicable theories, nor expect the sociologists to develop such theories. Following the leads of Haas and Cox, scholars of international relations must do it themselves.

Notes

1. Weber, M., *Economy and Society*, edited by G. Roth and C. Wittich, Vols. 1 & 3, New York, Bedminister Press, 1947. Also Weber, M., *The Theory of Social and Economic Organisation*, translated and edited by A. Herleson and T. Parsons, New York, Oxford University Press, 1967.
2. Barnard, C., *The Functions of The Executive*, Columbia, Columbia University Press, 1947.
3. Selznick, P., *Leadership in Administration*, Evanston, Ill., Row, Peterson, 1957.
4. March, J. and Simon, H., *Organizations*, New York, Wiley, 1958.
5. Crozier, M., *The Bureaucratic Phenomenon*, Chicago, Chicago University Press, 1964.
6. Parsons, T., *The Social System,* Glencoe, Ill., The Free Press, 1951.
7. Easton, D., *A Systems Analysis of Political Life*, New York, Wiley, 1965.
8. Apter, D., *The Politics of Modernization*, Chicago, Chicago University Press, 1965.
9. Almond, G., *The Civic Culture*, Princeton, Princeton University Press, 1963.

10. Keohance, R. and Nye, J., *Transnational Relations and World Politics*, Cambridge, Harvard University Press, 1971.
11. Haas, E.B., *Beyond the Nation-State*, Stanford, Stanford University Press, 1964, p. 29.
12. Haas, E.B. (1964) *Beyond the Nation-State*, Stanford, Stanford University Press, p. 29.
13. Ibid., p. 96.
14. Ibid., p. 105.
15. Ibid., p. 113.
16. Ibid., p. 116.
17. Especially Philippe Schmitter, Leon Lindberg, and Stuart Scheingold.
18. Haas, E.B. (1967) 'The Uniting of Europe and the Uniting of Latin America',

Journal of Common Market Studies, 5, pp. 315—43.
19. Caporaso, J., *Functionalist and Regional Integration*, Beverly Hills, California, Sage Publications, 1972, p. 37f.
20. Haas, E.B., loc. cit.
21. Schmitter, P., 'Three Neo-Functionalist Hypotheses About International Integration', *International Organization,* 23, 1969, pp. 161—66. Also Schmitter, P., 'A New Theory of Regional Integration', *International Organization*, 24, 1970, pp. 836—68.
22. Lindberg, L. and Scheingold, S., *Europe's Would-Be Polity*, Englewood Cliffs, N.J., Prentice-Hall, 1970.
23. Cox, R., 'The Executive Head: An Essay on Leadership In The ILO', *International Organization*, 23, 1969, pp. 205—29.
24. Ibid., p. 216.
25. Ibid., p. 226.
26. Ibid., p. 227.
27. Ibid., p. 230.
28. Ibid., p. 230.
29. Laitin, D. and Lustick, I., 'Leadership: A Comparative Perspective', *International Organization*, 28, 1974, pp. 89—117.
30. Axelrod, R., *Structure of Decision*, Princeton, Princeton University Press, 1976.
31. Haas, E.B., 'Turbulent Fields and the Theory of Regional Integration', *International Organization*, 23, 1976, pp. 173—202.
32. Hart, J., 'Structures of Influence and Cooperation-Conflict', *International Interactions*, 1, 1974, pp. 141—62.
33. Evan, William M., loc. cit.
34. Downs, A., *Inside Organization*, Boston, Little, Brown & Co., 1967, p. 24f.
35. Black, D., *The Theory of Committees and Elections*, New York, Oxford University Press, 1958.
36. Allison, G., *Essence of Decision*, Boston, Little, Brown & Co., 1971.

Selected Reading

1. Cox, R., 'The Executive Head: An Essay on Leadership In The ILO', *International Organization*, 23, 1969, pp. 205—29.
2. Easton, D., *A Systems Analysis of Political Life*, New York, Wiley, 1965.
3. Evan, William (ed.), *Interorganizational Relations*, Harmondsworth, Penguin Books, 1976.
4. Haas, E.B., *Beyond the Nation-State*, Stanford, Stanford University Press, 1964.
5. Haas, E.B., 'The Uniting of Europe and the Uniting of Latin America', *Journal of Common Market Studies*, 5, 1967, pp. 315—43.
6. Haas, E.B., 'Turbulent Fields and the Theory of Regional Integration', *International Organization*, 23, 1976, pp. 173—202.
7. Laitin, D. and Lustick, I., 'Leadership: A Comparative Perspective', *International Organization*, 28, 1974, pp. 89—117.

8. Lindberg, L. and Scheingold, S., *Europe's Would-Be Polity*, Englewood Cliffs, N.J., Prentice-Hall, 1970.
9. March, J. and Simon, H., *Organizations*, New York, Wiley, 1958.
10. Selznick, P., *Leadership in Administration*, Evanston, Ill., Row, Peterson, 1957.

PART TWO

CHAPTER FOUR

SOME PROBLEMS OF INTERNATIONAL SECRETARIATS
Mihály Simai

Among the plethora of problems concerning not only the U.N. but all
international organisation some of the most contentious are concerned
with the role of the secretariat. These give rise to discussions at
different levels and has many facets.

The history of the U.N. demonstrates however, that governments
establishing international institutions generally agree that in order to
ensure the normal functioning of a given institution in a variety of
circumstances, a special kind of personnel is needed who can arrange
the administrative and substantive preparation of the sessions,
elaborate decisions, resolutions, and their implementation, 'keep alive'
the institution, collect membership dues, help the states to maintain
their relations through the institution and the like.

Competence of Secretariats, Objective and Subjective Limits

The first level of the problems concerns the role and authority of the
secretariats. Even in the case of institutions which are considered
'supranational' by their founders, the issue remains concerning the
extent to which the secretariat can be 'supranational'. The question is
not simply organisational or legal; it is essentially a political question
whether the decisions of the bodies representing governments, such
as ministerial commissions for special organisational and representative
tasks, or councils of foreign ministers, should be supranational, and
merely implemented by the secretariats, or whether the secretariats
themselves are authorized to both take and implement supranational

111

decisions. The experts of the socialist countries generally regard both solutions as being unrealistic under such conditions when the role and decisions of states are still significant in international politics and the world economy. The decision-making role of national centres suggests that neither the international representative bodies nor the secretariats are able to extend their authority over governmental activities, and even collectively elaborated and accepted resolutions can only be enforced through the activity of the governments.

However, even under these conditions a great many things still depend on the secretariats especially for the promotion and implementation of the resolutions through the stimulation of government activities in the given field and the preparation of comparative studies with the help of the government bodies in the given country. Secretariats can also play a significant initiatory role concerning the activity of international institutions. Some matters could be initiated by being put on the agenda if they are deemed essential to the member countries and attention could also be drawn to problems in specific fields. The activity of secretariats could also be important in controversial political issues existing among nations as for example when the secretariat has a mediatory role in a critical situation or is active in the elaboration of resolutions which would be acceptable to the nations concerned. The position is similar in the problems of the world economy as well. Thus without doubt there are great possibilities for action by secretariats although this is often greatly influenced by the role and character of the given interstate institution.

Among the problems emerging in connection with the 'supra-national' character of the secretariat one of the most important is the following: how far can the personnel, recruited from different member countries be independent of the countries of their own nationality or from which they were recruited by the secretariat. This is an especially important question because in any institution there is the possibility that it will be utilized by one state more than by another and that in so doing such a state uses for that purpose its citizens on the staff of the secretariat. 'World citizenship' still does not exist, and individuals are connected with nations, through their language, cultural backgrounds and probably by their future perspectives as well and therefore it is not desirable to turn the working staff of the secretariats against their own nations. However, it is necessary that, as civil servants of an international institution, they should be objective and represent the mutual interests and tasks of the

112

given community. During the course of their activity their country should be regarded as one of the members of a given community of which everyone is equal with the others.

In some cases it is not excluded that in the fulfillment of his tasks in some specific question the staff member may enter into conflict with the special interest of his own country. Therefore it would be advisable to organise the internal work of the international institution in such a way that the possibilities of conflicts should be kept to a minimum. Efforts should also be made at the same time to ensure that the employees of the secretariat behave honestly, be unselfish and be prepared for sacrifices in the general interest.

Composition: Conflicts and Solutions

The composition of the secretariats is also a highly discussed issue, and can give rise to problems of an extremely delicate nature which could even paralyse the work of the given institution. Three questions must be regarded simultaneously — the national composition, the professional structure, and the duration of employment.

One of the most difficult problems is the national composition of the secretariat especially in global institutions such as the organs of the U.N. The situation in the U.N. and its specialized agencies is complicated by the admission of new members because the existing pattern of national representation has inevitably to be altered to take the new members into account.

It is justifiable for member countries to claim that their citizens should be employed as international civil servants in the secretariats. On the other hand it is reasonable that the tasks of the secretariats should be accomplished as effectively and as professionally as possible. The two demands cannot always be fully reconciled. The hierarchy of the secretariats makes the solution of the problem even more difficult, since the different levels of the jobs and the various possibilities in management concerning the activity of the organisation must also be taken into account.

To be realistic the composition of the secretariats cannot be independent from the differing importance of the member countries in international policy and the world economy. This often means that the opportunities for bigger countries are objectively better, in that they can supply more and better qualified experts to the given institution. Naturally the smaller countries have difficulties in lending their experts for a longer period to the international community and in the case of a small developing countries even the charge of 'brain drain' can be brought up.

The following principles underlie the composition and the general requirements of secretariats.

a) As far as the composition of secretariats is concerned the starting point is naturally the character and function of the given institution. The national composition has to be formed on the widest possible basis in an institution which has political functions as its prime concern. In institutions of limited or special functions the national or professional composition has to be developed according to the available expertise and tasks.

b) On a realistic basis, it would be advisable to relate the definition of the national composition in a global organisation with the quotas for contributions. The relationship between national and regional proportions is also a vital question especially when filling the so-called 'National Quotas' is not possible for other reasons.

c) The new tasks of the international institutions require the high qualification and specialized knowledge of the employees of the secretariats. It is no easy task to guarantee this because there is a big world-wide demand for highly qualified experts and the majority of the nations cannot spare their best experts for an extended period. Thus there is a need to develop organisational forms through which the national and common interests can be harmonized in such a way that an international institution can employ high level experts for special tasks for a short period of one or two years. Ad hoc consultants should be employed on a wide scale as well, and, in addition, advisory bodies should be involved in operative decisions.

d) The civil servants of the international institution should not stay on a permanent basis and international public service should not be a profession for life, but an important temporary stage in the life of civil servants. A complete break with the home country generally does not strengthen an international commitment, but rather creates an unstable status for the individual which can easily lead to a routine attitude to work. Conditions have also to be created whereby international civil servants who are returning to their home country should be provided with proper jobs according to their ability and skill so that they do not lose their seniority.

e) The rigid system of having persons of a particular nationality in a particular post has to be avoided in international institutions since it often means that the institution becomes rigid too. It can also lead to a situation that when new states join the institution they automatically increase the size of the staff. This does not

114

necessarily contribute to the efficiency of the institution.

f) Greater opportunities have to be opened for the training of such experts who would be suitable for work with the international institution. This must not be regarded as being limited to the 'training of diplomats'. It is especially important that the same training should be granted for the experts in specialist fields. The secretariats of international institutions should pay greater attention to giving more effective support to individual countries in the field of professional training.

The nature of the leadership of the secretariats also raises important questions. Usually, the double requirements of impartiality outside in the relationship among states, and a strong personality inside for the effective running of the secretariats is seldom met. The actual requirements of leadership of secretariats differ according to the levels and functions of the institution. Selecting the heads of secretariat in global institutions involves not just the delicate question of which nationality but also what region of the world is represented. In this respect problems encountered are less intractable in the regional institutions. Changing nationality in the leading bodies or within the main directing posts is more important than on the lower levels of secretariats. However, a situation may occur as a result of a compromise of the powers, in the policy forming bodies, according to which the head of the secretariat may be of the same nationality on a quasi-permanent basis. This is usually the case only if the directing and controlling bodies of the institution are effective and strong.

Some Alternative Views

In connection with the composition of secretariats other views have been expressed on both the general and specific issues. As a result of increasing global problems quite a few Western experts express their opinion that the role and independence of the secretariats has to be increased considerably. According to some other views the institution has to develop towards becoming a regional or world government and the role of the secretariats must be defined consequently. In the present situation and in the foreseeable future such proposals are unrealistic due to the divisions of the world and the continued importance of states.

Various problems which are developing demand an increased level and the intensification and deepening of international cooperation which will be reflected not only in organisational conditions but also at the personal level. These problems, however, cannot be solved separately from the reality of the world and any great gap between reality and needs could lead to disastrous results.

There are many different opinions also concerning the composition of the personnel of secretariats. Some experts (and even governments) envisage the secretariats of international institutions as being subordinate to national sovereignity. This means that international civil servants would become delegates whose activity would be guided by the government concerned.

According to this interpretation the secretariat of an international institution is an organic part of the member country's government, a sort of 'extended hand' which cannot initiate but can only provide executive functions. This concept is usually associated with the idea that a secretariat of an international institution should not have any independent activity. In fact all the member countries could practically veto all issues in the activity of the secretariat, thus hindering all kinds of steps which the secretariat might take.

Complete or partial implementation of such a concept could not serve, or only on a very limited scale, the advancement of international cooperation in the settling of common problems. Subordinating the selection of the members of the secretariats completely to the personnel policy of the national administration weakens the institution as well. Thus it may occur that governments 'get rid' of civil servants who are not working adequately within the national framework by passing them to international institutions. This could be especially harmful when the particular institution plays a central role from the point of view of the member countries.

The other extremity concerning the composition and selection of international civil servants is the concept of selection according to 'professional competence' apart from national quotas, which is also unilateral, unrealistic and may distort the composition of the secretariat on the basis of a subjective approach. Often this approach provides the opportunity for some states to acquire key positions for themselves on the secretariat at the expense of the others. Checking professional knowledge is not a simple task in itself. The multiple tasks and the specific environment make it impossible, in many cases, for the international institution to employ such professionals who have the exact skill for the specific job. There are, of course, some positions in the secretariats of an international institution which require narrow specialization. However, requirements of talent, the ability to adjust and convertible knowledge are the most important requirements which need to be related to the system of national quotas.

The increase of programme activities by the secretariats of certain international institutions raises many new problems concerning the fluctuations in and composition of the personnel of secretariats. Such institutions as the International Monetary Fund, the World Bank and regional international banks represent a special transition in this field. It is in their nature to function in such a routine manner that their directing bodies provide only a most general framework. The secretariats, therefore, not only have the tasks of simply carrying out resolutions but also have to give content to political decisions and adapt them to a given situation and, furthermore, they are also involved in some operative work as well. The secretariats of this sort of institutions naturally are of a different character from those of more general institutions which deal mostly with coordination or with special political relations and which are, of course, provided with different and greater authority.

In those global institutions established mostly for political purposes such as the U.N. or its specialised agencies, the appearance of operative tasks (like technical cooperation, emergency medical or other help, international meteorological surveys, or their coordination, organisation and preparation of actual agreements) has given rise to the establishment of operative departments within the framework of the secretariats of the institutions or attached to them. In order to implement these tasks it is evident that sufficient operative freedom is required. The composition of the secretariats has to be formed under different conditions in such cases. However, efforts have to be made in order to recruit the experts necessary for the accomplishment of the tasks of the institution from as many countries as possible.

In Conclusion

1. The different views and main fields of debate concerning the secretariats of international institutions are mostly connected with their authority, role and composition.
2. The size and composition of the secretariats depend mostly upon the character of the particular institution.
3. The national composition of secretariats, their permanent or temporary status, the skills and the like of civil servants are very important factors in the activity of the secretariats of international institutions. The extent to which particular institutions are able to fulfill their functions depends mostly on an adequate solution of these problems.

117

CHAPTER FIVE

A CONCEPTUAL TYPOLOGY OF INTERNATIONAL ORGANISATION

Paul Taylor

One of the great difficulties in teaching the academic subject called
International Organisation at any level is that the central themes are
very difficult to identify. This problem is intensified by the wide range
of relevant literature, which is increasingly specialised: a richness of
available writings is matched by the scarcity of good, comprehensive
texts. There are, of course, books which cover particular areas of the
subject with great skill, but few with the range of reference expected
by teachers of a general course on International Organisation. The
problems of identifying the texts is only matched by the difficulty
of obtaining agreement between any two teachers of International
Organisation about what their courses should contain. The increasing
range of international institutions, and the increasing number of
possible empirical references, has suggested to teachers the advisability
of picking out general themes in the subject such as those covered in
Inis Claude's *Swords into Plowshares*.[0] But there have been few
attempts to relate these themes, essentially an organising procedure,
to developments in the theory of the subject in recent years. Claude's
book, which remains the most widely used basic text on International
Organisation, is now some twenty years old, though it has appeared
in four revised editions.

In this chapter an attempt is made to present a typology of themes
in International Organisation which is roughly tuned to the range of
available literature in the mid-1970s. Students seem to find such a
typology a useful reference point for their work: it gives them some

feeling for the coherence of the subject and, additionally, allows them some measure, however illusory, of progress through a definable territory. There is, of course, inevitably a certain arbitrariness about such a typology — some themes and literature are difficult to classify precisely — but it represents at least a step towards obtaining a sense of the coherence of the subject, and provides a framework into which the teacher might fit a range of empirical references according to his own knowledge and enthusiasms.

In this chapter the word 'theory' is used in a number of rather different ways. It refers to any organised set of propositions about the present or future of international organisation, and not exclusively to a set of verifiable or falsifiable descriptive, explanatory or predictive hypotheses as would be required by a strict, 'scientific' use of the term. The word theory is used throughout, though some might label the more prescriptive writings as 'speculation', in the interest of economy of terminology, and in order to avoid entering into the argument about what is, or is not, a theory in the social sciences.

There are three major areas of concern in writings about International Organisation in the mid 1970s: these areas indicate the major overall problems to which the theory is related, and not the particular empirical reference of the theory.

The three main types of theory, then, are (1) adjustment theories, (2) integration theories, and (3) constitutional theories. The broad character, and the sub-divisions, of each of these types of theory will now be examined.

A. Adjustment Theories

Adjustment theories are concerned with the response of national governments to demands made upon them as a result of changes in their environment. Governments are continuously faced with the need to carry out new tasks, which may arise from political circumstances in the international system, or from technological change or other features of modernisation, or economic development, or from new demands made upon them by their own citizens. The tasks may also include the settlement of international disputes or the maintenance of international order. The essential point is that adjustment theories are about the ways in which existing governments cope with demands made upon them by working through international institutions and carrying through appropriate adjustments in their position. They do not see governments, or other levels of the state, as being fundamentally changed, and, accordingly they stress the range of inter-governmental

119

arrangements in international organisation. Governments are seen as the dominant actors, using international organisation to the extent that it serves their interests in the context of a changing environment.

Adjustment theories may be conveniently sub-divided into five major styles of inter-governmental co-operation in international organisation. The classification helps to overcome the rather naive prejudice — surprisingly widely held — that inter-governmental co-operation is a single kind of procedure. It has, in fact, several distinctive styles. The styles of inter-governmental co-operation which are found in the range of literature in the mid-1970s may be conveniently labelled supra-nationalism, co-ordination, harmonisation, co-operation and association. Particular theories or theses contained in a particular piece of writing, may be categorized according to these styles of inter-governmental co-operation. They represent a preliminary framework for classification.

Supra-nationalism may be regarded as a form of inter-governmental arrangement by which governments allow an international institution to manage an area of common interest on the basis of decisions taken either by majority voting, or by committees of independent civil servants. This unusual power is often exercised by the international institution in an area of narrow scope, and, it seems now generally agreed, it does so in the interest of existing governments both in terms of their perceptions of self interest and in terms of individual, collective and institutional views of the common interest. Supra-nationalism is a modern technique used by governments to assist them to survive, and satisfy new demands in the modern world. It may be viewed as a kind of partial federalism: powers are transferred to a centre, but they are to be exercised in an area the scope of which is narrowly circumscribed by participating governments. As its scope increases, so the range of independent power in the hands of the institution tends to decrease. Writings which consider this style of supra-nationalism include those on the High Authority of the European Coal and Steel Community such as Ernst Haas' *Uniting of Europe;*[1] and those which argue for compulsory international jurisdiction in disputes between states.[2]

Co-ordination involves the adjustment of government policies by a process of intensive consultation within an international institution in order to establish and maintain a programme which is designed to obtain goals generally regarded as being overwhelmingly important. In brief, there is a goal which it is believed can only be obtained through a common programme. The international institution

120

has the task of deciding the programme with the advice and consent of member states. In co-ordination, however, it is the state which retains powers and responsibility for executing the common task. States are pushed towards the adjustment of policy in the common interest — by a process identified originally in the Organisation for European Economic Co-operation (OEEC) as the confrontation of policy — but their status is confirmed in decision making procedures based on the principle of unanimity in the international institutions' controlling committees of governmental representatives. The realization of the programme depends upon a process of co-ordination which extends through a period of time; it involves adjustment of technical arrangements which demand a precision of control in relation to each other in order to facilitate the obtaining of the common goal.

Co-ordination has been detected in a wide variety of international institutions, but it was particularly clear in the case of the OEEC's drawing up of its Annual Programme, in NATO's procedure for drawing up the Force Plan, and in policy-making in the European Communities in the 1970s.[3] In the Organisation for Economic Co-operation and Development (OECD) and other agencies, it has been detected in the mechanisms for the co-ordination of aid programmes to the developing world. In the European Communities it may be regarded as a feature of the latest phase of the emergence of the Communities, which has been called the confederal phase,[4] and it seemed to become more readily identifiable, as the scope of the Communities widened, and as the aspiration to supra-nationalism was lost in the mid-1960s. The emergence into a position of importance in policy-making in the Communities of the Committee of Permanent Representatives illustrates the growth of co-ordination as the dominant style of the Communities. That Committee contains the permanent representatives of member states in Brussels and has become the main forum of the confrontation of policy between member states and between them and the Commission of the European Communities, the main representative of the interest of the Communities as a whole.

One of the advantages of classifying adjustment theories in terms of styles of inter-governmental cooperation is that it facilitates a greater clarity about, on the one hand, ways of proceeding in the taking of decisions, and on the other, *systems* of interactions. Collective security may be usefully viewed as one example of a security system, involving specific principles, such as general obligation, automatic operation, and the triggering role of an international institution. Other security systems are the *concert system*, which involves the leadership and greater responsibility of a smaller number of larger states in questions of security, which affect all members of the system; and the *balance of power*, involving, predominantly the principle of the restraining of one actor's use of power by countervailing power.

Each of these systems has corresponding styles of inter-governmental co-operation. The system of collective security, for instance, has as its most characteristic style that of co-ordination, though it could be argued that it sometimes moves towards supra-nationalism. States are expected to organise among themselves a co-ordinated programme for the taking of sanctions in the event of aggression by one of their number. The international institution has of course, a key role in the setting up and carrying out of this programme: the co-ordination procedure is underwritten by the general obligation entered into by participating states, and by their relinquishment in the collective security system of the right to judge when they will participate in the common enterprise against an aggressor.

Inis Claude has argued in *Swords into Plowshares* that collective security as an approach to peace (the title of his chapter 12)[5] may be contrasted with pacific settlement (chapter 11) and preventive diplomacy (chapter 14). One of the problems with organising the chapters in this way is that collective security is a system, while pacific settlement and preventive diplomacy are procedures, although in the latter case, the goal or product is particularly stressed. They are, in other words, two different kinds of phenomenon and are not alternative procedures, which may be considered by the potential peace-maker. Pacific settlement, which involves procedures such as mediation, arbitration, negotiation and conciliation, is perfectly compatible with a collective security system: states are encouraged to adjust their claims by peaceful means rather than fight. (It is also compatible with the balance of power systems, and with the concert system.) Preventive diplomacy, on the other hand, in that it relies on the ability of an international institution to insulate a dispute between minor states from the competitive, potentially conflictual, relationships between the dominant ones, is not compatible with collective security or with the multi-actor balance-of-power system of the kind outlined by Kaplan, but is compatible with the concert system.[6] This allows the international institution to exploit a stand-off position between the major states, members of the concert, and to act on the basis of a minimum of consensus between them, in disputes between non-members of the concert.

Discussion of preventive diplomacy, in contrast to collective security, may be conveniently related to the style of inter-governmental co-operation called *harmonisation*. This mode can be illustrated, first, by reference to the work of an institution which may at first glance appear to be very different — the Council of Europe.[7] Preventive diplomacy and the work of the Council are linked in that both styles rely upon the ability of the international institution to identify and exploit existing compatibilities between the states, and their reluctance to assert distinctive positions to the point at which there will be an escalation of conflict. The international institution is allowed an area of operation which depends upon two inter-related factors: the existence of actual compatibility of interests (or structures) which are to be harmonised, and the reluctance of states to act to endanger these compatibilities.

In the case of the Council of Europe, the actions of the institution in preparing for further harmonisation are not dramatic, but it is evident that part of its role must be to try to steer states around danger zones in which competitiveness and discord could originate. The Council of Europe's work in specifying particular areas for harmonisation is rather more concerned with technical, economic, social or cultural questions, than that involved in the technique of preventive diplomacy. The normal pattern of the Council's work is for similarities, in principle or practice, to be identified in the various states, for conventions embodying these similarities to be drawn up, and on this basis, for existing barriers to be dismantled and common structures or procedures established. An excellent example of the harmonization process of the Council of Europe was reported on 25th January 1977 (*The Times*, London, 25th January 1977, p. 6). A British Government Minister had been questioned in the House of Commons about the legality of doctors' taking a kidney for transplant purposes from a youth of 16, with his consent and that of his parents. The reply was that British law on this matter was at present ambiguous, but that action should wait until a Council of Europe Report, due shortly, had considered practice in member countries and recommended guidelines. The conventions usually take the form of what have been called *partial agreements*; a minimum of signatures ensures the activation of the agreement between assenting states while non-members are expected, and reminded, to join at a later date.[8] The list of the Council's partial agreements is impressive: it ranges from the European Convention of Human Rights and its associated Commission of Human Rights, and the Court, to a European students' cultural card, which allows rebates to students in member countries. In all these instances, it should be stressed, harmonisation involves chiefly identifying existing compatibilities on the basis of which common elements could be built with very little amendment. No major changes in existing practices or principles of the various states are expected: belief in the success of the process, as Harrison points out below, depends on the assumption of a natural convergence among the interests of states. At the least it establishes a ratchet mechanism which discourages future divergences and discords.

Preventive diplomacy is a product of the post-Second World War bi-polar international system in which the dominant security system, incorporated in the United Nations Organisation, is the *concert* system. This is reflected in the primary responsibility of the Security Council for matters of security, and the introduction of the veto into that institution: action in security questions depends, according to the Charter primarily upon the agreement of the permanent members of the Security Council that is, the leading powers of 1945. The ideas of Dag Hammarskjold on the use of *quiet* diplomacy, *conference* diplomacy, and peace-keeping forces illustrate preventive diplomacy in action: a minimum permissive consensus between the permanent members of the Security Council, particularly, of course, the two Super Powers, is the essential foundation for the action of the institution.[9] The institution then acts to restrain the use of violence between non-members of the concert (preventive diplomacy cannot be between the permanent members of the Security Council), by negotiation, in which it seeks to represent the common interest, or, if this fails, by the use of peace-keeping forces taken from non-permanent member states which are interposed between the warring parties.[10] It is fundamental to the idea of preventive diplomacy that the international institution is able to act because the major states recognise a compatability of interest (a harmony), and are anxious not to jeopardise this by involvement in issues which could increase the level of discord, and, that they expect that further compatabilities will be identified in future; the institution does not act directly in this case to *modify* policy in order to facilitate co-operation as it would in the process of co-ordination.

The dominant style of inter-governmental co-operative action in the classical balance of power system, insofar as it succeeds in preserving peace, is *co-operation*.[11] Co-operation is defined here as a limited involvement of states in a joint enterprise, limited both in scope and duration, and focussed upon a specific pre-determined objective. Obviously, in matters of security in a balance of power system co-operation will involve the techniques of negotiation, mediation, arbitration, conciliation or good offices, and the role of the international institution is to service such procedures between member states. It may provide a framework, informal advice, or secretarial facilities but is not itself an element in the stability of the system (in preventive diplomacy, if it is successful, it is such an element of stability as an essential actor in the concert system). The stability of the balance of power system depends essentially upon the ability of member states, to maintain a fluid system of arrangements between themselves, in which alliances are limited and capable of adjustment. The system stands or falls on the ability of the participant states to undertake specific acts of co-operation on their own behalf: in that system the international institution's role is a rather minor, incidental, one.

Although co-operation in this sense is the dominant style of international involvement in the balance of power system, it is evident that it is also found in the system of collective security as an agency of peaceful change, and in the concert system, where it works alongside and reinforces preventive diplomacy (in the United Nations system it is embodied in chapter 6 of the Charter on pacific settlement of disputes.) But it is distinguishable from the processes involved in attaining collective security (co-ordination). In the practice of the United Nations it is difficult to make a clear distinction between it and harmonization in preventive diplomacy. The one may be seen as reinforcement of the other.

Co-operation, as defined here, obviously takes place in the framework of a large number of international institutions and may be involved in political, economic, social or cultural questions. It has been argued that it is the dominant mode in relations between member states of COMECON in which the sovereign equal states of Eastern Europe co-operate on specific limited projects which they separately regard as being of benefit.[12] Co-operative arrangements may also be made, through an international institution, between two or more member states to further the interests of one state, as an exchange for future co-operative arrangements which further the interests of others. It is essential, though, that the objectives on these various occasions relate to matters which are not connected directly with each other.

Two styles of *association* may be identified. In the first an international institution employs high levels of expertise in the management of a sector of the technical infra-structure of international society which is generally accepted by states as vital. Governments tend to interfere in the work of these associations only when they are in a position to back their demands with appropriate specialist technical information. Such institutions include those which manage international air safety or maritime safety, or which manage international communications of all sorts. It is not argued that such institutions are non-political, but that the political issues involved tend to be cloaked or filled out with supporting research and expert opinion.

They can sometimes acquire considerable power in getting governments to accept the system which they think is most desirable. The main international air safety regulation body (I.A.T.A.) is influential, though its maritime equivalent (I.M.C.O.), is fairly weak. There is in the mid-1970s a considerable body of research on these association organisations,[13] but it is probable that of all the various styles of inter-governmental co-operation, association has the least impact upon elite political attitudes. It is specific, involves experts more than politicians and the public, and is concerned with management rather than policy alignment.

A second style of association is to be found in relations between countries such as Greece and Turkey and international institutions such as the European Communities. Although the scope of this style of association may be considerably wider, it does have in common with the first style the tendency to concentrate on practical, functional arrangements and to postpone or avoid associated questions of political commitment.[14]

These then are the major forms of adjustment theories. It is apparent that in this brief essay it is only possible to give a broad indication of the various ways in which they may be illustrated. But hopefully enough has been said to indicate that the processes of intergovernmental cooperation in international institutions can be usefully categorized in terms of these styles, and several are examined at length in succeeding chapters.

B. Integration Theories

These are theories which describe and explain a qualitative change in the context of decision-making: integration theories are about a fundamental change which is expected to be persistent at one or more of four levels of the state. These levels are:—

1. The people or citizens. (The popular level.)
2. Organised groups. (The level of the competing, non-governmental institutions in the state.)
3. The bureaucrats: elites in 'key institutional settings'. (The level of administration.)

4. The politicians/statesmen. (The level of the executive.)

In the literature of international organisation there are, in the mid-1970s, writings which concentrate on each of these levels. It may be noted that supra-nationalism, the most novel form of adjustment theory, forms a useful introduction to integration theories. Many of its aspects touch upon the considerations which recur in the theory of international integration.

The discussion of integration theory begins conveniently with theories which concentrate at the popular level on changes in mass attitudes and values. Such theories generally see such changes as the test or major dynamic of integration although they may be concerned with consequent or associated changes at other levels too. Generally, they are concerned with the development of community, or Gemeinschaft[15], at the popular level and see developments at that level as the main determinant of stability, be it in the states involved in the integration process, or in the emerging integrated system. Among the theorists who stress this view are Karl Deutsch, whose ideas onn the development of amalgamated and pluralistic security communities put great stress upon changes in popular attitudes.[16] He is concerned clearly with developments at three levels of the state: the changes in patterns of transactions (hence, he is sometimes called a transactionalist), the development of a community of attitudes of values, and the development of political amalgamation (patterns of institutional unity). But the critical development, the one of which changes in transactions are used as an indication, and on which the persistence of political amalgamation rests, is seen as being the development of a community of values and attitudes. It should be stressed here that Deutsch does not regard development in transactions as *equivalent* to developing community. It is also important to point out that it is the range and quality of changes in transactions that constitutes an indicator of community: too frequently Deutsch's ideas are criticized on the mistaken assumption that he sees *particular* transactions developments as indicators of community. The well-known R.A. index is one way of summarizing transactions changes in a form which provides, in Deutsch's view, an indicator of community.[17]

The functionalism of David Mitrany is also concerned primarily with attitude changes at the popular level. They provide the test and the dynamic of integration.[18] International institutions which concentrate upon specific tasks are seen as generating supportive popular attitudes, thus modifying loyalties to the nation state which are thought to sustain the more dangerously competitive conflicting aspects of international society. Once the process of transnational community building begins it generates new demands for international institutions to satisfy felt needs, which in turn, consolidate the emerging community. Eventually, international co-operation is seen to be sustained by the interdependencies and cross-cutting ties of international society which impose restraints upon the disruptive ambitions of governments, and by the existence of supportive attitudes. Unlike Deutsch, Mitrany places much more stress on the causal links between the various levels of the integration process: the processes of co-operation which may be linked with transactions, are seen to modify attitudes.

Attitude formation among the member states of the European Communities is one possible empirical reference, though work on attitude change in international institutions, such as assemblies and secretariats, may be taken from a wide variety of sources.[19] Professor Alger's work was one of the earlier examples of attempts to research into attitude change in international institutions.[20]

Transnationalism concentrates on the level of organised groups: the major empirical reference in the mid-1970s is the multi-national business organisation although there are many other examples which range from the Roman Catholic church to the Communist party. Transnationalism has as its main underlying focus the question of the manner in which developments in international interdependencies, particularly those of an economic kind, together with multi-national, non-governmental organisations, such as multi-national business, may have significantly changed the style and purpose of foreign policy-making. It suggests that new inter-dependencies and non-state actors may have fundamentally altered the context of foreign policy making so that the theory may be justifiably placed under the heading of integration. The question is asked of whether the developments have so detracted from the abilities of governments to control their own affairs in areas which they have come to regard as crucial that they are pushed to establish frameworks for control at the international level. 'International economy' is seen as giving way to 'world economy', with all the joint management arrangements which that implies. The literature on these developments is multiplying extremely rapidly in the mid-1970s: the volume edited by Keohane and Nye is well-known and broke new ground.[21] It may be usefully linked with writings on international business, such as the book by Raymond Vernon,[22] and work on effects on the making of foreign policy such as the articles by Edward Morse[23] and by Samuel Huntingdon.[24] Also useful are a volume of *International Affairs* which has several writings on transnationalism by Susan Strange and others.[25]

The working model of the transnationalists is essentially pluralist, unlike that of the functionalists or of Karl Deutsch. The latter believes that stability in society is dependent upon consensus, whilst the pluralists accept the dominance of competitiveness in society and see stability in a general acceptance of the rules of the game. The neo-functionalists also accept a pluralist model, and stress in their view of integration the pressures produced by interest group demands upon decision-making elites, amongst which bureaucrats occupy a key position.[26] Interest groups' demands are seen as stimulating decision-makers to apply the experience of successful integration to new areas: once integration begins further integrative decisions, which are seen as rewarding by interest groups, become more likely.[27] Bureaucrats are also faced with problems caused by previous integration in areas which are functionally connected and try to solve them by steps for further integration. They are also seen as being able to relate the political interests of politicians to demands of interest groups as they respond to such problems. They occupy a central position in integration and it is their work and changes in their behaviour (for instance, in establishing closer links with colleagues in the international civil service, and in other governments), which provides the key test and condition of integration. They are instrumental in creating a new transnational political system, the modalities of which come to be accepted by organised groups as they pursue their various competing interests. As a result of this process responsibility for performance of crucial tasks is transferred from national governments to new centres in international institutions.

The range of neo-functionalist writings and criticisms and developments of their ideas is very extensive. The work of Ernst Haas on the European Coal and Street Community (ECSC), and on the International Labour Organisation (I.L.O.), is of central importance[28], as is the volume of *International Organisation* on regional integration theory of the Autumn of 1970.[29] There are a number of useful brief critiques and developments. Hansen's critique is now a standard reference,[30] but reference should also be made to the insightful analysis of neo-functionalism by Ron Kaiser in the *Journal of Common Market Studies*, of 1972,[31] this should be related to Haas' own re-assessment of his theories.[32] There are also a number of summaries and critiques of neo-functionalist ideas contained in larger books on integration theory.[33]

At the level of governments there are a number of ideas about changes in behaviour and context which may be prop rly judged to constitute integration theory. These ideas may be labelled collectively as *process federalism*:

One example is the theory of Dag Hammarskjold about an emerging constitution in international society which has governments and states as its primary members. Hammarskjold detected a process of entrenching in international society, the practice of resorting to procedures which involved international institutions in order to settle disputes and in order to achieve common interests. He described the process of moving from a phase of 'primitive institutionalism' to a phase of 'sophisticated constitutionalism' among states, in which conventions of behaviour, increasingly adhered to as norms of the society of governments, were identified and followed.[34] The process was sustained by the experience over a period of years of *quiet diplomacy* in the corridors of the United Nations and other international institutions, and by *conference diplomacy* in assemblies of statesmen, such as the General Assembly of the UN or the Consultative Assembly of the Council of Europe. The accumulated wisdom and perspective of the institution itself, contained particularly in the international secretariat, would become an element in international diplomacy, continuously encouraging states to adjust their positions and attitudes so that peace could be maintained and order consolidated. These ideas, developed by Hammarskjold in a number of his writings and speeches, constitute an approach towards international federalism: governments are expected to be gradually merged in an international constitution, to be fixed by entrenched conventions in a co-ordinated global system.

The ideas of the functional federalists, such as Carl Friedrich, should also be considered in this context, as they also involve a view of a step-by-step movement towards a more highly integrated system at the levels of the governments. One useful comment and critique of the functional federalist approach is the article by von Krosigk in the *Journal of Common Market Studies*.[35] The ideas of Hammarskjold about the role of the United Nations may be developed by reference to the practices of multi-lateral diplomacy in the United Nations. There is a considerable body of writing on *quiet diplomacy* and *conference diplomacy* and about the role of international secretariats.[36] It is the case, however, that Hammarskjold's ideas also contained a strong prescriptive element and because of this they moved towards the style of theorising which is contained more clearly in the third section of this essay.

These then are the major integration theories arranged according to their level of concentration in the state. It is not claimed that any one theory concentrates entirely at the stated level, but rather that all attach particular stress to developments at that level and seek to explain developments at other levels in terms of changes there. Again, this typology gives the student a sense of order in this rather complex set of ideas and propositions about international society. The student should also recognise the different models of society which are implied, or stated, in the various approaches, and the differences in terms of methodology, be it social scientific, or more traditional and less rigorous. They should also recall that integration theories stress a variety of theoretical purposes, and range from the prescriptive to the essentially descriptive and explanatory. Succeeding chapters develop these points.

C. Constitutional Theories

These are theories which either prescribe an ideal future arrangement of international society or which discover an approximation to an established constitutional form in existing circumstances. The distinguishing features of the first form of constitutional theories are that they are essentially prescriptive, are also rather vague in their explanation of how to arrive at the end situation, and are static in the sense that they involve a notion of the ideal order. Integration theories, in contrast, invariably fasten onto developments in present circumstances and, on the basis of these, forecast future developments. Constitutional theories of this type specify what we should aspire to, or prescribe on the basis of things which we are *not* doing now.

The analysis and criticism of such theories is useful for a number of reasons: they are an indication of assumptions about the nature of international society in the minds of their creators. They also give an insight into the difficulties and dangers of prescriptions, and the problems of attaching them to an accepted reality. They also help develop a sense of the depth of international organisation, the range of problems with which they cope, and the variety of potential which they contain. Although the constitutional theorists do not usually consider themselves as speculative thinkers their wide-ranging ideas are a useful hook onto which to attach discussion of nascent forms in international organisation and in international society. The works mentioned are therefore well worthy of study. Ideas from recent times and previous periods should be considered.[37]

More recent examples include prescriptive federalism, be it radical in the style of Clarence Streit or evolutionary, in the style of the European

Federalist Movement.[38] This kind of Federalism is episodic in the sense that it postulates a condition which is to be obtained, as it were, at a single stroke, and which once obtained, it is thought, will establish the millenium. Another example is the writing of Clark and Sohn, as reflected in their work on *World Peace through World Law*,[39] which is to be obtained by drastic modification of the Charter of the United Nations, by world disarmament and by the setting up of an international army. These ideas have the one major disadvantage, that it is difficult to see how they could be realised!

In the second style of constitutional theories the attempt is made to characterise a particular stage of integration by reference to an established constitutional form. It is an attempt to sharpen the description of what is, and to illuminate and give coherence to the wide range of detail in existing circumstances. The specific structures, procedures, and institutions are given colour and an imputed conceptual setting by reference to the constitutional form. This has been most frequently attempted in studies of integration in Western Europe. The various stages of the integration process of the Communities have been characterised as the federal phase, from 1951 to approximately 1954, (after Altiero Spinelli[40]), as the neo-functionalist phase, from 1957 until 1965 (after Ernst Haas), and as the confederal phase, from 1969 until the present. The use of term such as federalism, and confederalism illuminate particular features of the pattern of interaction between participating states and other actors during this period. The federalist model illuminates the concentration of statesmen on rapid integration in highly salient areas, without regard to background conditions or the attitude of the people. It was an attempt at a rapid achievement of integration relying upon the creative arts of a small number of active committed statesmen. Although ultimately their attempts foundered on the rock of the failure of political will, particularly in France, the Federal model was the one which seemed to best illuminate their efforts.

The Confederal model of the period after 1969 suggests the primacy of the sub-systems in the Communities, the retention by states of their sovereignty and ultimate responsibility, but, at the same time, their involvement in regional arrangements at a variety of levels, and their recognition that they shared together a common position, both in geographical terms, and in terms of their broad interests in international society. They are contiguous both in the physical sense, and in the sense of inhabiting the same functional context. They are separate but bound together through existing

132

interests, and in anticipation of future compatibilities. At the same time though, there is no expectation of political union. The details of this phase have been outlined by the present writer elsewhere (see chapter 14), but it is a frame of reference into which may be fitted a range of the features of contemporary Europe. Confederalism has wide scope, a feeling for common interests, a preparedness to adjust the politics and structures, but a limitation of the implications of this for sovereignty. It is the setting of the co-ordination process in the European Communities, described elsewhere in this volume. It may be usefully compared with the idea of arabled legislation (see chapter 13), which is also a constitutional theory.

These then are the three broad types of theory in international organisation. It is possible to fit a wide range of concepts into this typology, and, to relate a wide range of empirical references to them in a coherent way. There are a number of themes in contemporary international organisation which might yet escape the typology and need to be considered separately. These include some aspects of the international institution as an *actor*, particularly those which are conveniently explained by reference to organisation theory. Perspective questions also fall outside the framework. (See chapters 17– 20 below.)

Detailed accounts of the working methods of the EEC, NATO, and various aid programmes, both at the regional and universal level may be related to the idea of co-ordination. The consideration of the problems of *controlling* the work of international institutions, may be conveniently related to a particular slot: the consideration of neo-functionalist integration theory. The reason for this is that neo-functionalism is one of the more sophisticated accounts of the processes whereby international institutions come to acquire and develop formal powers in addition to the ones extended to them in the founding agreements. It is of course the acquiring of powers which are independent of individual participating states which creates the problem of control. It is true, of course, that there are other ways of understanding the processes by which international institutions acquire such powers. But the important question here is to give a sense of the coherence of the subject. The neo-functionalists' slot is a *convenient* place for such a consideration rather than the *only* place at which it could be done.

There are two major kinds of problem of control. The first concerns the problem of control by governments, either as reflected in the international institution itself, particularly in executive committees, or as reflected in committees in the home government which co-ordinate the states' policy towards the institution and its response to it. Problems here include voting arrangements and questions of the pattern of influence in the decision-making of the institution. The volume edited by Cox and Jacobson provides an excellent account of this subject.[41] There is, however, a second crucial problem of control, which refers to problems at the popular level: how should, or can, the electorates control the work of international institutions in questions which affect them? Are governments adequate agents of their interests? Should electorates have direct representation? The discussion about the European Assembly is one context where such questions have been examined. Unfortunately, little has been written about the problem in general at the international level: some of the few examples are essays by David Mitrany, contained in the 1966 edition of his *A Working Peace System*,[42] and the book written by Willard Hogan.[43]

In the following chapters a range of contributions have concentrated on particular stages of the typology. The editors have not covered every step in the typology — this would have led to an unmanageable volume — but rather have encouraged consideration of particularly interesting aspects and perspectives. It is hoped that the merits of the approach will in this way become apparent.

Notes

0. Inis Claude, *Swords into Plowshares*, New York, Random House, 4th Edition, 1971.
1. Ernst Haas, *The Uniting of Europe*, 2nd Edition, Stanford, Stanford University Press, 1968. See below, chapter 10.
2. See L.S. Woolf, *Framework of a Lasting Peace*, London, Allen & Unwin, 1917. Also see Grenville Clark and Louis B. John, *World Peace through World Law*, Cambridge Mass., Harvard UP, 3rd Edition, 1966.
3. See chapter 9 below.
4. See Paul Taylor, 'The Politics of the European Communities: the Confederal Phase', *World Politics*, April, 1975 (Princeton), pp. 336–360.
5. Inis Claude, *Swords into Plowshares*, loc. cit.
6. Morton Kaplan, *System and Process in International Politics*.
7. See A.H. Robertson, *The Council of Europe*, (2nd edition), London, Stevens, 1962. See below, chapter 8.
8. See A. Glenn Mower Jr., 'The Official Pressure Group of the Council of Europe's Consultative Assembly', *International Organization*, Boston, Spring 1964, pp. 292–306.
9. See Y. Tandon, 'Consensus and Authority behind UN Peace-Keeping Operations', *International Organization*, Boston, Spring 1967.
10. See Alan James, *The Politics of Peace Keeping*, London, Chatto & Windus, 1969.

11. See Richard Rosecrance, *International Relations: Peace or War*, McGraw-Hill, New York, 1973, Chapter 5.
12. See chapter 6 below.
13. See Robert T. Thornton, *Governments and Airlines*, in Robert O. Keohane and Joseph S. Nye Jr. (eds.), *Transnational Relations and World Politics*, Cambridge, Harvard University Press, pp. 191–203. See also *International Organization*, Madison, University of Wisconsin Press, Vol. 29, No. 3, Summer 1975, on *International Responses to Technology*.
14. See chapter 7 below.
15. For an account of gemeinshaft and gesellschaft, see Paul Taylor, 'The Concept of Community and the European Integration Process', *Journal of Common Market Studies*, Oxford, Blackwells, December 1968, Vol. VII, No. 2, pp. 83–101.
16. See Karl W. Deutsch et al, *Political Community and the North Atlantic Area*, Princeton, Princeton University Press, 1957.
17. See the exposition and application of Deutsch's ideas by Donald Puchala in his 'International Transactions and Regional Integration', *International Organization*, Boston, Vol. XXIV, No. 4, Autumn, 1970, pp. 732–763.
18. See chapter 11 below.
19. See, inter alia, Ronald Inglehart, 'An end to European Integration?', *American Political Science Review*, March 1967.
20. Chadwick F. Alger, 'Personal Contact in Intergovernmental Organizations' in Herbert C. Kelman (ed.), *International Behaviour*, New York, Holt, Rinehart and Winston, 1965.
21. R. Keohane and J. Nye Jr., *Transnational Relations and World Politics,* op. cit.
22. Raymond Vernon, *Sovereignty at Bay: the Multinational Spread of US Enterprises*, New York, Basic Books, 1971.
23. Edward L. Morse, 'The Transformation of Foreign Policies: modernization, interdependence, and externalization', *World Politics*, Princeton, Vol. XXII, No. 3, April 1970, pp. 371–392.
24. Samuel P. Huntington, 'Transnational Organisations in World Politics', *World Politics*, Vol. XXV, April 1973, No. 3, pp. 335–368.
25. *International Affairs*, London, Royal Institute of International Affairs, Vol. 52, No. 3, July, 1976, and G.L. Goodwin and Andrew Linklater, *New Dimensions of World Politics*, London, Croom Helm, 1975.
26. See Paul Taylor, *International Cooperation Today*, London, Elek, 1971, pp. 50–79.
27. See chapter 12 below.
28. Ernst B. Haas, *The Uniting of Europe*, loc cit.; and, *Beyond the Nation State*, Stanford, Stanford University Press, 1964.
29. Vol. XXIV, No. 4, Autumn 1970, op. cit.
30. Roger D. Hansen, 'Regional Integration: reflections on a decade of Theoretical Efforts', *World Politics*, Princeton, January 1969, pp. 242–271.
31. Ronn D. Kaiser, 'Toward the Copernican Phase of Regional Integration Theory', *Journal of Common Market Studies*, Oxford, Blackwells, March 1972, pp. 207–232.
32. Ernst B. Haas, 'The Study of Regional Integration: Reflections on the Joy and Anguish of pre-theorising', *International Organization*, Boston, Vol. XXIV, 4, 1970.
33. See R.J. Harrison, *Europe in Question*, London, Allen & Unwin, 1974, chapter 4. See also chapter by David Mitrany, and by Nina Heathcote in A.J.R. Groom and Paul Taylor, *Functionalism: theory and practice in International Relations*, University of London Press, 1975.

135

34. See Dag Hammarskjold, Speech at the University of Chicago, 1st May 1960, in Wilder Foote (ed.), Dag Hammarskjold: *Servant of Peace*, The Bodley Head, London, 1962, p. 252.
35. Friedrich von Krosigk, 'A Reconsideration of Federalism in the Scope of the Present Discussion on European Integration', *Journal of Common Market Studies*, Oxford, Blackwells, March, 1971, pp. 197–223.
36. See text and bibliography in Paul Taylor, *International Cooperation Today*, loc. cit., chapter 4, pp. 80–102.
37. See S.J. Hemleben, *Plans for World Peace through Six Centuries*, Chicago, University of Chicago Press, 1943.
38. See R.J. Harrison, *Europe in Question*, loc. cit., chapter 3.
39. Grenville Clark and Louis B. Sohn, *World Peace through World Law*, loc. cit.
40. Atiero Spinelli, *The Eurocrats*, Baltimore, The Johns Hopkins Press, 1966.
41. Robert W. Cox and Harold K. Jacobson (editors), *The Anatomy of Influence: decision-making in International Organization*, London, Yale University Press, 1974 (2nd printing).
42. Quadrangle Books, Chicago.
43. W.N. Hogan, *Representative Government and European Integration*, Nebraska, 1967.

Selected Reading

1. Inis L. Claude, Jr., *Swords into Plowshares*, New York, Random House, 4th Edition, 1971.
2. Charles Pentland, *International Theory and European Integration*, London, Faber and Faber, 1973.
3. Paul Taylor, *International Cooperation Today*, London, Elek, 1971.
4. Leon Lindberg and S. Scheingold, (Eds.), *Regional Integration, Theory and Research*, Harvard, 1971.
5. R.J. Harrison, *Europe in Question*, London, Allen and Unwin, 1974.
6. Leland M. Goodrich and David A. Kay, (Eds.), *International Organization: Politics and Process*, Madison, University of Wisconsin Press, 1973.

CHAPTER SIX

COORDINATION AND COOPERATION IN COUNCIL FOR MUTUAL ECONOMIC ASSISTANCE

Mihály Simai

The marxist theory of international organisations is based on the recognition of internationalization in production, consumption, science, technology, culture, health and many other aspects of human activities. Internationalization is considered as an inevitable consequence of economic development. This process started by capitalism was recognized by Marx and Engels, as early as in 1848, when they wrote in the Communist Manifesto:

'The bourgeoisie has through its exploitation of the world market, given a cosmopolitan character to production and consumption in every country. To the great chagrin of reactionaries it has drawn from under the feet of industry the national ground on which it stood. All old established national industries have been destroyed or are daily being destroyed. They are dislodged by new industries, whose introduction becomes a life and death question for all civilised nations, by industries that no longer work up indigenous raw material, but raw material drawn from the remotest zones; industries, whose products are consumed not only at home but in every quarter of the globe. In place of the old wants, satisfied by the production of the country, we find new wants, requiring for their satisfaction the products of distant lands and climes. In place of the old local and national seclusion and self sufficiency we have intercourse in every direction, universal interdependence of nations. And as in material, so also in intellectual production. The intellectual creation of individual nations becomes common property. National one-sidedness and narrow-mindedness become more and more impossible, and from the numerous national and local literatures there arises a world literature.'[1]

In our epoch, internationalization in the spheres of economic relations is going on in a world of different economic and social systems and about 150 states, which have different levels of economic development and social structure. The two economic and social systems have several formally similar features. It is a common characterisitc, for example, that the process of internationalization speeded up on the basis of modern industrial development and in response to revolutionary changes in science and technology. Since states remained the basic political formations, the contradiction between internationalization and the national framework, is characteristic of both economic and social systems. The appearance, consequences, and tasks of solving emerging problems, and the tools and possibilities for their solution, are different in many important respects. Similar international organisational forms could however, develop on the basis of similar technology and problems.

The difference between the two systems are based above all on the fact that in the socialist countries the private ownership of the means of production has been abolished. With this step, the tool for national and international exploitation — one of the m ain source of conflicts among nations — was eliminated. There could, of course, be other sources of problems among socialist nations, but all these problems could be solved more easily since the sources of antagonistic contradictions no longer exist. The basic equality of socialist nations, the similarities in the patterns of internal social and economic order, could not, however, eliminate differences in the level of their economic development, in their size, in natural resources and the like. Nor could the national prejudices, which had developed during many centuries before the victory of socialism, be eliminated within a rather short period of time.

The marxist movement developed some basic views about the future relations among socialist nations before the victory of socialist forces in one state. It has been emphasized for example that their relations must be established on the basis of their complete and full equality. Only then can mutual trust and respect develop, whereby they come closer to each other, cooperate and finally merge.

On the basis of the success of Soviet policies in promoting the economic progress and integration of many nations and minorities in the revolutionary movement before the Second World War, views were expressed that the world of socialism will develop further by the territorial increase of the first socialist state, since the emerging proletarian republics will merge into one single country.

In reality, the emerging world system of socialism developed on different lines. It was born as a system of independent states. Historically, in a situation, when great differences in levels of development remained among the states the victory of socialist forces took a different path, and it occured on different continents; this was the only real possibility. This means that, at present, socialist countries are politically and economically independent sovereign states. They develop their economic, social and cultural life on the basis of their national plans and programmes. This also indicates that national differences will remain for a long time, and they will influence the place, role and policies of governments in their approach to any form of international cooperation.

The national (or multinational) state with its internal economic and socio-political structure, with its specific patterns of interests, is a decisive factor not only in the Western world but also in the socialist world system. National sovereignty therefore plays an important role in international law. The economic policy of the governments, and the system of national decision-making centres is a key factor in international relations.

With the process of increasing internationalisation, the role of states has not diminished. The nineteenth century concept of sovereignty, in which states represented a rather isolated unit in culture, defence, and economics, cannot be valid today, even theoretically. Modern socialist (or non-socialist) states cannot exist today outside international relations. Any accepted system of international relations means certain limitations for the member states. The economic needs of states and interests together with external realities determine the character and the degree of inevitable compromises. This does not mean that the relations among states based on interdependence are necessarily undermining political sovereignty nor that they are eliminating the role of states. International economic, political, ideological, legal, diplomatic and military relations among states or economic and social systems and the institutionalization of these relations in international organisations are playing an increasingly important role in the everyday life and activities of nations also in the socialist system. The participation of countries in any form of international organisation is based on the decision of national governments and it is implemented by government actions.

The marxist theory of international relations based on the general theory of marxism considers, however, that this situation is a temporary one and emphasises that historically it is necessary to create a world economy, directed by one plan. This is an objective tendency, because only in this way can the problems of mankind be solved. However, only after the global victory of communism can mankind achieve this goal.

The different international organisations are, of course, not equally important for the states of the world. For the socialist countries, those types of international organisations whose activities impringe upon vital economic and political areas are the most important. The international organisation of the socialist countries, the Council of Mutual Economic Assistance (C.M.E.A.), occupies, therefore, a central role. Thus CMEA is analysed in this chapter as a typical institutionalized example of international cooperation between socialist countries in the present world economy.

1. The Roots of the CMEA Cooperation

CMEA is an economic organisation. It was established in 1949 at the Moscow conference of representatives from Bulgaria, Czechoslovakia, Hungary, Poland, Rumania and the USSR. Politically it was a reaction of the Eastern European countries to the Marshall plan and to the beginnings of cold war policies. In economic cooperation its aims were to exchange information on economic problems, to extend mutual technical assistance and to grant mutual aid in the form of raw materials, machines and industrial equipment and other goods needed by the member countries.

At the very beginning it was declared that,

a) CMEA is an open organisation, to which other European countries may join, which accept the same principles and would like to participate in wide economic cooperation with the member countries. (The geographical limitation was removed in 1962.)

b) Decisions would be taken only with the approval of the interested country.

c) The periodical meetings would be held in the capital of each of the member countries in turn. The chairman of each session should be the representative of the country in whose capital the session takes place.

The members of CMEA in 1976 are the following countries: Bulgaria, Cuba, Czechoslovakia, German Democratic Republic, Hungary, Mongolia, Poland, Romania and the USSR. Yugoslavia participated in the work of CMEA in certain areas and has an 'observer' status at certain meetings. Finland, Iraq and Mexico have signed special cooperation agreements with the CMEA.

International organisations, especially those which occupy a central role in cooperation between countries, necessarily reflect the characteristic features of the member countries, their problems, policies and short and long term aims. Changes in the interests of the countries require changes in the level and forms of cooperation within the framework of the given organisation. CMEA is no exception to this.

The existing system of international economic relations within CMEA is still connected with the inherited and considerable differences of level of development of the countries and with the policy measures of earlier periods. The system of planning and management was also a function of the achieved level of economic development, and of the issues connected with it.

It is well known that the increasing interdependence of the Common Market countries which led to the creation of the European Economic Community had long historical traditions. The international division of labour between these countries was already well developed before the Rome treaty. Among the CMEA countries, there was very little contact before the war; they had very little to sell to each other (with the exception of Czechoslovakia), and the western industrial powers played a predominant role in their foreign trade.[2] The Soviet Union, because of the special conditions of her economic development, could not build an economy heavily dependent on foreign markets.[3]

International economic policy in the Soviet Union was formed in circumstances which necessitated the need to ensure independence and self-defence. The Soviet economic system was conceived and developed as a self contained unit: the extraordinary size and natural resources of the Soviet Union afforded possibilities for such a course. However, in the years after the Second World War, the smaller states which took the road to socialism were in a totally different situation.

It was, however, more or less inevitable that in the strained international situation of the late forties and early fifties the socialist countries adopted similar methods of development to those which had been applied in the Soviet Union under the conditions prevailing in the late twenties, without considering the obvious differences in circumstances. Every country strove rapidly to enlarge its industrial base and to raise its production of coal, steel and electricity.

This policy brought rapid and significant progress in industrialization, and increased the economic potential of the socialist countries. A new industrial belt emerged in the eastern part of Europe.[4]

In their manufacturing industries, most of the eastern European member countries inherited poor conditions from their past. Their industry was characterized by an economically unjustified diversification based on small scale production with very limited raw material and fuel bases: they were economically dependent upon the great industrial powers of the West. After the war these traditional connections were disrupted. Each Eastern European country developed more or less the same branches of heavy industry, neglected agriculture and light industry, increased the import of the same kind of machinery and raw materials, mostly from the Soviet Union, and as a natural economic consequence of this situation the Soviet Union became the most important market for their goods. In spite of the increase of foreign trade, there were strong tendencies toward import substitution in the pattern of industrialization. The CMEA countries neglected the advantages offered by the possibilities of establishing specialized large scale industries which could satisfy the needs of several nations, instead of the narrow markets of one country.[5]

Integration — as an expression was not even used in its official documents until the late sixties. The theoretical as well as practical issues of socialist integration were neglected by the social sciences in the socialist countries for many years.

It took another decade, from the mid fifties, until the socialist countries finally discovered the necessity to change the character of their international cooperation. Between 1954 and 1962 a new approach emerged in the CMEA region, in the focus of which there was an unrealistic attempt of *introducing common planning on an international scale.*

The reception of the idea of introducing common planning from one centre was by no means uniform, and the problems presented by the realization of these ambitious projects soon became evident. Integrated planning was frowned upon because central planning was acceptable only within a national framework. This attitude, resulting from historical-political traits, still has to be taken into account when planning new projects and programmes.

There were certain economic realities which were not conducive to

142

the development of integration.

It is well known from the history of the international division of labour that the advantage gained in the process of international economic relations are not equal for all the countries. All countries could gain benefits — but far from equally. The more developed a country is, the higher the technical level and the more elastic its economic structure, the greater the ability to produce different kinds of goods — among them those which are highly demanded in the world market — the greater will be the relative advantages. The countries on a higher level of economic development have relatively greater sources of saving partly because of the higher degree of processing in their industries so they are able not only to invest in their own country but, because of the relative abundance of investment funds, are much more able to participate in investments of in international character without substantial bottlenecks in their national investments. In addition, the accumulated technical skill of the population, the available research and highly skilled technical personnel make the economy of these countries more elastic in structure enabling them to follow more rapidly the shifts in the pattern of the international division of labour based on rapid changes in technology.

So international cooperation, between countries of different levels, could increase inequalities and this was neither the aim of the CMEA nor the consequence of the cooperation achieved so far. But because of the great differences of productivity the countries on a lower technical level with a lower labour productivity in their industries were reluctant to accept the given level of productivity as a criteria of specialization in industry or their given economic structure as a determining factor in the development of different branches of economy.

The idea of extending the centralized planning system to an international level was impractical for other reasons as well. (It is beyond the scope of the present study to deal with the probable effect of the over centralized national planning systems on the realization of joint planning on an international scale.)

One reason was lack of multilateralism. There can be no doubt that, in the initial stage of co-operation, the system of bilateralism that emerged in the CMEA countries from the economies based on plan directives had its positive effects, especially from the point of view of the less-developed countries, creating as it did, with the rapid pace of industrialization based primarily on the mobilization of internal resources, secure external markets.[6]

143

However, the then rigid system put a brake on efficient growth in each country. As the economy of CMEA countries became more developed, the internal changes in the needs of the countries demanded a new and higher level of international cooperation as well. Such problems as the impossibility of creating a convertible socialist world currency suited to fulfil all the functions of money hindered the progress towards multilateralism. The drawbacks presented by this and other problems made themselves felt in every domain of co-operation and international division of labour, resulting in difficulties of specialization and in launching joint ventures, in a lack of capital flows, in the difficulty of co-ordinating economic policies and plans on an international level, in the impossibility or complexity of compensation, and the like. The creation of a transferable currency and the achievement of multilateralism was a necessity which was especially emphasized by some Hungarian and Polish economists, not as an end in itself but as a necessary precondition for efficient co-operation.

A second group of issues deriving from those above related to the domestic and international situation regarding prices and exchange rates, and the system of quotas. This latter was closely connected with the fact that the co-ordination of plans based on physical indicators gave rise to a tendency to replace the exchange of equal values by an exchange of identical commodity patterns.

2. The Organisation and its Principles

The structure of the CMEA, and the forms of cooperation, are the results of far reaching changes in the attitude of the member countries in accepting the idea of moving from the stage of cooperation to the era of economic integration. An important document, a 'Comprehensive Programme for the Further Intensification and Improvement of Cooperation and the Development of Socialist integration of CMEA countries' has been accepted and the institutional structure of CMEA was reorganized in 1971 at the Bucharest session of the CMEA Council. The Bucharest meeting, and the changes implemented afterwards, represent a new phase in the history of CMEA relations. While accepting the unavoidable and necessary character of the developments towards economic integration of the member countries, some basic conditions remained unchanged as has been underlined in the new programme:

a) The development of socialist integration of CMEA members will be carried out also in the future in accordance with the principles of socialist internationalism and on the basis of respect for national

144

sovereignty, independence and national interests, of nonintervention in the internal affairs of nations and of total equality, mutual advantage, and comradely reciprocal aid.

b) Socialist economic integration is carried out on an entirely voluntary basis and it is not accompanied by the creation of supra-national organs, nor does it affect matters pertaining to internal planning or the financial and cost calculating activities of organisations.

c) CMEA cooperation is aiming to promote the over-all economic and social progress of the member countries and the equalization of their development level through the more rapid growth of the economically less developed member countries, with the assistance of the more developed ones.

Three important changes, however, have been decided and their implementation has already begun:

a) The principle of unanimity which characterized the decisions of CMEA organs was modified in one organisation, in the International Investment Bank. Unanimity is required on important questions, like the acceptance of the annual report, the distribution of income, the nomination of the chief managers. A two thirds majority is sufficient in other cases. For the time being, this change has limited importance. However, it could be more important in the future.

b) The possibility that certain steps will be taken only by the interested parties and not by the whole community indicates that countries, which are not ready to join in a certain programme, can no longer block the progress in the particular field. This latter principle, on the other hand, underlines even more strongly the voluntary character of the integration process in the CMEA.

c) The Secretariat was given greater opportunity to initiate steps and measures. Its tasks increased and it was decided that they should work as a collective body, as an entity. The increased role of the secretariat in the future may speed up the solution of technical problems in cooperation.

The organs of CMEA have, of course, been established gradually, and the implementation of the Comprehensive Programme represents no more than a given stage in the development of the organizational structure.

1. At the establishment of the CMEA only a Bureau was formed, with one representative from each country, and with a small secretariat, with mainly technical tasks.

2. The main organs of CMEA were founded in 1962–63, after a series of negotiations among the member states, like the *Council of the*

CMEA, the *Executive Committee* (consisting of the Deputy Prime Ministers), the *Secretariat*, and the *Standing Committees* (the main discussion forums for Ministries and chief government agencies).

3. The development of the organizational structure was continued in 1963–64, by the establishment of the International Bank for Economic Cooperation, the Common Wagon Pool, Intermetall, the United Electric Power Distribution Centre and many other international organs. All these organisations, were, however, considered as independent international bodies.[7]

4. Together with the Comprehensive Programme, several important organisational changes were initiated and implemented after the XXVth session. Three important Committees were established directly under the Council: the Committee for Cooperation in Planning, the Committee for Scientific and Technological Cooperation and, more recently, the Committee for Cooperation in Material and Technical Supply. The structure of the Standing Committees has been rationalized and new Standing Conferences have been organised. Three scientific research institutes were founded: the Institute for Standardization, the International Institute for Economic Problems of the World Socialist System and the International Research Institute for Cybernetics. A new bank, the International Investment Bank, was added to the existing one. New International Industrial Organisations were also set up, including one in the field of nuclear energy (Interatomenergo).

The structure of the CMEA system and the functions of the different organs requires further changes and additions in the future. In many cases their competence has already turned out to be insufficient to realize the tasks for which they were established. Their working mechanism is often hindered by certain shortcomings and limitations in the international financial system and by the existing weaknesses in the method of international settlements. The international legal framework is also mentioned by many experts as an important field requiring further improvements.[8]

The increasing complexity of coordination of different organs, the number of which will undoubtedly increase in the future, gives rise to the problem of establishing a logical hierarchy in the system and inevitably leads to the increase of the tasks and scope of responsibilities of the Secretariat. These issues are far from being solved at the present stage of development.

146

3. The Mechanism of International Socialist Integration

The basic importance of the states and governments as decision-making centres in the framework of CMEA cooperation influenced not only the character and the competences of CMEA organs but also the tools of international cooperation — the mechanism of international economic integration.

There are three important components of CMEA integration:

a) The coordination of national medium and long term development programmes.

b) Cooperation in production, science and technology.

c) Trade, monetary and credit relations.

a) *Plan Coordination*

The underlying importance of plan coordination is derived from the role of states in the integration process and also from the role of central planning in the economic development of the member countries.[9]

Plan coordination is a comprehensive activity in which the representatives of politically and economically sovereign countries are searching for mutually acceptable long term solutions and joint programmes for action in the framework of the CMEA.

Several important issues received special emphasis for such type of activities:

a) The development of specialization and cooperation in production in those branches where the importance of a rational scale of production based on sophisticated technologies is especially great.

b) The coordination of capital investment programmes which are of mutual interest especially for the expansion of the fuel and raw material base for the key industries.

c) The output and deadline for reciprocal supplies.

Plan coordination is both bilateral and multilateral and it has several stages and processes. The most important stages are the following ones:

1. Bilateral and multilateral consultations about long term economic strategies at the highest level, followed by discussions of the planning agencies.

2. The preparation of joint forecasts for the most important products and for science and technology.

3. Coordination of the long and medium term plans through a series of negotiations, with the participation of the representative of planning agencies, CMEA bodies, appropriate departments and Standing Committees.

4. Conclusion of multilateral and bilateral cooperation agreements,

147

which include a statement of reciprocal obligations and responsibilities of the member countries. These agreements cover the most important sectors where mutual interests require joint activities in the field of investments, production and deliveries, and in certain branches, joint planning as well.[10]

5. Plan coordination has several 'auxiliary' activities, which are at the same time important 'independent' fields for cooperation as well. The planning agencies of the socialist countries for example have direct and systematic relations for the purpose of the mutual exchange of information and experience about the methods of planning and management of national economies. The international banks of the CMEA are playing an important role in searching for coordination in the field of credit and monetary policies. There is a lot of concrete activity in the field of planning and coordination in the framework of the international organisations in the CMEA in the field of different industries, transport and the like. Coordination of scientific research activities by the Academies, Ministries and such bodies is also an important aspect of plan coordination, with separate agreements among the different participating bodies. The activities in the field of standardization and the acceptance of mutually agreed standards belong also to the category of the auxiliary activities, but at the same time, they represent a special field of cooperation which is important especially on the micro economic level. The developments in the field of plan coordination within CMEA expanded not only the scope of activities but the number of national institutions participating directly in international cooperation as well. New possibilities were opened for the establishment of direct and systematic relations not only in the sphere of macro economic institutions, but also at the 'mezzo' and micro level, which will inevitably influence the mechanism of cooperation and specialization in production. Cooperation, while decided on the level of macro economic institutions, has been carried out by the producing enterprises. In conclusion, it can be stated that plan coordination is not a supranational activity. The participating international organs have no supranational power. The mutually agreed measures are international, in the interests of the individual countries and, at the same time, in that of the whole community, but not supranational.

b) *Cooperation*

Coordination of plans among the CMEA countries as a macro economic process cannot be successfully implemented without the cooperation of those economic organisations which are directly responsible for production and its management.[11] The Comprehensive Programme called on the member countries to create the necessary conditions for the development of direct ties between ministries and other government organs, between enterprises, scientific research, planning and design organisations. Ties are to be established directly whenever there is a mutual interest of the parties to implement specific measures on a cooperative basis. It is quite clear that cooperation and specialization in production also require the establishment of direct ties.

Direct relations are to be developed with due regard to the existing system of planning and management in the various countries and they can not disregard or disrupt the ties of the particular national enterprise or agency within the national plan. Thus, direct ties cannot weaken the autonomy of the governments within the country in respect to planning. Plan coordination therefore has a higher position in the hierarchy of CMEA relations among the countries, since the establishment of direct ties must be in accordance with the national plans. In this sense, they are serving as a tool for the implementation of the coordinated plans. Cooperation, however, is not simply a tool and there are possibilities, opened by the Comprehensive programme, for government organs and economic organisations to form joint international enterprises, when it is feasible. These joint enterprises have their own property, they are subject to civil law, operate on a cost accounting basis and answer with all their property for their obligations.

The establishment of international socialist ownership is a major step in the framework of CMEA, and in the future, this may be an important lever of investigation. The proper working conditions of such joint enterprises, their relation to the national system of planning and management including financing, pricing and the like require further elaboration and improvement in the future.

Cooperation is not confined to production. There are several joint research organisations for the solution of scientific problems directly or indirectly fostering cooperation in technologically sophisticated areas. The further progress of scientific and technological cooperation is as much the function of financial incentives, realistic exchange rates and price calculation as other forms of cooperation in output or in services. The problems of financial incentives, prices, exchange rates and such questions, of course, influence most directly the market relations of the CMEA countries, which represent the third important factor of socialist integration.

149

c) *Market Relations*

Trade, credit relations and the flow of services follow the developments in plan coordination, and cooperation, but at the same time they represent an important link between the countries. The most important actors of the socialist market, are also independent states, with different internal planning systems and price structures.

This market is influenced not only by its own developments but also by the economic relations of the socialist countries with other areas of the world.

The socialist market is more stable, and safer for the member countries, than the non-socialist world market due to the fact that trade flows are conditioned by long term agreements based on the coordination of plans.

The problems and shortcomings in the mechanism of international economic relations, however, are reflected in the socialist market; they hinder the smooth flow of commodities and services and may reduce the efficiency of plan coordination.

Exchange rates, pricing, convertibility, greater mobility of the factors of production are therefore very important issues also from the point of view of plan coordination and cooperation among enterprises.

The working mechanism of CMEA integration proves that the harmonization of national sovereignty and international integration is not an easy task, and the emerging or existing difficulties may block even economically desirable processes and slow down the required progress.

4. External Relations of CMEA

CMEA is not a closed economic bloc. It is not only open to cooperation and agreements with non-member countries, but accepts the fact that the CMEA members must participate also in the wider, global international division of labour.[12]

The 'Basic Rules' (Constitution) in their present form authorize CMEA to enter into agreements with member countries, with other states and with international organisations.

CMEA is not a supranational organisation in the sense that it cannot undertake international obligations on behalf of its member states, without the agreement of the member states, or against their will. Special measures are required, when the agreements are also binding for the member states.

There are several possible forms of cooperation with non-member countries. They can participate as full members in some organs and as observers in others (like Yugoslavia). The traditional form however is the participation of representatives of the non-member countries in the work of the Council Session, as observers.[13]

There are other forms of cooperation, like the organisation of joint committees formed from the representatives of member and non-member states.[14]

Non-member countries could be represented as members or just observers in one or in several standing committees as well.

CMEA cooperates actively with several U.N. agencies and commissions, and it is authorized to establish working relations or cooperation with other integration organisations as well.

CMEA offers also fellowship programmes to postgraduate students and specialists from developing countries.

In its external activities CMEA represents a realistic approach to international economic and political relations also on a global scale. Its structure and practice corresponds to the present world reality, which is and for a long time to come will be the reality of states and not a world of supranational institutions. The content of national sovereignty changes, but it does not disappear. The loyalty of the people is and will be attached primarily to nation states for many more decades. The existence of any international institutions, communities and like bodies could be justified only to the extent that is required by their individual and joint interests and by the needs of states to find joint solutions to their common problems, the number of which is undoubtedly increasing.

In the future, CMEA countries will participate increasingly in international organisations, agreements and cooperation schemes, beyond the region. This is required not only by their changing economic structure, and their foreign policy aims, but also by the changes in the world, by the emerging global problems, in the solutions of which they must also play an active role. Most of their economic ties will remain within the group, which underlines the importance of improving the mechanism and performance of CMEA cooperation. Their relations with other countries, and economic groups are however expanding. To a great extent, the expansion of extra-CMEA relations depends on the partners outside the region, but still, at the same time, this process creates new possibilities and challenges to CMEA structure. At the meeting of UNCTAD IV in Nairobi, for example, some of the developing countries, important trade partners of the CMEA countries, raised the question of connecting their international settlement system with the CMEA transferable rouble structure.

All these and other external changes may bring new elements into CMEA cooperation beyond the present patterns and plans, they will increase the importance of the CMEA's external relations, and they could bring the organisation into the chain of future regional groups organizing and promoting global cooperation.

Summary

1. Within the CMEA a new type of institutionalized cooperation has developed between states belonging to the socialist system. The member states were on different levels of development but their internal socio-political and institutional structures were similar in many important respects and their long term political aims were identical.

2. The characteristics of the system and the sovereign equality of the member states determines the forms of cooperation. CMEA is not a supra-national organisation. The member states, which are looking for collective responses to their problems, are connected by a substantial proportion of intra-group trade, in their foreign trade through a number of cooperation, specialization agreements and with several other ties in the field of technology, monetary affairs and sciences. All these ties created a high degree of interdependence among them. The agreed forms of cooperation are implemented through the national plans of the member states, using mostly their own resources. There is relatively little movement of capital and labour among them.

3. Due to the central role of national planning within the states, the coordination of development strategies, national and sectoral plans and the joint planning of certain industrial activities play a crucial role in the system of cooperation.

4. Most of the problems and shortcomings of CMEA cooperation are rooted in the differences of their level of development, influencing the short and long term interests of the states, but they are also due to certain errors, committed by some of the member states in their economic policies at the earlier period.

5. The progress of CMEA integration is based on the long term Comprehensive Programme accepted in 1971. This programme has laid down the aims and suggested the means of the integration process for the next one and a half decades. The institutions of the CMEA, which are still in the process of expansion and improvement, were also structured by the Comprehensive Programme and brought to their present form by it.

6. CMEA is an open organisation with no geographic limitations.

Beyond the members, some other, even non-socialist countries concluded special agreements with it. It is beginning to play an increasing role in global economic relations. It is represented in the UN and has entered into negotiations with other regional organisations.

Notes

1. Karl Marx and Friedrich Engels, *Communist Manifesto*, London, George Allen and Unwin Ltd., 1954, p. 124–125.
2. In 1938 in the foreign trade of Bulgaria, Hungary, Poland, Czechoslovakia and Romania the proportion of the industrial West was 86 per cent, their mutual trade was 12–13 per cent of the total, and the share of the U.S.S.R. was about one per cent.
3. In 1931, the U.S.S.R. purchased about one third of the world's exports of machinery and equipment and in 1932, about half. The proportion of imports in the domestic demand for machinery was 21 per cent in 1928–29. It was reduced to 4.4 per cent in 1933 and to 0.9 per cent in 1937. (N. Smeljev, 'Avtarkichna li Socialisticheshkaia Economica', *Voprosi Economiki*, 1974, No. 4.)
4. The proportion of the CMEA countries in world GNP increased from 14–16 per cent in 1950 to 28 per cent in 1965. About 19 per cent was the proportion of the USSR and about 9 per cent of the other CMEA countries.
5. Analyzing the motive forces creating an autarchic economy in the case of the CMEA countries the late Professor Imre Vajda stated:
   'The policy of autarchy has its roots also in the subjective over estimate of our own strength, and in the belittling of the advantages of the international division of labour, facilitating a faster growth. This false view was applied less in the theories but more in the practices of the socialist countries in the early fifties. These factors had been augmented by the fact that they were countries starting their industrialization at a lower stage of development and following the Soviet pattern and they did not orient themselves in their industrialization programme to the possibilities offered by the international division of labour among the countries concerned... The shortcomings of the international division of labour in itself did not result automatically in autarchy but because of the parallelism in the economic development, in many cases these factors threw difficulties in the way of the development of an international division of labour.'
   Source: Imre Vajda, *Socialist Foreign Trade*, Budapest, Corvina, 1964, p.16.
6. The proportion of the intra-CMEA trade in their total foreign trade was about 60 per cent at the mid-seventies. The annual volume of their mutual trade turnover increased by 1300 per cent between 1950–1975. These patterns of CMEA cooperation could be especially interesting for the developing countries, which could find expanding markets for their exports more easily with deliberate regional specialization agreements.
7. These 'Joint Intergovernmental Organizations' (JIGO) were established on the initiative of the CMEA Council. Their function is to promote coordination of activities and to establish direct cooperation in different fields, like branches of the economy, in product groups and sometimes in the output of individual products. The establishment and the scope of activities of JIGOs are determined by intergovernmental agreements. The national

governments could authorize the participation of ministries, state committees, trusts as well as other organisations including enterprises. The JIGOs are financed by the participating governments. The typical structure of a JIGO is a governing council, composed of the representatives from the member states on an equal basis which directs the work of a secretariat recruited from the participating countries. The staff is paid from the budget of the given JIGO.

8. See for example J.S. Shiraev, *Economic Mechanism of Socialist Integration (in Russian)*, Moscow, Economica, 1973.

9. The members of the CMEA are centrally planned economies. The method of plan implementation is not identical in every country, and the organizational forms of the internal economic structure may also differ. The central plan, especially the 5 year plan, plays however a decisive role in every country. It determines the main proportions of production and distribution of GNP. Any international specialization agreement in output must be incorporated in the plan and implemented by the measures approved in the plan. There is very little room for those measures, which are not in the plan. It is important, therefore, that the countries should coordinate their long term development strategies, especially in those fields which influence the output patterns and the allocation of investments.

10. At the 30th session of the Council, (Berlin, July 1976) it was decided for example to initiate five important 'Joint special programmes', by selecting the following industrial blocks for international cooperative actions:
    a) fuel and raw materials
    b) machinery and equipment
    c) basic food products
    d) industrial consumer goods
    e) transport.
    Special long term cooperation programmes are to be worked out in order to help the solution of the existing problems in the given fields with joint efforts, like joint investments, specialization of production, joint designing, increasing mutual deliveries, establishing joint firms etc.

11. In a socialist economy, the enterprises, owned by the state, are working n in a given system of a Ministry, responsible for an industrial branch or in the framework of a Trust or General Directorate, organized also according to branches or product groups. Their rights in the decision-making process may differ not only by countries but also according to their size, and the type of goods they produce. They may receive most of their tasks from 'above' in the forms of directives or they may develop their own plans, based on contracts and they are regulated only or mostly by indirect instruments of plan implementation. In either case, they have their own costs-benefits calculations and work as independent units. Their direct participation in international economic relations may also differ accordingly.

12. CMEA declared for example the full support of the Organization for the Declaration on the New International Economic Order and to the Programme for Action.

13. At the 30th Session of the Council, the representatives of the following countries took part as observers: Peoples Republic of Angola, Socialist Republic of Vietnam, the Peoples Democratic Republic of Korea, the Peoples Democratic Republic of Laos.

14. In 1975 CMEA had such arrangement with Finland, Iraq, Mexico.

CHAPTER SEVEN

ASSOCIATION

J.N. Kinnas

The Emergence of Association as an International System

Association is a relatively new institution on the international scene, at least in its present form. It concerns several types of arrangement which have led to the creation of new international systems as subsystems of world society. Association is a form of institutionalised relationship established between one or more states and an international institution.[1]

Association permits the symbiosis of a nation-state with an international institution in regard to certain activities but not others, within a new systemic framework. It is a form of relationship between states, which allows the integration of some dimensions, while, at the same time, keeping others separate.

There is, in fact, no general agreement on what constitute the major characteristics of association, because it is a flexible institution which covers various needs and demands according to space, time and the particularities of the individual system under consideration. Indeed, the different frames of reference of the application of association complicate the situation and the business of research. This is one of the factors that may lead us to incorrect conclusions, such as the one that the association systems actually constitute an expansion of already existing systems with the partial addition of new sub-units. In general, association systems are not a mere expansion of existing ones differently labelled after expansion. They are new subsystems within the overall framework of the international system which serve different purposes and which are also different institutionally.

Association is an outcome of the methods and techniques introduced in international relations mainly after the Second World War, while its origin can be observed well before that period. In order to trace the origins of association as an *international* institution, we have to go back to the late twenties when the disintegration of the imperial systems was gradually accelerating. Some maintain that the association institution was applied for the first time through the Treaty of Versailles.[2] It stated the forms and conditions under which the Dominions would participate in the League, but it was not until the Statute of Westminster that association was, for the first time, officially introduced by an international institution — the then British Commonwealth of Nations, later modified to 'The Commonwealth'. This was the first step towards the introduction of association on the international scene and it worked very well indeed, taking into consideration the circumstances, its *raison d'être*, the diversity of goals and the proliferation of Commonwealth membership after the Second World War.

After the War, the emergence of new international actors as well as of new demands for rules of contact between them, played a crucial role in the establishment of new cross-national flows and, consequently, new forms of systems. It is during this period that the application and proliferation of a modified version of association systems occurred. This system is characterised by the existence of two opposite forces in respect to the position of the associate-state within the system: one leads towards the transcending of the nation-state identity, as between members of the IGO and the associate for those matters covered by the association agreement, and the other leads towards the rebuilding, or at least the maintenance of the nation-state, because the association is specifically limited to certain dimensions. Thus the so-called dominant (usually the most powerful) actor of the association system, that is the IGO, usually seeks to transcend the nation-state, and the dependent actor, the associated state, tries to preserve it. It is difficult to trace whether these trends of transcending or preserving the nation-state are a consequence of the dominant-dependent relationship between the actors or whether they are due to other major factors as well.

Association systems currently exist between developed countries as in the case of nearly all of the European association systems, whether on a permanent or transitional basis.[3] On the other hand, there is a large number of the countries of the Third World which have very close ties with and dependence on the former metropoles and this is the reason that these countries, although outside Europe, have tried to maintain such close links with the countries of the old continent and particularly with a powerful institution like the EEC through association agreements.[4] Of course, some scholars[5] maintain that such a 'bridge' was established as a new form of exploitation and neocolonialism rather than as a cooperative effort on the part of the former imperial systems, and that it is aimed at exploiting the newly-independent countries of the Third World. It is difficult to assess whether in such international coalitions the assets or liabilities are greater for the Third World countries.[6] However, the Lomé Agreement was certainly an improvement on its predecessors.

Association provides a state with a way between isolation and adherence to an international institution as a full member. Paradoxically although an association system may involve many states it is essentially bilateral in character since there are usually only two parties — the IGO and the associate. Where the IGO has many association partners the relationship is still on an individual bilateral basis even though the negotiation may have been by a group of associates as in the Lomé agreement. At the same time association and its bilateral character allows the maintenance of political neutrality if desired. Economic incentives for integration have on occasion been checked by reluctance to accept the political effects which usually accompany economic integration, since all economic policies are finally based on political decisions. For example, Finland has treated her relationship with the EEC with considerable caution.

As already mentioned, it was through economic instiutions that association was introduced in the postwar era. The International Trade Organisation (ITO) became (through the Havana Charter) the first indirect formal sponsor of association after the Second World War.[7] The GATT (General Agreement on Tariffs and Trade), considered in general to be a substitute for the Charter, which was never implemented, did not,however, acquire the form and the powers planned for the ITO.[8] Even in the predominantly economic context of the GATT, political motives are often plainly apparent and underlie the definitions of a 'customs union' or a 'free trade area'.[9] Therefore, although association dealt with economic matters, it has a basis in political circumstances, whether in a negative way to avoid political repercussions, or in a positive way, to lead, through the 'functional imperative', to political achievements. It is significant that all the currently effective association agreements involving GATT members are based on paragraphs 8 and 10 of Article 24 of GATT so that GATT can be viewed as a major sponsor of association in the postwar era. It is on the basis of this Article that the European economic association systems operate, with the difference, however, that the association provided by GATT refers to future full members and not to associates of a permanent form, such as those of the Lomé Agreement. However, in certain association systems provision for future membership for the associates is explicitly made in the text of the relevant Agreements.[10]

Following the pioneering introduction of association by the Commonwealth, the postwar *de facto* association systems appear for the first time with the United Nations Economic Commission for Europe (ECE). The system of the Council of Europe-the Saar, which followed, remained the only one of the association systems introduced on a purely political basis in the postwar era. The OEEC association scheme with the United States and Canada was established on a *de facto* basis. The associate status of the two North American countries with the OEEC continued until the OEEC was succeeded by the OECD in 1961. Today, OECD confers a special status on Yugoslavia, which can be classified as an association system. This system also presents some similarities with the association system established in 1964 between CMEA and Yugoslavia. Both of these systems refer to the functional cooperation of each of the two organisations with Yugoslavia in certain economic and technical fields. The same refers also to the character of the association system between the ECE and Switzerland (and, later on, the two Germanies).

The European Communities have given rise to several association agreements within the European area. The first association of the then Community of the Six concerned the special relationship established between the United Kingdom and the ECSC. In the Paris Treaty establishing the European Coal and Steel Community (ECSC), no provision is made for association but in spite of that, an Association Agreement with Britain was signed. This association system ceased to operate after the full membership of the United Kingdom in all the three European Communities in 1973.

Under Article 238[11] of the Treaty establishing the European Economic Community, the Rome Treaty 'introduced' association status, which as far as European countries are concerned, was implemented for the first time in connection with Greece in 1961.[12] As part of the Rome Treaty, an association of the EEC with the ex-French and Belgian colonies was also established.[13] While the association of EEC-Greece was under negotiation, another European organisation, EFTA, introduced an association system within the

European area. It involved EFTA and Finland, and, although of a purely free trade character, it was shaped by political considerations.[14] Greece was followed in its association with the EEC by Turkey. In all of these arrangements the bilateral character of association systems was preserved. The greatest number of association systems involve Europe. Their importance varies according to the purpose of each system and its role. 'Small' association systems, such as those in which Finland or Yugoslavia are involved, are of vital importance as regards the possibility of a *rapprochement* between East and West Europe. In this connection other small association schemes, like that of OPEC with Gambia (which in 1975 became a full member of OPEC), can also be of some importance in providing an element of flexibility in institutional arrangements to satisfy felt needs.[15]

Some of the association systems have become defunct, some have been modified and others have been enlarged. The Council of Europe — the Saar system is already defunct, due to the incorporation of the Saar in the German Federal Republic after the 1955 Referendum. The ECSC-UK system has been transformed and expanded to full membership of the associate (U.K.). Finefta is modified in membership[16] and the Yaoundé association system was replaced by the modified, enlarged Lomé system (EEC-CAP). The above developments give evidence of the mediating role and dynamic character of association operating as an international system.

The different purposes the association institution serves and the flexible characteristics it possesses makes association, both in its role and achievements, unique among the various international subsystems of the world system. In spite of the flexibility and the unique nature of each association system, some models have been informally developed so that a rough classification can be made. Such a classification is attempted below.

Operational Characteristics of the Association Systems

Association systems involving an IGO and an associate can be classified as follows: permanent collaborative, transitional, regional, non-regional, functional. The main characteristic which differentiates the permanent collaborative systems from the transitional association systems is the fact that in the former the actors concerned intimate their desire not to integrate fully, as for example, in Finefta on the part of Finland and in the EEC-Greece association system on the part of the EEC during the period 1967–1974. In transitional systems the intention is to establish an interim arrangement between the interested parties leading in the long run to full membership (EEC-Turkey). The non-regional systems, contrary to regional association systems, are hardly ever of a transitional character. They include, predominantly, actors with 'complementary' interests but which remain disparate in many ways, for example, in the EEC-Lomé association system. The countries of the Third World are therefore most frequently members in non-regional association systems. As regards regional association systems Europe is the area most involved. The functional relations developed through the establishment and operation of the association systems may become stronger with time but for those systems which are not expressly transitional they usually fall short of providing the prerequisites for full membership since this requires an act of political will. The functional imperative may give rise to a propitious climate for full membership but this is rarely 'automatic'. The development of functional relations, however, usually plays a crucial role in the establishment and operation of association systems but even in this instance political considerations also play a decisive role in the adoption of association, particularly by neutral or non-aligned countries such as Switzerland or Yugoslavia.

The area covered by associates or special relationship partners (regional association systems) in Europe encompasses, geographically-speaking, a long corridor beginning with Finland in the North and extending to Greece in the South. These countries can be strictly neutral (Austria, Switzerland) or non-aligned (Finland, Yugoslavia) or with links either with the West (Greece) or with both the East and West (GDR through inter-German trade). Therefore, it can be maintained that a kind of association 'corridor' is gradually being formed which impinges upon several parts of Europe through functional ties.[17]

In this connection the role of Finland and Yugoslavia, which maintain close economic links with both Eastern and Western European institutions must be emphasised. For Yugoslavia CMEA appeared to be preferable to isolation while for Finland no alternative other than association with EFTA was feasible because of the proximity of one of the super Powers. On the other hand, Greece plays a decisive bridging role through her improved relations with the Balkan countries, a role comparable to that of Denmark in respect to EFTA. The GDR with her special economic links with the EEC through the Federal Republic also constitutes a more or less informal associate and a key piece in the East-West European jigsaw. The EEC rules do not apply to inter-German trade so that exports from the GDR reach the Federal Republic free of duties and levies.[18] In spite of the official diplomatic relations, which followed the mutual recognition of two Germanies, each belonging to different political systems, the trade of the Federal Republic with the GDR is neither included in the former's foreign trade nor in the domestic trade. It is classified under a special category — 'inter-German-trade'.[19] Such trade contributes to the intensification of links between the two Germanies. In general, East-West relations have been intensified with the substantial assistance of the ECE[20] and form part of the association corridor running from North to South. To a certain degree this provides an example of the operation of the functional imperative tempered as it is by political factors.

There is a high degree of mobility in capital and labour between the actors of most of the association systems. However, this does not increase substantially the overall links of the associated states between themselves and does not apply to the relations between the associates of the EEC in Africa.[21] The strictly bilateral character of the association does not encourage direct links. On the other hand, functional links between the IGO and the associate usually have some political consequences for the latter.[22]

It has been maintained that the setting up of an association framework may encourage creative policies towards non-member countries, as happened with the Lomé Convention. Association systems involving European countries and developing countries of the Third World — whatever their defects, particularly as regards the potential exploitation of the developing countries by the developed Western European countries — encourage a more positive approach towards co-operation. Their long survival and enlarged membership is some evidence of this. The main features of the evolving relationship between the countries of the EEC and developing countries outside Europe are, the association system which linked some African states (mainly ex-French colonies) with the EEC at its foundation, the Arusha Agreement[23], and, recently, the EEC-CAP Agreement (Lomé) which actually merged the above systems and expanded their membership bringing the number of the associated countries to forty-six.[24] It is likely that such association systems consolidated the institution and secured its further application on the international scene.

Association systems do not necessarily strengthen regionalism although they may do so. However, the *raison d'être* of association systems is to avoid supranationalism. 'Regional' and 'supranational' are terms which are used nowadays in a rather different way from when they were introduced into international politics. While a number of association systems have been developed on a regional basis, regionalism in general is not a predominant characteristic of or a prerequisite for the establishment and operation of association systems.

In both functionalism and association the primary focus is the network of transactions between the actors involved in a system where boundaries are more or less functionally determined. Functionalism refers to certain activities and not to the whole spectrum of the exchange between two or more actors. A crucial problem arises when the functional links do not seem compatible with political links (for example in the EEC-Greece system during the period 1967–1974). The association system may then stagnate since any further spillover from the functional level to the political level is ruled out, perhaps only temporarily, because of political factors. In such cases it is the IGO and not, as is more usually the case, the individual actor which is seeking to preserve its autonomy and values.

Association systems are established in order to avoid a close relationship of the federal type, although the IGO concerned might itself be a federation. Indeed, the actors of an IGO may strive for a federation with the associate. However, functional association is usually introduced by actors who wish to have full commitments only in some particular dimension(s) while not being fully involved in an institution, federal or otherwise. For example, the I.T.U. has officially introduced association status for any potential member.[25] The same applies to OPEC.

Association is shown to be linked both with the theory and practice of integration and, when compared, most association systems present remarkable common denominators, notwithstanding their unique characteristics. These can be classified into a) background conditions, that is the situation of the partners of an association system before its establishment, and b) process mechanisms, that is those forces (the presence of which follows from a new system) through which pressure is exerted on the decision-makers to produce integrative or disintegrative responses.[26]

Background conditions are usually characteristics such as geographical contiguity and cultural homogeneity. Although after 'take-off' the cohesion between the associated actors is further reinforced, whether they are geographically contiguous or not, the functional imperative is felt most in cases of geographical contiguity (e.g. Finland with the members of EFTA, Yugoslavia with the members of CMEA), because contacts and exchanges are easier than with distant countries. However, the functional imperative can be in evidence between countries at

162

opposite ends of the globe as in the relationship between Britain and New Zealand or in OPEC which extends to three continents.

Geographical criteria are only important to the extent that they promote transactions. Such transactions are the basis of the functional imperative so that the links formed by the establishment and reinforcement of such transactions can guarantee the survival of the system on a functional level whatever the eventual difficulties or strains at the official level of the relations of the actors of the association system. The diversion of the transactions can lead to the disappearance of the association system, but up until now only cases of upgrading the status of the associate state have been observed. The functional imperative may have contributed to the attainment of full membership for the actor concerned and the demise of the association system.

The possible dependence (financial or otherwise) existing in the past between the actors of an association system can lead after the establishment of the association system to an informal dominant-dependent relationship. Such a relationship is found mostly in the association systems of the developed with the developing countries. It has been argued that the imperial systems presented a dominant-dependent relationship among and between their actors. This view has been transformed into what today is called 'neocolonialism' between the 'metropoles' and 'peripheries'. This situation arises in part from the fact that the societies of the Third World continue, in spite of their national independence, to be subject to a deep-rooted structural dependency of a different magnitude from the dependency in raw materials of the industrialised countries on the Third World. However, economic factors constitute only a part of structural dependency although association systems can in some cases overcome it (as in the relations between the GDR and the Federal Republic). Nevertheless, in other cases structural dependence is supplemented by institutional dependence which includes the operation of the association systems concerned. Any new independent state may have the external formal characteristics of independence but the essential dominant-dependent relationship of the pre-association situation remains.

The decision-making process, if it locks a variety of actors, official and unofficial, into a propitious situation can further the momentum of an international system towards either partial or full integration and secure the survival of the system. This is particularly the case if it creates a climate in which an act of political will to enhance still further the degree of integration appears to be both necessary and in order.

163

Other major process mechanisms can be summarised as follows:

1. Rising transactions, that is the expansion of already-existing or the development of new dimensions of transactions after 'take-off'.

2. The involvement of powerful external actors, not only those interested in the formation and course of the association systems.

3. The special institutions or mechanisms introduced by the systems concerned.

4. Finally, elite socialisation plays an important part in strengthening the links between the actors of the systems after 'take-off'. This last common denominator is usually found among the association systems which involve actors both from the developed and the developing world.

These common denominators are not always readily apparent but this does not diminish their importance and their impact on the operation and effectiveness of the association systems. The differences existing among association systems are usually connected with the degree to which a particular common denominator is operative rather than to its overall presence or absence. The difference existing between and among the various association systems are due to the dynamic nature of every international system. Diversity is a great incentive for improvement, though conflict usually accompanies such a diversity. The dynamic nature of international systems is preserved in the association systems, indeed, the flexibility of association as an international institution leads to a remarkable diversity of the aims and policies of the association systems and explains the growing role it is playing in contemporary international relations.

Implications of Association for Modern World Society

Association is predominantly an open, decentralised and collaborative system. It is open because it provides access to new associate members. It is decentralised because control is exercised from a variety of points, and, it is collaborative, because collaboration is its predominant goal as well as its usual method of operation. It also sometimes serves as a brake on further integration (Finefta).

Indeed, a restricted kind of partnership is the very goal that has led the two parties concerned to engage in an association system. The main purpose of association systems is to promote the mutual interests of the associated parties and to create favourable circumstances for the successful development of common interests shared between the actors concerned, if full membership is excluded. Association, as a formal agreement, is usually based on an existing or hoped for system

164

of transactions in one or several dimensions, whether of a largely instrumental or attitudinal character. It is a flexible institution which refers to several types of arrangement for a close relationship, either between a state or states and an IGO (whenever the former does not intend to become a full member of the latter) or between a group of states, temporarily or for an indefinite period of time.

Association also serves as an institutional bridge between two major international subsystems: the traditional East-West system, which seems to dominate relations within the European continent, and the North-South system which is concerned with the mitigation of conflict situations between the developing countries (the so-called Third World) and the industrialised countries (the North). The latter system has become of considerable importance recently and association provides one crucial institutional bridge which keeps the parties concerned within the same framework whilst minimising conflict. Nevertheless, it is useful to bear in mind that the development model of the dominant actors (implemented or planned for the dependent actors of the association systems) is not usually ideal for the needs and aspirations of the developing countries which may have a wholly different view of development.[27] However, such different views cannot always be reconciled not only because of the already existing structural links between the dominant and dependent actors of the association systems (in the case of ex-metropoles with ex-colonies) but also because of strong ethnocentric tendencies.

In assessing the prospects of association systems, clearly those of the European Communities are being affected by the enlargement of the Community. The enlargement of the EEC in 1973 affected the membership of Finefta by reducing the number of the members of the dominant actor (EFTA) of the Finefta system and created a number of new associates (the EFTA members). It also affected the existence of the ECSC-United Kingdom system, as well as the association system with the countries of the Third World. The previously operating association systems of the EEC had also to adjust themselves to the new membership of the EEC by applying the association agreements to the new members.

The present situation in world society, wavering between old and new models of the International System, has a direct impact on developments in Europe and the association systems will probably affect overall efforts for establishing a durable peace. It is not association itself which will secure peace, but it is a catalyst which contributes towards that end. However, if association does not achieve all its objectives this does not mean that it is not useful. Association seems to provide one suitable vehicle for resolving the problems arising out of the relationship between the developed and the developing world which seem to dominate current international politics. The larger the scale of implementation of association, the greater the possibility for a more complete and fruitful consideration of world problems.

Notes

1. Parts of the present text are based on the Ph.D. dissertation of the author, *The Politics of Association of European States with European Organisations; a Comparative Approach*, University of London, 1973.
2. L. Ananiadès, *L'Association aux Communautés Européennes*, Paris, Librairie Generale de Droit et de Jurisprudence, 1967, p. 13.
3. It can be maintained that the associated actors of the systems comprising EEC and Cyprus, Greece, Malta and Turkey, respectively, are at an economic level lower than the average of the Nine. However, the criteria for participation for the above countries are not only economic, given the fact that their European identity, the overall similarity of values and even public enthusiasm for a United Europe played an equally important role in their establishment.
4. Currently the Lomé Agreement, known also as the EEC-CAP Agreement (CAP standing for Caribbean, Africa and the Pacific) and the association agreements established between the EEC and countries of the Maghreb, on an individual basis and not collectively. Although each state is associated with the EEC individually on a bilateral basis this is done through a collective agreement signed by all parties concerned.
5. For example see Tibor Mende: *De l'Aide à la Recolonisation: les leçons d'un échec*, Paris, Seuil, 1972.
6. I. William Zartman: 'Europe and Africa: Decolonization or Dependency?' *Foreign Affairs*, Vol. 54:2, January 1976, p. 325 et seq..
7. *Final Act and the Havana Charter for an International Trade Organisation with Related Documents*, London, HMSO, Cmd 7375, 1948, Article 44, paras. 1, 2, 4.
8. GATT is viewed in some quarters as a 'spokesman' of the rich countries while UNCTAD, established later, seems to represent, more or less, the Third World views. GATT played a substantial role in postwar international trade relations.
9. The difference between a customs union and a free trade area is that the common external tariff of the former does not apply in the latter. See Article 24, para. 8.
10. For example in the EEC-Greece Association Agreement, signed in Athens in 1961, provision is made for the negotiation of the 'extension' of association status to full membership (Article 72). Disregarding that provision, the recent Greek application for full membership was submitted to the EEC under Article 237 of the Rome Treaty, which applies to European States whether having a transitional link with the Community or not. Article 237 was used in the case of the application of Britain, Denmark and Ireland to become full members of the EEC. The Greek application probably provides a precedent, given the fact that it is the first European associate to apply for full EEC membership.

11. Article 238 reads: 'The Community may conclude with a third State, a union of States or an international organisation, agreements establishing an association involving reciprocal rights and obligations, common actions and special procedures'.

12. The appropriate article in the treaty establishing Euratom is Article 208.

13. Annex III to the Rome Treaty, Implementing Convention relating to the Association with the Community of the Overseas Countries and Territories. This association was named Yaoundé I. Yaoundé II followed after negotiations between the then six and the 18 African ex-colonies at Yaoundé. As we have seen the Lomé Agreement have superseded and changed the character of these relationships.

14. Finland is always cautious not to offend her big neighbour, the Soviet Union, while maintaining closer links with Western Europe and Scandinavia in particular. Cf. M. Jacobson: *A Study of Finnish Foreign Policy since the Second World War*, London, Evelyn, 1968.

15. Under article 7 of *The Statute of the Organization of the Petroleum Exporting Countries*, Vienna, November 1971.

16. Present membership includes: Austria, Finland (associated), Iceland, Norway, Portugal, Sweden, Switzerland (and Lichtenstein). As from January 1973, the United Kingdom and Denmark ceased to be members of EFTA, since they joined the EEC as full members. However, special agreements were signed so that the financial links will continue on the same, or about the same, level as before. These agreements were signed between the EEC and the members of EFTA again on a separate bilateral basis.

17. A.J.R. Groom, 'The Functionalist Approach and East-West Cooperation in Europe', *Journal of Common Market Studies*, Vol. 13:1–2, 1975, p. 57 and J. Kinnas, *op cit.*.

18. Ulrike Stahl, 'Economic Relations between the Federal Republic of Germany and the Comecon Countries', *Euro-cooperation; Economic Studies on Europe*, Nos. 14–15, 1976, p. 67.

19. Ulrike Stahl, *op cit.*, p. 66.

20. J. Siotis, 'The Secretariat of the United Nations Commission for Europe: The First Ten Years', *International Organization*, Vol. 19:2, 1965, p. 198 and *Work of the Economic Commission for Europe*, 1947–1972, New York, United Nations, 1972.

21. For example, recently about 380 out of the 832 intra-African telephone channels were operating through Europe. Cf. *Pre-Investment News*, July–August 1970, UNDP. New York, p. 4. The situation has improved since then, but not substantially.

22. For example, after links were established between Yugoslavia and the OECD and the EEC some indirect political influence on Yugoslavia has been exercised through such economic relations.

23. Signed at Arusha on 26th July 1968 (Kenya-Tanzania-Uganda and the EEC). It did not provide clauses for financial and technical cooperation.

24. The Convention was signed by the Nine members of the EEC, 37 African and 9 Caribbean and Pacific states. It was signed at Lomé on the 28th February 1975. On the Lomé Convention, cf. Charles Vallée, 'Regards sur la Convention de Lomé', *Revue Iranienne des Relations Internationales*, No. 4, Automne 1975.

25. Article 1 of the *Convention establishing the International Telecommunication Union* (Montreux, 1965), ITU, Geneva. There, association status is provided for non-members or non-sovereign areas.

26. See J.S. Nye, 'Comparing Common Markets: A Revised Neo-Functionalist Model', in *International Organization*, Vol. 24:4, op. cit., p. 803.

167

27. K.J. Holsti, 'Underdevelopment and the 'Gap' Theory of International Conflict', *American Political Science Review*, September 1975, No. 3 and J. Galtung, 'The Technology that can alienate', *Development Forum*, Vol. 4:6, July–August 1976.

Selected Reading

1. W. Feld, 'The Association Agreements of the European Communities; A Comparative Analysis', *International Organisation*, 1967.
2. S. Henig, *External Relations of the European Community: Associations and Trade Agreements*, Chatham House, PEP, London, 1971.
3. J. Kinnas, *The Politics of Association of European States with European Organisations; A Comparative Approach*, Ph.D. dissertation, University of London, 1974.
4. I.W. Zartman, 'Europe and Africa: Decolonization or Dependency?', *Foreign Affairs*, Vol. 54:2, January 1976.

CHAPTER EIGHT

HARMONISATION

R.J. Harrison & Stuart Mungall

Scope of the Activity

A contemporary phenomenon of international behaviour, evident at various levels, is the attempt to ensure that the separate policies of a number of states are in concordant alignment with each other. The label harmonisation readily suggests the nature of this activity. In musical use it connotes the contemporaneous pursuit of separate themes within a conventional framework, avoiding discord. International 'harmonisation', in this metaphor requires a 'score' of common information, common interpretation, and agreement on relevant values in pursuing separate policies. In practice, the attempt to compose this commonality and agreement usually involves some kind of international organisation but, essentially in our conception, the functional activities themselves remain the responsibility of the separate states.

The term is further 'refined' in the present work, beyond popular usage, to distinguish this level of activity from 'cooperation', a term reserved here for the piecemeal working out of specific agreements to adjust a nationally conducted policy for a specific purpose.[1] There is no attempt to define an overall framework of policy guidelines. Cooperation is therefore more limited in scope than harmonisation. We distinguish also 'coordination' which denotes policy adjustment by international prescription, laying down a specific policy obligation for states rather than a principle to which their individually shaped policies must conform.[2] In our stripulation then, harmonisation is wider in potential scope than 'cooperation' and less specific in its policy implications than

169

'coordination'. Characteristically it results in Conventions expressing principles in a number of fields, under the aegis of one international organisation.

Relevant Assumptive Framework

Such harmonisation stands in no explicit, or obviously implicit, relationship to any coherent philosophy of, or approach to, international politics. The closest thing to a coincidental rationalisation of it, perhaps, may be found in Benthamite utilitarianism. While Bentham is emphatic that there is no natural harmony of interest between individuals so that 'on every occasion, the happiness of every individual is liable to come into competition with the happiness of every other',[3] he takes a different view of the interests of states or nations. 'Between the interests of nations, there is nowhere any real conflict: if they appear repugnant anywhere, it is only in proportion as they are misunderstood.'[4] This assertion (heavily qualified in the development of Bentham's argument) depends on two basic assumptions: the first is that a state or nation is an artificial construct, not to be considered as a person. It has its property, its honour, its condition, but other things being equal it may be attacked 'in all these particulars without the individuals who compose it being affected'.[5] Private ownership and public sovereignty are all too easily confused.[6] Bentham's second assumption is that there is a natural economic harmony of interests which makes attempts to secure trading preferences and overseas territories pointless and wasteful. Blood and treasure must be expended on securing and maintaining them. And any attempt to encourage a particular trade, or direction of trade, necessarily and *pro tanto* discourages some other, which might have been more profitable[7] — a classical free trade argument.

Bentham recognises that these two abstracted deducible realities are very much obscured in international behaviour by prejudice and confusion — a social artifice of habit and convention which results in unnecessary and damaging wars between states who genuinely believe they are defending the 'right'.[8] There are, of course, wars *mala fides*, undertaken for the perfectly rational objective of despoiling another state. The wars of antiquity are examples. So too, Bentham suggests were the wars of the New Zealanders (Maoris) — for while the conquered fry, the conquerors fatten.[9] And it may be quite proper, on calculation, to resist such predatory aggressors and form alliances against them in war. But for the nations of today, who act for the most part, Bentham thought, *bona fides*, a different course recommends itself.

For the individual state, the object of its behaviour should be the general utility, avoiding injury to, and promoting the good of, other nations, saving the regard proper to its own well being. For all such states, the mutual objective would be to work out a code of written and unwritten agreements in matters where the interests of states are capable of collision; to reduce the possible area of dispute by instituting general liberty of commerce, and to reach previous agreement on such matters as boundaries, new discoveries and the rules which should apply. In sum, the individual states would follow the line of least resistance in the pursuit of their own interests,[10] but would cooperate in the elaboration of a code which would reduce the possibilities of encountering resistance in areas of interdependence. Bentham suggested that a common international court of judicature, without coercive powers, might well play a useful role in interpreting such rules and agreements.[11]

Unlike the functionalist, David Mitrany, Bentham did not contemplate the possibility that internationally performed functional services would reduce the role of national governments and make them 'meaningless'. He shared the functionalist view of the illusory and artificial nature of the nation state system and its arbitrary and often detrimental relationship to man's welfare interests, but he was too much of a realist to suppose that the system could be fundamentally changed by direction.

Operational Experience

Contemporary harmonisation conforms with the Benthamite model in that it depends operationally on the possibility that states will at least act in good faith to achieve what are presumed to be generally compatible though not identical interests. Harmonisation suggests itself where discussion between national policy makers may discover an existing value consensus which can be the ground for a wide range of agreements.

Still in line with Bentham's model, the prescriptive implications produce only a limited structural impact on international society. The relevant international institutions may be equated with so called 'forum' organisations as distinct from the more highly developed 'service' organisation.[12] That is to say that their role is limited to facilitating the development of a common framework of principles according to which member states will regulate their own activities. The discussions and agreement serve to legitimise national activities both domestically and internationally, characteristically, by the formulation of open

171

conventions like the International Labour Conventions and the Convention on Human Rights of the Council of Europe. A secretariat may exist for the collection, analysis and dissemination of information relevant to discussion by governments.

The International Labour Organisation (I.L.O.)

In its early years, after its foundation in 1919, the I.L.O., for example, was primarily concerned with framing international labour standards. It brought together, in a tripartite Labour Conference, representatives of governments, employers and workers. All three sections met separately to prepare their positions for plenary sessions. This was a design which exploited the distinction between the citizen and the government of the sovereign state; it might very well have been approved by Bentham. It exploited, too, the potential commonality of interest of like sections of different national communities. This commonality was, to a considerable degree, realised in practice by the two non-governmental groups in expanding the role of the Organisation. The International Federation of Trade Unions (Amsterdam International) which coordinates union action in the I.L.O., provided very considerable support for the first Director, Albert Thomas, a French Socialist, enabling him to take initiatives both in the negotiation of Labour standards and in proposals for social policy. This was archetypically 'harmonisation' — creating standards implemented as policy by the individual states in their own ways.[13]

After 1948, however, the organisation changed its character moving into active services such as technical assistance and cooperation, and the balance of its funding shifted from the contributions of the member states to a major funding from United Nations Development Programme sources.[14] The Soviet Union, which had been hostile to the interwar organisation, joined it in 1954, whereupon ideological controversy began to wrack the proceedings. The change suggests that there may be inherent in highly successful harmonisation a transformation potential: the organisation will be tempted to expand into service activities or into specific policy prescription for member governments with quite different and much more significant political implications. It will move into policy areas where there is little or no reason to expect an easily defined value consensus let alone a consensus on the policies by means of which the values are to be achieved. Within the I.L.O. this transformation potential was inherent in the tripartite organisation. On the one hand the non-governmental organisations (N.G.O.s) were relatively easily able to agree on values and frameworks, fulfilling the harmonisation objective. On the other, they provided the political base of support from which the organisation in the person of its Director was able to launch initiatives for the more ambitious service activities which followed the appointment of David A. Morse of the U.S.A. in 1948. One analysis of budget information indicates that from 1950–1967 the ratio of forum to service activity in the I.L.O. changed from 80:20 to 16:84.[15]

It is not clear that this development has in any way contributed to a change in the political environment, but it has meant that the organisation itself, because it has become more significant politically, may be adversely affected by ideological and diplomatic differences. Preoccupation with Cold War quarrels, for example, has conflicted with the demands of Third World members that there should be, first of all, attention to their problems. All three parties, USA, USSR and Third World, seem to have become more uncertain about their allegiance to the organisation so that there has been a reduction of its effectiveness at least in its role of legitimising national activities both internationally and domestically. In June 1970, the US Congress actually suspended its contribution to the I.L.O. budget because of the appointment of a Soviet citizen as Assistant Director-General.

The Council of Europe

The Council of Europe is another obvious agency of harmonisation. It is a 'forum' rather than a service organisation. However, in the intention of some of its creators, it was to be an agency of integration which would produce a United States of Europe rather than merely a device to maintain harmony between separate member states. This federalist pressure, evident in post-war Europe, was expressed in the demand made at the Hague Congress in 1948 that 'the nations of Europe must create an economic and political union . . . and for this purpose, must agree to merge certain of their sovereign rights'. Something of this appeal may be detected in Article 1 of the Statute of the Council of Europe.

'The aim of the Council of Europe is to achieve a greater unity between its members for the purpose of safeguarding and realising the ideals and principles which are their common heritage and facilitating their economic and social progress.'

However, as Robertson points out,[16] the phrase 'greater unity' is an eschewal, not an avowal, of the supranationalist goal sought by the federalists. Its use indicates the triumph of the intergovernmentalist forces which sought to rebuild Europe by reinforcing the nation state.

These competing conceptions of the road ahead for Europe, the federalist method and the intergovernmentalist method, were institutionalised in the two organs of the Council: the Consultative Assembly of Parliamentarians – a sop to federalist aspirations – and the Committee of Ministers composed of the representatives of the government of each nation-state – the intergovernmental organs. Given the allocation of decision-making power, intergovernmentalism proved ascendant. Only the Committee of Ministers had powers of decision-making. Except in questions arising out of the findings of the Commission of Human Rights (discussed later) their decisions had to be unanimous. Only consultative and recommendatory functions were given to the Assembly.

For the first two years of its existence the Assembly attempted to act as if it were the legislature of a supranational authority. However, it lacked effective support amongst the peoples and interests of Western Europe. It, therefore, resorted to a less ambitious goal – that of providing some of the conditions upon which a union might in future be built. This involved the mundane task of identifying and giving expression to common interests and values, and, through recommend-ations and resolutions, urging the Committee of Ministers to establish Conventions and Agreements in an effort to harmonise elements of national policies.

The catharsis of two disastrous wars between the nations of Europe in the twentieth century had created a general consensus that relations between nations had to be improved. Clearly this was one factor which assisted the limited objectives of the Council of Europe. Two related factors reinforced this favourable climate of opinion. The Cold War and the domination of the American and Russian superpowers pressed Western Europe to give voice to her identity. With an eye to the reputedly totalitarian regime in the U.S.S.R., the Preamble to the Statute of the Council of Europe expressed the devotion of its states 'to the spiritual and moral values which are the common heritage of their peoples and the true source of individual freedom, political liberty and the rule of law, principles which form the basis of all genuine democracy'. Common values and the need to establish a separate identity assisted the harmonising efforts of the Council.

The list of conventions and agreements that are the outcome of these pressures is large, wide in scope and somewhat recondite. By 1974, some twenty-five years after the setting up of the Council, the list had

174

eighty-four items.

The first Convention is the best known and the most significant politically. This is the European Convention of Human Rights and Fundamental Freedoms, concluded on November 4, 1950. The Convention set up two institutions, the Commission and the Court of Human Rights, to examine and adjudicate on grievances brought before it. The Convention obliged the contracting parties to secure, for all persons under their jurisdiction, the rights and freedoms stipulated therein. It also bound them to accept the decisions of its institutions. The Convention was not finally ratified by all the members of the Council until France and Switzerland attached their signatures to it in 1974.

Although initially the Convention was seen as a block to totalitarianism it has also come to be seen as a standard from which the constitutional principles of Western European democratic states can be measured. These principles are set out in the Statute in Article 3 of Chapter II which deals with membership. 'Members must accept the principle of the rule of law and of the enjoyment by all persons within their jurisdiction of human rights and fundamental freedoms.' The failure of Greece, between 1967 and 1973, to live up to the standards thus set forth indicated that she was out of harmony with the stipulated common values of other members of the Council. It was on the basis of fundamental criticisms of the Greek regime in this period by the Human Rights Commission, that the E.E.C. suspended economic relations with that country. Greece was obliged to resign from the Council of Europe in 1969. A similar disharmony between the values embraced by the Council and those of Spain and Portugal (until recently) has prevented their membership of the organisation. The stipulated values have provided a useful lever on their governments for the parliamentarians in the Consultative Assembly to urge caution in giving support to Spain during the Franco regime and to urge support for democratic elements in Portugal following the overthrow of the Caetano dictatorship.

Apart from human rights, the conventions and agreements cover a large variety of subjects; social (e.g. European Agreement on 'au pair' placement (1969)); cultural (e.g. European Cultural Convention (1954); patents (e.g. European Convention on the Formalities required for Patent Application (1953)); broadcasting and television (e.g. European Agreement for the Protection of Television Broadcasts transmitted from stations outside National Territories (1965)); legal (e.g. European Convention on the International Validity of Criminal Judgements

(1970)); public health (e.g. European Agreement on the Exchange of Blood-grouping Reagents (1962)); international travel (e.g. European Agreement on Travel by Young Persons on Collective Passports between the Member Countries of the Council of Europe (1961)); environment (e.g. European Agreement on the restriction of the use of certain detergents in washing and cleaning products (1968)).

While the setting of standards and principles is the most characteristic method of harmonisation, it is by no means the only method. Of considerable importance are activities designed to socialise significant national actors towards common international objectives, and to encourage the development of an international identity from which policy alignments may follow. The Council of Europe has encouraged such activities by sponsoring specialised conferences. At the instigation of the Assembly, and with the eventual support of the Committee of Ministers, a European Conference of Local and Regional Authorities has been sponsored. Further example include the European Parliamentary and Scientific Conference, the Conference of Ministers of Education and the Conference of European Ministers of Justice. In an attempt to increase public awareness of the activity of the Council of Europe in 1975, it sponsored European Architectural Heritage Year.

Although the Council of Europe and the institutions of the E.E.C. are coextensive neither in interests nor in memberships there is a considerable overlap. Particularly following the increase in the membership of the E.E.C. in 1972 to include Britain, Ireland and Denmark, the Council has been overshadowed. The development of the European Council of Heads of States and Governments has produced far broader perspectives than that adopted by the central institutions of the E.E.C. and this has further undermined the position of the Council of Europe. It was the European Council which, for example, decided to offer funds to Portugal to aid her democratic development. The persistence of the Council of Europe is due more to the desire to give a continuing voice to non-E.E.C. members in a European organisation. However, the Assembly of the Council offers a place for the ventilation of the views of other international organisations which lack a parliamentary body, for example, the O.E.C.D., whose Secretary-General gives an annual report to the Assembly.

The O.E.C.D.[17]

Although the O.E.C.D. came into being only on the 30 September 1961 its historical roots can be traced to the formation of the Organisation for European Economic Cooperation (O.E.E.C.) in 1948. We need briefly to consider the evolution of this latter organisation in order to set the context out of which the former grew.

Post-war economic reconstruction in Western Europe was, to a large extent, financed by the American Marshall Aid Plan. One of the conditions attached to the disbursement of this American largesse amongst the recipient countries was that they should work together. The United States refused to take the responsibility themselves for allocating the aid and instead promoted an international agency, composed of the recipient countries. This led to the formation of the O.E.E.C. Its functions were not limited to determining the allocations of aid resources amongst applicant countries. It sought also to harmonise the specific national recovery programmes and to achieve trade liberalisation and the restoration of full currency convertibility.

The procedures and devices developed to supervise and administer reconstruction are important, as some at least have been retained by the O.E.C.D. In an effort to coordinate the recovery programmes each national strategy was subject to periodic review. Furthermore, national officials underwent mutual cross-examination, under the auspices of the organisation's own officials, in an effort to ensure a wider awareness of the specific national responses to particular problems and also with the hope that a sensitivity to the international ramifications of national actions would develop. Despite these procedures it cannot be said that coordination was achieved. Individual countries pursued their own recovery programmes without much attention to the assumptions underlying other programmes. Attempts to draw attention to incompatibilities did not normally have much effect. This reluctance to use Marshall Aid as a weapon of even partial 'integration' is explained by the prior need to create a strong bulwark to communism in Western Europe — economically strong if not economically unified. Discussion over a proposed coordinated programme could have impeded this goal and only limited time was thought to be available.

As far as trade liberalisation and the restoration of full currency convertibility is concerned, the O.E.E.C. was able directly to affect national policies. Access to credits from the European Payments Union for the financing of trade deficits was dependent upon adherence to the rules of behaviour and the goals outlined in the Code of Trade Liberalisation. This asset tended to reinforce rather than counteract national predilections. The relation between trade and economic growth was generally conceded: the problem of achieving trade liberalisation was more a matter of timing than of conversion to the desirability of the goal.

177

The lack of substantial independent financial assets distinguishes the O.E.C.D. from the O.E.E.C. Although the Financial Support Fund of the O.E.C.D. and the creation of the International Energy Agency (both to be dealt with later) in the recent past, suggest the situation may be changing, the question of why the O.E.C.D. has historically been deprived of assets that might have allowed a coordinating rather than a harmonising role directs us to the politics surrounding its formation and continuation.

As reconstruction gave way to economic growth, the interests of the O.E.E.C. shifted towards productivity, manpower and education and into the field of nuclear energy. Nonetheless with the restoration of currency convertibility and the achievement of a substantial level of trade liberalisation, the utility of the O.E.E.C. began to decline. However, the split between member countries into the E.E.C. and E.F.T.A. threatened serious disharmony and indicated a continuing need for a forum which included both groups of states.[18]

Coinciding with these developments was a shift in the balance of economic power from the United States to Western Europe. The United States' balance of payments setbacks in this period and the further threat to its position posed by the protectionism of the E.E.C. drove it to seek an expanded forum for the discussion of the economic issues facing industrialised capitalist states. Furthermore, the United States wanted to shift some of the burden of giving aid to the increasingly vociferous developing states to the shoulders of the Western Europeans. It sought to impose this new orientation on the successor to the O.E.E.C.

Amongst major members of the O.E.E.C., France seems to have been the only one to favour the termination of the organisation once its functions had been achieved. However, she was ready to acquiesce in the desire of the E.F.T.A. neutrals to have some say in an international forum and to support a common aid programme within an expanded organisation. Britain supported the continuation as a check on E.E.C. supranationality and protectionism while West Germany saw the proposed new organisation as a means of retaining access to markets outside the E.E.C.

The outcome of this reappraisal was the signature of the Convention on the O.E.C.D. on December 14 1960. In the same year, a Development Assistance Group was set up reflecting the new interest in the Third World. When the O.E.C.D. formally came into being in 1961, it absorbed the D.A.G. as one of its major committees, though not all members of the O.E.C.D. are members of the Development Assistance

Committee (D.A.C.).[19] The outward-looking purpose of many members was thus given organisational form.

The European basis of memerbship which had applied to the O.E.E.C. was altered by the entry of the U.S.A. and Canada into the new organisation. Japan became a member in 1964, Finland in 1969, Australia in 1971 and New Zealand in 1973. The global spread of the membership signified a further shift in perspective. There are now twenty-four members and one associate member, Yugoslavia.

With the exception of Yugoslavia, the member states embrace a common belief in the market economy, the rights of private capital and the efficacy of private enterprise. Although not all members are advanced industrial capitalist economies the O.E.C.D. countries are enormously important in the world economy. Sixty per cent of world industrial production; seventy-three per cent of world trade and eighty per cent of development aid emanate from them, although they have only twenty per cent of the world's population. It is the place of its members, as a whole, in the world economy and their consequent interdependence which, as much as their common economic values, make the O.E.C.D. potentially a very significant organisation.

Common economic values (one must stress economic values because the organisation includes members whose governments have reflected antidemocratic values: for example Spain, Portugal and Greece) and common economic interests have provided the background for a harmonising organisation. The stated aims of the organisation, as outlined in Article 1 of the Convention, are of a generality that one might expect when the purpose is to aid nations to achieve their own goals rather than impose international goals upon them. The aims of the O.E.C.D. are:

a) to achieve the highest sustainable economic growth and employment and a rising standard of living in member countries, while maintaining financial stability, and thus to contribute to the development of the world economy;

b) to contribute to sound economic expansion in member as well as non-member countries in the process of economic development; and

c) to contribute to the expansion of world trade on a multilateral non-discriminatory basis in accordance with international obligations.

In distinct contrast to the albeit ambiguous goals of the Council of Europe, the purposes ascribed to the O.E.C.D. by its founders eschew supranational pretensions. Moreover, constitutionally, the executive body of the O.E.C.D., the Council, cannot, unlike its O.E.E.C. predecessor, pass binding decisions. All decisions have to be ratified by due constitutional process before they are so regarded.

Significantly, in terms of its capacity to affect the policies of national actors, the O.E.C.D. did not retain the operation of the Code of Trade Liberalisation as one of its functions. This was allowed to lapse as a result of pressure by the U.S. Congress and the French government. For the latter, this meant that tariffs against outsiders could be established for the E.E.C., while Congress was able to concentrate its interest in trade matters on the G.A.T.T.

At its origin then, the O.E.C.D. was uniquely prepared for all the limitations and possibilities of a harmonising role amongst its member states. It had been stripped of the coordinative assets possessed by the O.E.E.C. through the lapsing of the Code of Trade Liberalisation and the termination of the European Payments Union in 1958. Constitutionally its executive organ lost the admittedly weak decision-making prerogative of the O.E.E.C.'s Council to the national decision makers. Its purposes were explicitly economic and non-contentious, avoiding intrusion on sensitive areas of national sovereignty. Moreover, until the latter years of the sixties, global economic conditions generally sustained the goals of economic growth and development, financial stability and trade expansion. Understandably in these favourable circumstances, the O.E.C.D.'s role as a harmonising agent was relatively easy.

The financial instability which has developed in the international economic system since the late sixties, the rise in the rate of inflation in the seventies and the major recession the capitalist economies are at present suffering have all radically altered the circumstances in which the O.E.C.D. operates. The oil crisis and the more insistent demands of the developing world for a greater share in the resources of the developed world have added to the dislocation and have produced interesting responses from the organisation. Before discussing these recent developments, we shall consider the four techniques available to the organisation for harmonisation. No comment shall be made, at the moment, regarding the separate or collective utility of these techniques nor their significance in comparison with other pressures upon member states to pursue similar goals.

The first technique is research: that is the investigation, collation and distribution of information against which national policies may be judged or from which national policy-makers may be able to create or modify their own policies. Furthermore, research involves examining the implications of national policies, whether proposed or actual, against the interests of the other O.E.C.D. members, against other policy areas and indeed, against the needs of the national actor concerned. In order that such research may be useful to governments it must cover important areas of policy, it must be constantly alive to the shifting concerns of government and it must be presented in a fashion that reflects fairly accurately the complex interrelations of issues facing governments.

Responsiveness to the changing problems of government is thus a vital element in determining the likely importance of the research technique in harmonisation. In this respect, three developments in the organisation of research within the O.E.C.D. since the late sixties should be noted. The first has been the broadening of the interests of the O.E.C.D. as reflected in its committee structure. Although still organised around the axial principle of economic growth, committees on tourism, science policy, environment policy, international investment and multi-national enterprise and the like have been formed in addition to those carried over from the O.E.E.C. or which were established at the origin of the O.E.C.D. such as the Development Assistance Committee. Second, but obviously related to the first development, has been the shift in emphasis from a quantitative to a qualitative concern for economic growth. In this respect, the formation of the science policy committee mentioned above indicated a recognition of the disenchantment in public opinion about the effects of scientific development. The environment committee, also set up in 1970 (although built around the preceding Committee for Research Co-operation) reflected a similar preoccupation — water and air pollution, car and aircraft noise and so on. Throughout such adaptations, the goal of economic growth was sustained. For example, one concern of the environment committee was to find out how anti-pollution measures could themselves be a spur to economic growth. The O.E.C.D. was certainly not evolving into a radical critic of the goals defined at its origin. Its continued 'respectability' in the eyes of governments was thus assured. The third development was the so-called horizontal approach introduced at the initiative of the Secretary-General Emile van Lennep shortly after he took the office in 1969. Essentially, this involved an effort to develop relations between committees in different specialist fields in order to reflect the interdependence of the fields. The sectoral analysis of the earlier years of the O.E.C.D. was replaced by a broader based analysis. An example of the developments of the second and third type mentioned above is evident in the changing role of the

O.E.C.D.'s Nuclear Energy Agency. Originally, this was established to explore the possibilities of a new source of energy. The growing commercial application of nuclear power pushed the organisation's concerns into safety problems, the problems of regulating and controlling the uses of nuclear power and environmental issues. Organisationally this meant that linkages between committees in different specialist areas had to be developed.

One further resource which the O.E.C.D. has most recently attempted to exploit in order to improve research as a technique for harmonisation has been the growing awareness amongst its members of their interdependence. As a centre for information, analysis and expert advice derived from an international perspective, O.E.C.D. research has gained increasing status. The Secretary-General has, in recent years, made significant statements, of an analytic and prescriptive nature, about inflation[20] and the energy crisis[21] which undoubtedly affect the climate of opinion in which governments have to make their decisions.

The second technique for harmonisation is that of reviewing the national policies of member states in specific areas of activity. Normally this is carried out annually and it is a technique employed by many of the specialist committees of the O.E.C.D. The most important review is that carried out by the Economic and Development Review Committee which results in the publication of Annual Economic Surveys of members states. The technique is also employed, for example, by the Development Assistance Committee and more recently by the International Energy Agency, where the concern is to review energy conservation measures. Officials of the O.E.C.D. conduct the review in cooperation with national officials in the relevant ministries. A comparison is made between the principles and methodological or statistical assumptions employed by the O.E.C.D. in its analysis of the issues and those employed by the national officials. Deficiencies and disagreements in the respective analyses can thus be isolated and the reviews allow rational policies to be judged against the interests of the O.E.C.D. as a whole. Moreover, officials of other member states are able to comment upon the policies of the member under review and thus impart their preferences.

An interesting extension of the review technique both in itself and as an illumination of limits and possibilities of harmonisation, is the system of notification and consultation activated by the O.E.C.D. Council in 1971 in the field of environment policy.[22] Voluntarily and without legal restraint member countries have agreed to notify the O.E.C.D. whenever they propose or pursue policies which introduce pernicious materials into the environment. Consultation follows, in which the action can be assessed against the principles already evolved by the O.E.C.D. in dealing with environmental matters (e.g. the Polluter Pays Principle) and the consequences for other countries can be aired. The important points to be noted are the voluntary nature of the notification, the lack of legal sanctions and the reliance upon persuasion and consultation as a means of exercising influence. The aim is to achieve a concern for the consequences of an action by one member state for conditions in other member states. The transfrontier nature of some pollution is thus exploited as a means of attaining harmony: this is another example of interdependence between members aiding the purposes of the organisation. Attempts to impose policies from the international centre are avoided and the issue of national sovereignty is sidestepped.

The third technique, like the second carried over from the O.E.E.C., is the mutual cross-examination between high national officials responsible for particular areas of national policy. This technique evolved from confrontation' in the O.E.E.C. but the term no longer seems to be in general use in the O.E.C.D. In the opinion of the present Secretary-General:

'The impact of the action of the organisation derives to a very large extent from the fact that high level policy-makers from the capitals meet in Paris (the Head-quarters of the O.E.C.D.) and are able to compare and collate their views directly and to keep each other in touch with policies pursued in various countries.'[23]

The technique involves the periodic (normally annual) examination, country by country, of some aspect of the life of member states held to be of interest to all members. Such aspects are the economy, social welfare system and energy resources. Each state presents a report to the relevant O.E.C.D. committee outlining the situation with regard to this aspect of national life and explaining the policies used to attain certain ends and the assumptions underlying these policies.

This report is then examined by the Secretariat and becomes the subject of an internal report. On the basis of this internal report a high national official is questioned by his peers from two other member states. The assumptions, international consequences and fidelity to the principles of the organisation involved in each country's activities are scrutinised. Other member states are able to join in the examination in order to inform themselves and inject their interests into the debate.

This process does, of course, get very close to that of coordination (see Chapter 9): the main difference lies in the stress, in this case placed upon mutual information and advice, rather than on amending policies and structures in the interest of a common programme.

The scrutiny and debate are carried out in secret and the confidentiality allows a frankness about politically sensitive issues which a public forum would preclude. Since officials rather than politicians are involved a greater degree of detachment is also possible.

Clearly the technique will, on the one hand, heighten the awareness of the international consequences of national actions and provide an opportunity for informed comment on the desirability of the action even from the member's own parochial perspective. On the other hand, it allows other members to acquire an understanding of the premises upon which policies are based and on the political pressures that impinge upon the government of the examined country. Finally, , it increases the distribution of knowledge of how other countries have handled similar problems and may thus assist useful innovation. The most important application of the technique is in the field of economic policy where it is operated under the aegis of the Economic Policy Committee. Economic Reports are, however, approved by the states involved before publication. It is also employed by the Development Assistance Committee and, as we saw earlier, the Environment Committee.

Clearly the technique of mutual cross examination is markedly different in style and even substance from the conventional forum, which, we have argued, is associated with harmonisation. It does not conform to the defining criterion of setting standrads on the basis of common values. Rather, it assumes these common values, and stresses instead the interdependence of member states and the mutual dangers of pursuing divergent policies. And here policies stand to values in much the same way as ends to means. The scope of the technique can be as extensive as the awareness of trans-frontier consequences of national actions. Finally, it conforms to the criterion that functional responsibility should be retained within the member state. Binding agreements are not an outcome of this technique: the examined official is not a plenipotentiary.

The final technique to consider, now, is the conventional one we have ascribed to harmonisation: the forum. For activities of the O.E.C.D. take place within the executive organ, the Council, the various specialist committees, and within the working parties and ad hoc groups set up to consider areas of activity or particular issues.

From the research activities undertaken in these various organs and from the discussions conducted therein, declarations of principle or guidelines for future behaviour may emerge. The research upon which these discussions are based is carried out by the Secretariat of the O.E.C.D. Those involved in the resulting discussions may be Ministeres of the member states, in the case of the Council; permanent representatives of the members; national officials drawn from their own capitals on a temporary basis, and finally, in the case of some ad hoc groups, experts drawn from various walks of life.

Two recent, important examples of declarations of principle have been the so-called Trade Pledge of May 1974 (renewed in May 1975 for a year) and the Delcaration of Relations with Developing Countries of May 1975. With the former, the member states renounced the use of restrictive trade devices as a means to encourage economic expansion or to overcome balance of payments deficits. The pledge was felt to be important in a period when capitalist economies have plunged into recession and oil price increases had created massive trade deficits for the O.E.C.D. as a whole. The Declaration on Relations with Developing Countries was meant to reassure the Third World that the industrially advanced capitalist economies were aware of their conditions and were willing to participate in a constructive dialogue towards improving them.

It is probably fair to distinguish such declarations of principle from the setting of standards or guidelines from which national policies may develop or towards which they may progress. Such guidelines are likely to be the outcome of specific research activities, established initially on the initiative of the Secretary-General, and they will normally be reinforced by the techniques of review and confrontation. Examples of such guidelines are to be found in the areas of health and safety in the operation of nuclear reactors, and in tackling the pollution of the environment. In the latter case, the 'Polluter Pays Principle'[24] has been formulated and rules for the control of transfrontier pollution have also been made. At present, the organisation is seeking guidelines for the treatment of migrant workers.

Although normally these guidelines are of a non-binding nature, a binding guideline does exist to control the production, movement, and use of polychlorinated biphenyls. The agreement on their control was announced in February 1973 following research by a sub-group of the Environment Committee and a meeting of natural representatives to examine the need for common measures. The decision to establish a binding agreement was then made by the Council. Two points should be noted for their reflection on the nature of harmonisation. First, the substantive decision was taken by the member states. Second, the function of the organisation and the source of its influence was its ability to raise awareness amongst its member states of the utility of collective action.

These four techniques for harmonisation — research, review, mutual cross-examination between high officials and conferences — clearly overlap and it is consequently difficult and perhaps pointless to attempt to weigh them. The general picture, however, is of an organisation struggling to achieve harmonisation by raising the awareness of its member-states of their own interdependence, to the similarity of the problems they face and to the compatibility of related assumptions and principles.

We do not wish to give the impression that the O.E.C.D. is solely a centre of research and dialogue, however constructive. It also performs some 'service' functions. The Nuclear Energy Agency operates reactors in Britain and Norway. The Development Centre provides technical aid to the developing countries. The Centre for Educational Research and Innovation is involved in the development of educational techniques. Moreover, two important recent developments have strengthened the service side of the O.E.C.D.'s activities. These are the Financial Support Fund, which in fact is still awaiting ratification at time of writing, and the International Energy Agency, which is an autonomous body within the O.E.C.D. Both are products of the world recession and energy crisis which has, on the one hand, plunged the O.E.C.D. countries into overall trade deficit and, on the other, exposed the dependence of these countries on oil imports from O.P.E.C.

It was proposed that the Financial Support Fund should have assets of US $25 thousand million dollars which could be used as a backstop credit facility for countries with serious balance of payments deficits. The O.E.C.D. was regarded as a suitable instrument to operate this fund because O.P.E.C. would have presented obstacles to its effective use had it been located in the I.M.F. Although the fund was regarded as a potentially useful device to encourage congruent national policies by acting as a sanction behind the O.E.C.D.'s prescriptions, this is one of the reasons why its ratification has not been hasty and is, indeed, in doubt. Member countries feel credit may be gained elsewhere with less onerous conditions. Furthermore, balance of payments upheavals have not been as large as expected following the rise in oil prices and the pressure to establish the fund has been lessened.

The International Energy Agency is the most important development because it deals with a long term resource problem of major consequence for member states. For our purposes, the significance of the Agency is that it performs several functions which are coordinative rather than harmonising in nature. That is it involves policy adjustment by international prescription. Policy obligations not principles are set out. The objectives of the I.E.A. are: '(1) to reduce members dependence on imported oil through a threefold programme of (i) energy conservation, (ii) accelerated development of alternative energy sources and (iii) research and development; (2) to devise a comprehensive information system in monitor developments in the international oil market; (3) *to put in place a system of oil allocation between members for use in an emergency* and (4) to establish new relations with oil producing and developing countries.'[25] Although the principle coordinating function is a latent one — the operation in an emergency of an allocation system — the coordinative implication of the Agency is marked by the system of weighted majority voting for all but those decisions which involve a revision of the International Energy Programme. Important achievements so far of the Agency have been the setting of a minimum safeguard price (MSP) for oil at $7 per barrel to protect investments in alternative energy sources, the setting of conservation targets for aggregate oil imports and the fixing of minimum levels of oil reserves for each of the eighteen participants in the Programme. The Agency is also funding major research and development schemes in such fields as coal technology, nuclear safety and waste heat utilisation.

Interestingly, the coordinative implications of the I.E.A. have moved it into a controversial position. France, at the moment, is not a member because she sees it as producing confrontation with O.P.E.C. and threatening her standing in the Arab world in particular. Australia, because of her special links with Indonesia is, likewise, not a member. Nor are Iceland, Finland, Portugal or Greece although the reasons vary from Iceland's dependence on Russian oil to Portugese instability. Norway is not yet a full member. The O.E.C.D. is largely protected from this political imbroglio, but the tendentious political aspects of coordination are underlined in the work of the Agency.

One may perhaps infer from these developments that the O.E.C.D. is manifesting some latent transformation potential which, as we noted with the I.L.O., may be inherent in successful harmonisation. The extension of the scope of the O.E.C.D.'s activities following the attachment of the I.E.A. and the proposed support fund are responses to world economic and political developments. The O.E.C.D. has been

187

able to offer an attractive locus composed of expert staff, a tried organisational structure, political modesty and a high level of responsiveness to the issues and problems of the day.

There is an awareness within the organisation of the limitations involved in harmonisation. One is that agreements or congruent policies do not in themselves ensure either their timely introduction or that, collectively, they do not produce greater effects than that expected by individual national actors. For example, the priority given to anti-inflation measures in 1974 by the Economic Policy Committee resulted in an overreaction, as individual members failed to weigh their own anti-inflation policies against the transmission effect from such policies in other member countries. A second and major limitation is that, devoid of major sanctions, the organisation can seek only to persuade member countries to modify their policies. It cannot coerce. Its weapons are actor socialisation, moral reprobation, reasoned and well researched discussion and the transmission of information to show the pernicious or beneficial implications of national actions. To break through these limitations would mean the organisation would have to develop supranational instruments, or, more accurately, would have to be granted them, in a transfer of sovereignty, by the member states.

Appraisal

The preceding examination of three major organisational manifestations of harmonisation suggests the circumstances that are conducive to this type of approach to international organisation. These were already alluded to in the assumptive framework outlined at the start of this chapter but can be briefly restated here. First, a common set of values and a common store of information and interpretation is required. Second, an awareness of interdependence, and an acceptance of the view that transfrontier consequences of national actions ought to be a matter of concern for the national actors, has to exist or to develop. Third, a presumption in favour of the retention of sovereignty within the nation-state is an imperative. Any aspiration for supranationalism threatens the national political actors who alone possess the political resources from which to undertake actions in the interest of the international collectivity.

Of course national actors need not be governmental actors. We have already noticed this in the case of the I.L.O. but numerous less ambiguous examples exist. For example, in January 1976, an international maritime industry forum met in London. It discussed ways of dealing with the oil tanker problem and considered ways of planning the flow of new tankers. We can see that common values, information and its interpretation operated to stimulate action as did an awareness of interdependence and a respect for actor sovereignty.

In such cases the forum established need not be permanent. It may be an ad hoc response to specific problems. The Montreal International Conference on highjacking which produced a Convention[26] on the problem would seem to fall into this category. Special United Nations conferences can also be included such as the 1974 Conference on Food and Population problems[27] and the 1976 Conference on the Law of the Sea. The International Conference on Economic Cooperation held in Paris in December 1975 is a further example although, from this, four specialist committees have been set up to continue research into particular problems.

The major advantage of harmonisation in achieving policy congruence amongst various national actors is that it explicitly avoids intruding on national sovereignty. Individual members have 'maintaining' rather than 'transforming' objectives. The organisations that manifest this approach do not claim or seek supranational authority. They are servants rather than aspirant masters and while their influence is not thereby negligible, the techniques open to them for the exertion of influence are inevitably undramatic. Pressure has to be applied through the language of national interest and not through the rhetoric of idealistic, collectivist goals. A comparison between the E.E.C. Commission and the O.E.C.D. illuminates the difference between an organisation with a formally dynamic, coordinating role and one which eschews supranational goals. The former has been an object of acute political controversy as it has been perceived by some member states as using its mandate for uniting Europe against their interests. On the other hand the history of the latter is marked by the absence of controversy about its operations, its legitimacy or its organisational aspirations. Such controversy as there has been, say over alternative assessments of national economic prospects (a recent example of this is the sharply different forecasts for economic growth in West Germany produced by the O.E.C.D. and the West German government), is likely to be seen in the long run as a potentially productive technical disagreement rather than a matter for highly coloured political debate employing all the symbols of nationalism or supranationalism.

While harmonisation may be an eminently suitable strategy for an international organisation in a world of nation states, what can be said regarding its utility as a device for achieving policy congruence while retaining functional responsibility with the national actors? It is tempting to rush to a conclusion based upon examination of the declared goals of the organisation, the principles and guidelines it has established, and the declarations of intent that have been made. Have the goals been attained? Are the guidelines adhered to? Has the intent been matched by action? In some cases of standard setting, it is possible to establish a relationship between the action of the organisation and the behaviour of national actors. A survey by Yemin,[28] for example, suggested that following the adoption by the I.L.O. of the Termination of Employment Recommendation in 1963, the principle embraced in the recommendation, that 'a worker should not lose his job without a valid reason', was more rapidly adopted by member countries than would have been predicted from past trends.[29]

But the important point about harmonisation is not whether a specific outcome weighs more or less heavily with a government facing a particular decision. Rather it derives from the fact that officials of that government participate in the process from which the guideline or principle evolves. The real test of the utility of harmonisation is whether, *over time*, organisations manifesting this characteristic can extend the areas over which national actors find it useful to interact with their fellows. By a rather crude rule of thumb, that of whether the organisation has evolved, or has had attached to itself, a widening number of interests, the O.E.C.D. stands out as the most successful of the harmonising organisations we have considered. While the International Labour Organisation has evolved a substantial set of service rather than forum activities it has lacked the organising principle, such as economic growth in the O.E.C.D., around which novel interests can be woven. The Council of Europe is limited by the static nature of the values it embodies: they are declarations of identity rather than dynamic, constantly evolving, commitments. Economic growth and development, financial stability, trade and aid expansion are concrete goals of government amongst the member states of the O.E.C.D. Attaining or maintaining these goals is a substantial validation of political regimes at least in the eyes of the political elites. It is for this reason — that political elites are interested in the same questions as those examined by the O.E.C.D. — that the organisation stands out as important compared to the others we have considered.

Evidently changing political objectives on the part of member states could alter the relative status of these organisations. Socialist states may be more impressed by the work of the I.L.O. if working conditions come to be perceived as a basis for their domestic political support. If popular support for European union suddenly emerged, the weightiness of the statements and actions of the European Council of Europe would undoubtedly be enhanced. The ideological implications of the European Security Conference and the developments in Greece, Portugal and Spain have undoubtedly allowed the Council to enhance its status, however marginally, by calling for actions to be made in accordance with the values enshrined in its Statute.

A further aspect of the problem of utility is the extent to which international organisations overlap each other in terms of functional interests. This overlap is often deliberate. For example, Working Party No. 3 of the O.E.C.D.'s Economic Policy Committee is composed of the same members as the 'Group of Ten', indeed, they are the same people. The Group of Ten is, in fact, serviced by the O.E.C.D., the I.M.F. and the Bank of International Settlement in Basle. As Working Party No. 3 in the O.E.C.D., the Group of Ten 'is concerned with the impact of economic policies on the international payments situation, the adjustment and financing of payments imbalances and with the likely evolution of payments patterns over the longer term'. The location of this Group within the O.E.C.D. is an appreciation of the fact that an adequate picture of the world's monetary problems was not given within the I.M.F. It was necessary to deal with the underlying economic problems and the O.E.C.D. seemed the more appropriate institution for this approach.

Such a potentially creative overlap is by no means inveriably the case. Other overlaps are simply the product of separate organisational development and although a creative competition may be one consequence, another may be duplication of effort and the squandering of scarce resources. Such cases of overlap abound: E.E.C.'s Euratom and the O.E.C.D.'s Nuclear Energy Agency; the environment protection work of the E.E.C. and the O.E.C.D.; efforts of the Council of Europe and the European Council to harmonise foreign policies.

The vital factor determining the utility of a harmonising international organisation in terms of its functional scope is the level of awareness amongst member states of their interdependence. Interdependence, the situation in which the action of one affects the environment or conditions or the behaviour of one or several others, provides conditions in which the national interest can be seen to coincide with a collective, international interest. The issue of

191

sovereignty is sidestepped. What this seems to suggest is that harmonising international organisations can work most effectively in areas where actors operate in a self-interested manner and these are not only areas where values are congruent but where the operational goals of governments coincide. Interdependence is thus both an asset of such organisations and a condition of which they must make member states aware.

Increasing levels of economic specialisation, world-shrinking communications, and a widening perception of global resource depletion and environmental pollution together suggest that both the awareness and actuality of interdependence are expanding phenomena. In such circumstances, the scope for harmonisation will increase.

It is important to stress once again that this likely development reflects the continued supremacy of the states — whether national or otherwise. Harmonisation may well reflect a desire to conduct affairs between states more rationally, it may even spur on this development. But it will not lead, in itself, to the supercession of the nation state. This is because the sources of political support, the legitimacy of major actors upon the international stage — the national political elites — lie within the confines of each individual state. This is why supranationalist organisations with an elite rather than a mass following normally have insubstantial effects upon national political systems.

But within the marginal structural impact achieved by such organisations a problem does arise. To the extent that such organisations impinge upon specific national policies do they thereby undermine national political processes? There are probably two extreme answers which can be given to this question. The first is that the question is irrelevant because in a context of value congruence, and operational goal coincidence, harmonising efforts are more likely to lead to the better or faster achievement of national goals and thus reinforce the national political process. In effect, harmonisation provides mechanisms for expert cross-examination and diffusion of knowledge. The negative answer would be that through processes of actor socialisation, bureaucratic interpretation and such like, valid alternatives open to national actors are perceived to be progressively closed. Moreover, in the context of the problem of partisan control of administration, contacts between high level national officials may well result in implicit agreements or dispositions which bias the presentation of evidence and options by the official to his political master.

In stating the problem we have probably given more importance to the answers than they are worth, at least within the context of the influence of harmonising organisations upon their members. However the opinions and pressures generated by the organisation are only one factor in determining specific national policy decisions and where the goal set by the organisation is couched in terms of an ideal rather than from an awareness of practical politics, the influence of the organisation may well be marginal. For example, the Development Assistance Committee of the O.E.C.D. has struggled to raise the level of aid given by the wealthier O.E.C.D. members to one per cent of their G.N.P. This is in line with a U.N. figure. Countries such as Sweden and Germany are responsive to such appeals while others such as Austria are almost indifferent. But these different responses do not reflect a greater or lesser degree of influence by the O.E.C.D. because elements within these countries already support such goals, or oppose them as the case may be. As with all international organisations, the relative standing of the organisation in the eyes of each national community is a vital determinant of the comparative degree of success of their decisions or declarations or guidelines. In the case above, Sweden and Germany (West) attribute a higher degree of worth to the decisions and declarations of international organisations than does Austria.

As a corollary to the previous comments, the degree to which such decisions or declarations reflect political realities, will enhance the prospects that the organisation's output will be accepted and adhered to. Harmonisation by its nature involves a humble approach in terms of achieving structural transformation. It operates within the actual political realities by eschewing supranationalism and appealing to the self-interest of each actor in achieving mutual resolution of the problems of interdependence.

Notes

1. See chapters 5 and 6 on this concept.
2. See chapters 5 and 9.
3. *The works of Jeremy Bentham, Published under the supervision of his Executor, John Bowring* (11 vols., 1843), vol. ix., p. 6.
4. *Ibid.*, vol. ii, p. 559.
5. *Ibid.*, vol. ii, p. 539.
6. *Ibid.*, vol. ii, p. 554.
7. *Bowring*, vol. ii, pp. 557–559.
8. *Bowring*, vol. ii, pp. 539–540.
9. *Bowring*, vol. ii, p. 557.
10. *Bowring*, vol. ii, p. 535.
11. *Bowring*, vol. ii, p. 552.
12. The distinction is made in these terms by R.W. Cox and H.K. Jacobson in

their *The Anatomy of Influence: Decision-Making in International Organisation*, New Have, Yale University Press, 1973, p. 5.

13. See E.J. Phelan, *Yes and Albert Thomas*, London, Crescent Press, 1949.
14. Cox, *op. cit.*, p. 136.
15. *Ibid.*, p. 105.
16. A.H. Robertson, *European Institutions*, 3rd edition, London, Stevens and Sons, 1973, p. 36ff.
17. This account is partly based on interviews in Paris with O.E.C.D. officials. The authors thank those concerned for their assistance.
18. M. Esman and D. Cheever, *The Common Aid Effort*, Ohio, Ohio State University Press, 1967, p. 35.
19. Greece, Iceland, Luxembourg, Portugal, Spain and Turkey are in O.E.C.D. but not members of D.A.C. The Commission of the E.E.C. is a member of the D.A.C. but not of O.E.C.D.
20. Secretary-General, *The Present Problem of Inflation*, O.E.C.D. Paris 1970.
21. Secretary-General, 'Energy Policy and its Effects on the International Monetary Situation', *O.E.C.D. Observer*, No. 74, March-April 1975.
22. See for a summary account of this activity, *O.E.C.D. at Work for Environment*, 2nd edition, O.E.C.D., Paris, July 1973.
23. Emile van Lennep, Secretary-General O.E.C.D., *Activities of the O.E.C.D. in 1970*, Paris O.E.C.D. 1971, p. 12.
24. O.E.C.D. Publication, *The Polluter Pays Principle – Definition, Analysis, Implementation*, Paris, O.E.C.D., 1975.
25. The International Energy Agency, Paris, O.E.C.D., April 1975, p. 1.
26. Convention for the Suppression of Unlawful Acts against the Safety of Civil Aviation.
27. A permanent World Food Council was set up at the behest of the Conference.
28. E. Yemin, 'Job Security: Influence of I.L.O. Standards and Recent Trends', *International Labour Review*, January–February, 1976.
29. Note also the possible link between the Trade Pledge, against protectionist measures, taken by O.E.C.D. members at a Council meeting in May 1974, (and renewed in May 1975) and the, largely successful, resistance by governments to pressures for such restrictions in the face of balance of payments deficits.
30. O.E.C.D. Department of Economics and Statistics, Paris, O.E.C.D., 1975, p. 9.

Selected Reading

1. E.J. Phelan, *Yes and Albert Thomas*, London, Crescent Press, 1949.
2. A.H. Robertson, *European Institutions*, 3rd edition, London, Stevens & Sons, 1973.
3. Emile van Lennep: Secretary General O.E.C.D., *Activities of the O.E.C.D. in 1970*, Paris, O.E.C.D., 1971.
4. E. Yemin, 'Job security: influence of I.L.O. standards and recent trends', *International Labour Review*, January/February 1976.
5. Robert W. Cox and Harold K. Jacobson, *The Anatomy of Influence*, New York, Yale University Press, 1973.

CHAPTER NINE

COORDINATION IN INTERNATIONAL ORGANISATION
Paul Taylor

This account of coordination, together with the accounts of other
types of cooperation, illustrate further the view that inter-governmental
cooperation, far from being a uni-dimensional phenomenon, opposed
sharply to supranationalism or federalism, is capable of sub-division
into a large range of styles. Coordination is a way of producing
common policies among actors which have legal, or formal independence
in the areas to which the policies refer; it involves adjustments in the
initial positions of the actors in line with the agreed policy and it
assumes the acceptance of the overriding importance of common
objectives as reflected in a programme of action which is to run over
a period of time. These three elements, then, are the major elements in
coordination: the actors have an area of discretion; policies are
adjusted by them in an agreed direction; and policies are fitted into
a programme which is seen to be of mutual advantage. Although this
procedure may be followed at any level of society, it is particularly
interesting and complex at the level of international society in
international institutions because of the principle of the sovereignty
and equality of the principal actors, namely, the states. In the following discussion, examples will be taken mainly from the experience of
the North Atlantic Treaty Organisation in producing its annual reviews
and, more recently, the Force Plan; and from the institutions of the
European Economic Communities in their role as coordinator of
Community policy. Some examples are also taken from the
experience of the Organisation for European Economic Cooperation

(OEEC), which in 1961 became the Organisation for Economic Cooperation and Development (OECD),[1] in working out its Annual Programme. Other examples of coordination may be found, however, in the practice of a wide range of international institutions.

The freedom of the actors to reject policies which are the object of coordination is reflected in the use of techniques of influence or persuasion to change their position in the agreed direction, and not those of power or coercion. Influence involves the changing of the actors preferences among policies, from one which was originally preferred more, to one which was originally preferred less, by the promise of rewards such as economic or political gain by other states or by an international institution. It should be stressed that movement is between policies which are more or less preferred, and which are each conceivable ways to the same general end, and not from one which was preferred to one which was definitely opposed. (This would follow from the use of power or force.)[2] The rewards of the coordination programme are seen by the participating states as outweighing the costs of such adjustments in policy: there is a superordinate goal.

The process is greatly assisted by the recognition by the actor of the high skills of the staff of the international institution, a circumstance which is encouraged by the exchange of highly rated staff, possibly on a short term secondment basis, between the home civil service and the international civil service. This occurs between national administrations and the international civil services of NATO and of the OECD, and to some extent between them and the Commission of the European Economic Communities. (In the latter case national governments have a considerable direct representation through the permanent delegations and the officials linked with the Council and the Committee of Permanent Representatives.) The role of the institution is also greatly enhanced by the availability to it of a wide range of accurate, and comparable information in the area of its competence. Among the basic tasks which faced the OEEC in its early period, and NATO, was the introduction of techniques for collecting and organising information, such as economic statistics in various states, which allowed effective collation and comparison at the international level; the EEC has also devoted considerable effort to this task, though much remains to be done in this area.[3] (e.g. it was not until the 1st January 1966 that a harmonised nomenclature for the foreign trade statistics of the EEC countries came into operation; this contained some 4828 headings.)

The acceptance of the high status of the staff of the international institution by national officials may greatly assist the process of gathering comparable information, and of maintaining the confidence of states in its reliability. Indeed, it has been argued that national bureaucracies are sometimes more prepared to allow to international officials the right of inspection in sensitive areas, than they are to members of their own country's elected assemblies: scrutiny by fellow specialists, even international ones, can be more acceptable than scrutiny by nationals who may have a political interest.[4] Comprehensive information about the common programmes should, however, also be available to the separate actors. They are more likely to respond to influence if they are placed in the position of feeling that they too have acquired an accurate oversight of the proposed arrangements. The role of the institution in relating information to the programme, and the importance of national confidence in the scheme, are illustrated in the context of the provision of international aid as follows:

'If several potential doners are aware of a development plan in its entirety, and if they have had the opportunity to pass judgement upon it, or if a trusted mutual agent, such as the World Bank, has confirmed its feasibility, the more likely are they to support the interlocking projects and programmes that the plan requires.'[5]

These remarks equally apply to coordination in NATO or the OEEC-OECD or in the EEC. It should also be stressed that this linking of the functions of a mediator of high status with the availability of a wide range of information, adequate to the formulation of a convincing oversight on the common programme, is more likely to be achieved through a formal institution: 'informal exchange among donors is not likely to provide the sustained and intensive information flows and discussion that effective co-ordination requires'.[6] International institutions have an important role in the construction of a coordinated programme.

In the execution of the agreed programme the participating actors, not the international institution, are the responsible agencies, though the international institution may sometimes act 'in the field' in their name. This contrasts with the behaviour of the archetypal supranational agency in which responsibility for execution is thought to lie with the international institution. The appropriate constitutional analogy for the latter system is federalism: powers are legally transferred to the centre in a range of aspects of the formulation and execution of policy. In coordination the parallel analogy is confederalism: in the distribution of coordinate powers and responsibilities the separate actors remain supreme. Coordination may be seen as reflecting a limited or partial confederalism: the programme reflects a commitment, by states, a perception of convergent interests, and a sense of their common setting in the global functional context; thus the actors retain their sovereignty — their primary role and responsibility are unchallenged.

In most schemes of coordination a transfer of resources or skills from one country to another is involved; this is true of the NATO force programmes, and of the OECD annual programmes, and of the coordinated aid programmes, and, of course, of the operations of the EEC. But in conducting these transfers it is important that participating donor states should feel that outflows of resources are proportional to their capacity and to the inflows of political or material values which follow from the programme; some states will certainly contribute more than others because of inequalities in circumstances, and others will receive more. The idea of *proportionality* requires, however, that inflows should be felt to be in scale with outflows and the level of available resources. This is called, in the terminology of EEC politics, the idea of the *juste retour*, which was stressed by the British during the 1974—75 renegotiation of the conditions of their membership in the European Communities and which increasingly has become a feature of the Communities in the 1970s. It does not mean, of course, that there should be an immediate balancing of accounts, but, rather, that accounts should be felt to be balanced over the period of the programme, or over a fairly limited period such as one or two years. Some items in this account are difficult to quantify — hence, the reference to a feeling of balance.

There is a tendency for the policies and actions of the state to diverge in the area of the programme, despite the wish for an alignment of policies and activities, because of the technical complexity of the programme concerned, and the existence of competing interests in related areas.

The international machinery has the task of continually correcting the divergences in policy among the participating actors. The latter task is a predictable aspect of coordination, particularly where it is attempted in areas of policy which are more highly salient, such as security, or the restoration of domestic economies. The programme which emerges from the coordinating process is, therefore, inevitably in part a declaration of intent, which may be honestly pursued by the sovereign national actors, but which they cannot be compelled to follow. The coordinating machinery generally includes steering procedures — which may even include scholarly reports — which attempt to alter the course of governments within the programme so that they stay in convoy. The value of the objective to be obtained by participating states provides one dynamic of the steering mechanism. But the continuing tug-of-war between the centrifugal forces inherent in the decision-making procedures of sovereign states and the centripetal forces of the programme is very much a part of the character of co-ordination. In areas of lower salience, however, though the centrifugal force, may be considerably weaker, the values to be gained are also much smaller.

One of the central processes for co-ordinating policy may be summarized under the heading of the *confrontation of policy*, a term that was coined to describe a technique which was first identified in the OEEC.[7] It refers to the close examination of the policies of each actor by other actors and by the international institution. The state which bears the examination is made to defend its departures from the proposed programme, and the international institution explains and defends it. The sense is conveyed during the confrontation process that the availability of the benefits of the programme is conditional upon successful co-ordination. In this way the policy of each participating state is confronted with the policy of every other participating state in the context of the overall view of the institution: it is a two-way juxtaposition, international institution with each state, and states with each other.

These points may now be illustrated and developed with reference, first, to the experience of NATO in constructing the Force Plan; some points may be illustrated further by reference to the earlier Annual Review procedure, particularly that of 1958. The First Force Plan was constructed in NATO in 1966 for the period 1966—7. They are now designed to plan for a five-year period, though the planning cycle is repeated every two years, with states being formally committed to the Plan only for the first year.[8] It is important to stress at the outset that the machinery involves a continuing and carefully organised dialogue between the various parties concerned in order to achieve the maximum contributions of member states to the agreed common plans by which the NATO area is to be defended jointly against attack from the outside. But the operation of the machinery cannot be understood until it is realised that the actors are not homogeneous entities: different elements of each state actor build relations with comparable elements in other state actors, and the international institution, and establish common cause with them against elements in their own state at various points in the co-ordination process. It will be helpful to describe the major institutional elements involved, in order to illustrate this point. This ambiguity of roles is a recurrent feature of co-ordination procedures.

First, there are at the headquarters of NATO in Brussels two groups of civil servants which have rather different functions but which are nevertheless largely interchangeable. There are the civil servant representatives of state administrations which make up the national delegations, containing senior personnel from defence and foreign ministries in the main; and there are civil servants of the international staff, many of whom have transferred from positions in national civil services, either for a short-term or a long-term period. Members of permanent delegations usually make up the Defence Review Committee (DRC) (together with main military commanders and representatives of the Military Committee), which is chaired by a member of the International Staff (the Assistant Secretary-General for Defence Planning and Policy); the Defence Planning Committee, which is a committee which has senior status (parallel with the Council) in military/strategic questions, may meet at the political level (National Defence Ministries), but may equally meet at the level of permanent delegations. (The Secretary General, Head of the International Staff, is Chairman of the DPC.) Links between national administrations and international staff are close; they meet in a number of working committees and have a natural sympathy with each other. It is not surprising that in working on NATO policies, such as the Force Plan, there is a tendency for national delegations in Brussels, at some stages in the coordination process, to veer in their nuancing of policy towards the position of the international staff.

The second element is the political representatives of the states who come to Brussels from time to time to take part in the meetings of senior committees, such as the Defence Planning Committee, or the Council (also chaired by the Secretary General). These individuals are usually elected politicians and are accompanied by advisors from their national ministries. They are inevitably more in touch with the variety of demands upon scarce resources in national capitals, and the interests of rival departmental chiefs, than are members of the permanent delegations or the international staff.

The third element is the military one. In the co-ordination process this is represented in three main institutions: the Military Committee which consists of the Chiefs-of-Staff of the member states; the offices of the major military commanders, who are Commanders-in-Chief of the various NATO regional command areas with international responsibilities, (who naturally have a particularly strong interest in the states which are involved in their regions); and the Defence Review Committee, which includes, as already stated, the major military commanders, together with state representatives, and members of the Military Committee. It is likely that the national military representatives will have a sympathy with the problems and intentions of the commanders. This leaning is likely to be increased by the interactions between NATO military staffs in the various command administrative head-quarters, such as SHAPE, at Mons, near Brussels. The military element, together with the administrative/bureaucratic elements at the national delegation and international level in Brussels, are groups within which there is a continuing potential for the convergence of interests, which, in turn is potentially in opposition to the political interests of national ministers of the various states. These alignments inevitably affect the way in which disagreements between the participating states are reconciled during the co-ordination process.

The co-ordination process may be divided into three major phases. In the first phase is the formulation of the Force Goals: this is the NATO plan for arranging and improving the common defensive effort in the light of the perceived threat from the Soviet Union. The Military Committee first assesses the military challenge as it may face the alliance for the five years of the planning period (national military element). This is augmented by the so-called Ministerial Guidance which adds in political and economic factors (national political representatives). In the light of this advice the major commanders then put forward their force proposals on a country-by-country basis (international military commanders). These proposals are probably the most international elements in the co-ordination process, because the military commanders are close to the day-to-day working deficiencies of the alliance and are particularly immersed in alliance planning. The force proposals are then co-ordinated by the Military Committee, before being sent to the Defence Planning Committee (usually, delegations), which in turn sends it to the Defence Review Committee (national delegations plus commanders plus Military Committee representatives). The Defence Review Committee consults the Military Committee, and refers to the Ministerial Guidance, and, on this basis, constructs its account of Force Goals in the light of what appears to be desirable, because of fore-seeable contingencies, and the practical requirement of asking states to attempt to achieve what they judge can be attained. The Force Goals are, finally, approved by the Defence Planning Committee.

In the second phase, Force Plans are produced by the various member countries in response to the account of Force Goals and in a series of meetings between international military and civilian staffs and the national delegations, and between the national representatives themselves, the attempt is made to iron out any incompatibilities between *goals* and *plans*. To initiate this process Force Goals are sent to the various national governments who respond in their plans with an account of their achievements in specified areas, their intentions as regards future deployments, and equipment and force levels, and the available finance: they are intended to cover a five-year period. The question arises, of course, of why it is, after such protracted efforts to produce a statement of goals, a process which included contributions from national delegations at various points, that country plans should now come to represent different views and intentions. The answer is that country plans represent the input into the co-ordinating process of the *political* interests of the collectivity of the national ministers, in their own capitals, who compete for scarce resources of the states, whereas the Force Goals largely measures the extent of the national delegation (administration) and international staff alignment, together with the views of the national and international military personnel. The country plans, therefore, generally take a rather more pessimistic view of the extent of available finance, and tend to reflect a greater preparedness to take risks in the military/strategic area, or to discount military/strategic expert opinion. The alignment of goals and plans is attempted first, at the level of military/international staff/delegations and officials together with commanders' representatives. Success or lack of it is reported to the DRC, which, if necessary, then organises a series of multilateral examinations, by delegations, of the 'difficult' countries' position.

The multilateral stage of this process can sometimes be quite complex. G.L. Goodwin, who studied the comparable process, the Annual Review, in 1958, reported that the scrutiny of a country's position started with the preparation of a list of questions by the international staff and the NATO military.[9] About two weeks were allowed between notification to the designated delegation and the examining session. It was interesting that not all delegations participated in each examining session: seven states studied the position of the United Kingdom, only four studied that of France and the United States, and six studied Italy and West Germany.[10] On the other hand the United States was designated to study all fourteen other members, while France studied nine, the UK seven, and Italy and Germany four each. In this is to be found evidence of a wish to achieve proportionality on the part of the largest donor, that is, to ensure that others gave in proportion to capacity as much as itself. As Goodwin points out the process also allowed the United States to assess the necessary level of mutual aid required for each state, in a form which avoided some of the embarrassment which might arise if the necessary investigation were conducted on a bi-lateral basis.[11] In this way co-ordination processes may sometimes provide the opportunity for up-grading general standards on the instigation of a leading member of the process in a fashion which does not challenge the susceptibilities of the various national governments.

The third and final phase of the co-ordination of the NATO Force Plan occurs when the DRC with the advice of the Military Committee reports to the Defence Planning Committee. The Military Committee assesses the degree of risk inherent in what the DRC has been able to achieve. Eventually the Plan is approved by the Defence Planning Committee, and its adaptation by the Ministers meeting in the Council is recommended.

As in any process of co-ordination between sovereign states, three kinds of achievement result from the adaption of the NATO Force Plan. In the first place, there is the achievement of establishing standards and laying down guidelines which are generally believed to be closely attuned to the common task. The Ministerial Guidance is one aspect of this (document MC70 in the case of the Annual Review, M–DPC–1 (75)11 in 1975): in 1975, for instance, standards and guidelines were to include measures for 'rationalising tasks and functions as between nations,' to increase the 'flexibility and optimum deployment of all forces available,' to standardise equipment and increase inter-operability, and to improve co-operation in the 'development and production of military equipment.'[12] Strategic elements were added by the Military Committee and specific force adjustments by the military commanders. Secondly, departure from the ideal standards and guidelines were measured through the information collecting process, and the extent to which the actual achievement added up to this ideal was evaluated. Thirdly, a series of pressures on states to fit into the desired framework, to measure up to required standards and follow appropriate guidelines, were set up. These derived in the case of NATO from the pressures upon government of opinion among their peers and from the entrenchment of accepted practice. More detailed requirements were then added to these broad stipulations.

There are of course a host of examples of failure to live up to these standards in NATO, and of failures in member states to make stipulated changes. They cannot be compelled to do so, but the co-ordination process establishes a minimum standard, a point of reference, or a pole of attraction in national defence decision-making, and it helps to define an area within which co-operative defence ventures, such as joint research and production and infra-structure programmes, are acceptable.

Goodwin concludes that 'the impact of the Annual Review on governmental attitudes and policies is very difficult to measure, and will naturally vary from country to country, but on some issues, or on some occasions, a country may be open to suggestions while remaining adamant on others'.[13] But 'it can help to focus minds on the collective needs of the Alliance, and, in the process, not only to smooth off the rough edges of national policies but also to enduce a frame of mind not rooted exclusively in narrowly conceived national interests. The pressure it exercises may be gradually accumulative'. This judgement applies equally to the later Force Programmes of NATO.

Policy-making in the European Communities reveals, perhaps surprisingly, the same elements of co-ordination that were discovered in NATO although many of them take a rather more complex form. Programmes exist at three levels: there are those programmes which are associated with a particular *area* such as Commercial Policy, the Comman Market, the Common Agricultural Policy and Regional Policy; there is the programme of programmes, the common framework into which the particular programmes are to be fitted, which could be called the co-ordinated economic system of the European Communities; and there are the focussed programmes within the area programmes, which are intended to achieve specific objectives in the arrangements of the member states, such as the protection under stated conditions of the right of individuals to remain in the territory of another state. There are many examples of the working out of an operational programme at the first and third levels but the scope and nature of the second level is still the subject of debate and argument, and it is by no means certain that it will ever be attained. A further complicating feature in the EEC compared with NATO is that it was for some time a forum of contending concepts. In the period after its foundation in 1958 until the mid-1960s it was expected by many supporters of European integration that the supra-national elements would prevail and that there would be a steady increment of powers and authority to the centre, in the shape of the Commission, at the expense of the participating states. There was also the expectation that there would be a transition as was required by the Treaty of Rome,

204

to a majority voting system in the Council of Ministers. The ascendancy of this concept of the potential of European integration, which was sustained by the style of the Hallstein Commission, and by the theories of the neo-functionalists, was challenged fiercely by the French Government in the crisis in the Communities in 1965;[14] the concept declined in its relevance fairly rapidly with the confirming of the continuation of the system of voting on the basis of unanimity in the Council of Ministers in the Luxembourg agreement of 1966, and was clearly replaced by the concept of confederal Europe after the assertion of West German diplomatic strength in the late 1960's, particularly at the Summit Conference at The Hague in December 1969, and the accession of Britain, Denmark and Ireland in January 1973.[15] The process of the co-ordination of policy in the setting up and managing of the programmes of the European Communities, is very much a feature of this later confederal phase. This has emerged more clearly with the declining relevance of the concept of supra-national centralisation.

As in the NATO setting the key element in co-ordination is a process which it is useful to identify as the confrontation of policy. The central importance of this process in the Community system is probably immediately attributable to the confirmation of the system of taking decisions on the basis of unanimity in the Council of Ministers, the main decision-making body on which governments are represented. In the Treaty of Rome a qualified majority voting system should have applied to an increasing range of areas in the second and third (final) phases of the transitional stage. The use of majority voting would have discouraged the appearance of several of the procedural and institutional devices which have become familiar features in the confederal phase in the 1970s. It would have encouraged the Commission, which is the main initiating body in the Community system, to concentrate, in its relations with the Council of Ministers, upon a single policy, or a very closely-related cluster of policies, and to introduce into that policy a much stronger European element. It would have had a lesser incentive to employ the existing technique of linking a wide range of areas together in what has been called a *package deal*[16], which involes the trading-off of the interests of one state against those of another in relation to various elements of the package. The Commission would have been encouraged by majority voting to try to build coalitions of support in the Council for more European solutions, and to risk offending a disapproving minority. Furthermore, the need for unity on any important issue is the foundation upon which the very complicated system of consultations among participating actors was developed: the Commission had to work for consensus among the actors by using extensive consultation and amendment and confrontation before the decision was taken. The stress upon these procedures led directly to the development of an institution which has now come to rival the Commission in the co-ordination process, the Committee of Permanent Representatives. This is a committee of permanent delegations based full-time in Brussels, which meets every week, and attempts to establish agreement between delegations and between them and the Commission.[17]

Policy-making in the European Communities has become crucially dependent upon the co-ordination of the position of national actors through their permanent delegations in Brussels.[18] The importance of the issues involved for member states is illustrated by the high status of permanent delegations' officials, and by their number and the range of home departments which they represent. Heads of permanent delegations are of ambassadorial rank and normally come from the Foreign Offices of member states (in 1977 the UK Ambassador to the Communities was Sir Donald Maitland). Other officials may be transferred from senior positions in a wide range of national ministries. Delegations vary in size; the number of senior staff in the British delegation, in 1976, was forty-five above the level of Second Secretary. The convention has emerged that the Committee of Permanent Representatives may itself take decisions on the less controversial issues after due consultation, but any more controversial political issues, are forwarded for decision to the Council of Ministers. The Committee is, of course, responsible to the Council, and in a sense stands in for the Council when it is not in session. Since the Hague Conference of December 1969, a further layer of decision-making has, however, emerged in the Communities which also demonstrates the assertion of the separateness and sovereignty of the states in the co-ordination process in the Communities in recent years. Increasingly, crucial decisions on Community policy are left for Summit meetings of Heads of State or Government, now christened European Councils, which meet at regular intervals. In the opinion of some commentators the introduction of this third level has slowed down the work of the Community. It certainly reflects a further step away from the supranational model supported by pro-Europeans in the early 1960s which envisaged the development of the role of the Commission together with the introduction of majority voting into the Council of Ministers.

These tendencies in decision-making in the Communities were

confirmed in the meeting of the Heads of Government of the Community in Paris, December 9–10 1974. Heads of Government then agreed to meet three times a year, but requested that the Council of the Community in the particular form of the foreign ministers, should act as initiator and co-ordinator, though this should not affect the 'rules and procedures laid down in the Treaty, or the provisions on political co-operation in the Luxembourg and Copenhagen reports',[19] and 'greater latitude will be given to the permanent representatives so that only the most important political problems need to be discussed in the Council. To this end, each member state will take the measures it considers necessary to strengthen the role of the permanent representatives and involve them in preparing the national positions on European affairs.'[20] They also agreed that they would 'renounce in the Council the practice of taking decisions on all issues on the basis of unanimity,' as had been agreed at Luxembourg on 28 January 1966.[21] They did not say, however, which issues would be voted by majority and it is difficult to believe that this development will now make any difference to the working of existing institutions or to the essential hard fact of Community life, that any development of importance requires the assent of participating governments. The strengthening of the powers of the permanent representatives might also be expected to make the work of the Council of Ministers less important and therefore the precise manner of its voting procedures less critical.

The process of co-ordinating policy in the European Communities may be considered under the same three headings that seemed appropriate in the case of the NATO Force Plan. It is indeed possible to find equivalent elements at each stage, and these will be indicated. Some are functional equivalents, rather than precisely parallel institutions, and in the EEC some stages of the process are rather more complicated. The argument is illustrated mainly with examples taken from the Community's experience of the Common Commercial policy.

The first phase is equivalent to the production of force goals in NATO; in the EEC the equivalent of force goals is the draft proposals of the appropriate Directorate-General of the Commission. It begins with the statement of general objectives and intentions in the particular area of policy, which may be contained in the Rome Treaty (articles 110 to 116 on commercial policy), or in statements made in the Communiqués of Summit Meetings, (for example, in the Final Declaration of the Paris Summit, October 19–20 1972; on commercial policy see paragraphs 11, 12, 13 and 14[22]), or in sessions of the Councils of

207

Ministers, or in generally approved Grand Designs such as the Commission's Action Programme of 1962.[23] Such statements are generally about the first level of programmes and refer to policy areas rather than the focussed programmes of the third level: they refer to expectations in the area of common commercial policy, rather than intentions in specific areas of policy such as anti-dumping. Commitment at this stage is likely to be expressed more forcibly where the area is felt to be less salient, and where it is less specific; the more salient the area, and the more specific it is, the greater the level of caution indicated at this stage. The views of Ministers or Heads of Government, even when codified in the shape of the Rome Treaty, may be seen as the equivalent of Ministerial Guidance, or MC70 in NATO, and the rather wide-ranging, non-specific advice and evaluation of government specialists, such as economists, may be seen as the functional equivalent of the preliminary statement of the Military Committee. Long-term goals, strategies, and problems, such as changes in the position of the 'enemy', in the shape of such factors as inflation, or international monetary crises, or the cost of raw materials, are evaluated.

The next step is the Commission's response to the advice, requests, initiatives of the Ministers. An initiative is now taken at the third level of the focussed programmes in the appropriate Directorate-General of the Commission. (Directorate-General One in the case of commercial policy.[24]) It is worth remembering that the majority of programmes at level one can be split up into a large number of focussed programmes: in the case of the commercial policy the extent of the range of these programmes is extremely imprecise, but the following matters seem to follow from the treaty or from related 'ministerial guidance'. (It is noticeable that the achievement of the common external tariff which was completed in June 1968, and its supervision since that date, does not conventionally fall within the accepted range of the common commercial policy): methods for identifying the country of origin of goods entering member countries from third countries; the reduction of quotas on imports from third countries and the establishment of an agreed list of liberalised products; the setting up of procedures for managing trade agreements with third countries, and for abolishing bi-lateral trade agreements; (This programme applied particularly to relations between the Communities and Eastern Europe: it was not until 1973 that trade arrangements with COMECON countries became a Community responsibility.); procedures in the event of dumping and other 'unfair' trade practices by non-members; equalising arrangements for financing exports, particularly the export credit systems. In producing its focussed programme the Commission works in one or other of these areas. For mainly political reasons, little progress was made in any of them before the late 1960's.[25] Since then, however, there has been limited progress on a number of specific areas.

In producing its draft proposal the Commission staff consults with representatives of organised European interest groups, with experts, and with the members of the permanent delegations of member states. In the case of the commercial policy — on the quota system for instance — it consults the representatives in Brussels of various affected manufacturing industries. At this stage it is attempting to inform itself about the kind of arrangements which would be ideal in, for instance, the liberalisation of imports or action on dumping, and the kind of arrangements which might prove acceptable to member states. At this point the advisers from state delegations are not necessarily in close touch with home ministries about the specific topics under discussion and the chances are therefore greater of a convergence of interest between delegations and the Commission sustained by a shared expertise. It is not, of course, that delegates will now support advanced schemes for European integration, but rather that they are more 'expert', 'rational', and individual and less restricted by political directives. The discussion at this stage is analogous with the discussion in the first phase of the Defence Review Committee in NATO, with the Directorate-General roughly in the position of the military commanders, and the national delegations adopting rather a similar general stance in relation to the international staff. At the conclusion of this process the draft proposal (c.f. Force Goal), in the form of a Commission initiative, will have emerged.

The second phase of the co-ordination of policy in the EEC is dominated by the confrontation of policy between national positions and between them and the views of the international institution. It begins when the Commission itself (now thirteen senior international civil servants), following the so-called *collegiate* principle,[26] decides to accept the proposal, and send it on to the Council of Ministers for decision: any General Report of the Communities contains an account of the wide-ranging proposals which are sent by the Commission, in its role as initiator of Community legislation, to the Council, the main decision-making body and law-maker in the Community (it makes around 300 *regulations* per annum). The Commission proposal is then forwarded to the Committee of Permanent. Representatives, which now, in its formal deliberations, begins the process of evaluating the acceptability of the proposal for its members. This is a second style of work of the Representatives, quite different from the first, co-operative, informal style: they are now in the position of obtaining politically informed reactions from home governments, in response to the Commission's proposal, which are analogous with the country force plans of the members of NATO. In addition delegations submit them to their own experts and consult relevant interest groups: they may also seek clarification and possibly modification from the Commission. In its formal meetings the committee, and supporting sub-committees, will attempt to reconcile national views on the proposal, and, if successful, the agreed draft will be approved without reference to the Council: if agreement cannot be established the *confrontation*, in the presence of Commission representatives, will be transferred to a meeting of full Council. At both Committee and Council levels national ministries are fully engaged; as with country *force plans* the political element is now very evident. It reflects the co-ordinated positions of the ministries in national capitals. The dual role of the delegations which focus upon the Committee of Permanent Representatives as informal advisers to the Commission and as forums for the confrontation of policy is a crucial mechanism in reconciling the international goals of the international organisation and the interests of member states.

The Commission's proposals do not always enter new territory. A particular proposal may be the latest in a series of linked proposals which seek to expand co-ordination in a focussed area. For instance, regulation (EEC) No. 1439/74 of the Council of 4 June 1974 on common rules for imports and dumping, referred to eleven previous regulations (all passed since 1968) in the same area, and each of these followed from a Commission proposal. The Commission is therefore aware, because of past experience and because of its consultations at the time, of the likely response of the states to its proposals. But, in some areas, where the initiative does break new ground, the proposal may be extremely contentious, as with the proposal to transfer responsibility for trade arrangements with East European countries to the Community,[27] and in this case, the confrontation of policy may be prolonged. (Under these circumstances it would take place at Council level or even at a Summit Meeting.) In new areas, in particular, the package deal technique may be an aspect of confrontation: several proposals, which may be in different areas, are linked together by the Commission in a total package. States are persuaded to give concessions to other states on some proposals contained in the package in order to gain concessions from them on proposals from which they expect to benefit. Package deals are invariably made at Council level. The two stages of confrontation, in the Committee of Permanent Representatives and the Council, are broadly analogous with the stage in NATO of discussions between national staffs and delegations on country force plans, and the stage of the final examination of national positions, respectively.

The third stage of co-ordination follows the making of the regulation in the Council, which is analogous with the acceptance of the NATO force plan by the Defence Policy Planning Committee and the Council. There are, however, important differences between the consequences of having passed the regulation and having adopted the Force Plan, although there are a number of interesting 'functional equivalents'. An EEC regulation has a legal status, in that it is directly binding on members, and on individuals and groups within the state, whereas the NATO force plan is not so binding. As was discovered, the latter is a useful pressure in the agreed direction and keeps states very aware of common goals and the problems of others, but there is no way of enforcing its conclusion. A regulation, on the other hand, *requires* changes in the behaviour of the actors to which it is addressed which are reinforced by the law of the Community: disobedience may lead to the instigation of proceedings against the offender and the use of legal sanctions. The practical results of a successful act of co-ordination are therefore very obvious.

The lack of compulsion behind the Force Plan finds a functional equivalent, however, in a trade-off in a large number of EEC regulations between, on the one side the legal requirement to introduce specified changes, and, on the other, the establishment of a range of so-called *safeguard procedures*. The states often include in the co-ordinated programme a statement on the circumstances in which they might avoid implications or consequences which they judge to be undesirable. Although the immediate pressures to co-ordinate are certainly stronger in the EEC than in NATO, states generally retain the right in both contexts to protect themselves from changes which they might come to dislike.

There are a wide range of safeguard procedures in the Treaty of Rome, and in regulations, by means of which states seek to protect their status as separate actors in the co-ordinated system. These largely refer to courses of action which are open to states in emergency situations such as a severe adverse balance of payments.[28] There are, however, general reservations and exclusions; for instance, all the

Community's regulations which allow employees and self-employed persons to reside in another member's territory, to work there, and to receive social welfare benefits equivalent to those received by nationals are subject to the terms of Article 48, paragraph 3, which allows states to exclude individuals on 'grounds of public policy, public security or public health'. Article 9 of the Council's Directive of 17 December 1974, which greatly strengthened the rights of 'nationals of a member state to remain in the territory of another member state after having pursued therein an activity in a self-employed capacity', repeated the term of Article 48 in stating that 'member states may not derogate from the provisions of this directive save on grounds of public policy, public security or public health'.[29] States also refused in the Rome Treaty, to allow nationals the right to take employment in 'reserved' occupations, such as the civil service[30]: in Germany university teachers are civil servants, in France teachers, nurses and even postmen are counted as civil servants, and hence, these are occupations in which non-nationals cannot be employed. Another exclusion from the terms of the rules of the Community, perhaps less surprisingly, are goods or information deemed essential to national security[31]; a list of products which were judged relevant to national security was drawn up by the Council in 1959, as required by article 223 (para. 3), but it has not been published.[32] These various exclusions, limitations and safeguards, do, however, together constitute a formidable legal defence of the interests of national actors against unacceptable inroads from the Communities.

A typical arrangement of safeguard procedures may be found in the context of the commercial policy in the regulation of 4 June 1974 on common rules for imports.[33] In the preamble member states are empowered, provided that their actions are on an interim basis, to take protective measures individually. The regulation adds to the list of liberalised products, that in the event of changes in the trading patterns which 'threaten to cause injury to Community producers' (article 7), such as dumping, a three-stage procedure may be instituted.[34] The first is surveillance, which requires importers to obtain a licence from member states; second is action by the Commission to limit the offending imports (article 12); the third is action by member states (article 14),[35] which may also be taken where such measures are justified by a protective clause contained in a bi-lateral agreement between the member states and a third country. (Art. 14, r (b))
In the third procedure, the Community must be consulted after steps have been taken at the national level, but in the second procedure the

states may require the Commission to act within five days (Art. 12, para 4). The Council has the right to override any action proposed by the Commission (Art. 12, para 5). In the event of disagreement between members and Commission about the gravity of the situation the Commission is liable in practice to accept the members view. The member states are therefore placed in a strong position because of their ability to trigger a Community procedure, and to challenge it through the Council if they disapprove of it, and by their right to act unilaterally if they judge it necessary, without much fear of effective action by the international organisation.

The position of the states in relation to a co-ordinated programme in the EEC is, therefore, not as unlike that in NATO as would appear at first sight. Indeed, there are a number of similarities at various stages of the co-ordination process, and quite a number of functional equivalents. In both cases, however, co-ordination emerges as a distinctive style of inter-governmental co-operation. This helps to establish the wide variety of forms of the latter. It is not just of a single type, to be contrasted, sharply with supranationalism, but rather, as is suggested by the approach of this volume, is part of a wide spectrum of styles of co-operation between governments.

Notes

1. For a further account of the work of the O.E.E.C. see Diebold, William Jr., *Trade and Payments in Western Europe*, New York, Harper, 1952; see also chapter 8 on harmonization above.
2. See Peter Bachrach and Morton Baratz, *Power and Poverty: Theory and Practice*, London, Oxford University Press, 1974, pp. 17–30.
3. See William Wallace (RAPPORTEUR), 'The Administration Implications of Economic and Monetary Union within the European Community' in *Journal of Common Market Studies*, Vol. XII, No. 4, 1974, p. 431.
4. See Hugo Young, *The Sunday Times*, London, September 26th 1976, p. 16 for a comparison of the British Department of Education and Science's differing reaction to scrutiny by a team from the House of Commons, and by a visiting delegation from OECD.
5. Milton Esman and Daniel S. Cheever, *The Common Aid Effort*, Ohio State University Press, 1967, p. 252.
6. *Ibid.*, p. 252.
7. See M. Palmer, John Lambert, et al., *European Unity: A Survey of the European Organizations*, London, Allen and Unwin, 1968, pp. 88–89.
8. The following section on the NATO Force Plan is based mainly on informal interviews conducted during two visits to NATO Headquarters in March 1976. A brief account will be found in NATO Information Service, *Facts and Figures*, Brussels, October 1971, pp. 95–99.
9. G.L. Goodwin, NATO, *The Functional Approach to the Problem of Community Building*, unpublished memorandum, p.14.

10. *Ibid.*, p. 16.
11. *Ibid.*, p. 26.
12. *Introduction* to *Ministerial Guidance 1975*, Annex to M–DPC–1(75) 11, Brussels, 1975, p. 5.
13. G.L. Goodwin, loc. cit., p. 28.
14. See Leon N. Lindberg, 'Integration as a Source of Stress on the European Community System', *International Organization*, Vol. XX, No. 2, Boston, Spring 1966, pp. 233–265.
15. See Confederalism chapter 14 below.
16. See Roy Pryce, *The Politics of the European Community*, London, Butterworth, 1973, p. 67.
17. *Ibid.*, pp. 67–69.
18. The following section is based in part on interviews conducted in the Commission, and in the Office of the British Delegation, in March and April 1976.
19. Communique of Meeting of the Heads of Government of the Community, Paris, 9–10 December 1974, as in *Eighth General Report on the Activities of the European Communities*, Brussels, 1975, Paragraph 3, p. 297.
20. *Ibid.*, para. 7, p. 298.
21. *Ibid.*, Para. 6.
22. See The Declaration of the Heads of State or Government in *Sixth General Report on the Activities of the Communities*, 1972, Brussels, February 1973, pp. 14–15.
23. See account of the Action Programme in *Sixth General Report on the Activities of the Communities* (1 May 1962 – 31 March 1963), Brussels, June 1963, pp. 21–26.
24. The Commissioner in charge from January 1977 is M. Ortoli.
25. See European Community Information Service, *Commercial Policy of the European Community*, Brussels, January 1973, p. 5.
26. See E. Noel, O.B.E., *How the European Community's Institutions Work,* Community Topic, 39, Brussels, 1974, pp. 7–9.
27. See Ralf Dahrendorf, 'The Foreign Policy of the EEC', *The World Today,* Royal Institute of International Affairs, London, 1973.
28. See Article 73, *Treaty Establishing the European Economic Community.*
29. *Official Journal of the European Communities*, 20 January 1975, (75/34/EC), No. L.14, p. 12.
30. Article 48, para. 4.
31. Article 223.
32. According to advice given to the author by the Legal Section of the European Communities, October 1975.
33. Official Journal of the European Communities, No.L.159, 15 June 1974. Regulation, (EEC) No. 1439/74 of the Council.
34. *Ibid.*, p.3.
35. *Ibid.*, p.5.

Selected Reading

1. Helen Wallace, William Wallace, Carole Webb, (editors), *Policy Making in The European Communities*, London, Wiley, 1977.
2. Francis A. Beer, *Integration and Disintegration in NATO: Processes of Alliance Cohesion and Prospects for Atlantic Community,*

Columbus, Ohio State Press, 1969.

3. Robert S. Jordan (editor), *Multinational Cooperation: Economic, Social and Scientific Development*, London and New York, Oxford University Press, 1972.

4. Robert W. Cox (editor), *The Politics of International Organization Studies in Multilateral Social and Economic Agencies*, New York, Praeger, 1970.

5. Peter Busch and Donald Puchala, 'Interests, Influence and Integration: Political Structure in the European Communities', *Comparative Political Studies*, Vol. 9, No. 3, October 1976, pp. 235–254.

6. Robert W. Cox and Harold K. Jacobson, *The Anatomy of Influence: Decision-making in International Organization*, New Haven and London, Yale University Press, 1974.

CHAPTER TEN

ELEMENTS OF SUPRANATIONALISM: THE POWER AND AUTHORITY OF INTERNATIONAL INSTITUTIONS

Paul Taylor

The concept of supranationalism concerns the interplay between the state and international institutions. It has been most frequently used in discussions of relations between states in the developed world and international institutions which are thought to have interfered in some sense with the traditional pattern of exclusive control by state authorities of their own internal governmental affairs. The concept raises questions about the power and authority of international institutions and about the way in which developments there may have weakened the authority of states and their capacity to survive in their traditional form. The question is also raised of whether supranationalism may in some sense have served the interests of the state, by helping it to adapt to the ever increasing demands and expectations of its citizens and the changing circumstances of international society.

Beloff writes that 'what supranationalism means is that there is a recognised interest within a political grouping of several nations which is different from, or dinstinguishable from, the interests of any one of them and which thus claims institutional expression.'[1] Such a recognition is fundamental in the circumstances of supranationalism; it affects the authority of the international institution, the role allowed to it by the states, and its methods of taking decisions. Beloff adds that 'the difficulty lies not in the conception of policy but in its authorisation and execution.'[2] Supranationalism depends upon the states willingness to allow the international institution a range of powers and an area of independent initiative which are comensurate with the allocated tasks.

Powers are allocated in specific, limited areas, to a new centre. Decisions are taken there by a majority voting system of some sort, and their execution is supervised by the international institution, rather than by the state. A number of developments in the areas of law, organisation, communication and attitudes are found in relations between the states, which both follow from the authority of the international institution and help to sustain it. In sum, supranationalism consists of a pyramid of interrelated elements at the peak of which is majority voting in an international institution, which reflects the dominance of the latter over member states in a limited functional area. In this chapter these elements are considered, and their role in the development of the authority of international institutions is evaluated. Examples are taken mainly from the experience of the European Communities, though as will become evident, the Communities in its present form are not themselves a supranational organisation.[3]

There are three headings under which the following discussion of the main elements of supranationalism are organised. They reflect a convenient way of organising the materials and ideas in relation to the two main actors involved in the relationship, the international institution and the state. The relationship is seen as having two main components in its impact on the latter. The first heading therefore, refers to changes in the structure and powers of the international institution; the second refers to challenges to the exclusive competence of the state in its own territory; the third refers to challenges to the separateness or 'integrity' of the decision-making structures in the states. The last two categories should perhaps be explained in greater detail.

They reflect two facets of the sovereignty of states which are affected by supranationalism. The first (the second heading) is the exclusive competence of a government within its territorial frontiers which is generally understood and widely accepted as essential in sovereignty. In the United Kingdom it means that laws passed by Parliament prevail within the frontiers of that country, and that laws passed by, for instance, the French government, have no legal standing and will not be upheld by British courts. A discussion of supranationalism should be concerned with the possible effects of the work of international institutions upon this exclusive competence of the state.

The second (the third heading) is the integrity of decision-making structures in the state. It is possible to conceive of circumstances in which the decision-making structures of the state are so affected or controlled by outside forces that the legal effect of *exclusive* competence disguises a *de facto* subjection to external control. The elites of one state may subscribe to an ideology which disposes them normally to follow detailed instructions from another 'government' or agency outside its frontiers. It is conceivable that the members of one government could be in effect placed in office by another government, and, habitually follow the others instructions because of loyalty, physical dependence, or bribery. An example of this would be the Nazi-dominated government of Austria before the invasion by Hitler of 1938. The exclusive competence of the government to make laws for its territory was perserved, but the integrity of the government had been so undermined that the legal forms concealed a *de facto* breach of sovereignty. It is conceivable that a breach of the integrity of national decision-making structures could result from an accumulation of pressures and interventions from international institutions, like the IMF, or international non-governmental institutions, like the oil companies, or large foreign corporations, like Lockheed. It is, however, extremely difficult to judge the point at which a government's ability to control its own affairs had been so reduced that it could be said that it faced serious challenge to this aspect of its sovereignty. A situation in which more than 50% of a national budget was allocated according to the wishes of foreign businessmen, who were bribing national officials, might be accepted as constituting such a challenge. But a single intervention, such as the much discussed letter sent to the International Monetary Fund (IMF) by the British Government in 1967, which allowed IMF inspection of British Treasury activities, is not enough. An increasing range of interventions in the internal affairs of states could, however, have implications for sovereignty which are similar to those which follow from the placing of personnel by an out-side power, or the subjection of the state's own personnel to an ideology through which they could be manipulated.

This argument illustrates the point that sovereignty has two facets, first an exclusive competence, and, second, the relative independence of law-making entities from outside intervention. A discussion of supranationalism should be concerned with both of these facets in that they represent fronts on which sovereignty may be actually or potentially challenged. In this chapter groups of elements of supranationalism are organised so that they can be related to each in turn. They are concerned respectively with *legal* questions and with the development of transnational *political* systems. They are considered after an examination of the supranational elements which have been found in the international institutions themselves. The stages of the argument are set out in brief at the end of this chapter.

The governing bodies of international institutions normally have two major elements, a group of international civil servants, and a group of state representatives, where decisions are taken on the basis of either unanimity or majority voting. A third element is sometimes found: an assembly of delegates from national parliaments which support one or other of the main bodies, provide additional expertise, and in some cases try to ensure accountability. Distinctive, supranational features, have been found in each of these elements. In this chapter attention is focussed on the first two.

In the case of the group of international civil servants factors conducive towards supranationalism are those which allow the definition and pursuit of policies which reflect the longer term common interests of member states and which transcend their short-term individual interests. Support for supranationalism is found, first, in the condition of independence of the secretariat. In the case of the European Communities the independence of the members of the High Authority and of the Commission was required by the founding Treaties of Paris and of Rome. The Treaty of Paris, which established the European Coal and Steel Community (ECSC), contained one of the few instances of the actual use in a treaty of the term *supranationalism*, and it is significant that it is used in the context of discussing the requirement of independence of members of the High Authority: they 'will refrain from any action incompatible with the supranational character of their duties. Each member state undertakes to respect the supranational character.' (Article 9, ECSC.) Although the term is not mentioned in the article which replaced Article 9 (ECSC) in the Treaty of Merger of April 1965, under which the High Authority of the ECSC and the Commission of the European Economic Community (EEC) and EURATOM were merged, members were still told that they shall 'in the general interest of the Communities be completely independent in the performance of their duties.' (Merger Treaty, Article 10, paragraph 2); and that 'they shall neither seek nor take instructions from any government or from any other body,' and 'shall refrain from any action incompatible with their duties.' (Merger Treaty, Article 10, paragraph 2). As Professor Mathijsen has pointed out these conditions underline the requirement that the High Authority and the Commission should represent 'the Communities' *general* interest and must be in a position to take a stand against any government which tries to put national interests first.'[4]

A further condition of independence of the Secretariat and one which may be of great importance in allowing it to strive actively for the general interest is a measure of budgetary independence. In the case of the European Coal and Steel Community this independence was established from the beginning by allowing the Community the right to its own finance from a tax directly levied on the coal and steel industries of member states. In the case of the EEC the acquiring of a right to independent finance took a considerable number of years: the EEC and EURATOM depended upon the contributions of member governments until the mid 1970s. It was only with the Council of Ministers' decision of 21 April, 1970, that steps were taken towards the granting to these two institutions of their 'own resources'. By 1976 considerable progress had been made towards the removal of the Communities from dependence on the member governments' contributions by allowing them finance from the levies on food imports and tariffs on imports of manufactured goods from third countries. There was, however, continuing uncertainty about the percentage of value added tax — the third source of the Communities own resources according to the 1970 decision — which should go directly to Brussels.

These conditions of independence are only significant in so far as they are exploited by the members of the Secretariat. Less tangible factors such as the quality of leadership in the institution, its energy and even its mood also play a role. The independence of members of the Secretariat from direct instructions from governments is, however, a *sine qua non*. But a Walter Hallstein or a Jean Monnet can be decisive in the definition and pursuit of interests which are separable from those of the states.

Methods of exercising control in international institutions, in committees of intergovernmental representatives or international civil servants, are frequently thought to be good indicators of supranationalism. Reynolds writes that 'the word supranational is of relatively recent origin and refers to institutions which have been created for the performance of specific functions, and which have power to take decisions binding on the members whether they have participated in the decision or not.'[5] He refers to the High Authority of ECSC as one example of such decision-making, and also the Committee of Ministers of Western European Union, which could, in certain circumstances, prevent, by majority voting, the United Kingdom from reducing the level of her forces in Western Germany below an agreed level. The voting arrangements of the Council of Ministers of the EEC, according to the original form of the Rome Treaty, would also qualify as evidence of that institution's supranationalism. There are, therefore, two situations in which a member could be said not to have participated in a decision taken by an international institution: the first would be when a binding decision is taken by a group of international civil servants according to rules previously agreed to by member states (as with the High Authority); the second is when the decision is taken by a committee of representatives of national governments according to a system of majority voting. Conversely, member states participate in a decision when it is taken by a committee of governmental representatives on the basis of unanimity or on the basis of a system which gives them the right to say whether they will accept a decision which has been taken by other members. A *binding* decision is one which is not only taken according to the agreed forms and procedures, and is therefore binding in the legal sense, but is also effective in the sense that it is carried out.

Executive committees of international civil servants and of government representatives may take decisions by majority vote which have two major kinds of effect: either the decision upholds a framework of policies or arrangements already approved by governments, for instance, in a founding treaty, or it initiates new arrangements and policies. The High Authority and the Commission's decision-making role was the quasi-legal one of supporting arrangements already approved by governments rather than of initiating new elements of the framework. The institutions of the European Communities do, however, possess a power which is regarded as supranational, even in the taking of decisions of this kind: governments agreed that the institutions should act directly in relation to individuals and groups within the state without immediate supervision by state authorities (the legal framework and its implications are discussed more fully below). The High Authority acted to impose the rules of the common market in coal steel and scrap, as agreed by the states which signed the Treaty of Paris. Even in this role, however, the record of the High Authority was rather mixed: it failed, for instance, to obtain in the 1950s the rearrangement of West German coal selling cartels which seemed necessary to the proper working of the common market in coal. The Commission of the European Communities also takes decisions independently only in areas already agreed by member governments: although it is the main initiator of community legislation it does not decide what changes should be accepted. That task is reserved to the intergovernmental Council.

The existence of majority voting in a committee of government representatives may be misleading as an indicator of supranationalism. The committee should not have a *permanent* majority and an *unchanging* minority — it should have a *fluid* majority voting system — and should be backed by communication procedures, attitudes and structures which sustain a general confidence in the majority vote. A majority voting system such as that in the General Assembly of the United Nations could not be said to be supranational; one indication of this is that its decisions are mainly in the form of recommendations; another is the lack of fluidity among majority groups in relation to a wide range of issues. Minorities and majorities tend to solidify and to become either sullen, or over-impressed with the validity of their positions. In addition, of course, the lack of a sufficient consensus among states leads to majority votes being discounted or judged as trivial or irresponsible. It may also, as in Western European Union, lead to a deliberate avoidance of the possibility of majority voting. The British decision to reduce the size of her forces in Wester Germany in the late 1950s, in order to concentrate on nuclear weapons, was not put to the vote in WEU, although the institution was legally entitled to stop such reductions by qualified majority. The states lacked sufficient confidence in each other: the institution therefore lacked the authority to act in this situation. In the EEC the Council of Ministers has also retained the principle of unanimity (see qualification of this in Chapter 9 above), and the Communities lack this critical element of supranationalism. Although a range of independent powers in administering an agreed framework may be accepted as an element of supranationalism, the ability to take decisions by a fluid majority which initiates new policies and structures is a more convincing indication.

Rigid majority voting systems may indeed help to destroy the foundations on which a more fluid system might be built. They may help to amplify the disagreements of contending groups and discourage the use of the mechanisms for reconciling their interests, and the development of linking structures, and the softening of hostile attitudes. They lead to mere vote-counting by the majority, rather than consensus building.

The argument is now concerned with elements of a supranationalism which relate to the facet of the integrity of decision-making structures, and the development of transnational political systems. (I turn to the legal facet below.)

The structures which link states with each other and with the international institution are the mechanism through which the common interests are expressed. They reflect and generate interdependence amongst states, particularly among the developed states, which now find that their search for economic stability and for increases in the level of welfare can only be satisfied within a cooperative framework. Andrew Shonfield has picked out some aspects of these structures of interdependence in the context of the European Communities and discusses their implications. He writes that 'the dramatic improvement in communications, the greatly increased mobility of people and money, and also the huge concentration of corporate power in the hands of international businesses, taken together, demand the establishment of a new dimension of international public power. At the same time there is a parallel movement, less obvious, but beginning to be significant, among the associations of private and professional persons — farmers, trade unionists, certain scientists, even specialist professional civil servants, who find that the natural links for much of what they wish to accomplish are with their professional colleagues abroad rather than with their own national governments. The transnational lobbies that are thus created look for some international political counterpart'. 'Now I call this amalgam of private groups and agencies transcending national frontiers, together with the official political agencies that have been established in and around the European Community supranational'.[6] Shonfield also points out that these structures do not stand above governments, but include parts of them.

The structures which have developed across national frontiers in Western Europe are certainly numerous (about 300 examples of one type of structure, interest groups, have been counted in Brussels) but they have not as yet developed their full potential as elements of supranationalism. The reason is that groups which are active in attempting to affect immediately the allocation of values still concentrate their efforts at the national level, and have developed rather weak umbrella organisations at the European level. That they have been able to develop mechanisms for articulating a residual common European interest is an achievement which should not be underestimated but transnational structures are often divided within themselves on national lines about a large number of more salient

223

issues. Their common interest is as yet clearly defined rather infrequently, and rarely exists in a form which could be sought without reservation by various parts of the groups at the national and international level.

Many tests of the emergence of such structures as stronger elements of supranationalism are conceivable. One possibility concerns the attitude of the various sub-systems in the structure to the distribution of resources: on the one side the sub-system might be expected to come to rely on obtaining resources from the international level, and to perceive that its activities at that level produced appropriate reward; on the other side the members of the sub-system should be prepared to accept variations in the distribution of resources, sometimes to the obvious greater advantage of members of another sub-system. They should, in other words, not see short-term maldistribution as being contrary to the common interest. The more groups within the state which are encouraged to plan on the basis of the expectation of transnational involvement, the stronger the pressure towards strengthening this element of supranationalism. Planning committees attached to groups and governments within the state which regularly called on regional resources for specific projects are particularly likely to learn to think in regional terms and to choose solutions which are compatible with the general interest. They are likely to be more aware of the problems of creating regional resources, be more convinced of the need to manage them efficiently (not, for instance, to over-exploit them in the short term), to be more frequently in touch with the international institution, (and hence aware of its preferred solution), and more understanding of the needs and interests of competing groups in other countries. This is, of course, conditional upon the availability of resources at the supranational level.

The development of a system of supranational structures depends upon and encourages the process of *legitimizing* the values of the supranational institution. The arrangements mentioned by Shonfield have already encouraged the acceptance of goals which may be defined as 'European' into the political cultures of member states: the European solution is something which has become a generally acceptable option, even though it may not always prevail. It is possible for the bureaucrats in European states to consider 'general interest' solutions without putting themselves in danger of being thought to be 'selling out'. It should indeed be stressed that the alternative to a situation in which common values, expressed in this case through an institution, are accepted as legitimate is one in which they are thought to involve betrayal or even treachery. The terminology is suggestive of the fact that the legitimization of the goals of Europe in national political processes involves an amendment of concepts about what was previously thought to be reserved to the nation.

A large number of civil servants and politicians now contact colleagues in corresponding ministries in other states, or in Brussels, as part of the routine processes of decision-making. They do not consider they are betraying their country by doing this and are not so regarded by their colleagues. Even in the inter-war period states were far more sensitive about the kind of information which they were prepared to exchange: in 1922, for instance, only four years after the conclusion of the 'war to end wars', negotiations between France and Britain about the possibility of agreeing contingency plans between General Staffs to cope with any new German attack were broken off by the British on the grounds that such plans involved giving too much away to another country. In NATO West European states now exchange information on security/defence arrangements in a routine way, and similar changes have taken place in the economic area. The legitimization of European values has proceeded rather slowly, but it is easy to overlook the remarkable character of this development: that such values have now been accepted in the European states is a measure of the development of a transnational political system. Conventions in communication have developed between international institutions and member countries, and between member countries themselves, which only a short while ago would have been judged as a betrayal of the sacred interests of the separate nations.

Various pieces of evidence illustrate these developments and the limits upon them in structures and values in Western Europe. The picture of national bureaucrats presented by Feld and Wildgen's statistics is that national bureaucrats prefer specific or limited forms of integration;[7] a substantial group were, however, opposed to political union and rather resented long-term assignment to the Community.[8] Mennis and Sauvant further illustrates the acceptance of the legitimacy of European solutions in their study of German business elite attitudes: they write that 'there are differences of opinion regarding the European Community, but for the most part they concern the degree of regional participation preferred and not the issue of the desirability or legitimacy of European integration itself';[9] 'the issue of whether or not Western European integration is probably a dead one'.[10] At the same time, though, German elites support Europe because it serves their current interests and rewards material and value expectations defined in the existing national settings.[11] The view that European goals have been legitimized (this, of course, does not mean that they are always thought to be correct) is also supported by the fact that the issue of membership in the European Communities has played little part in national elections in the original six member states since the mid-1960s.

Both the EEC and the UN are involved in a legitimization process. But in the United Nations, and indeed in specialized agencies, such as the International Labour Organisation, or the I.M.F., legitimization is a process which results from the accumulation of interstate agreements: it follows from an overwhelming general sanction given by member states, and any measure of support short of this is likely to reduce the level of legitimization by offending opponents. The legitimization process in the United Nations tends to take the form of individual states or groups of states seeking to get their individual policies accepted by overwhelming majorities in the General Assembly. The legitimization of anti-colonialism by the overwhelming adoption of a sweeping anti-colonial declaration in 1960, and subsequently, is a good example of this.[12] In the European Communities, however, the *Commission's proposals* (i.e. those of the institution) are generally legitimized, in the sense that they are usually accepted as constituting an attempt at the general interest, without regard to whether or not they have been approved in the Council. Commission proposals may be regarded as inappropriate, or even just wrong, but they are rarely seen as threatening or partisan. At the same time there is a sense among members of national governments that certain national goals are legitimate whilst some others are out of bounds.[13] The larger number of states with which the UN deals, the nature of the areas within which it is asked to act, and the failure to spell out in the Charter a long term programme of action for the Secretariat, within which it could exercise a right to initiate, are all difficulties in the way of an incremental extension of the area of legitimate supranational action in the United Nations.

The argument is now concerned with elements of supranationalism which affect the second facet of sovereignty: the exclusive legal competence of the state within its own frontiers. They affect the states' monopoly on law-making within its own territory. In its most obvious first form the challenge is in the shape of the development of a rival legal system which has priority over the municipal law of the state within its frontiers. In a second form it consists of changes in attitudes at the popular level which indicate an increasing reluctance

226

on the part of the people of the state to obey the law as handed down to them by their particular government. This second form of the challenge to the exclusive competence of governments touches on some of the arguments in the classic debate on sovereignty such as those contained in John Austin's *Lectures on Jurisprudence*. These arguments are considered shortly. It may be noted here, however, that there is a clear distinction between changes in attitudes which affect, to put the matter in a rather over-simple form, the *loyalty* of citizens — and which may affect the sovereignty of states — and changes in attitudes towards the *purpose* of law, regulation, or decision, which may involve the legitimization of supranational goals in national decision-making systems. Where loyalty is undermined, disobedience is the result; where the purpose of the law is changing as supranational goals are legitimized we may find a perfectly loyal citizenry supporting the increasingly supranational ambitions and objectives of its government, or its agents, and other policy-making elites, in a community system.

The one extent example of the setting up of a rival legal system within the state is, of course, that of the European Communities, although lawyers are by no means agreed on how far this constitutes a threat to national sovereignty. It is clear, however, that the member states of the European Communities now accept that law made by the institutions of the European Communities in Brussels should have direct effect in their territories: Community law is followed by domestic courts without the requirement of any special act of approval by national governments or national assemblies. Furthermore, under the terms of the Treaty of Paris (see, for example, articles 41, 42, 43, 44 and 92) and of the Treaty of Rome (article 177) it is the Court of the Communities which meets at Luxembourg which is the final court of appeal on Community questions and which acts as interpreter of the Treaty. It is not just that Community laws are to have direct effect within national territories but governments are also to lose their right to decide how that law is to be applied and interpreted. In the event of clashes between domestic law and Community law, furthermore, domestic courts are to give precedence to Community law (in the UK according to section 2(4) European Communities Act). In order to ensure compliance with Community law, institutions such as the High Authority and the Commission are given extensive powers under the founding treaties: the High Authority had a particularly wide range of powers to fine firms which broke the rules of the ECSC (see articles 65 and 66) and 'decisions of the High Authority which impose a pecuniary obligation shall be enforceable . . . Enforcement may be suspended only be a decision of the Court' (of the ECSC) (article 92). The Commission may also act directly, without the legal intervention of national governments, in areas such as those covered by articles 85 and 86 (EEC) on cartels, concentrations and abuse of dominant position. It is this unique character of the law of the Communities, together with the powers of Community institutions to enforce and interpret that law, which some lawyers have considered to be the most important, supranational element of the Communities.[14]

There are, however, various difficulties in the way of evaluating implications for the sovereignty of states of this penetration of national legal systems by the Communities, though the very existence of such difficulties is some measure of the challenge to traditional ideas about sovereignty. That there exists a body external to the member states which makes, enforces, and interprets law, which is directly applicable in the states in the areas covered by the founding treaties, cannot be denied; and the conclusion that this represents a challenge to the exclusive competence of the state to make law in its own territory seems to follow in a straightforward fashion. But the difficulties are, first, that it is the Council of Ministers which in effect makes the law by its regulations, directives and decisions, and this institution is made up of representatives of member governments who act on the basis of unanimity. (Member governments *do* in fact agree to Community laws which are to operate within their frontiers, although when they do so they are acting in a Community institution); second, that national assemblies, such as the British Parliament, agreed, when they allowed Community law to operate in their states, merely, to restrain themselves from challenging that law. 'What has really happened is that Parliament (in the UK) has identified an area within which Community legislative power will operate. Within that area Parliament intends to refrain from exercising its own legislative power.'[15] (The conclusion is that Community law is allowed its status in the United Kingdom by an Act of Parliament, and that Parliament could equally change that status. In some EEC states the rejection of Community law would involve the special processes of constitutional amendment); third, states could under international law decide unilaterally that they are no longer bound by the Treaties of Rome and Paris, and, if they did this, though the political consequences would be serious, there would be little that their partners could do.

The conclusion is that as governments and national assemblies at various points in the establishment of the basic agreements, and in the drawing up of the detailed, day to day, decisions, agree to be bound, they could equally disagree to be bound — they could take back what they have given and, the argument runs, this does not amount to a breach of sovereignty. The procedures are novel, the Community legal system is indeed unique, and may be justifiably called supranational, but it is still an expression of the states' adjustment to new conditions: it serves them, at their discretion. In this argument, again, the supranational elements help states to survive rather than tend to replace them in new integrated structures.

There is, therefore, a contradiction between the appearance in contemporary Western Europe that the exclusive competence of states has been undermined by the Communities' legal system — and national sovereignty therefore breached — and the various legal safeguards to which states can in theory resort if that legal system displeases them. One way of resolving the contradiction is suggested by the idea of 'entrenchment':[16] the safeguards remain as possibilities but resort to them becomes increasingly unlikely because of the accumulation of adjustments in national laws and habits of law-making to take account of the Communities' legal system. The latter is, therefore, *entrenched* in the national legal system; it becomes increasingly difficult, though legally perfectly possible, to revise the mass of national legislation so that it could be separated from Community law. The idea of entrenchment applies particularly to the United Kingdom's adjustment to membership in the European Communities: the European Communities' Bill did not immediately deprive Parliament of a legal sovereignty, but entrenchment would in practice in time make it increasingly unlikely that Parliament would reassert itself in the areas of law-making transferred to the Communities. This could lead to a *de facto* limitation or loss of sovereignty. The penetration of national legal systems by legal systems managed by an international institution, as has happened in the Communities, together with the possibility of entrenchment, are further elements of the supranational relationship between international institutions and states.

Entrenchment, though discussed most frequently in the context of Britain's relationship with the EEC, is also an important aspect of the relationship between other member states and the Communities. Even in those countries where international treaties, such as the Treaties of Rome and Paris, become a part of the national constitution, there is no certainty of continued adherence to the treaties: withdrawal is made rather more difficult, in that it requires special processes. But the practice of assimilating treaty obligations into constitituons should be seen as a way of encouraging the same elements of obligation and commitment which, it is hoped by supporters of European integration, will prevail in the United Kingdom, namely, the process of entrenchment. Continued adherence to the Treaties of the European Communities depends upon that process, regardless of whether the treaties are assimilated into the constitution or not, the major difference being that withdrawal from the treaties would involve the slightly more complicated procedure of constitutional amendment, whereas in the United Kingdom withdrawal could be effected by the normal processes of legislation.

The process of developing international institutions envisaged by Hammarskjold is surprisingly similar in some respects, as is the process of maintaining international 'regimes', such as is found in international monetary and financial arrangements. Hammarskjold spoke of the need to build in international society a sophisticated 'constitutionalism', and to move away gradually from the present 'primitive institutionalism'.[17] He saw this sophisticated constitutionalism in the building of conventions about appropriate procedure, for instance, in the event of threats to the peace; he envisaged the construction of an increasingly dense network of accepted practice focused upon the United Nations by which governments would manage international society. Entrenchment is found in this case in the way in which the conventions of international government are gradually built into the processes and structures of national governments, and in the way in which an increasing part of national law, particularly, in the first instance, in public administration and commerce, is made in the light of emerging international practice. Two levels of governmental practice and law are detected, the higher one in international society, being developed and strengthened by involvement and entrenchment in the lower one, at the national level. These ideas clearly reflect Hammarskjold's interest in the *regulation* of relations between the nation state members of international society, and his acceptance of a Lockean model of man's, and the nation's, involvement in society.

Another way of resolving the contradictions between the appearance of a breach of sovereignty, such as is suggested by the penetration of national legal systems by the legal system of the Communities, and the existence of continuing legal safeguards for state governments and assemblies, is the refocusing of popular loyalties away from national governments towards international institutions. In this situation sovereignty could be said to have been lost by the state, and the supranational character of the international institution strengthened as a direct challenge to the state's survival, by the reluctance of citizens to obey national law and their willingness to obey the 'law' of the international institution. The contradiction is thus resolved in favour of the international institution by removing from the state an essential element in its sovereignty: the loyalty of its citizens. The exclusive competence of the state to make laws for its own territory is challenged not directly by external intervention, but from within by a weakening of its authority.

The concern here is not so much with the evidence of actual changes, but more with their implications if they do happen. The writings of John Austin are one useful starting point for this discussion. They describe the role of popular loyalties in the sovereignty of the state.

He writes that 'if a determinate human superior not in a habit of obedience to a like superior, receives habitual obedience from the bulk of a given society, that determinate superior is sovereign in that society, and the society (including the superior) is a society political and independent.'[18] 'The generality of the given society must be in the habit of obedience to a determinate and common superior.'[19] Austin makes the point that the sovereign of a state cannot be the subject of any higher law giver. But Austin also says that he is sovereign in his state because his citizens are in the habit of obedience. It is indeed surprising that so many students of sovereignty have concluded with MacIver that Austin's notion of sovereignty involved 'an extreme master-servant relationship'. 'More like a slave-plantation or a menagerie than the actuality of political life.'[20] Austin does in fact reinforce the meaning of his 'habit of obedience' when he points out that 'all obedience is voluntary or free. . . That acquiescene which is purely involuntary, or which is purely the consequence of physical compulsion or restraint, is not obedience or submission . . . in every society political and independent, people are determined by motives of some description or another, to obey their government habitually.'[21] The motives for following the habit of obedience are found in two circumstances of the state: first that the membership of the sovereign entity partially overlaps that of the subject; second that both sovereign and subject are liable to common traditions and experiences within their state which produce mutually accepted 'principles and maxims'[22]; in almost every independent political society there are principles or maxims expressly adopted or tacitly accepted by the sovereign and which the sovereign habitually observes. The act of a sovereign may be judged 'unconstitutional' or otherwise wrong (though not illegal), if it contravenes those principles of morality or constitutionality which are found among law-makers and which the subjects have themselves habitually recognized and supported.

Austin's arguments point to the possibility that as a sovereignty is dependent upon a 'habit of obedience' so the weakening of that habit may undermine sovereignty. The development over a period of time of new habits, traditions, and generally accepted 'principles and maxims' could support the emergence of a new sovereign. If international institutions, by ensuring the regular involvement of citizens and increasing their rewards, succeed in attracting popular loyalties they may over a period of time succeed in creating a 'habit of obedience' to themselves at the expense of the sovereign states. This constitutes a further possible element in a supranational relationship between international institutions and the state.

These then are the major interrelated elements of supranationalism. In this chapter they have been deduced mainly from the experience of the European Communities, but it is apparent that they have not been fully realised, and the Communities could not be said to be supranational. Its central organisation in Brussels lacks many of the powers, and the background resources of supranationalism. It may be, indeed, that the elements of supranationalism outlined here can only appear when the scope of integration is rather narrow. The wider the scope of the enterprise, the more diluted the elements of supranationalism become. This is because as scope increases, supranationalism gets closer to Federalism: while supranationalism, as partial Federalism, serves the existing states — it helps them to adapt to new needs and problems — Federalism challenges their existence fundamentally. States might, therefore, be expected to resist any tendency for partial Federalism to turn into Federalism. In practice even the ECSC was short of several essential features of supranationalism, particularly a body which could take decisions on the basis of a majority voting system which could initiate new structures or principles of policy: it bore the same relationship to supranationalism as was borne by the League of Nations to the idea of collective security — an ideal which was not attained.

The main components of the argument are set out in schematic form below.

Summary of Elements of Supranationalism

Recognition of a general interest

a) *International Actor*
   1. Independence of international civil servants from instructions of national governments.
   2. Financial independence.
   3. Voting on policy initiatives by 'fluid' majorities.
   4. An effective leadership and bouyant mood in the international secretariat.

b) *National Actor: Integrity of Decision-Making*
   1. Development of extensive procedures for consultation about the general interest linking governmental and non-governmental institutions.
   2. Legitimization of goals of the international institution in the national and collective systems.
   3. Focus upon international institutions in order to obtain 'supranational' resources: acceptance of temporary discrimination in favour of other sub-systems.

c) *National Actor: Exclusive Competence*
   1. Penetration of national legal system by extra-national legal system of the international institution.
   2. Allowing to international institution of decision-making capacity to maintain common legal system within states.
   3. Development of 'entrenchment' of legal system.
   4. Development of habit of obedience to new international actor: 'compliance'.

Notes

1. Max Beloff, in Carol Ann Cosgrove & Kenneth Twitchett (eds.), *The New International Actors*, London, Macmillan, 1970, p.95.
2. *Ibid.*, p. 95.
3. One of the earliest references to the concept is to be found in the Fabian Society's Draft Treaty, described in L.S. Woolf: *Framework of a Lasting Peace*, London, Allen & Unwin, 1917, although in this case it is 'supernationalism'. The purpose was to construct a supranational authority which would be made up of two components, an International High Court to deal with 'legal' or 'justiciable' disputes, and an International Council, which would help to codify international law and mediate or arbitrate in political disputes. The system was to be supported by a variety of covenants outlawing war, a comprehensive range of economic sanctions, and a permanent

Secretariat. The scheme had the objective of achieving the 'superordinate' goal of outlawing war. The Fabian Society insisted that 'what is suggested is no merging of independent national units into a "world state", though to this Utopia future ages may well come. No impairment of sovereignty and no sacrifice of independence are proposed.' (p. 92)

4. P.S.R.F. Mathijsen, *A Guide to European Community Law*, London, Sweet & Maxwell, 1972, pp. 139–140.
5. P.A. Reynolds, *An Introduction to International Relations*, London, Longman, 1971, p. 26.
6. Andrew Shonfield, *Europe: Journey to an Unknown Destination*, Harmondsworth, Penguin Books, 1972, pp. 16–17.
7. Werner J. Feld and John K. Wildgen, 'National Administration Elites and European Integration: Saboteurs at Work?', *Journal of Common Market Studies*, March, 1975, Vol. XIII, No. 3, p. 255.
8. Of the 81% which said that they felt pressure to conform with the 'norms' of their departments only 44% favoured political union, whilst of these 68% favoured economic union. *Ibid.*, p. 260.
9. Bernard Mennis and Karl P. Sauvant, 'Describing and Explaining Support for Regional Integration: An Investigation of German Business Elite Attitudes Towards the European Community', *International Organization*, Autumn, 1975, Vol. 29, No. 4, p. 984.
10. *Ibid.*, p. 984.
11. *Ibid.*, pp. 993–994.
12. See Inis L. Claude, Jr., 'Collective Legitimization as a Political Function of the United Nations', *International Organization*, Summer, 1966.
13. The demand by the British government for a separate seat at the 1976 Paris Conference on basic resources aroused not only political opposition among other EEC members but also a feeling that the British demand was in a deeper sense 'wrong': it was in bad taste, a contravention of the emerging conventions of behaviour in the Communities.
14. See J.D.B. Mitchell, 'Community Legislation', in M.E. Bathurst, K.R. Simmonds, N. March Hunnings and Jane Welch (eds.), *Legal Problems of the an Enlarged European Community*, London, Stevens, 1972, pp. 87–103, especially p. 88.
15. Geoffrey Howe, 'The European Communities Act 1972', *International Affairs*, Vol. 49, No. I, January 1973, p. 6.
16. See J.D.B. Mitchell, S.A. Kuipers and B. Gall, 'Constitutional Aspects of the Treaty and Legislation Relating to British Membership', *Common Market Law Review*, London, Stevens, May 1972, Vol. 9, No. 2, pp. 134–150, especially pp. 143 and 145.
17. See Dag Hammarskjold in Wilder Foote (ed.), *Loc. cit.*, p. 252.
18. John Austin, *Lectures on Jurisprudence: the Philosophy of Positive Law,* abridged and introduced by Robert Campbell, New York, Henry Holt, 1875, p. 82.
19. *Ibid.*, p. 83.
20. R.M. MacIver, *The Modern State*, Oxford, 1926, p. 14.
21. John Austin, *Loc. cit.*, p. 126.
22. John Austin, *Loc. cit.*, p. 106.

Selected Reading

1. Leon L. Lindberg, 'Political Integration as a Multi-Dimensional Phenomenon Requiring Multi-Variate Measurement', *International Organization*, Boston, Vol. XXIV, No. 4, Autumn 1970, pp. 649–731.
2. Ernst B. Haas, *The Uniting of Europe*, (2nd Edition), Stanford University Press, Stanford, 1968.
3. Max Beloff, 'International Integration and the Modern State' in Carol Ann Cosgrove and Kenneth Twitchett (eds.), *The New International Actors*, London, Macmillan, 1970, p. 95.
4. Amitai Etzioni, 'The Dialectics of Supranational Unification', *American Political Science Review,* Vol. LVI, No. 4, pp. 927–935.
5. Francis Rosenstiel, 'Reflections on the Notion of Supranationality', *Journal of Common Market Studies*, November 1963, pp. 127–139.
6. Ronn Kaiser, 'Toward the Copernican Phase of Regional Integration Theory', *Journal of Common Market Studies*, March 1972, pp. 207–232.

CHAPTER ELEVEN

FUNCTIONALISM: THE THEORY OF DAVID MITRANY

Paul Taylor

In this chapter some of the main features of the functionalism of David
Mitrany are considered. His ideas were particularly important in the
development of thinking about the role of international organisation,
and are the starting point of much of modern integration theory. They
should not be confused, however, with functionalism in other fields,
such as sociology, (as in the structure-functionalism of Malinowski)[1]
or in biology. A group of American scholars, now generally called
Neofunctionalists, took Professor Mitrany's ideas as one of the starting
points of their own thinking about integration between states,
particularly in Western Europe.[2] There are also intellectual links
between functionalism and other recently formed islands of theorising
about international organisation and international relations; these
include transnationalism, the world society image of international
relations, and linkage politics.[3] The existence of these links is one
reason for discussing Mitrany's ideas here; another is that in being
analysed and reconsidered, his ideas have sometimes been amended so
far as to lose much of their original form and value; and their influence
among both students and servants of international organisation, which
illustrates a belief in the continuing relevance of the theory of
contemporary problems, is a further justification.

Professor Mitrany produced his writings mainly in the inter-war
period and during the Second World War. His major contribution
appeared in 1943 under the heading of *A Working Peace System*.[4]
Although he produced a number of essays after the War, including one

as late as 1974,[5] his central ideas are from the earlier period.[6] The timing of their emergence is, indeed, of some significance, as is the location of their development: although born a Rumanian in Bucharest in 1888, Professor Mitrany worked and lived most of his life in England and was acquainted there with a number of Fabians and other Liberal-Left scholars such as G.D.H. Cole, Leonard Woolf, Norman Angel and Robert Cecil. His theory reflects a number of assumptions which were also accepted by this group, such as a belief in the desirability of increasing the public provision of welfare for the citizen, and the possibility of 'engineering' improvements in society by deliberate, rational means; he was also impressed by the problems and opportunities produced by economic development. But he reacted strongly against some of the implications of their arguments, which, he thought, would lead to the isolating of states more completely from each other, in the attempt to develop better national welfare schemes, than had previously been the case. Rather, in his vision of a working peace system, he adapted them to the task of bringing states more closely together in fruitful partnership, and by these means eventually outlawing war from international society.

In pursuing this task he was sharply critical of the grand theories of the political/social order of the pre-First World War period, which, he believed, were increasingly inappropriate to the understanding and solution of the pressing problems of a new age, both within the state and in international society.[7] Indeed, in linking together national and international problems, he was one of the first to develop the idea of 'world politics' which is now supported by a number of scholars, such as John Burton, Johan Galtung, James Rosenau, Joseph Nye and others.

Professor Mitrany thought that classical philosophers such as Hume, Burke, Mill, and so on, had been concerned with the discovery and description of an ideal system of relations between the various elements of state and people; they seemed to believe that there was an ideal order which could be achieved, and, once achieved, maintained. The setting up of arrangements such as Federal/Confederal constitutions, was one aspect of this style of approach. Mitrany concluded, in contrast, that the elements of change in society, in the demands and expectations of the people and in the problems posed by the need for the proper management of the economy, were such as to make this prescriptive, overarching approach a futile one. Society was changing so quickly that any attempt to fix the ideal order was doomed to failure, and, indeed, the very attempt to fix an ideal system could itself make the solution of immediate, pressing problems more difficult. In functionalism

Mitrany believed he had discovered a real alternative to grand theory, one which could cope with change, and which was orientated towards the more effective solution of immediate problems.

The essential starting point of this new approach, according to Mitrany, was to concentrate in the first instance upon the particular task, problems or function, and to attempt to exclude from this analysis the distorting elements of ideology, dogma, or philosophical system. Mitrany was convinced that it was possible to discover a kind of irreducable set of 'relations between things',[8] which were distinguishable from relations suggested by a constitution, or a dogma, and which, if left to themselves, would suggest the ideal geographical extent in which the problem could be tackled, and the most appropriate administrative arrangements. Hence the oft-quoted functionalist dictum that 'form follows function': the function, problem, or task itself suggests the extent of the area and form of the administration within which it is to be tackled.[9] It followed that the discontinuities in areas and administration were also ideally suggested by the function, though an ideology, such as nationalism, could impose such discontinuities in defiance of the 'relations between things'. Such intervention it was thought would inevitably add to the problems and make them more difficult to solve. In sum, functionalism laid great stress on the importance of allowing interrelationships and inter-dependences to develop according to the requirements of the function. Indeed, the theory was based upon the assumption that to isolate, as with nationalism and its various constitutional appendages, was to reduce, to trap, or to limit, while to allow interdependence according to function was to add, to complete, to generate.

Functionalism could cope with change, it was thought, because it worked from the particular problem and the relations suggested by it, rather than from some constitutional system, or idealised set of political or social relationships which were imposed upon it. Mitrany argued further that the irrelevance of traditional theories was particularly clear when it came to welfare problems or 'service' problems in their broadest sense which had become more pressing in recent years. 'No form of government, no constitutional or traditional claim is now immutably set: in the last resort the form of government and its laws and constitutions are shaped and re-shaped by the restless flux of the communities' social pressures.' 'Government is no longer a guarantor of a set social order, but the servant and instrument of change.'[10] In the manner of most theories in politics which claim a comprehensive relevance, Mitrany did not hesitate to infuse his

238

description with prescriptive elements: he added to the view that these social forces were in fact overwhelming the plea that they should be encouraged to be so. There were advantages in terms of world peace, and a better society, in choosing to work on welfare problems and thus harnessing the pressures which they generated. Man should respond positively to these by developing structures and procedures which allowed 'form' to follow 'function'.

By doing this, long standing problems could be solved in a new way. Within the nation state, in Britain, for instance, demands for social welfare had created a new, major, social-political problem: the problem of the lack of effective representation of the people in the government system. The development of the 'community's social pressures' had led an outdated style of administration and government to defeat attempts to obtain popular control by widening the franchise. There is now more management, and the state was increasingly pervasive, but management escaped the constitutional forms, including those newly established for obtaining popular control, with 'a pragmatical authority of a welfare state which refused to be shackled to any constitutional pillars'.[11] The result was that the 'old democratic remedy of widening the electorate has only served to dilute still more the scope of popular initiative and control. All the aims of political democracy were to control government: all the claims of social democracy end in control by government.'[12] The answer to this difficulty, in Mitrany's view, was to develop stronger representative institutions in areas of activity which directly touched upon the lives of the people. We should set up representative assemblies to look after particular sections of our life, such as health or energy, or transport, rather in the manner of meetings of shareholders in public companies. These new assemblies would establish control over the crucial areas of government more effectively than old style parliaments (which in some ways had become a positive hindrance to open government) because they would involve people who were directly affected by the work being done, and who would be more knowledgeable about the technical details of the activities involved. Traditional style parliaments, in contrast, tended to lack expertise, and were increasingly remote from the places where the real decisions were made. Professor Mitrany believed that in international institutions, such as the International Labour Organisation (I.L.O.), and later in the European Coal and Steel Community (E.C.S.C.) and in UNESCO, the more specialist assemblies recommended by him already existed. In the ILO, for instance, there was an assembly containing representatives of the three major interested groups, labour, management, and

239

the government; in this area, at least, international organisation was ahead of national government. ECSC also had an advisory specialist, consultative council of producers and consumers.

Mitrany prescribed that this particular aspect of *form* should follow from the new *functions* of the welfare state. Other aspects of the method of obtaining effective control and efficient management should also be adjusted to the nature of the function: some functions needed strong, rapid direction with the possibility of later correction; others needed to be decentralized in relatively strong regional offices, or, conversely, concentrated in more highly centralized ones; the composition and responsibilities of the committee of management would also vary with the function. How much of the detail of this would follow from the function was left rather unclear; as indeed was the more basic question of whether functions needed to be transplanted, as it were, into a society, or whether they would spring up of their own volition.

In developing states, such as India, Mitrany argued 'mass voting and sporadic elections were spurious democratic tools for illiterate, inexperienced populations'.[13] It was much better to build representative systems by functional means, by encouraging participation in the tackling of specific tasks and service industries. In this way an inexperienced people could learn about control over government by acting in areas in which they were immediately involved and therefore more likely to respond. But it may well be that functions would have to be introduced into the society in order to begin the attempt to solve the larger problem of control and representation. In the USA, however, the tasks of the Tennessee Valley Authority (T.V.A.), which was Mitrany's favourite functional model, was seen to be so self-evident and pressing that the problems of the sovereignty of the various states which impinged upon the Valley were set aside in a flood of Federal initiatives.[14] In this case, it seems, form did indeed follow more immediately from the pressing requirements of the function.

Professor Mitrany's advice to concentrate upon function in the interests of greater efficiency in the provision of welfare, and in the attempt to solve a number of linked tasks, such as the obtaining of a better system of representation, and overcoming the barriers of dogma, prescription and constitutionalism, is therefore not quite as straightforward as it would appear at first sight: sometimes function seems to impose itself upon the form (as with the T.V.A.); sometimes the form has to be moulded by man in a positive way, because existing constitutional structures resist change (as with the form of

240

representation in England); and sometimes functions are not at all self-evident and have to be introduced in order to facilitate the obtaining of some linked goals. There is, however, an increasing range of tasks and problems within the state, between them and transnationally, which have emerged as a result of technological change and development, which demand control and solutions of a specialised, technical kind, in which it seems a matter of common sense that the role of ideology should be minimized. Such tasks and problems apparently need to be tackled on their own terms and where necessary across national frontiers. The idea that benefits will accrue by concentrating on a particular task, service, function is revealed as indicating a most worthwhile general direction.

In its application to international society functionalism is an extension of the above arguments. As already explained the theory is conceived as relevant to circumstances within states and among them. Even the theory of the origin of war is implied by Mitrany's view about the value of concentrating upon 'relations between things'. The essential point — one which is very often misunderstood — is that functionalism sees the solution of a problem, not in the obtaining of specific, unchanging conditions (to do so would be to move dangerously close to an acceptance of a prescribed, fixed, order) but in the dynamic 'process' elements between one condition and the next. It is the case that war may be caused by particular circumstances in the functionalist eyes, as fixed conditions may interrupt the area or administration in which a function might be best tackled; such circumstances might include physical deficiencies, lack of food, shelter, clothing and also educational facilities which influence national perspectives in favour of war, or persuade national leaders that it might be the lesser of the range of evils. But the solution to war is not simply a correction of such deficiencies: it is the process of dealing with such deficiencies within organisations which, it is believed, produces the new dynamic of peace. There is, in other words, a lack of symmetry between Mitrany's views on the causes of the problem of war and its solution, which is perfectly consistent with other aspects of functionalism theory. The cause may be a constant or a condition, the solution, however, is a process of involving people in organisations devoted to the improvement of their circumstances and situation.

Critics of functionalism who argue that Professor Mitrany believed that war could be cured by satisfying man's wants have got the stress somewhat wrong. Inis Claude, for instance, quotes Charles Malik with approval: 'The poor, the sick, the dispossessed, must certainly be done

241

justice to. But to suppose that there will be peace when everybody is materially happy and comfortable is absolute nonsense.'[15] Professor Mitrany would agree with this view; his point is rather that it is the *process* of helping the poor, the sick and the dispossessed within an increasing range of organisations which helps to put things right rather than the actual attainment of these goals (they never could be obtained in any absolute sense). He did point out, however, that the participation of the people in the work of the international organisation is a sine qua non: it should be a response to 'felt needs'. Without such involvement the organisation might be judged to be an agent of exploitation, as is the case, sometimes, with multinational business organisations. It is important also to read Professor Mitrany's own views on this question in the context of their related arguments. He wrote in 1944: 'Give people a moderate sufficiency of what they need and ought to have and they will keep the peace: this has been proved time and again nationally but it has not yet been tried internationally.'[16] The context suggests that the stress again is on the process of giving, or trying to fulfil the welfare needs, rather than simply the consequence of their fulfilment.

Two aspects of the process are thought by the functionalists to be particularly promising in their implications for the chances of solving the problem of war. These are, first, the changing attitudes of people involved in the organisations and experiencing the benefits derived from their operation: it is assumed by functionalists that the establishment of a range of mutual contacts in the course of attempting to perform common tasks will change attitudes in the direction of greater amity, or, at least, towards a growing support for co-operation; and second the development between states in economic, technical, or welfare areas of a widening range of interdependencies which are seen to enmesh governments. These interdependencies would be expected to be successful in achieving the enmeshment of governments to the extent that the governments feel that the cost of their severance by war is unacceptably high. The process of functional integration is therefore seen as changing attitudes and creating costs of disruption – the enmeshment process – which make war less likely.

In this century there has developed in international society a wide range of governmental and non-governmental organisations which are expanding at a remarkable rate. These organisations are paralleled by an increasingly dense range of transactions between states which reflect a growing international, economic, trade and monetary interdependence, the growth of multinational business, and the exchange of ideas and

242

individuals. The functionalist theory illuminates these developments and finds in them a potential for peace; it also prescribes the approach of adding to the level of international organisation whenever this is suggested by the task or function.

These two aspects of attitude change and enmeshment are core elements in the functionalist view of international integration. The process starts when international institutions are set up in the area where they might act most efficiently, which is suggested by the nature of the task or function: institutions might also be set up in areas within the state according to the function with which they deal. The immediate initiative for such steps could be either private groups or individuals or national governments. It should be remembered that *A Working Peace System* was published during the Second World War and that it was addressed to national governments as advice on how best to guarantee peace at the conclusion of the war. Mitrany advocated 'a network of international agencies penetrating deep into German economic life'[17] as a way of restraining her aggressions in future, a proposal which was very like the 1951 European Coal and Steel Community, and quite unlike the Morgenthau plan. Once established, the international institutions would set in train pressures for further institutions: a number of people would be directly involved, and, it was expected, convinced of the benefits of co-operation, a larger number would realise that their welfare level would be likely to rise as international co-operation increased, and would suffer if it were restricted in favour of autarchic nation states. There would, therefore be set in motion a process of gradually changing popular attitudes as a result of the perceived benefits of international organisation and these would be shaped into an international socio-psychological community reflecting a co-operative ethos which would push for further international organisation and help 'form to follow function' across national frontiers. At the same time, fanatical loyalties to the nation state would be softened as international understanding increased.

The functionalist view of how this process might end is reflected in various dispersed passages of Professor Mitrany's writing. But it is clear that the intention is not to abolish governments though it is expected that their choice of goals for themselves would increasingly come to be predicated upon the survival of the co-operative framework. In the terms of modern social-science theory the zero-sum model would become less useful a model of international politics, while the non-zero-sum model would become more appropriate. It has been rightly pointed out that functionalism is an *indirect* approach to the problems of war; it does not seek to confront governments directly or expect that they will undertake commitments of which they disapprove. This indirect approach is illustrated particularly clearly by the rather different concepts of *spillover* found in functionalism compared with neo-functionalism. In Neofunctionalism the classical style of spill-over — one which has been frequently advocated in Western Europe and criticized as being too mechanical by Professor Dahrendorf[18] — holds that successful integration in an area of lesser salience, leads to a series of further linked integration measure, which culminate in overwhelming pressure to integrate in the high political areas closest to the heart of sovereignty. Problems resulting from one step in integration can only be solved by further integration: attitudes among elites about the most appropriate ways for obtaining their existing interests increasingly support integration. There is a kind of accumulation of implications of integration which gradually impinge upon decision-makers so that eventually they accept consciously the desirability of integration in areas of high politics — foreign policy and defence — as the best way of furthering their interests. Responsibility for these is transferred to a new common centre, the international institution. In its earliest form this process was thought to have a kind of deterministic quality which led to its being called 'the necessary logic' of neofunctionalism, or the 'functional imperative'.

The functionalist view, in contrast, regards spill-over as involving two stages. The first stage differs from that of the neofunctionalists in that it puts much greater stress upon pressures from, and changes in popular attitudes. The integration process proceeds from areas which are thought to be less contentious, and which particularly concern questions of welfare, and is pushed on by the 'felt needs' of the citizens. These reflect an increasing concern with welfare issues and a deepening realization of the costs of national frameworks: they suggest functions which are taken up by international institutions and which operate, as has been pointed out, across national frontiers according to the requirements of the particular function. The functionalists, however, believe in the educational effects of successful integration: the hierarchy of tasks from high to low politics is to be ironed out so that the salience of particular functions is changed as the process proceeds. Issues which were thought to be closer to the heart of sovereignty are no longer believed to be so.

The indirectness of the functional approach becomes particularly evident in the second stage. This is the stage at which it is thought governments are themselves involved in the education process. The

244

essential point here is not, as in the neofunctionalist approach, that decision-makers have reached the point of integrating what they have always believed to be important, but rather, that their views about what is important have changed. They become more involved in questions which relate in the broadest sense to welfare: the question of whether or not to hand over responsibility for defence and foreign policy, for instance, to a new common institution is bypassed because it has become irrelevant. The substantive issues of politics, even high politics, have changed. Governments have been approached indirectly and a new framework created without their full realization of its implications. On the other hand, the continued survival of governments, and of identifiable states, within this framework is perfectly compatible with functionalism. The functionalist approach, indeed, allows the view that there is no point at which the state would *necessarily* lose its sovereignty, in the sense that power would now need to be finally transferred, or that the state would lose its legal right to act, if it so wished, against the wishes of the functional agency. It holds, rather, that the issue of sovereignty becomes irrelevant to the important issues in the emerging world society.[19]

As the state is not thought to be necessarily losing its sovereignty, so there is to be no single place in international society which is necessarily gaining it. Functionalism is not, however, either Utopian or teleological in its view of international integration: rather it stresses central principles in the attainment of a more effective 'working peace system'. International society is seen as being made up of an increasing number of international institutions with competence in particular functional areas the territories of which intersect and overlap with each other. No ideology or political scheme must be allowed to impose a co-extensiveness upon these territories: the function must prevail. It is because of this that Professor Mitrany opposed movements towards regional political unification such as that in Western Europe. There are indeed many functions which should be organised on a regional basis, such as coal and steel in European Coal and Steel Community. But Professor Mitrany pointed out that there are many others which are best organised on a continental or a universal basis: the nature of the function determines this. The political objective of some supporters of the European Economic Community, in contrast, would lead to the fracturing of the natural overlapping functional areas, and would lead, if successful, to the recreation of all the traditional problems of international society on a bigger scale. The essential task of involving and enmeshing an increasing number of units, and of re-educating people in favour of co-operation, in order to reduce the chances of war, would be completely lost in the interests of yet another regional super-state.

In evaluating the contribution of functionalism to our understanding of international organisation, it is appropriate to return to the two aspects of the approach which seemed central to it, namely attitude change and enmeshment.[20] First a number of critics have focussed on points related to the problem of attitude change: is it really possible, they ask, that attitudes can be changed by involvement in international organisation or by experiencing the effects of international institutions? On the one hand is the evidence of common sense, and of everyday experience, on which functionalism lays a great deal of stress; what people do together, if they do enough of it, leads them to greater involvement with each other and to full participation in common institutions. Within the state it seems these methods are one of the steps towards the improvement of relations between groups which are mutually suspicious of each other. It is thought by some to be the most promising way of attempting the solution of the problem in Northern Ireland in the 1970s. At the international level, however, the evidence, which is collected in the face of considerable research problems, is somewhat inconclusive: there is as yet little evidence to suggest that international institutions are capable of becoming the focus of loyalties at the expense of the nation state.[21] But there is evidence of a softening of attitudes towards each other among those who work in international institutions and of an increasing readiness to avoid group criticisms on the basis of in-group out-group distinctions. The worst forms of hostility, usually based on ignorance or prejudice, tend to be less extreme. There is some evidence of a softening of support for the nation state in regions such as Western Europe which may be attributable to the work of the international institutions. But the conclusion must be that the evidence about attitude change is as yet not particularly encouraging for those who expect international organisation to find its own basis of support in popular loyalties. On the other hand, it is very difficult to refute the functionalist claims in this area, though this may itself be a problem in its formulation as a 'theory' — that it is hard to falsify. The supporter of the functionalist position can always resort to the proposition that enough co-operation over enough time will generate support for integration in the long term, and that a softening of attitudes, and a preparedness to accept involvement, is itself a valuable change in the short term.

A further crucial aspect of attitudes and attitude change is concerned with governments and their expectations. Supporters of the traditional power politics approach to the academic subject of international relations argue that the re-education process which the functionalists stress is a most unlikely development. They argue that governments are bound to retain to themselves ultimate control over their interests and more importantly that there can be no gradual process of integration because there are no areas in which international co-operation is likely to have any consequences whatsoever for a governments's determination to do what it wants in terms of its traditional interests and values. There are eternal verities in power politics, it is argued, and it is impossible to transcend these: the primacy of the separate, high political interests of governments cannot be amended.

The absence of any impact upon power politics at the end of the process is matched in the arguments of the critics of functionalism by the view that there is also no easy way in which the process can begin. The argument here is about the so-called separability thesis; critics of functionalism have argued that Professor Mitrany distinguished between political and non-political areas, which included welfare, and that this is a logical requirement of his gradualist approach.[22] The criticism is offered that such a separation of welfare from politics is entirely unrealistic, and that because of this there can be no easy way into the process of integration: there is, indeed, no possibility that the experience of integration could release a dynamic which made integration in other areas more likely, and eventually modified high politics itself.

It is probably true that functionalists have not been careful enough in their arguments about the relationship between power and welfare or between high and low politics. On the other hand, the criticisms of functionalism in this area have themselves been too blunt and even perversely unsympathetic: there are various ways of relating power and politics to welfare without denying the functionalists their gradualist integration process. Groom has pointed out that any issue can involve either high or low politics: the important distinction is rather between legitimized and non-legitimized relations, and there can be a process of legitimizing relations between actors where they have previously possessed rather low levels of legitimacy.[23] Furthermore, although no area can be essentially or entirely 'non-political', it is possible for there to be more or less contentious issues in the sense that they involve more agreement among specialists or experts, and attract less disagreement among politicians. It is also possible, as Groom implies,

247

for a particular subject to be moved out of the realm of high politics as others may be moved into it. The functionalists might be allowed the possibility of starting their integration process in less contentious areas and of re-focussing the object of politics upon welfare issues and upon issues which lay greater stress upon an acceptance of the co-operative framework without implying that they believe that some areas are essentially matters of high politics and others essentially matter of low politics. Politics in either event is not to be excluded, but rather is to be re-focussed, as the area of legitimized relations is expanded.

In his treatment of functionalism, Inis Claude has questioned the viability of the functionalist approach in these terms:

> 'Is it in fact possible to segregate a group of problems and subject them to treatment in an international workshop where the nations shed their conflicts at the door and busy themselves only with the co-operative use of the tools of mutual interest?'[24]

'Groups of problems' are not to be segregated, but rather identified; the nations are not expected to shed their conflicts at the door, or anywhere else, but rather to attempt to locate less contentious issues and to focus on these to the advantage of the separate states, and of their societies; and the 'tools of mutual interest' are nothing unless they are recognised and freely accepted by the separate governments.

A second criticism is that the development of systems of trans-national transactions, which functionalism recognises and fits into a strategy of peace, does not trap states in interdependences or confine them within a co-operative framework. The comment has been made that 'international welfare issues have emerged as high political questions in our time' and that 'in contrast to international politics, partnership, beneficence and threat are all likely to be conceived, perceived, and evaluated economically rather than militarily'. But 'the new politics of international economics seems a major dimension of the substance of international politics in the 1970s.'[25] In other words, governments' involvement in the economic affairs of states, i.e. in welfare, and the number of inter-governmental disputes about the international and economic system, seem to some commentators to have increased as a result of increasing co-operation, rather than to have decreased, and their disputes seem to be as intractable as the earlier disagreements about territory or status. Integration has simply increased the range of opportunities for governments to exercise their national muscle and pursue their interests and, within the state, they have involved themselves consistently in more areas of life than before. More issues, within and without the state, are, in other words, becoming politicised.

Two major points can be made in response to these comments in defence of enmeshment. First it seems that the development of the interdependences has been associated with changes in the kind of objectives which governments normally seek: they are much more likely to stress economic or developmental objectives, and much less likely to stress the acquisition of territory or other symbols of national prestige. This is mainly in response to the rising tide of expectations, at the popular level, and it is associated with the appearance of a different style of managerial, technocratic, politician. These changes, themselves, tend to strengthen the acceptance of the pre-existing co-operative framework in international society; a system of rules has to be accepted in order to allow the separate national economic interests to be obtained. Despite intense dispute about the details of the economic or monetary systems in the 1970s, it was generally accepted that there should be a system and that it should possess certain broad characteristics. As Professor Morse has pointed out:

> 'One principle characteristic of foreign policies under modernised conditions is that they approach the pole of co-operation rather than the pole of conflict. Conflictual or political activities, therefore, take place within the context of predominantly co-operative arrangements.'[26]

Any student of the development of trade unions in the modern state is similarly aware of a countervailing influence on the spread of government influence. Government may be more pervasive, but it is not as dominant. It may be involved in more but it is the master in less. Within the co-operative framework of the welfare state more issues seem to involve political questions than formerly, a development which mirrors the process in international society. Politicisation does make for a more messy political system, involving a greater range of actors, each with their own interests, but its existence, both within and without the state, ultimately depends upon the existence of the co-operative framework. Growing internal interdependences are an aspect of a widening governmental presence; they are also an aspect of the declining governmental authority and its partial submerging in a widening system of legitimised political relations within the state. Politicisation, again, may be seen as a consequence of developments which fit happily in the functionalist theory, rather than evidence of its irrelevance.

The further problem arises, though, of how far the enmeshment process is reversible and how far it need go before the state is unable to escape its hold. At present the answer can only be stated in imprecise terms. The costs of breaking interdependences are rising — France has felt this both in the EEC and the NATO context — and the acceptance of the cost depends ultimately upon the priority attached by politicians to alternative values: but the more the enmeshment, the higher the cost of severance, and the more difficult the political choice. On the other hand, if the worst happens, if war breaks out, the functionalist theory probably has little to offer: it may help to build the underlying conditions of peace, but if these prove insubstantial, it has little to offer crisis management.

The student of international organisation should make the attempt to become familiar with the writings of the functionalists, particularly the work of David Mitrany as reflected in his *A Working Peace System.* He should not accept them uncritically, but rather should treat them as a starting point for his thinking about the subject and the prospects of international organisation. It reflects a large number of unstated assumptions, mainly of a liberal/rational kind, which cannot be identified in full in this brief chapter, and it is part of a much larger philosophical structure of ideas with implications both within the state and in international society. It is valuable despite its lack of rigor in the sense of modern social science. The student should also examine the conventional criticisms of functionalism, and remember that there is an orthodoxy here too which should not go unchallenged.

Functionalism is revealed as a useful antidote to the power politics approach to the study of international society. It is, however, essentially modest and pragmatic: it does not claim to eliminate the pursuit of power, but only to consider the circumstances in which it might be limited or redirected, and it accepts that different standpoints might reveal valid insights. It also leads to a concern with practical, short term steps for improvement, and is not encumbered with a sense of the hopelessness of trying to improve man's condition. That hopelessness lies at the dead heart of power politics.

Notes

1. See Dorothy Emet, *Function, Purpose and Power,* London, Macmillan, 1958, and B. Malinowski, *A Scientific Theory of Culture*, University of North Carolina Press, 1944.
2. See bibliography with Chapter 12 below.

3.   See Paul Taylor, 'Introduction' in David Mitrany *The Functional Theory of Politics*, London School of Economics and Political Science and Martin Robertson, London, 1975.

4.   David Mitrany, *A Working Peace System*, London, Royal Institute of International Affairs, 1943.

5.   David Mitrany, 'A Political Theory for a New Society', in A.J.R. Groom and Paul Taylor, *Functionalism: Theory and Practice in International Relations*, London, University of London Press, 1975, pp. 25–37.

6.   See inter alia his *The Road to Security*, Peace News Pamphlet, No. 29, National Press Council, 1944; *The Progress of International Government*, London, Allen & Unwin, 1933; *The Functional Theory of Politics*, London London School of Economics and Political Science and Martin Robertson, 1975.

7.   David Mitrany, *The Functional Theory of Politics*, 'A Political Theory for a New Society', Loc. Cit., p. 25.

8.   'The Making of Functional Theory: a Memoir', in *The Functional Theory of Politics*, loc. cit., p. 37.

9.   See *A Working Peace System*, loc. cit., pp. 72–73.

10. 'A Political Theory for a New Society', loc. cit., p. 27.

11. *Ibid.*, p. 28.

12. *Ibid.*, p. 31.

13. 'Memoir', loc. cit., p. 33.

14. *A Working Peace System*, Chicago, Quadrangle Books, 1966, pp. 56–57.

15. Inis L. Claude, Jr., *Swords into Plowshares*, University of London Press, 3rd edition, 1964, p. 353.

16. *The Road to Security*, loc. cit., p. 15.

17. *The Road to Security*, loc. cit., p. 13.

18. R. Dahrendorf, *Plädoyer für die Europaische Union*, Piper Verlog, 1973, pp. 78–79 and passim.

19. See *A Working Peace System*, Loc. Cit., pp. 30–31, and see especially pp. 65–66. Mitrany spoke of 'slices' of sovereignty being *'transferred . . . through a function'*, though he implies that the transfer is to many centres not a single, new centre (p. 31). Elsewhere, however, he speaks of *sharing* sovereignty, and argues that 'specific functional arrangements would not *steal* the crown of sovereignty.' (p. 66).

20. For a consideration of the problems of testing functionalism see R.J. Harrison, 'Testing Functionalism', in A.J.R. Goom and Paul Taylor (eds.), *Functionalism*, loc. cit., pp. 112–138.

21. See Peter Wolf, 'International Organization and Attitude Change: a
]   reexception of the Functionalist Approach', *International Organization*, Vol. 27, Summer 1973, pp. 347–371.

22. See Ernst B. Haas, *Beyond the Nation State*, Stanford University Press, 1964, pp. 47–48. It is not intended to suggest here that Professor Haas is linked with supporters of the power politics school in general opposition to Functionalism. But he has criticized at loc. cit. this particular aspect of the approach.

23. See A.J.R. Groom, in Groom & Taylor (eds.), loc. cit., pp. 99–100.

24. Inis Claude Jr., loc. cit., pp. 353–354.

25. Donald Puchala and Stuart Fagan 'International Politics in the 1970s: the Search for Perspective', *International Organisation*, Madison, Spring 1974, Vol. 28, No. 2, pp. 263.

26. Edward L. Morse, 'The Transformation of Foreign Politics: Modernization, Interdependence, and Externalization', *World Politics*, April 1970, p. 382.

Selected Reading

1. David Mitrany, *A Working Peace System*, Chicago, Quadrangle Books, 1966.
2. David Mitrany, *The Funcational Theory of Politics*, London, London School of Economics and Political Science and Martin Robertson, 1975.
3. A.J.R. Groom and Paul Taylor (eds.), *Functionalism: Theory and Practice in International Relations*, London, University of London Press, 1975.
4. Ernst B. Haas, *Beyond the Nation State*, Stanford, 1964.
5. J.P. Sewell, *Functionalism and World Politics*, London, Oxford University Press, 1966.
6. Andrew Wilson Green, 'Mitrany re-read with the help of Haas and Sewell', *Journal of Common Market Studies*, September 1969.

CHAPTER TWELVE

NEOFUNCTIONALISM

R.J. Harrison

The neo-functionalist conception of international organisation finds direct expression in the European Community. The Community in its early stage was the inspiration for the thesis in the form of which it was originally offered by E.B. Haas in his study *The Uniting of Europe*. He examined the European Coal and Steel Community and provided an academic rationalisation of the strategy and goals incorporated in the Treaty. In summary form these had been made clear by M. Robert Schuman in his Declaration of May 9 1950, introducing the proposal for the new Community. He said:

> 'Europe will not be made all at once, or according to a single, general plan. It will be built through concrete achievements, which first create a *de facto* solidarity ... The pooling of coal and steel production will immediately provide for the setting-up of common bases for economic development as a first step in the federation of Europe.'

In this statement, in concise summary, are some of the most important neo-functionalist tenets. First, the object of the exercise is stated quite clearly to be *federation*, (though in elaborations of the neo-functionalist argument and in later political debate, the vaguer term *political union* has often been used). Second, the strategy is basically 'functionalist' in conception. Indeed, Mitrany, the father of 'functionalism', when he refers to the European Community experiment and its underlying theory,

253

calls it 'functional-federalism'. It is, clearly however, functionalism with a difference. Thus, though Schuman talks about the need to create a *de facto* solidarity, and later in the Declaration talks about the importance of building a wider and deeper community between countries, the social-psychological overtones of the term 'community' are not given the weight that they are accorded in Mitrany's argument and in his conception of community. And though the notion of a transfer of loyalties to a new regional centre was visualised by neo-functionalist theorists in their original conception of the dynamic process of integration, this is specifically abandoned by Haas as a necessary component in later reflections on the Community experience and its implication for the theory. In any case what Haas and Schuman stress is the importance of a fusion of *economic* interests and the sector which Schuman chose for the first step in the master plan was seen as one of vital economic importance: coal and steel production and marketing. It was thought to be so important that its integration would make any future war between France and Germany 'not merely unthinkable but materially impossible'.[1] Another vital part of Schuman's strategy and of neo-functionalist theory which differentiates it from that of functionalism is the setting up of central institutions for the proposed Community — institutions that are supposed to be capable of playing a creative role in the realization of the overall objective, and are distinctly federal in the sense that decisions made by them within their formal powers are binding on the member countries. Ernest Haas' study of the Community a few years after it came into effect is a theoretical vindication of its economic and institutional emphasis.

He saw it as particularly appropriate to the advanced industrial pluralist societies in which it was being tried. Haas was a proponent of the view that the politics of the international arena are not markedly different from domestic politics. 'As a major premiss', he stated in an earlier work,[2] 'We assume that the ends of foreign policy are qualitatively similar to ends implicit in any other field of politics. Whatever 'laws' of political behaviour, group conduct and elite leadership can be isolated and identified in the domestic field are therefore considered applicable to the international field as well. In both cases the agent of action is man acting within a group. We doubt that this group is necessarily identical with that called the nation, hence we have attempted to synthesize the study of political behaviour and social action with an analysis of international relations as one manifestation of group aspirations.' This major premiss is a vitally important one in the neo-functionalist thesis. All the original states of the European Coal and Steel Community were advanced industrial pluralist democracies. That is to say, they had highly developed party organisations and activity and there were pressure groups purporting to represent almost every conceivable sphere of activity and interest which might impinge upon government. These, it was argued, were the background conditions most favourable to the strategy of integration by stealth, that is, by incremental, concrete, economic achievements which build up de facto 'engrenage' or enmeshment of one national political and economic system with another. Haas recognizes that the policy which emerges from group competition in such societies does not in every single instance represent a common or community interest. But it is critical to this thesis that group activity by its long-term results does engender commitment, at least, to constitutional procedures. With the right strategy, Haas thought, that commitment could conceivably be transferred to the regional level. Pressure groups and political parties are, he says, 'singled out as significant carriers of values and ideologies whose opposition, identity or convergence determines the success or failure of a transnational ideology.'[3]

If anything, in Haas' conception, the interest groups are more important than parties. They are the dynamic element of political process in advanced pluralist democracies, and this is especially true of the groups which operate in the economic sector. Haas says 'almost universally economic groups seem to be in the forefront of those who clamour for the recognition of common needs.'[4] If groups can be caught up in the integration process, therefore, they could push it forward, overcoming even the resistance of national governments. They would generalise the commitment to integration and promote that solidarity which Schuman thought necessary.

These assumptions about the group basis of politics are fundamental to the neo-functionalist theory. It was best to pick the economic sector for the first measure of integration, because this is where the groups are most active. The possibility of collaboration in other sectors like education, social policy and defence does of course exist, but according to the theory, the most fluid, adaptable area in the advanced, industrial democracies is the economic area, and this is also the area in which the major, organised, interest group activity is concentrated. If the groups active in the economic area are affected by integration it is very likely that they will become involved. To involve groups and parties the initial integrative step must be fairly important and fairly controversial. It must not be so controversial that states feel that their vital interests are affected, since this might very well arouse the opposition of national political elites who feel their power and vested interests are threatened. But strains and distortions should be felt, as a consequence of integration, which will give rise to a need, and consequently a demand, by affected groups, for adjustment. That adjustment could well be by means of further integration. This is most likely if the initial integrative task itself is inherently expansive; that is, if the joint activity is larger than the sum of the original, independent activities.

The demands for task-expansion expressed by pressure groups and parties would be felt originally at the national level. However, as regional central institutions are given more power and functions in response to pressures, the theory is that the demands, the expectations and the loyalties of groups and parties will gradually shift to the new centre of decision-making, — not entirely, but significantly. Central institutions will respond and become, thereby, the driving force or 'motor' of the process of community development. Thus, in this conception, 'the process of community formation is dominated by nationally constituted groups with specific interests and aims, willing and able to adjust their aspirations by turning to supranational means when this course appears profitable'.[5] Haas, in other words, expects the regional community to be very like the national communities which make it up, only writ larger. He is quite explicit about this: 'Group conflict is a given and expected form of conduct in the nations under study . . . a larger political community . . . may well be expected to display the same traits'.[6] This is the main reason why the advanced industrial democracies whose interest groups, as Haas puts it, 'pulsate with life and vigour',[7] are considered the best, perhaps the only possible candidates for integration.

The building of community then, in the neo-functionalist theory does not depend initially upon mass support. It is directed towards political union, but identical aims on the part of all the participants in the process do not have to be assumed. There may be different advantages in integration for different groups. As Haas points out, 'the European Coal and Steel Community was initially accepted because it offered a multitude of different advantages to different groups'.[8] He argued that this *compatibility* rather than *coincidence* of group interests provides the basis for an expansive logic of integration, which includes what he calls the 'spillover' effect. Haas defines 'spillover' as something which occurs when 'policies made pursuant to an initial task and grant of power can be made real only if the task itself is expanded.' Leon Lindberg, who most closely follows in Haas's footsteps, with his study of the European Economic Community, re-states the definition so that it denotes the process whereby 'a given action, related to a specific goal, creates a situation in which the original goal can be assured only by taking further actions, which in turn create a further condition and a need for more action, and so forth.'[9] Now spillover according to these definitions could occur in a number of ways. A given step in integration might very well alter the conditions of competition in a manner that calls for new central policy decisions, either to restore something like the original competitive balance of advantage within the sector affected, or to open up new opportunities for all the affected parties. Or, the alterations, strains, and distortions resulting from one integrative step may result in pressures by groups for their correction. Their pressures ensure that the spillover effect works itself out productively for further integration. For example, a transport and road system, relatively uncoordinated, might continue to impede the flow of goods and services after the elimination of tariffs, so that steps would have to be taken in the transport sector itself. An original agreement say, on tariffs, might be evaded by some of the member states of the nascent community, or by constituent groups, through actions which fell outside the literal scope of the obligations created. An agreement on tariff elimination for example, might be negated by the imposition of differential transport rates, or border health inspections and.regulations, and other non-tariff barriers to trade; yet the original agreement though ineffective or only partially effected may have aroused expectations among business and other groups who planned accordingly. These groups are likely to press for agreement on further measures which will make the first step effective, and so vindicate their plans. Spillover may also occur because an integrative step is redistributive in its effects, *between* states. That is, it benefits some states more than others. The disadvantaged states will look for ways in which they can redress the balance in their favour, possibly in another sector altogether.

This is the essence of what has come to be called package-dealing within the European Community. This involves the reaching of complex agreements in a number of what may well be disparate areas, tied together, as it were, in a package which in one way or another satisfies all the member states of the European Community. It can be argued that, as integration develops from sector to sector, increased scope would exist for a resolution of conflicts over income redistribution by such bargains between sectors. Spillover may also occur either because the effects of an integrative step, although they produce no clear balance of advantage or disadvantage for states or groups, clearly show the likelihood of benefit from, or the need for, further integration in some way which can be readily agreed, or because the integrative step has automatic integrative implications in other sectors. Haas is emphatic that 'sector integration . . . begets its own impetus towards extension to the entire economy even in the absence of specific group demands and their attendant ideologies . . . (thus) while not in principle favouring the control of the scrap trade with third countries civil servants in the Council of Ministers decided on supranational administrative measures just the same merely in order to make the common market for steel a reality.'[10]

Lindberg offers another example of this impetus at work in the Acceleration agreement of 12 May 1960. He suggests that 'business circles, after initial reactions ranging from cautious support to outright hostility, had accepted the Common Market as a *fait accompli* and jumped in with almost breathtaking speed to form a network of agreements within the Six. An acceleration of the realisation of the Common Market, far from exceeding the pace desired by business groups, would only catch up with the pace they had already set . . . it was from business circles that much of the political pressure for acceleration originated.'[11] Another example of this impetus at work was the way in which agreement on agricultural prices in the 1960's immediately had implications for exchange rates among the Six. European officials congratulated themselves on having achieved exchange rates stability without negotiation merely as a bi-product of their agreement on agricultural prices.

There are, then, possibilities of spillover without direct group involvement, but group activity is seen as the most likely and dynamic element in most examples of the process, bringing about an increasing 'politicization' of integrative activity, moving further and further into the areas of traditional concern of political elites.

A distinction which may be drawn between 'negative' and 'positive' integration helps to clarify the notion of politicization 'Negative' integration connotes policy agreements which remove existing barriers to communications and transactions of all kinds between countries. The removal of tarriffs, for example, has this aspect. The effects of negative integration may be far reaching but the policies do not, singly detract very much from the powers of national governments to fulfil what has become their primary role in most states, whatever their stage of development — the management of the national economy. As measures of negative integration are multiplied, however, the cumulative effect does begin to touch on government's ability to perform this important role. To remove the tariff weapon, the import quota, and the elaborate fair competition rules which regulate the circumstances in which subsidies and tax concessions can be provided by national governments; to fix prices for agricultural products which, as we have noted, inhibit exchange rate flexibility, is to begin, noticeably, to impair the management capability of governments. It raises the question whether, in the circumstances, the regional community institutions should not assume management responsibility for the regional economy, including such basic problems as sectoral and regional unemployment, demand management and exchange rate stability. In other words, it raises the question of the need for an economic and monetary union — or what may be termed 'positive' integration. Given the pragmatic decision making style in advanced industrial pluralist societies, the perception of this need by bureaucrats will, it is presumed, lead to proposals for its fulfilment in ways which upgrade community decision-making to higher, increasingly 'political' levels. Policies will be redistributive across national frontiers because they serve the interest of the community as a whole as it is perceived by people in key institutional settings, national and international.

There would be, in fact, according to this thesis, a virtually ineluctable 'interpenetration of elites', national and international, governmental and non-governmental, brought together in the various meetings and institutions of the regional organisation. There would be, therefore, a process of 'elite socialisation' 'as the immediate participants in the policy-making process, from interest groups to bureaucrats and statesmen, begin to develop new perspectives, loyalties and identifications as a result of their mutual interactions.'[12]

The attempt to build the European Community has proved a concrete test of neo-functionalist theory and it must be conceded in the light of experience that many of the expectations have been disappointed particularly those relating to the role of groups and of regional institutions. The actual goals laid down in specific terms in all three of the European treaties, and the institutions that are created, and the relations between them which are specified, give the Schuman, or neo-functionalist strategy, an operational definition. The goals laid down in the treaties are to be achieved incrementally rather than all at once. Some are immediate and some are remote. The EEC treaty, for example, provided for the three stage removal of international customs duties and quotas, and it required, at the same time, a common external tariff to be completed, also in three stages, totalling twelve years, with provision for extension of each of the stages, should the task prove too difficult. The details and the time limits for the completion of other tasks were specified more generally. There was to be free movement of labour and capital by the end of the period, there were to be special provisions for agriculture to be worked out by the Community institutions. There was to be harmonisation of social policies. A European Investment Bank was to be set up. There was provision for the creation of an Association of Overseas Territories and for creating a Development Fund for their benefit. Parliament was to draw up plans for its own direct election. The Council of Ministers was to adopt majority voting, or qualified majority voting in some cases, in clearly specified ways and in specified stages. Some goals then were laid down in detail, others were left to the institutions of the Community to work out and develop.

The institutional structure of all three Communities in their premerger state, that is before 1967, was basically the same. The Assembly and the Court of Justice were common to all three Communities. The Assembly is a body made up of delegates from the member state parliaments, selected from their own numbers as they decide. The other common institution, the Court of Justice has nine members appointed unanimously by all the member governments, and is charged with the responsibility of ensuring that the treaty provisions are adhered to and authoritatively interpreted. Each Community was also given a Council of Ministers, one member of the government of each state, and each Community had an executive or Commission. Finally each Community was given an Economic and Social Committee (in the European Coal and Steel Community, the Consultative Committee) of tripartite representation, that is, of employers, employees and a 'miscellaneous' category.

In the 1950's there were a number of presumptions about the role which Community institutions might play. These are apparent in the text of the Treaty in the formal allocation of powers and they provide the inspiration for the neo-functionalist conception of the role of central institutions in an integrative process. At the heart of it all was the provision for what has been called 'the dialogue' between the Commission and the Council of Ministers. These two institutions embodied respectively the 'community' and the 'nationality' principles and they were required to sit together to consider the policy of the Community. Other elements in this institutional framework, the

260

Parliament, the Economic and Social Committee and the Court (also, by their appointment and composition, 'community' bodies) have relatively minor roles, lending an air of democratic legitimacy and judicial authority to Community activity — providing, as it were, environmental support for the dialogue. ECOSOC and Parliament provided 'official' fora for group and party activity of European scope. To a considerable degree, the expectations which were focused on the dialogue depended on the role assigned to the Commission of the Community. In all these respects the Commission resembled a national government. This made neo-functionalist assumptions about the transferability of modes of analysis of, and hypotheses about, the domestic politics of pluralist societies to an international regional integration context more credible and helped to give the theory the high status and acceptability it so quickly gained in academic circles. Furthermore, under the Treaty the dialogue has to be initiated by the Commission. Proposals were its monopoly. Only the Commission could offer an amendment to its own proposals unless the Council were unanimous. The power was one of the bases of an envisaged 'motor' role for the Commission. In the neo-functionalist conception it was expected that the Commission would become the focus of the informal pressures of the various national groups and of European-wide 'umbrella' organisations for the regional groups, making their demands for integrative measures which would promote their interests, or at least helping the Commission to ensure that its own promotive role was conducted in a way that would maximise the involvement and support of as wide a range of groups as possible within society. Another legal Treaty basis for the 'motor' role of the Commission, and, therefore, another reason why it should become the focus of interest of affected groups, was the rule-making power which was given to it. Either on Treaty authority or by subsequent decisions of the Council of Ministers, the Commission was enpowered to make regulations directly applicable in each member state. Further, it could issue directives which bind the state or firms or individuals to whom they are addressed. It can also issue recommendations and opinions which, though not binding in themselves, might provide a behavioural guide to the states or private bodies in the community.

Other powers given to the Commission though less directly related to policy promotion and the galvanizing of group support were certainly not supposed to detract from it. The Commission has, for example, under the Treaty, a supervisory watch-dog role ensuring that Treaty obligations are met. In exercising this role the Commission can bring suit against individual firms and states who offend its interpretation of the rules. The Commissioners, furthermore, have the overall administrative responsibility; and they are to represent the Community in negotiations with foreign governments. The Treaty included also a whole range of protective measures designed to ensure that the Commission's European orientation and status are preserved and to prevent it being deflected from its promotive role by conservative national pressures. The commissioners, (now 13 in the merged Communities) are appointed by the Council as a whole, unanimously. There is a nationality balance, but they are not national representatives. As a corollary, the individual nations are not to seek or accept instructions from the governments of their countries. They can only be dismissed as a group by the Parliament, so that they have, in effect, security of tenure − a fixed term of four years, renewable. They were to take secret majority decisions if they voted, thus ensuring that the individual national commissioners could not be attacked by their governments if they voted in ways contrary to the conceived interests of their member states. The Commission was, furthermore, empowered to recruit its staff directly.

All the devices and powers of the Communities institutions have, in the neo-functionalist conception, practical power implications. The policy role of administrators, by analogy with national governments, was expected to fall on the Commission, strengthened by the specific Treaty provisions, particularly the initiatory power. It was supposed, second, that the Commission would be able to play and exploit an arbitral, mediatory role stemming from its well protected Community orientation. It was supposed, also to be able to utilise Parliament and the Economic and Social Committees as supports. Together, they were to ensure that the pressures of spillover worked themselves out productively.

In practice, there have been a number of problems with this conception and they have reflected on the theory. First, the ultimate power of the Council in the institutional structure has made it the dominant institution, reducing the significance of the initiative and amendment monopoly of the Commission. The formal power to decide is the Council's alone. The formal initiatory power enjoyed by the Commission is still important to it, but in a mediatory concilatory role rather than a creative one. The obligation on the part of the Commission to put forward a Community interest has had to give way, in spite of all the informal assets of the Commission, and the political skills of the individual Commissioners, to the brutal realities of the non-distribution of formal power, and the consequent need to present something that will get through the unit-veto procedures of the Council of Ministers. For the Council of Ministers did not become a majoritarian body at the stages and in the way prescribed by the Treaty, and only in the past two or three years, since the Dublin summit, has it departed from the unanimity principle. The proposals therefore which the Commission has made to the Council have, for the most part, been a product of the quasi-diplomatic sounding-out of national government attitudes and opinions, and the incorporation into proposals of the appropriate concessions and compromises. This consultative process has been institutionalized through the Committee of Permanent Representatives, the ambassadors of the member countries to the Community. This committee, in conjunction with various special committees and working groups which study Commission proposals and suggest revisions, has in practice partially usurped the Commission's initiatory role, bringing national governmental elites very early into the process. The 'dialogue' is therefore, not between equals but between master, (the Council) and foreman.

A second problem is that there does seem to be a genuine conflict between administrative tasks and policy leadership. The analogy which was drawn with the influential role of national administrations was incomplete. Bureaucratic competence without the support of political leadership tends to be ineffective, incapable of taking charge of problem situations and giving direction and purpose to their solution. It would seem too that the very qualities that are associated with the bureaucratic ideal: impartiality, expertise, hierarchical structure and anonymity are inimical to a political leadership role. This is precisely what David Coombes finds in his study of the Commission. He considers that its 'mediative and administrative functions rather than its initiative and normative functions now characterise it as an institution'.[13] Because they lack a popular base 'the Commissioners in this system perform only a bureaucratic function in relation to the member governments. The Commission's organisation under such circumstances must be perpetually threatened by the 'dysfunctions' known to result from a delegative, impartial and hierarchically structured organisation. Unless there is some form of independent, central, political leadership for the Commission the latter cannot be relied upon to take its own initiative or to lay down its own norms. Only the member governments can do that on its behalf.'[14] It seems clear then that the provisions made by the Treaty for creative leadership were inadequate. The hopes focused on the institutions by neo-functionalists like Haas and Lindberg, by Deutsch and by Etzioni, by Schmitter and others were unrealistic.

A critical weakness of the domestic politics model which they incorporated into their integration process model was that it tended to relegate the formal, legal and coercive powers of the state to a relatively insignificant position. Haas himself characterised the study of regional integration as 'concerned with tasks, transactions, perceptions, and learning', rather than questions of governance and power. Neo-functionalist theory is based on a primarily consensual model of a political community in being an idealised conception of a self-regulating pluralist society whose unity and stability rest on mutual adjustment between groups, following accepted norms. No adequate theory is offered, however, of consensus formation mechanisms and their relationship to formal institutions in the international regional setting. But formal powers and questions of sovereignty have proved important in Community experience, and quasi-governmental powers have not proved enough to ensure the realisation of task expansion and spill-over through the European 'system-elite'. The Treaty provisions were inadequate because the initiatory role and administrative competence of the Commission was in latent and, it proved, actual conflict with the deciding role of the Council of Ministers. Leadership in the Community is not sustained by an effective, accepted pattern of consensus formation, simplifying choice and legitimising decision. The consensual support of the Council of Ministers is fragmented among the member countries. Divergent views have to be resolved at the highest-level, namely the Council itself. The Council was originally, and has remained, an intergovernmental body, not a regional governmental institution. This has limited the potential for effective action. The absence of any real powers in the Parliament and the Economic and Social Committees has reduced their usefulness. In particular, the interest and involvement of political parties and pressure groups has not been stimulated to any great extent. There is no electorate for the parties to organise. There is no point in pressure groups exerting themselves very energetically at the Community level.

This is also partly because, not surprisingly, the policy achievements of the Community have been relatively low. Schuman's expectations have not been fulfilled. Customs union was achieved with relative ease, mainly because it was specified in the Treaty in some detail and because its effects were very difficult to determine. They were certainly not clearly adverse to any one state's interest. Free movement of labour, a degree of harmonisation of social policies and competition rules have been achieved. None of these can be considered serious limitations on the powers of the government of member states. None involve obvious redistribution, across the state boundaries, of Community income. Only one policy that the Community has initiated is redistributive to any major degree. This is the common agricultural policy which sets the retail price minima of agricultural products and requires Community intervention, buying if these prices are not reached on the market. This policy has, most of the time, benefitted the French and Dutch at the expense of the Germans and Italians. The agricultural policy was achieved only after exhaustive nationalistic bargaining which very much reduced Community enthusiasm. It is the major achievement of the Community in that it is the policy most like national policies, redistributive in the conceived interests of the whole Community. It is the policy which most closely conforms with Haas' highest category of conflict resolution-'upgrading' the common interest' rather than mere 'splitting the difference' or even settling on 'the lowest common denominator' of interests. It has created, however, vested interest among the beneficiaries and resentment among those who pay, rather than solidarity as Schuman would have hoped and as the neo-functionalist thesis with its emphasis on critical tasks as the most productive and expansive would lead one to expect. It made a regional policy, even the very small one which the Community finally did agree upon, very difficult to achieve. Germany quite simply did not want to pay for any more re-allocation. In general those who have to pay can be expected to veto any important redistributive schemes and those who benefit from existing policies have an interest in preventing any changes, so that the French remain the ardent champions of the agricultural policy.

The first and most obvious critical point then, to be made about the neo-functionalist argument is that there is no evidence in the Community experience of the beguiling automaticity of step-by-step economic integration, leading eventually to political integration. What has been achieved within the Community has depended upon political leadership by national elites and by political agreements between national governments. As the President of Germany, Herr Scheel has put it, 'Only political impulses will unite Europe . . . Europe has grown beyond the blind belief that political unity will automatically and inevitably follow communal institutions in the economic field. This conception has unfortunately shown itself to be false.'[15]

However, undue optimism about the potential promotive role of 'quasi-federal' or supranational' rather than genuinely federal institutions is not the only weak point in the neo-functionalist argument. The argument too readily glosses over, or ignores, the differences between domestic and international politics, between sovereign government and international organisation. This fault in itself results from the tendency on the part of the theorists of pluralist society as we have seen to under-rate the importance of the formal powers of central government in a political process, and to over-emphasize the importance of group activity and informal power relationships. Behavioural studies generally have tended to neglect the importance of constitutional arrangements and formal power as systemic variables affecting behaviour. The ultimate formal power, in fact, of the Council within the range of powers and functions of the Community has proved a decisive factor. The residual and still overwhelmingly dominant powers of member state governments have not only determined the behaviour of the Council, which represents them, but have continued to determine the behaviour of parties and interest groups.

Yet another weakness in the neo-functionalist argument is that interest groups do not really, in fact, anywhere fulfill the role described for them in the pluralist apologia which is so important a part of the neo-functionalist thesis. They fall short of it. First they do not compromise and channel in any society, to any marked degree, the demands of their members. They have become more or less remote oligarchies, and the mass membership is neither much involved, nor committed through them to procedures for conflict resolution. They cannot, therefore, in any significant sense be looked to as possible creators of 'community' or 'significant carriers'[16] of an ideology of integration. Second, the competition between groups in pluralist societies does not ensure that, on the whole and in the long term, a community interest is represented to government as a product of countervailing interests which make themselves felt. Countervalency in most societies does not obtain to any general degree. Some groups are very much more powerful than others. Some interests go virtually unrepresented. Third and finally the institutionalisation of pressure group consultation with government accentuates both the tendencies mentioned above. Group leaders, through their association with government develop a different view-point from their members. The recognition of one group rather than another for consultation accentuates the disparity of power between groups. It may even effectively shut off the voice of dissent. Group leaders, in other words, are part of a *national* leadership complex. The internationalisation of national group leadership is not likely to be any easier than the inter-nationalisation of political leadership. To suppose that group leaders will perceive common interests with like groups in other countries and combine with them to promote policies at a new international regional level is quite unrealistic. Whether the orthodox model of the pluralist society ever corresponded to an existing reality is open to argument. It does not depict any contemporary reality but it is, unfortunately, a part of the framework of neo-functionalist assumptions.

Some of these weaknesses of the neo-functionalist theory and approach to international organisation have been recognised, at least in part, by the early proponents of the thesis. Haas himself has noted the extent to which spillover, though its logic may be apparent, is checked by what he calls 'the built-in autonomy of functional contexts'[17] (what I have called elsewhere[18] circumscription and counteraction: conservative, equilibrium restoring forces in any social system which limit and reduce the impact of any change). Leon Lindberg, faced with the example of General de Gaulle's intransigent opposition to the expansive logic of integration has, noted, sorrowing, that 'the evidence indicates that the governments can avoid the logical consequences of integration for an unexpectedly long time'.[19] They act as 'gatekeepers' against expansionist, spill-over pressures. Lindberg was also the first to recognize and point out that a successful integrative step might actually have a negative effect on the prospects for further integration, creating stress rather than solidarity among the participant states, reinforcing the gatekeeper effect. This could happen both because negotiations were protracted and harshly competitive and because the policy in action was redistributive in its effects. The European Community agricultural policy is an obvious example.

There are other respects in which the academic theory of neo-functionalism may be challenged. More relevant for our purposes, however, is the identification of the central problem of the European Community itself, since it was the inspiration for the theory and remains the unique actual example of the strategy. We have pointed out that the architects of the Treaty believed that they had created something new in international relations and organisation. What was new, and believed to be unique, was its institutional framework, which was said to be not federal but 'quasi-federal' or 'supranational' — federalism in prospect. Its distinctive feature was the dialogue between a designedly federal body — the European Commission with its autonomous, protected powers, and the Council of Ministers — a deliberately inter-governmental body with its unit-veto procedures. The Treaty was, there-fore, like the Council of Europe before it, a compromise between federalism and intergovernmentalism. In the Council of Europe it was the Assembly which embodied the federal principle. When that experimental compromise was seen to be a total victory for inter-governmentalism (as it was after the failure of the Assembly's Strasbourg Resolution of 1950 to make any headway in the Council of Ministers) the ECSC was designed with a much stronger federalist component. What is evident, after more than two decades of trial of the new design, is that, in any sort of compromise between inter-governmentalism and federalism, the triumph of the former has a certain logic about it. Unit-veto decision making procedures impose themselves on any organisation in which they play an integral part. They restrict its organic growth and its policy potential and they tend to be self-sustaining.

In neo-functionalist theory the very general conceptualisation of central institutions, or what Etzioni calls vaguely 'system-elites', though capable of embracing the ambiguities of the institutions of the Community, is a major weakness. Given the role anticipated for such illustrations there are necessary questions of detail about requisite structures, formal powers, rules, consensus, procedures, which are neither raised nor answered by neo-functionalists.

Notes

1. Quotations from the Schuman Declaration are from U. Kitzinger, *The European Common Market and Community: a selection of contemporary documents*, London, Routledge and Kegan Paul, 1967, pp. 37–39.
2. E.B. Haas and A.S. Whiting, *Dynamics of International Relations*, New York, McGraw Hill, 1956, p. vii.
3. Haas, E.B., *The Uniting of Europe*, 2nd edition, Standford University Press, 1968, p. 5.
4. Haas, E.B. *Beyond the Nation State*, Stanford U.P., 1964, p. 46.
5. *The Uniting of Europe*, p. xxxiv.
6. *Ibid.*, p. 5.
7. *Beyond the Nation State*, p. 37. citing R.C. McCridis, 'Interest Groups in Comparative Analysis', *Journal of Politics*, XXIII, 1961, 45.
8. *The Uniting of Europe*, p. xxxiii.
9. Leon Lindberg, *The Political Dynamics of European Economic Integration*, Stanford, Stanford University Press, 1963, p. 10. Haas's definition is from his 'International Integration: the European and the Universal Process', *International Organisation*, XV, 1961, p. 368.
10. *The Uniting of Europe*, p. 297.
11. Leon Lindberg, *op. cit.*, p. 170.
12. See Lindberg L. and Scheingold, S.A., *Europe's would-be polity*, Englewood Cliffs, Prentice Hall, 1970, p. 119. And J. Nye, *Peace in Parts*, Boston, Little Brown, 1971, pp. 69–71.
13. Coombes, D., *Politics & Bureaucracy in the European Community*, London, Allen and Unwin, 1970, p. 272.

14. *op. cit.*, p. 274.
15. Address by Herr Scheel to the Annual Congress of the Free Democratic Party, of which he was Chairman, in November 1973.
16. Haas, *The Uniting of Europe*, p. 5.
17. International Integration, *op. cit.*, p. 376.
18. *Europe in Question*, London, Allen and Unwin, 1974, p. 187.
19. 'Decision making and integration in the European Community', *International Political Communities* (an Anthology), New York, Doubleday, 1966, p. 228.

Selected Reading

1. R.J. Harrison, *Europe in Question*, London, George Allen and Unwin, 1974.
2. Ernst B. Haas, *Beyond the Nation State*, Stanford, Stanford University Press, 1964.
3. Ernst B. Haas, 'The Joys and Agonies of Pretheorising', *International Organisation*, XXIV, 4, 1970.
4. L.N. Lindberg and S.A. Scheingold, *Europe's Would-Be Polity*, Englewood Cliffs, Prnetice Hall, 1970.
5. Paul Taylor, *International Cooperation Today*, London, Elek, 1971.
6. R.D. Hanson, 'Regional Investigation: Reflections on a decade of theoretical efforts', *World Politics*, 21, 2, January 1969.
7. A.J.R. Groom and Paul Taylor (eds.), *Functionalism: Theory and Practice in International Relations*, London, University of London Press, 1975.

CHAPTER THIRTEEN

THE PARALLEL NATIONAL ACTION PROCESS: SCANDINAVIAN EXPERIENCES

Gunnar P. Nielsson

Introduction

The parallel national action process differs from harmonisation, co-ordination and cooperation in the sense that, while it involves all of those processes, it goes beyond them in the degree to which it develops continuously expanding integrative behavioural codes of conduct among the participating states and thereby expands the scope and intensity of common activities into an integrative network. The maintenance of autonomous state authority is a basic premise of the parallel national action approach. Consequently, there is no expectation that it may lead to regional political unification. However, the parallel national action process could lead to political integration in the behavioural sense that the states adopt identical or highly similar domestic and foreign policies as a result of continuous consultation, joint investigation and common deliberation which become constant factors in the national decision-making processes. For the analyst of parallel national action, therefore, the focus must be on the behavioural manifestations of identical and coordinated actions performed by national actors without the use of supra-national decision-making authorities.

The more detailed elaboration of the parallel national action process presented in this chapter is based on experiences among the five Nordic States of Denmark, Finland, Iceland, Norway and Sweden.[1] Previous scholarly work on Scandinavian cooperation has concentrated on the Nordic Council as a regional intergovernmental organisation comparable to the Council of Europe.[2] It is our contention that the analysis of the competence, procedures, and participants in the brief annual sessions of the Nordic Council's Plenary Assembly is an insufficient basis for gaining an understanding of the operating characteristics of the Nordic integrative network. It deals only with the tip of the iceberg, as it were, and gives the impression of discontinuity which characterizes the harmonization and coordination processes discussed elsewhere in this volume.

When Scandinavian relations are analyzed in the parallel national action perspective, the Nordic Council organisations can be viewed as instruments which assist in providing continuity to the interaction process among different types of actors. That is to say, integrative behaviour, involving Nordic transnational groups, parliamentarians, members of political executives and civil service administrators from the five states is *facilitated* by the Nordic Council organisations, but it is *not fundamentally dependent upon the regional institutions.*

The following discussion of the parallel national action process has been organized in four sections. A general overview of regional integration theories is presented in the first section which addresses the central thesis that a shift in analytical focus is needed, moving away from preoccupation with the supra-national institutional characteristics of integration processes toward a concentration on changes in the behavioural codes of conduct among states.

The Scandinavian experiences are discussed in the following three sections. First, three basic conditions governing the parallel national action approach to regional integration are discussed. Second, the structure and process characteristics of the Nordic cooperative network are analyzed within the developmental perspective of incremental, formal institutionalization leading to the establishment of Nordic Council organisations. The pattern of development demonstrates that cooperative behavioural codes of conduct among the five national actors emerged before they achieved expression in regional institutional form. Third, the outcomes of the Nordic parallel national action process are reviewed in terms of what has been achieved in regard to equalizing legal and socio-economic conditions, removing national barriers to interaction, pooling of resources, and coordinating foreign policy positions in extra-regional relations.

The Parallel National Action Process in Theoretical Perspective

In the perspective of theories of international cooperation and integration, the central thesis of this chapter is the necessity to change analytical focus by developing alternative conceptual frameworks and

271

methodological models. The neo-functionalist theories have been dominated by 'structural tunnel vision' with their emphasis on visions of potential, political structural formats which could be the outcome of dynamic integration processes. It is our contention that the focus should be turned to the process of change in the behavioural codes of conduct among states acting within the existing decentralized international structure of sovereign states.

Throughout the 1950's and 1960's, the academic, theoretically-oriented literature on international regional integration focused on the process of creating larger political units. The ultimate outcome of political integration was seen as a basic political structural transformation whereby a number of previously separated states become fused into a larger political unit whether federal, confederal or 'harmonized union' in format. The integration process involved the formation of a political community through the transfer of coercive, utilitarian and identitive powers to a new centre of authority.[3] A new structure would be created within which the political process was channeled.

According to the earlier theorists, there were four major approaches to this process of political community formation. In the first place, *military conquest* could be used to superimpose authority by one state on another political community. It assured an immediate transfer of coercive power and could also quickly lead to the establishment of effective utilitarian power. It was very difficult, however, to assure the transfer of symbolic power to the conquering state authority because it involved the self-abnegation of the previously existing community loyalties. Hence, structural transformation based on military conquest was a short run solution. It often created irredentist movements around cultural nationalist loyalties which were sources of 'liberation movements' struggling to regain a degree of autonomous political structure which could protect and express the particular cultural values tying a group of people together.[4]

A second approach to political structural transformation was *constitutional fusion*. This involved political unification through the single act of creating a new political structural framework by consent among diverse cultural groupings. A number of previously autonomous political units would come together voluntarily to establish a constitutional structure with binding authority in both high politics and low politics issue areas for all the participating actors.[5] The formation of the federal constitutional framework for the United States of America represents a case in which structural transformation occurred

272

through a series of major changes taking place within a relatively short period. The evolutionary development of the Swiss 'Confederation' represents a variant case where the constitutional fusion process has taken place over a longer period of time.[6] The establishment of federal political structures in Canada, India, Yugoslavia, Nigeria and Czechoslovakia represent more recent manifestations of the constitutional fusion approach. The main features of the approach were that adjustment to changes in conditions governing the political process took place through adoption by legal fiat of a new political structure, and that the existence of several institutionalized political communities based on cultural nationalism was a permanent condition. The constitutional fusion approach could, over time, lead to new strong societal bonds based on the mutual advantage which larger, more centralized (and therefore supposedly more effective) utilitarian power bestows on the participating groups. It could also lead to acceptance of centralized coercive power within limited jurisdiction. It would not necessarily lead to increased symbolic power because the federal or confederal structure usually guaranteed the protection and maintenance of distinct cultural identities.

A third approach to structural transformation was based on *classical functionalist* theory.[7] It postulated that cooperation must begin in low politics issue areas which can be 'decoupled' from the more symbolically and ideologically charged political processes. Cooperation in low politics issue areas could be achieved by granting to administrative experts a mandate with sufficient authority to negotiate, formulate, and implement new policies. It was assumed that such a low politics problem-solution process would lead to utilitarian advantages for more and more separate segments within the states involved. That, in turn, would create cross-cutting ties decreasing the ability of the political elites of the states to mobilize all their societal resources for the purposes of adopting power politics responses to demands for changes in the environment. According to the thesis that 'form follows function', the political structural transformation which would result from a classical functional approach would be the creation of a global-scope cobweb of functional ties based on a perceived superiority of utilitarian advantages which would under-mine the centralized coercive power available to state authorities. The territorial principle of political organisation created through the process of politically mobilized, assertive cultural nationalism would give way to a global network of administrative organizations based on the principle of functional advantage. However, Mitrany consistently maintained that cultural diversity would not disappear, that is, nationality identity would remain as the font of symbolic, identitive power, but pragmatic orientations would prevail in regard to solving problems involving utilitarian advantages. The concern with increasing socio-economic welfare would become the basic dynamic in relations among groups who would recognize the self-defeating strategy of dealing with the welfare issues by power politics responses.

The fourth approach to political unification was *neo-functionalist regional international economic integration.*[8] The neo-functionalist approach accepted the necessity to start the integration process at the level of low politics issue areas, but it could not be achieved by non-political, administrative leadership. The economic integration process was an integral part of the political process in which the states were active participants. New political elites would emerge through the creation of regional institutions with supranational authority in specific, limited jurisdictions involving issue areas which the state authorities recognized they were unable to solve individually. The regionally oriented elites operating the new regional decision-making institutions would foster a spill-over process based on their ability to solve problems on a regional instead of a single state basis. Such a spill-over process would result in expansion of tasks for the regional institutions and consequently creation of new regional loyalties. These regional decision-making authorities would expand incrementally from non-controversial, low politics to more politically sensitive high politics issue areas as the integration process expanded from economic to social and finally to symbolic, identitive political issue areas. The integrative spill-over dynamic would result in the gradual erosion of the individual state's authority culminating in the political structural transformation of forming a new, larger state in the region.

The experiences gained from attempts to demonstrate the viability of the neo-functionalist integration process indicated that the expectation of political structural transformation was unrealistic. Consequently, the more recently published, theoretically oriented works on regional integration indicate a trend away from the 'structural tunnel vision' of the earlier literature.[9] It is in this context, that the conceptual framework of parallel national action processes is proposed as an alternative analytical perspective. At a minimum, it is hoped that it could add a complementary dimension to the existing theoretical frameworks which have guided much of the scholarship in

274

this subfield of international relations.

Such a conceptual framework must, in the first place, be based on a differentiation of societal and community sources of solidarity. A community can be defined as a human group tied together by affective feelings usually based on cultural identity which is manifested by shared perceptions of common values, of the common public good, acceptance of the legacy of a shared past and the expectation of a shared future. Nationality identification is characterized by community attributes. A society, on the other hand, can be defined as a human group tied together by functional interdependence manifested by mutual advantages derived from role specializations, division of labour and increased material benefits.[10] Using the terminology proposed by Herbert Kelman, community bonds are based on 'sentimental' values whereas societal bonds are based on 'instrumental' values.[11] A political system can be composed of a single community or the coexistence of multiple communities tied together by societal bonds. The single-community political system is a pure type nation-state in which community and societal bonds combine as the basis upon which state authority is legitimized. In the multi-community type of political system, state authority is legitimized predominantly on the basis of societal bonds.[12] National integration can thus be defined as the process of transforming societal relationships into community bonds. Neo-functionalist international political integration can be defined as the process of expanding the basis of legitimization from several political systems to a larger single political system. Its structural attribute is the unification of several state authorities into a single state structure by 'incremental federalism'.[13]

The initial stages of the parallel national action process is characterized by a process of continuous intense *cooperation* among state authorities without the expectation of structural transformation in the form of political unification. It may result in *socio-economic integration* of an international region through which *societal* bonds are intensified, but the community bonds remain the basis of legitimized, separate state authorities. Hence, parallel national action is a method of adapting to growing international societal interdependence. State authorities commit themselves to pursuing a parallel national action process because it allows them to be responsive to the changing socio-economic conditions according to which they must operate, but with minimum political consequences in regard to their politico-structural autonomy.

As the scope of cooperation among state and non-state actors increases, the consultative and deliberative aspects of their interaction networks become institutionalized on a regional basis. The increased political interdependence which develops as a result of intensified cooperation is indicated in a change in the behavioural code of conduct among the participating states. The key indicators of the resultant *political integration* are to be found in the degree to which policies are formulated and implemented through identical or highly similar action by the separate political structures of each state. Hence, the indicators are not to be found in the formation of regional supranational decision-making authorities, but by the identical and closely coordinated *behaviour* of the formal governmental elites as well as the non-governmental groups within the region.

This discussion represents only a first step in the formulation of a more fully explicated model. The development of operational definitions and indicators of the parallel national action process, which would allow more precise empirical testing, has not been attempted here, but is in progress. Therefore, the descriptive analysis of the Scandinavian experiences presented in the following sections of this chapter serves only as an empirical illustration of how the parallel national action process might be a useful conceptual framework for future studies of how separate states maintain their structural autonomy while behaviourally becoming politically integrated.

Governing Conditions for the Nordic Integration Process

The parallel national action process in the Nordic region has occurred within parameters which facilitate changing behavioural codes of conduct among state units through intensive integration in the low politics issue areas without the expectation of political structural transformation leading to a new regional state. Before analysing the parallel national action approach in detail, a brief discussion is provided of the historical experiences which established the basic conditions governing the present structure and process of Scandinavian integration.

A political union existed in the Nordic region in the fifteenth and early sixteenth centuries.[14] The Kalmar Union was a loose confederation based on dynastic ties. The confederative jurisdiction was in the high politics issue areas of security policy, foreign policy and external commerce. Beyond that, the Kalmar Union was characterized by extreme decentralisation in the low politics areas of socio-economic relations both within and among the component states. It was also based on a regional structure of near-equal capability to exercise power. Consequently, no single state could compel unification by force.

In other words, there was no equivalent in Scandinavia to Piedmont in the Italian or Prussia in the German unification processes.

Intra-regional warfare between the kingdoms of Denmark-Norway and Sweden-Finland followed the collapse of the Kalmar Union. The competition for dominance of the Nordic region drew the two states into different coalitions with larger states and they became participants in the broader balance of power politics which character-ised European international politics. In the eighteenth century, the two kingdoms declined in stature as significant actors in Northern European relations and they became *objects* of balance of power policies by such larger European states as Russia, Prussia, France and Britain.

The Napoleonic Wars clearly demonstrated that the Scandinavian states had become pawns in European balance of power politics. The outcome of the wars led to a significant change in the structure of the Nordic state system. Finland was ceded by Sweden to Czarist Russia and became a Duchy within that regime. Denmark ceded control of Norway which was annexed into the Swedish kingdom while preserving considerable local autonomy.

Through the nineteenth century, relations among the Nordic states changed dramatically. The reduction in stature which the states had experienced through defeats in war and the emergence of larger political units in Central and Southern Europe resulted in a general withdrawal by the Scandinavian states from constant involvement in European balance of power politics. The confrontationist threat system which had been the dominant characteristic of Nordic inter-state relations subsided as the governing elites adapted foreign policies commensurate with their small state stature. One method of adaptation was the use of joint declarations of neutrality in conflicts among larger powers in Europe. Such an approach to security policy issues had been practised intermittently in the mid-eighteenth century until the Nordic states were drawn into the Napoleonic wars. It was used with renewed emphasis by Denmark and Sweden-Norway in response to the Crimean War in 1853 and the Franco-Prussian War in 1870.

Another method of adaptation was the attempt which was made in the 1860's to achieve political unification by the constitutional fusion approach. It was based on the combination of an emerging idealistic Pan-Scandinavian Movement, sustained predominantly by the academic profession and university student organisations, and the members of the governing elites in Denmark and Sweden who tried to

277

exploit the Pan-Scandinavian sentiment in coping with important foreign policy problems.[15] The governmental elites involved viewed potential political unification as a compensation for the dwindling stature of their states in European power politics. They decided to utilize these sentiments to form a confederation resembling the Kalmar Union. While the three states — Denmark, Norway and Sweden — would maintain their separate governments, a dynastic union was to be established through a Family Pact whereby the Danish Royal House and the Swedish-Norwegian Royal House would be fused by marriage. State Councils and a Confederal Parliament were to be established as common institutions with supra-national authority in the three issue areas of security policy, foreign policy and external commerce.

The plan to confederate collapsed because its foundation was undermined by power politics. The Danish Government's expectation of Swedish-Norwegian military assistance in its conflict with Prussia over Schlesvig-Holstein was unacceptable to Swedish interests. The commitment to a Scandinavian political union was revealed to be disguised nationalism by the Danish Government and a personal interest by the Swedish-Norwegian monarch. The unification scheme was without broad popular support in any of the three states and was considered an unrealistic approach to Nordic relations by important members of the Swedish Government.

The failure of the constitutional fusion approach demonstrated the lack of Scandinavian identification in the high politics issue areas. It had severe consequences for future cooperative relations. The constitutional fusion approach as well as the ideologically oriented Pan-Scandinavian Movement were totally discredited. The ideological overtone of the Scandinavian Movement was replaced by a concentration on 'practical Scandinavianism' as the Movement began the process of regaining legitimacy by emphasizing the need to build popular support 'from the bottom up'. Only a functional approach to integration in low politics issue areas could establish the infrastructure from which cooperation among states could proceed. Any scheme which could be characterized as involving political structural transformation in the direction of formal confederal or federal unification became viewed among the Scandinavian elites — even ardent advocates of closer low politics integration — as the visionary expression of naive fools. Hence, since the 1860's, Nordic political unification has not been legitimized as a high politics objective sustained by 'dramatic-political elites' operating in domestic conditions of 'permissive consensus'.[16] That is the legacy of the constitutional fusion experiment and in its failure lies one of the important governing conditions of twentieth century parallel national action approaches to Nordic integration.

In the second half of the nineteenth century, Scandinavian regional relations were dominated by the mobilization of new political forces based on cultural nationalism and democratisation of the political process. The resultant nation-state building process led to a fragmentation of the existing dynastic unions. After the loss of Schleswig-Holstein, the Danish political system became preoccupied with domestic economic development and democratic reform. The agrarian-bourgeois political organisations laid the foundations for pluralistic democracies which the emergent industrial labour movements in both Denmark and Sweden expanded into extensive welfare state democracies through the evolutionary socialist approach. In Norway, the democratisation process was combined with an especially intense upsurge of cultural nationalism as the Norwegians gained complete independence by separation from Sweden in 1905. At the end of the First World War, Finland gained independence by breaking away from the newly formed Soviet Union. After the Second World War, Iceland completed its gradual separation from Denmark and became an independent republic in 1948.

Except for a brief civil war in Finland, the fragmentation of state structures occurred under peaceful conditions in the Nordic region. The intense cultural nationalism was ameliorated by strong Scandinavian ties among the various labour movements although 'Labour Scandinavianism' was held suspect by the non-socialist political organisations. However, the Nordic solidarity within the labour movement was not allowed to interfere with the predominant nationalist emphasis on separate and full equality of all the Nordic states.

Hence, strong popular support within each of the five Nordic states for the continuation of separate, legitimised nation-states is the second important governing condition for the Scandinavian approach to integration. It is a reflection of community-based cultural nationalism and democratisation of the political process.

Until the formation of NATO in 1949, Nordic inter-state relations in the high politics issue area of security policy developed into a pattern of parallel national action responses in the form of joint neutrality declarations. This method of successful small state adaptation to major power conflict in Europe was used by Denmark, Norway and Sweden in the First World War.

The Nordic states did accept continuous active involvement in international politics through coordinated action in the League of Nations in the 1920's and used the League arbitration machinery to settle remaining territorial disputes in the cases of Greenland and the Aaland islands. However, the Scandinavian states quickly withdrew from active involvement when the League proved ineffective as a conflict resolution mechanism, demonstrated by its inability to impose effective economic sanctions against Italy in response to Mussolini's Abyssinian War in the mid-1930's. Instead, the Nordic states attempted in the late 1930's to revert back to non-involvement in a new large scale European war by negotiating a new joint neutrality declaration. An attempt to institutionalize that policy by establishing a Nordic neutral league failed.

The differences in the degree of involvement in the Second World War by the Nordic states set the stage for the diversity in their contemporary security policies. Finland's extensive warfare experiences against the Soviet Union — first separately in the 1939—40 Winter War and subsequently in alliance with Germany — led to its present precarious neutrality which is maintained by conducting very cautious relations with the Western states in order to assure its credibility as a neutral as far as the USSR is concerned.[17] Finland's relations with the other Nordic states have been a testing ground on how far it can go in relations with the West. Sweden's armed neutrality policy has become a tradition sustained by successfully remaining out of European armed conflict since 1815. It has been a major determinant in Swedish decisions to stay out of alliance commitments and not to join the European Communities after the Second World War. Its neutrality policies are partially justified by the Swedes as adding to the credibility of Finnish neutrality by avoiding the destabilizing effect western alliance membership would create in Finno-Soviet relations.

The occupation of Denmark and Norway by German forces during the Second World War created different perceptions of the necessary conditions for national security. The Norwegians' concern with national security has been expressed by a firm alliance commitment to NATO, a commitment initially reinforced by a strong Anglophile orientation as a result of their wartime experiences and by their perceived need for American support in defending a very long North Atlantic coastline. Denmark's national security interests have been perceived and interpreted in light of Germany's role in European international power politics since the unification of Germany. The attempt to return to neutrality after the Second World War (through a joint neutral Nordic alliance or a Swedish-Danish alliance) was dashed by an 'occupation generation' which sought new ways of coping with the problem of protecting a nationally autonomous existence as a small neighbour to a large state with a history of aggression in the twentieth century.[18] The Danes became committed to NATO membership reluctantly after the pursuit of neutrality policies in a Scandinavian context proved impossible. Both Denmark and Norway contribute to conventional force capabilities as part of NATO's integrated command structure. But they do not allow the stationing of non-indigenous forces or the positioning of nuclear arms on their territories. Iceland became a NATO member due to strong Anglo-American influence through their naval activities in the Second World War and because of its naval strategic significance in the North Atlantic. Iceland maintains no forces of its own, but has agreed to the stationing of allied air forces in Keflavik.

This constellation of relatively low level NATO commitment by Iceland, Denmark and Norway, armed neutrality by Sweden and a precarious, Soviet-conditioned neutrality by Finland comprise the structure of security policies identified as the Nordic Balance. It provides the Scandinavian states with a high degree of autonomy in the conduct of European as well as intra-Nordic relations. However, it contains the latent potential of superpower involvement in case of intensification of East-West hostilities.

In the perspective of Scandinavian integration, the diversity of national security policies which the concept of Nordic Balance connotes has resulted in the third major governing condition that security policies are excluded from the parallel nation action process.

The historical development of an intensive cooperative network among the Scandinavian states which has evolved into a parallel national action approach to integration are governed by the conditions of 1) the avoidance of the constitutional fusion approach; 2) the expectation that the political structure of five autonomous nation-states remains the unalterable basis for regional integration in low politics issue areas; and 3) the exclusion of the high politics issue area of national security policies from regional integration processes.

The Structure and Process of the Scandinavian Parallel National Action Approach to Integration

Scandinavian integration is characterised by a consensus-building process. The use of force or non-violent coercion are unacceptable practices. Reliance on close majority voting in formal decision-making

281

institutions is eschewed. Persuasion is the dominant instrument. Following the dictum of 'building cooperation from below', it starts with involving the parties most directly affected by the intended cooperative action, then working informally from the level of the individual through the level of secondary, socio-economic groupings to the level of formalized governmental agreements.

The Scandinavian integration process is dominated by pragmatism. Contrasted with the so-called Benelux Procedure,[19] which involved a high level elite decision on far-reaching principles that served as a mandate on the basis of which investigations could be undertaken and implementing institutions could be established, the Scandinavian approach starts without fixed, long-range political goals by initiating investigations and consultations from which it proceeds to deliberation and recommendations. If strong opposition develops to a proposed Nordic cooperative scheme, based on nationalistic emotions, violation of perceived national interests, fear of socio-economic disadvantage or pressure from outside the Scandinavian region, then the proponents try to meet it and overcome it by new rounds of investigations and consultations until well-founded, expert documentation and argumentation demonstrate mutual advantages for all parties concerned.

The primary, if not exclusive, tasks of the general Nordic institutions are those of initiating, investigating, deliberating and recommending proposals for cooperative actions. These tasks are carried out through calling conferences which include interest group representatives, parliamentarians, governmental ministers, and national administration experts; setting up *ad hoc* committees of investigation; deliberating in standing committees; and making recommendations to the five national political executives either by expert, senior civil servants to inter-Nordic meetings of Government Ministers or by the Nordic Council's Plenary Assembly during its brief, annual Plenary Session.

Nordic cooperation agreements are implemented through the process of parallel national action which takes the form of adopting identical laws and regulations by the five national political systems. There are no regional law-making institutions with supra-national authority. The legal or constitutional basis of Nordic integration practices are based on highly similar or identical national laws. In issue areas concerning joint action in extra-Scandinavian relations, implementation occurs through close coordination of policy positions and strategies of negotiation or through one state representing Scandinavian interests in executive organs of wider European or global-scope international institutions.

282

In considering the structural characteristics of the parallel national action approach, to focus exclusively on the formal Nordic Council organisations as the key to understanding the approach is to miss major components in the dynamics of the extensive network. The pattern of interactions involved includes four basic types of actors: 1) national interest groups and their Nordic transnational institutions; 2) political parties and their national and Nordic parliamentary institutions; 3) the political executives[20] acting in their national ministerial roles and their Nordic roles, formally through the new Nordic Council of Ministers and informally through their regularized inter-Scandinavian meetings; and 4) the National Civil Administrations with their Nordic Contact Man System. It is the behavioural code of conduct adopted in the patterns of interaction among these four types of actors which constitute the structure of the Nordic cooperative network.

In a developmental perspective, formal institutionalization of the Nordic cooperative network during the past twenty-five years represents efforts systematically to consolidate already existing cooperative behavioural codes of conduct which have developed incrementally, informally and in an *ad hoc* manner. It has truly been a case of the classical functionalist axiom that 'form follows (or should follow) function'.

In order to provide some impression of a time perspective, the Nordic cooperative network will be described according to the role of trans-national institutions, *ad hoc* cooperative practices by both political executive and parliamentary actors, and the administrative Nordic Contact Man System before the Nordic Council organisations are discussed.

The Nordic Transnational Infrastructure

Contrary to the experiences in the European Communities where Community-wide interest groups and associations have developed *in response to* the establishment of 'supra-national' decision-making institutions, the dynamic of Scandinavian integration is dominated by interest groups and parliamentarian groups acting as initiators and coordinators of proposals for Scandinavian-wide actions.

Since the late nineteenth century, a transnational infra-structure has developed based on the voluntary formation of Scandinavian-wide organisations — federations, congresses, associations, and unions — at the level of economic interest groups, professional associations, and social groupings. It is impossible within the format of this short chapter to provide a more detailed description of the present transnational institutional network. To give an impressionistic profile of the early phase of their development, a list of some of the main inter-Nordic organizations, arranged in chronological order, is provided.

Partial Overview of the Development of a Scandinavian Transnational Institutional Network

1860's: Nordic School Teachers Congresses
1870's: Nordic Congress of Economists
1872: Nordic Assembly of Jurists
1876: Association of Nordic Railway Men
1886: Nordic Congress of Trade Unions
1888: Nordic Shipping Companies' Association
1888: Nordic Agricultural Congress
1907: Nordic Employers' Association
1916: Nordic Trade and Commerce Association
1917: Nordic Council of Craftsmen
1918: Nordic Association of Consumers Cooperative Societies
1918: Nordic Civil Servants Federation
1919: Norden Association
1922: Nordic Tourist Industry Committee
1925: Nordic Telecommunication Congresses
1925: Nordic Journalists and Broadcasters Association
1931: Nordic Organization of Savings and Loan Association
1935: Nordic Union of Road Techniques

This partial list shows only the establishment of Scandinavian institutions at a 'peak-association' level. In many cases, inter-Scandinavian congresses, federations, associations and unions are established on lower geographical or narrower functional levels such as specific branches of industries or professions. While no complete description of the extent of transnational institutions has been completed yet, a group of researchers at Gothenburg University in Sweden recently reported the completion of a representative survey of 300 Swedish organisations. Of the 180 organisations which responded, 75% had had at least one meeting with their Nordic 'sister organisations' during the previous five years and nearly two-thirds of them participated continuously in permanently established Scandinavian institutions.[21]

The result has been that a very intensive and extensive institutional network exists which had developed roots prior to the institutionalization of Scandinavian integration at the governmental level. The Nordic non-state actors cooperate by means of regular congresses for representatives of the national branches, continuous consultation and coordination through committees and active participation in the investigations and planning phases of Nordic integrative activities. The interest groups focus predominantly on objectives which are narrow in scope such as standardization of nomenclature and technical specifications; equalization of working conditions; exchange of personnel and information; identical or similar Scandinavian legislation in the areas of the right of establishment (for commercial activity), trust laws, social welfare, insurance, industrial safety rules, patents, navigation; coordination of timetables and schedules for tourist travel; harmonization of school systems and joint Nordic textbooks in various subject areas; and joint radio and television broadcasts. The trade union and employers associations were more politicized in the early phases with establishment of joint strike funds, agreements on sympathy strikes, agreements not to hire workers striking in another country and not to ship commodities involved in industrial disputes into the country where it was taking place. But by the 1930's, the industrial interest groups had become predominantly technical and more narrow-scope occupational in orientation.

None of the Nordic transnational organisations promote a Pan-Scandinavian ideology striving for political unification. The only organization which deliberately promotes a general Nordic cooperation line is the 'Norden' Association. Formed in 1919, it has developed 500 branches in the five Scandinavian states with a membership of 120,000 in 1959.[22] It has worked most actively in the area of cultural cooperation and has promoted such projects as a friendship cities programme more general people-to-people exchanges, Scandinavian literature, and jointly authored texts on Scandinavian history to eliminate national prejudice. It has also been a consistent supporter of initiatives in Nordic cooperation in every sphere of activity. The absence of a commitment to use supranational authority in Scandinavian integration is indicated by the fact that the national Norden Associations did not establish a common Nordic Federation with a secretariat until 1965.

In general, the transnational institutional network has been dominated by a focus on 'practical Scandinavianism' which is characterized by acceptance of the existing five state structures, concentration on the least politically controversial issue areas, and operating through the parallel national action approach to integration. As such, the non-state actors have been crucially important as participants in expanding

Scandinavian integration.

Ad Hoc Intergovernmental Cooperation

Intergovernmental cooperation developed on an *ad hoc* basis during the first half of this century. It can be viewed as a response to the development of transnational infrastructure activity and to general European international political pressure. At the level of infrastructure activity, the Nordic Assembly of Jurists was instrumental in establishing, in 1901, the Joint Nordic Legal Commission which was the first Scandinavian intergovernmental body with the task of investigating the extent to which laws could be made identical or very similar throughout Scandinavia. In 1906, the Nordic Inter-Parliamentarian Union was established for the purpose of assuring participation by parliamentarians in the planning and deliberative phases of harmonizing legislation. It also reflected the rise of inter-Scandinavian contacts and conferences among the political parties in the Nordic states. Although no thorough research has yet been published on the role of political parties as transnational actors, most analysts of Scandinavian cooperation point to their significance as an instrument in forging the Scandinavian integrative network. While practically all the political parties in Scandinavia have participated actively, the 'Scandinavianism' of the Nordic Labour/ Social-Democratic parties has been especially important in raising cooperation to the political executive level during the 1930's and 1940's. The Nordic Inter-Parliamentarian Union provided a forum for the evolution of continuous discussion of Nordic cooperative proposals and for caucusing within the wider European Parliamentarian Union which was formed in 1899.

Regular meetings at the political executive level began with the Nordic Ministers For Social Policy in 1926. However, it was not until after the Second World War that such behaviour patterns became institutionalized. In 1946, regular meetings were begun by the five Scandinavian Ministers of Justice, Culture and Education. At that time, special standing commissions composed of senior civil servants, ministers and, in some cases, parliamentarians, were established in Legal Affairs, Cultural Affairs, and Social Policy Affairs. Since the late 1940's, regular meetings among members of the Scandinavian political executives have become an established behavioural code of conduct. Such meetings have been most extensively practiced by the ministers of Foreign Affairs, Justice, Culture and Education, Social Policy, Transportation and Communication, and Trade, Economy, and Commerce.

286

In the early 1950's, members of committees in the five national parliaments also began to meet on an *ad hoc* basis to deal with specific issue areas in Nordic cooperation. In May, 1950, the Danish, Norwegian and Swedish Parliamentary Committees on the Judiciary met in Copenhagen to discuss the proposal for a uniform citizenship law and in 1951 the respective Parliaments agreed to establish a Joint Nordic Parliamentary Committee for Traffic Freedom which laid the groundwork for the Nordic Passport Union established in the mid-1950's. Parallel national action at the Parliamentary Committee level was also used in 1960 to consider the proposal for uniform Nordic copyright laws.

High level intergovernmental cooperation also developed in the area of general foreign policy, but that was a response to European international political pressure, not a result of an intra-regional integrative dynamic. The primary purpose of cooperation in foreign policy was to defend and give enhanced political credibility to the Scandinavian states' neutrality postures in European balance of power politics. In response to the outbreak of the First World War, the three Scandinavian Monarchs and their Foreign Ministers met in Sweden in December, 1914 to issue a joint declaration of neutrality. It represented a case of parallel national action in which the three states coordinated their diplomatic behaviour as a basis for a 'Neutrality Entente' in Northern Europe. Throughout the First World War, both the Prime Ministers and Foreign Ministers met regularly to issue joint protest notes concerning violation of neutrality rights as well as to reach agreement to abstain from a mediatory role in the war (1916). Due to the effectiveness of the naval blockade, Scandinavian economic cooperation increased very dramatically and intra-Nordic trade rose from 10% in 1914 to 30% in 1919, but declined to 12% in 1922 when more normal trading patterns were resumed.[23]

Regular Prime Minister and Foreign Minister meetings were discontinued in 1922, but resumed in 1933 (the Finnish Foreign Minister began to participate in 1934). Throughout the 1930's, the Nordic states attempted, by parallel national action, to repeat their joint neutrality policies in response to the increasing international crises in Europe. The 1934 Nordic Foreign Ministers meeting declared that the Scandinavian States would not be divided by large state rivalries in Europe and a renewal of a joint neutrality declaration was issued in 1938 and in September, 1939. In 1937, special Nordic Neighbour Country Boards were established to prepare for the stockpiling of strategic economic materials based on a quota system and to promote intensified intra-Nordic economic cooperation in response to the increasing threat of war. With the failure of the Nordic Defence Pact in 1948–49, a joint Nordic Economic Cooperation Committee was formed in 1948 to investigate the prospect for a Nordic customs union. That was a response to United States pressure to form regional groupings as a prerequisite for qualifying for Marshall Aid.[24]

The purpose of this brief review has been to show that Nordic integrative patterns of behaviour developed to a considerable extent by the early 1950's. Although the Scandinavian states had failed to agree on the key issue areas of security policy and foreign economic policy, a considerable number of integrative schemes and interactions had developed both at the transnational and the intergovernmental levels.

Transnational Governmental Bureaucratic Interaction: The Contact Man System

As Nordic integrative practices have expanded at the intergovernmental level, senior civil servants in the five national administrations have become increasingly involved in the work of Nordic standing commissions, *ad hoc* committees and the regular ministerial meetings. They provide the staff services in the investigative and consultative phases of proposals for Nordic integrative schemes as well as monitoring and administrating Nordic integrative activity.

A Nordic Contact Man system was instituted by the five Ministries of Justice in 1959–60 as a response to the growing involvement by the five national administrations. While the Nordic Contact Man system has been adopted in most of the ministries, we shall use the system established in the ministries of Justice – where it is most developed – as our illustrative description of how the system works.[25] Within each of the national ministries, a senior civil servant, usually at the level of Undersecretary of State, is designated as the Nordic Contact Man. His responsibility is to coordinate Nordic legal cooperation within the home country and to maintain contact with his counterpart in the other four states. He must keep himself informed continuously about proposed new laws and legislative revision work being planned or acted upon in other ministries in his home country which might be relevant in a Nordic perspective. The initiative for new laws or revision of existing laws with possible Nordic ramifications can come from the various national ministries, the Nordic Ministers of Justice meetings, the national parliaments or from the Nordic Council. After an initiative with Scandinavian-wide relevance is taken, the Minister or the Nordic

Contact Man can decide to establish committees within each of the five national ministries involved. These committees work in parallel and hold periodic joint Nordic meetings or exchange views by correspondence or by telephone. The committees present reports which are dealt with, first, by each country's administration, including preparation of each special administrative department's position on the proposal, followed by the Nordic Contact Men meeting as a group. The joint position arrived at is then presented to each national Minister of Justice for political executive action. If further deliberation is needed, it takes place at the next Nordic Ministers of Justice meeting. After the planning phase is completed, the proposal is submitted in identical or highly similar texts to the five national legislatures for deliberation and possible enactment. Before legislative action is completed, the final version of a bill is presented to the Nordic Contact Men for comments and recommendations. Hence, Nordic cooperation is very intensive and extensive *within* the national administrations. As a Swedish Nordic Contact Man has commented:

> ' . . . it is no exaggeration to state that during the law-making (or revision) process, I discuss the issues with my Nordic colleagues almost as often as with my colleagues in other departments of the Swedish Administration.'[26]

As an indication of the scope of Nordic cooperation at the administrative level, the Swedish Contact Man estimated that about half of the sixty committees working on proposals for new laws or revision of existing laws in the Swedish Ministry of Justice are involved in subject areas of relevance for Nordic cooperation.

The Nordic Contact Man in a ministry is usually assisted by a more junior civil servant who coordinates the subject areas involving Nordic integrative processes in the various sections within the ministry. For example, the assistant to the Nordic Contact Man in the Swedish Ministry of Education coordinates proposals in the area of schools, higher educational institutions, and research, dealt with in various sections of the ministry. Additionally, he maintains close liaison with the Minister of Culture since all these issues areas are dealt with as one is area of Nordic cultural cooperation. The organisation of the Contact Man System varies from ministry to ministry because the tasks vary and civil administration structures in the five states vary. In some ministries, Nordic cooperation involves parallel national action in regard to monitoring and administering existing Nordic integrative programmes.

Some difficulties have been experienced when the Contact Men's activities involve different ministries; for example, the Swedish Ministry of Justice cooperating with the Danish Ministry of Commerce, but satisfactory procedures develop over time. Some of the Scandinavian states have institutionalized the coordination of Nordic Contact Man activity at the national level. In Finland, a single person has been given the task of coordinating all Finnish Nordic Contact Man activity. In Sweden, the Ministry of Justice provides central coordination of all Nordic cooperation issues through a special section of the Ministry. In Norway, the national coordination is done within the Prime Minister's Office where a State Secretary is responsible for coordinating both Nordic Contact Man activities and Nordic Council activities.

A recent development has been the extension of the Nordic Contact Man system into the international sections of the various functional service ministries. Their task is to investigate, plan and deliberate about adopting identical positions in negotiations in international institutions and jointly prepare for international conferences. For example, the five Nordic Health Departments have prepared joint positions on activities in the World Health Organisation, and the Ministries of Education have prepared joint positions on activities in UNESCO. Hence, in addition to the national, vertical coordination between the individual functional service ministries and the Ministry of Foreign Affairs, there is Nordic, horizontal coordination among the five Nordic functional service ministries concerned and among the five Nordic Ministries of Foreign Affairs about a subject matter to be dealt with in a general international institution or conference.

The Nordic Contact Man System is an indication of the degree to which Scandinavian integration through parallel national action has penetrated nearly all components and aspects of the decision-making processes in the five Scandinavian political systems.

The Nordic Council Organisations

The Nordic Council organisations represent a further institutionalization in the incremental growth of the parallel national action process. They are the only joint bodies within the wide integrative network comprising the national interest groups, transnational institutions, parliaments, political executives and civil administrations of the five national political systems. They serve as a source of initiative in proposals for Nordic integrative action and in promoting support for them among the general publics, as instruments of continuity by monitoring and coordinating the development of such proposals into parallel national action (in that respect, they can be viewed as a Scandinavian regional pressure group), and they provide a forum for consultation and deliberation in which the Scandinavian perspective can be maintained.

The development of the Nordic Council organizations has been characterized by an aversion to bureaucracy-creating measures which would involve Nordic supra-national authority. The organisations have evolved because of a combination of responses to extra-Nordic international developments and recognition of the need for more efficient organizational practices as a result of the expanding scope and magnitude of Scandinavian integrative activities. While the formation of the Nordic Council in 1952 can be viewed as an extension of the Nordic Inter-Parliamentary Union and the evolving practice of inter-Scandinavian meetings of parliamentary committees, the impetus came from the failure to form a Nordic Defence Pact and a Nordic Customs Union both of which demonstrated a new political division among the Scandinavian states.[27] It is indicative of the caution with which the Scandinavian states approach institution-building that the subject areas of cooperation and the formal role of the Nordic Council organizations were not identified and expressed in treaty form until the 1962 Helsinki Treaty of Cooperation — a.decade after the Nordic Council was established. The decision to elevate the behavioural code of conduct into treaty status was a response to external developments in Europe. With the decision of the Danish and Norwegian governments to apply for membership in the European communities in 1961 and 1962 respectively, it was felt necessary to demonstrate to the other European states that an integrative network existed. The Helsinki Treaty was also to serve as a basis from which, during negotiations with the European Communities, the Scandinavian states could gain recognition of their claims to protect and maintain Scandinavian integration. The amendment of the Helsinki Treaty in February, 1971, involved a significant reorganization of the Nordic Council which enhanced the role of the Presidium, established permanent secretariats and a Nordic Council of Ministers. The changes reflected the need to make the Nordic Council organisations more effective and efficient as well as the need to integrate the governing institutions of the proposed Nordic Economic Union (Nordek — which failed) with the existing organisations.[28] The descriptive overview of the Nordic Council organisations which follows is based upon the revised, 1971 Helsinki Treaty.

The Nordic Council organizations consist of the Plenary Assembly, the Standing Committees, the Presidium, the Secretariat and the Nordic Council of Ministers.

The Plenary Assembly consists of 78 members elected from the five national parliaments and about fifty members of the five political executives. Sweden and Norway each have 18 elected members, Finland 17, Denmark 16, and Iceland 6. The semi-autonomous territories of the Faeroe Islands and Aaland Islands have two and one elected members respectively. The national delegations are apportioned according to the distribution of political party representation in the national parliaments. The five national political executives are usually represented by the Prime Ministers, Foreign Ministers and the Ministers of Justice, Education, Culture, Social Affairs, Transporation and Communications, and Commerce, Economics and Finance. The Plenary Assembly meets annually for a week-long session although it can be called into extraordinary sessions. The annual session is conducted according to general parliamentary procedures. Both individual members and government representatives can initiate a proposal which, in turn goes through a first reading, committee investigation and reporting, a second reading with debate and finally a vote.[29] The Nordic Council is an advisory body and it can only pass recommendations for action to be taken by national governments. While the governmental representatives participate in both general debate and committee stages of proposals, only the elected members can vote on recommendations. During the first decade of its operation, i.e. from 1953 to 1962, the Plenary Assembly passed 241 recommendations. One hundred and twenty-five recommendations (or 52%) were completely or partially implemented, 61 (or 25%) were either in process of being implemented or under investigation, while 55 recommendations (or 23%) were rejected by the national governments.[30]

The Standing Committees of the Nordic Council consist of the Legal Committee with 13 members, the Cultural Committee with 17 members, the Social Policy Committee with 13 members, the Traffic Committee with 13 members and the Economic Committee with 22 members. The Standing Committee members are usually senior members of the corresponding national parliamentary committees. During the annual Plenary Assembly meetings, the Standing Committee meetings are attended by the five national ministers concerned with the particular subject matter designated to each of the committees. When the Standing Committees meet outside the ordinary, annual session, the minister of the host country attends as a representative of the Nordic Ministers Meeting.

The Presidium of the Nordic Council is composed of five members — a President and four Vice-Presidents plus their deputies. Presidium members are usually the chairmen of the national delegations of the elected members to the Plenary Assembly. The Presidium represents the entire Nordic Council between sessions. It can convene extraordinary sessions of the Plenary Assembly, as well as make representations to the Nordic Council of Ministers and to the national governments on behalf of the Nordic Council. Presidium statements of representation now have the same status as recommendations by the Plenary Assembly. It can also receive reports on the status of recommendations from the national governments and it is usually represented in Nordic Council committee meetings.

A Nordic Council Secretariat was established in 1971 to supplement the previous practice of separate national secretariats. The Board of Secretaries is composed of the Secretary of the Presidium and the five national General Secretaries and has its office in Stockholm. The tasks of the Secretariat are to prepare the meetings of the Presidium and conduct the day-to-day affairs of the Council.

The establishment of the *Nordic Council of Ministers* was the most significant innovation in the 1971 reorganisation. It was formed because of the recognition that the governments had no organisation which could provide continuity and overview at a level corresponding to the parliamentarians' organisations. It was decided that each state would appoint one of its ministers responsible for Nordic Cooperation Affairs, and these five ministers comprise the Nordic Council of Ministers. However, as with the European Communities Council of Ministers, different ministers can also act as the Council of Ministers if and when an important decision is to be made. In fact, while the Nordic Council of Ministers was given competence to deal with the whole area of Scandinavian cooperation, it was stipulated in the 1971 Helsinki Treaty that the regular ministerial meetings by heads of functional service ministries would continue parallel to the Council of Ministers. Typical of the Scandinavian approach to integration, the decision as to what format a meeting would take, whether formalized as a Nordic Council of Ministers meeting or kept informal as a regular meeting of ministers, should depend on the matter at hand and should be decided on the merit of each case. Hence, the regular ministerial meeting could, in the same session, move to become a Council of Ministers meeting and back to the informal setting of a regular meeting

The Council of Ministers operates by unanimity in substantive decision taking and its decisions are binding on the individual member states except where parliamentary approval is needed.

The main task of the Ministers For Nordic Affairs, acting as the Council of Ministers, is to provide coordination of policies at the highest level of the political executive in the five member states. It must assure continuity in the relationship with the other Nordic Council organisations as well as monitor the development of Plenary Assembly recommendations in favour of adopting Nordic integrative schemes by parallel national action. The Council of Ministers gives an annual account of current Nordic integrative activity, including the status of government action on Nordic Council recommendations, by issuing a report which becomes the basis for the opening general debate in the Plenary Assembly sessions. A very significant institutional development was the establishment of a Permanent Secretariat for the Nordic Council of Ministers in July 1973 with offices in Oslo. The Secretariat is staffed by senior civil servants who are not responsible to the national governments. Cultural cooperation has also become further institutionalized by the 1971 Treaty of Nordic Cultural Cooperation. The Scandinavian Ministers of Education and of Culture will now act as the Nordic Council of Ministers for Cultural Cooperation. The Council is assisted by a Senior Civil Servants Committee on Cultural Cooperation. A Permanent Secretariat for Cultural Cooperation with a Director was established in January, 1972 with its office located in Copenhagen.[32]

The recent institutionalization of the Nordic integrative network is a *responsive* development through which the five Nordic political systems have adopted the parallel national action process due to a combination of, on the one hand, intra-regional pressures for more effective and efficient methods of integration than the *ad hoc* behavioural practices which emerged in the post Second World War years, and on the other hand, the extra-regional pressures created by the growing institutionalization of Western European integration.

The structure of the Nordic integrative network is based on the continuous interaction among the four types of actors: 1) national interest groups acting individually or through their Nordic trans-national institutions; 2) national political parties acting through national as well as Nordic parliamentary institutions; 3) the national political executives acting through the Nordic Council's Plenary Assembly, the Nordic Council of Ministers and regular, informal

Nordic ministerial meetings; and 4) the national civil administrators acting through the Contact Man System and Nordic Standing Commissions and Committees of Senior Civil Servants. The extensive diffusion of channels of direct interaction among the five states' governmental organisations was given formal legal recognition in the 1962 Helsinki Treaty of Cooperation. Article 38 permits direct interaction through bypassing the Ministries of Foreign Affairs except in subject areas which ' . . . by their nature or for other reasons . . . ' are still to be handled through the traditional, established diplomatic channels.[33]

The major task of the Nordic Council organisations is to facilitate interaction among the four types of actors. They perform that task by initiating contacts and proposals for integrative action, by providing impetus and continuity through the investigatory and deliberative stages, and by monitoring developments until parallel national actions are implemented.

The organisational chart (see page 316) is an attempt to provide a summary overview of the interaction flows which characterise the Nordic integrative network, The impression the chart is designed to convey is the continuous communication and consultation processes among national, transnational and Scandinavian regional actors. A Norwegian Nordic Council official described the integrative inter-action processes as follows:

'There are always many, many channels which can be used. Private sector, political, and governmental officials have multiple options for communicating, and multiple options for attempting to gain support for their position. One may choose a national strategy, a Nordic one, one emphasizing governmental channels or non-governmental ones; one emphasizing governmental sectoral counter-parts or complementing interests. Governmental officials may lead directly, through diplomatic channels, through political party linkages, through Nordic Council machinery, through international bodies, or through counterpart administrative machinery.'[34]

While implementation of policies occurs through parallel national action by the five political systems, the increasing institutionalization of the policy formulating process demonstrates that the Nordic dimension has penetrated the national political system in every issue area except national security and military alliance policies.

Achievements in Nordic Integration

The outcomes of the parallel national action process in Scandinavia have been extensive and impressive. They can be dealt with only in a brief, summary manner here. The discussion of the achievements has been organized in three categories. In the first place, we will provide an 'inventory-overview' of Scandinavian integration which has resulted in removing those barriers to interaction which were manifestations of previous intense national exclusivity and in equalising societal conditions in a large number of issue areas. Secondly, integrative activity involving the pooling of resources and skills will be discussed. Finally, cooperation in the conduct of diplomacy outside of Scandinavia is briefly considered.

Removal of Barriers to Interaction and Equalization of Societal Conditions

It is in the area of public law that equalization of conditions has progressed most. Uniform laws have been enacted by parallel national action in practically every aspect of the five states' legal systems. Identical or very similar laws exist in citizenship law, family law, inheritance law, property laws, bankruptcy laws, laws on purchases, commercial practices, stocks, bonds, insurance, patents, brand names, copyright, maritime law, air travel law, law on nuclear energy installations, and penal law. In some areas of the legal systems, Scandinavian conventions have been adopted. This is the case, for example, in regard to family law, child support, bankruptcy, inheritance and in penal law where court decisions are mutually enforceable. Uniform legal procedures have been established leading to Scandinavia-wide equalization of judgements. Since 1959, a joint collection of legal cases entitled *The Nordic Collection of Judgments* has been published annually. As shown in Table I,[35] between 1880 and 1965 there have been 78 cases of parallel national action in the legal subject areas listed above. Denmark, Sweden and Norway have been the most active; (they participated in between 88 and 92% of the cases), and these three states set the pattern of legal cooperation into which Finland and Iceland have been drawn during the past forty years (Finland participated in 50% and Iceland in 41% of the cases). In 62 of the 78 cases (79%) parallel national action involved at least three states while 19 cases (24%) involved all five states. It is important to point out that these subject areas do not include Scandinavian participation in general international legal agreements and conventions which set global or European-wide standards. They

TABLE I:
PARALLEL NATIONAL ACTION IN LEGAL AFFAIRS AMONG THE NORDIC
STATES, 1880–1965

	1880–1913	1914–1945	1946–1965	Total
Involving all five states	1	11	7	19
Involving four states	5	10	7	22
Involving three states	5	8	14	27
Involving two states	0	5	5	10
Total	11	34	33	78

Source: 'Oversikt over lagar tillkomma genom nordiskt samarbejde', Stockholm: Nordiska Raadet, Nordisk Udredningsserie, 1965:2.

involve subject areas normally considered as exclusively 'within-state' jurisdiction.

Uniformity in social security and social welfare conditions has been achieved through the establishment of a Nordic Convention on Social Security. The Convention came into effect in November 1956 and integration in this subject area has been expanded by amendments of the Convention in 1962, 1967 and 1969. It creates equality of eligibility for all Nordic citizens for unemployment insurance, industrial accident insurance, partial disability insurance, health insurance, old age pension, widow and widower pensions, invalid pension, public assistance during pregnancy and childbirth, and child support. As a consequence, a Scandinavian citizen moving from one Nordic state to another can claim the same social security and social welfare benefits in the new country of residence as in the 'home country'. A mutual reimbursement system was adopted in the early years of the Convention, but it was dropped after a few years. In the cases of old age, invalid and widow and widowers pensions, three years' residence in the new country is required, but the 'home' country continues payments during the transition period.

Extensive Nordic integration exists in the areas of travel and transportation. A Nordic Passport Union was established in 1955 which allows for completely free travel by Scandinavians in the Nordic region. Furthermore, only one inspection is required for non-Scandinavians entering or leaving the region. Uniform rates for railway transportation of goods have been established as well as an agreement of uniform 'through-goods' rates. Domestic rates on mail services exist for the whole Scandinavian region arranged through the Nordic Postal Association which has been in existence since 1946.

Achievements in the area of economic integration have been more modest and closely linked to general European developments. A Common Labour Market for the Danish, Finnish, Norwegian and Swedish industrial work forces was established by a Nordic Convention in 1954. Workers can seek employment in the Nordic region (except Iceland) without work permits and the four national employment offices cooperate in providing information on employment opportunities as well as providing statistical analyses of employment trends and coordinating employment policies. So far, the interchange of industrial workers has been relatively low. Table II provides a partial overview of the major trends in worker migration in 1967. The total of 114,000 migrant workers represents only 1.2% of the entire Nordic work force of 9,381,000. The main flow of migrant workers has been from Finland to Sweden. The Common Labour Market Convention was expanded between 1966 and 1970 to include doctors, dentists, nurses and pharmacists and it is expected that other professions will be added in the near future.

TABLE II:
THE FLOW OF NORDIC MIGRANT WORKERS IN 1967

Working In	Denmark	Norway	Sweden	Finland	Total work force in 1965
Coming From					
Denmark	–	2,000	18,900	–	2,252,000
Norway	–	–	13,200	–	1,504,000
Sweden	–	5,500	–	–	3,450,000
Finland	–	500	71,800	–	2,175,000
Scandinavian Seamen		2,000			

Source: See footnote 36.

Removal of barriers to trade and the equalization of conditions for production and distribution of goods and services have not developed on an exclusively Scandinavian basis. Proposals and plans for a Nordic Customs Union were made in 1950 and 1957.[37] Plans for an extensive Nordic Economic Union (Nordek) were made in 1969.[38] In each instance, the plans failed because they were overtaken by general European economic integration developments. The Scandinavian national economies

298

are all heavily dependent on foreign trade. However, their trade patterns are based on greater interdependence with non-Scandinavian states, especially the United Kingdom and the Federal Republic of Germany, than among each other. During the critical stages of industrialization in the first half of the twentieth century, the Nordic national economies became internationally competitive rather than regionally complementary. Until the 1960's intra-Scandinavian trade accounted for only 12–15%, of the total foreign trade by the five states. Therefore, the main economic interest groups in each of the five national economies viewed the plans for a Nordic Customs Union as an imposition on the broader international trade patterns. While it would have had few direct economic benefits, it was argued, a Nordic customs union was considered a change which contained an unacceptably high risk of disadvantageous trade diversion caused by retaliatory actions by non-Scandinavian trade partners in response to discriminatory features of a Nordic common market.

In the late 1940's and throughout the 1950's, the Nordic states pursued a policy supporting proposals for the widest possible European free trade area and treated the potential of increased Scandinavian economic integration as a secondary, 'fallback' position when the plans for wider European free trade arrangements failed. A partial solution was found with the formation of the European Free Trade Association in 1959. Throughout the 1960s, Scandinavian economic cooperation expanded enormously within the EFTA umbrella under which foreign economic relations with the United Kingdom were covered and with the impetus provided through a new commitment by Scandinavian industrial interest groups to develop the growth potential of a Nordic regional market as a compensation for expected losses in economic relations with the European Communities. Table III provides a rough indicator of the tremendous growth in intra-Nordic trade. While the value of exports in current prices does not control for the effect of inflation, a six-fold increase for the regional total clearly demonstrates a significant increase which, except for Iceland, has been experienced by each of the Nordic states, and especially by Finland. As another measure of this trend, intra-Nordic trade increased as a percentage of total exports by all five states from 17.3 to 26.0 between 1960 and 1971.[39]

In short, utilizing the Scandinavian market as a basis for remaining competitive internationally was viewed as a compensatory feature which was manifested by a very high rate of increase in commodity

DEVELOPMENTS IN INTRA-NORDIC TRADE, 1962–1974
(In Millions of U.S. Dollars at Current Prices)

	1962	1968	1974	Percent Increase 1962–1974
Exports to the Other Four Nordic States from:				
Sweden	469.5	1,221.3	4,158.3	540
Denmark	286.1	650.1	1,977.7	591
Norway	236.8	474.4	1,841.3	678
Finland	120.0	276.7	1,252.0	943
Iceland	15.0	13.8	40.6	171
Total	1,307.4	2,636.3	9,269.9	609

Source: Direction of Trade Annual 1961–66; 1966–72; and *1970–74.*
Washington, D.C., International Monetary Fund and International Bank
for Reconstruction and Development, 1967, 1973 and 1975 respectively.

exchanges as well as an increased division of labour in production and
distribution within the region. Hence, while the recent growth in inter-
Scandinavian economic interdependence occurred almost inadvertently
because of unfavourable conditions for each of the Nordic states'
relations with larger non-Scandinavian trading partners, the effect
has been that intra-Nordic economic relations have become an important
factor in future foreign economic policy for each of the Nordic states.
For example, in 1972, the Danes and the Norwegians together bought
more industrial goods from Sweden than the original six members of
the European Communities and Sweden has replaced West Germany as
Denmark's second-most important customer.[40] The 1969 Nordek plans
for a Nordic Economic Union was advanced to consolidate and promote
these significant developments in Scandinavian economic integration. In
the context of a perceived prolonged stalemate concerning the enlargement of membership of the European Communities, Nordek would
have provided a 'fall-back' solution through which economic integration
in Scandinavia could have continued and a stronger bargaining position
vis-à-vis the European Communities could have been developed. When
the prospects for the British, Danish, Norwegian and Irish applications for
membership of the European Communities improved in late 1969, the
Nordek plan was rejected by Finland because of the implication which the

Finns perceived such a prospect would have for their precarious neutrality relations with the Soviet Union and the plan was dropped in 1970.[41]

In spite of the significant increase in Nordic economic interdependence, the Scandinavian national economies remain closely integrated with the rest of Western Europe. The twenty million Scandinavians are the most important consumers of West German exports and, in 1972, the Scandinavians bought more British industrial goods than Germany and France combined.

Since 1973, the Nordic states have been incorporated into the emerging general Western European common market, but by different policy positions. Denmark has become a member of the European Communities. Along with most of the EFTA member states, Sweden and Norway have entered into a transition phase in their relationship with the European Communities leading to a general Western European free trade area in industrial goods by 1980. Iceland and Finland have established special commercial treaties with the European Communities. So far, economic relations among the Nordic states have not been seriously affected by the differences in policy positions and intra-Nordic trade continues to expand.[42] Whether Danish membership of the European Communities will remain compatible with full participation in the Nordic integrative network remains an important, open question for the future.[43]

The main point about Nordic economic integration is that it is an issue area in which the Scandinavian region has been of insufficient significance for the five national economies to make a special arrangement among themselves which contained the risk of retaliatory damage to relations with non-Scandinavian trading partners. Hence, equalization of economic conditions has taken place within the wider framework of general European cooperation without, so far, creating impediments to expanded economic interdependence within the Nordic sub-region. However, it is an issue area which clearly demonstrates the limitations of the Scandinavian parallel national action approach. Issues concerning Scandinavian economic integration, especially when they require a formal structure, have been turned into high political questions when they have been seen as possibly detrimental to extra-regional links, particularly in matters of national security.

Sharing Resources and Skills Within the Region

The achievements by parallel national action in sharing resources and skills have developed to the greatest extent in the areas of higher education and research. Scandinavian higher education is becoming a truly integrated system. The universities and academies, and polytechnic institutes recognize the validity of completion of examinations and diploma certification in a single discipline in one Nordic higher educational institution as the complete or partial fulfillment of the equivalent degree programme in the other Nordic institutions. In several academic disciplines, Scandinavian-wide rules for curriculum structures and examination validity have been established. Fellowships, grants and loans paid by one state to a student can be used for study in other states' higher educational institutions. An intensive division of labour has occurred in the area of research where specialized Nordic research institutes have been established. An integrated transnational structure in higher education and research has been established. As shown in Table IV, there are nearly a hundred Nordic professional academic and research institutions which publish 81 joint Nordic journals, 18 of them in English.

TABLE IV:
NORDIC ACADEMIC, SCIENTIFIC AND PROFESSIONAL TRANSNATIONAL ORGANISATIONS AND PUBLICATIONS

Field:	Number of Organizations	Number of Journals	Of which in English
Humanities	7	13	5
Social Sciences	6	18	7
Natural Sciences	6	15	3
Applied Sciences	44 (a)	7	2
Agricultural Sciences	10	3	—
Medicine	22	25 (b)	1
Total	95	81	18

Source: Compiled from *Nordisk Samarbete inom forskningens och den hogre undervisningens omraade:* Stockholm: Nordiska Raadet, Nordisk Udredningsserie, 1967:2.

(a) Many of these organisations consist of Coordinating Committees for specific industries.
(b) In addition, there are fourteen joint Nordic medical textbooks published regularly in updated editions.

The integration of higher education and research activities has become highly organised by the establishment of formal regional institutions jointly funded by the five states and many of them with supranational administrative authority. Table V demonstrates this trend of growing institutionalization. There are proposals pending for a consolidation of these new Nordic supranational institutions under the direction of the Nordic Council of Ministers for Cultural Cooperation and its Permanent Secretariat in Copenhagen.

The Nordic Council has been promoting harmonisation of the structures of primary and secondary school systems, but so far it has only led to establishment of cooperation in planning school curricula and research on pedagogy.

Nordic integration in general adult education and promotion of the fine arts has also progressed very significantly. Financial support for Nordic cultural activity — higher education, research, general education and the fine arts amounted to 18 million Danish kroner in 1967—68. That was more than four times the funds spent for comparable purposes by the Council of Europe and equivalent to eight percent of UNESCO's budget for global scope cultural cooperation.[44]

In the area of transportation, the most significant achievement has been the establishment of an integrated airline company. The Scandinavian Airline System is jointly owned and managed by Denmark, Norway and Sweden. Cooperative organisations have been established among Finland, Norway and Sweden for the development of a road system in the northern section of the Scandinavian Peninsula (Nordkalotten) and between Denmark and Sweden for the development of a bridge over the narrow sound separating the two countries.

In the area of communications, joint educational radio programmes are produced and NORDVISION is the organisation through which regular education and entertainment television programmes are broadcast. The technical aspects of these cooperative arrangements are administered through the Nordic Telecommunication Council and the Nordic Council for Telesatellites.

Nordic Integration in External Relations

Parallel national action in international politics is based on an informal, unwritten behavioural code of conduct among the five Nordic states. It is characterized by continuous, extensive consultation, planning, coordination and joint policy actions. As a former Danish Foreign Minister once described it, 'In our voting in the United Nations, in the Council of Europe, in OECD and elsewhere, we must always bear in mind how our statements, our voting and our actions affect our relations with the other Nordic countries. It is, in fact, one of the permanent factors in the foreign policy of our countries.'[45] The Scandinavian Foreign Ministers meet at least twice a year to consult and coordinate

TABLE V: NEW NORDIC COMMON ADMINISTRATIVE INSTITUTIONS

Issue Area	Founded	Location
A – *Higher Educational Institutions*		
1 – Nordic Graduate School of Journalism and Press Research	1957	Aarhus, Denmark
2 – Nordic Institute on African Studies	1964	Uppsala, Sweden
3 – Nordic Graduate School of Domestic Science	1963	various places
4 – Nordic Central Institute for Asian Area Research (CINA)	1966	Copenhagen, Denmark
5 – Nordic Graduate School of Public Health and Welfare	1962	Gothenburg, Sweden
B – *Research Organizations*		
1 – Nordic Institute for Odontological Material Testing	1971	Oslo, Norway
2 – Nordic Institute for Theoretical Nuclear Physics (NORDITA)	1971	Copenhagen, Denmark
3 – Nordic Council for Applied Research (NORDFORSK)	1947	Rotates among Nordic capitals every 3 years
4 – Nordic Committee for Arctic Medical Research	1969	Uleaaborg, Finland
5 – Nordic Committee for International Politics Research	1966	Stockholm, Sweden
6 – Nordic Council on Criminology	–	–
7 – Nordic Institute for Maritime Law	1963	Oslo, Norway
8 – Nordic Board for Research on Alcoholism	–	–
9 – Nordic Institute of Social Planning (NORDPLAN)	1968	Stockholm, Sweden
C – *General Education, Fine Arts, and Information Dissemination*		
1 – Nordic Peoples' Academy	1968	Stockholm, Sweden
2 – Nordic House in Reykjavik	1968	Reykjavik, Iceland
3 – Nordic Council Literature Prize	1962	–
4 – Nordic Institute for Poetry	1959	Aabo, Sweden
5 – Nordic Cultural Fund	1967	Rotates based on resident country of chairman of Fund
6 – Nordic Coordinating Organization for Scientific and Technological Information and Documentation (NORDOK)	1972	Oslo, Norway
7 – Nordic Statistical Secretariat	1969	Copenhagen, Denmark

Sources: Faellesinstitutionerne i Norden, Stockholm, Nordiska Raadet, Nordisk Udredningsserie, 1960:2 and *Nordiska institutioner,* Stockholm, Nordiska Raadet, Nordisk Udredningsserie, 1972:5.

foreign policies. At the early autumn meeting, Scandinavian policies are coordinated in regard to issues to be dealt with at the forthcoming United Nations session. Consequently, the Scandinavian states have consistently voted identically in nearly all of the issues treated in the General Assembly.[46]

A very high degree of coordination among the Nordic states occurs in their participation in international institutions. Jointly planned policy positions are adopted by the Ministries of Justice in negotiations on legal cooperation in the United Nations, the Council of Europe, the Hague Conference and the Rome Institute for Private Law. The Transportation and Communication ministries coordinate their positions within the Universal Postal Union, the International Telecommunication Union and the International Air Transportation Association. The Ministries of Social Welfare and Labour and the Public Health Authorities coordinate their policy positions in the International Labour Organizations, the United Nations Economic and Social Council, the UN Social Commission, the World Health Organisation and the Council of Europe's Public Health Committee. In the areas of cultural and educational affairs, Scandinavian cooperation has moved one step further in that it was decided to divide among the states the responsibility for coordinating the *Nordic position* in international institutions. Thus, Denmark coordinates the Nordic position on culture and education in the Council of Europe, Finland in UNESCO, Norway in the OECD, and Sweden in CERN. In economic issue areas, the Ministries of Trade, Commerce, Economics and Finance coordinate their positions in the International Monetary Fund, the International Bank for Reconstruction and Development, in the OECD, in the UN Economic Commission for Europe and in the EFTA (for the latter, without Denmark since 1973).

In international conferences, the Nordic states have often acted as a group or a caucus. In both permanent international institutions and in international conferences, the individual states become spokesmen for a Nordic position on various executive boards and in committees. The greatest success in integrating their foreign policies occurred in 1966–1967 when the Nordic states agreed to negotiate as one unit in the GATT Kennedy Round negotiations on tariff liberalization. A single, Chief Negotiator was given authority to act on behalf of the Scandinavian states and he and his four national deputies confronted the key actors of the United States, the European Communities, Japan and Britain with a completely integrated negotiation posture.[47] The aggregate economic capability of the four Nordic states (Iceland was excluded) was of such a magnitude (for example, the Nordic states combined were a larger customer of the European Communities' products than the United States), that it led to the Nordic bloc being treated as the equivalent of a key state throughout the negotiations.

The Nordic Chief Negotiator and his four national deputies formed a steering group which supervised a staff of sixty experts drawn from the four national administrations according to expertise needed throughout the negotiation process in Geneva. Consequently, the Scandinavian states gained concessions on intra-regional economic interests which they would not have received on an individual basis and the Nordic bloc contributed significantly to more liberalized trading policies.

The Nordic States have also shared resources and skills in the conduct of international relations outside the region. Through their Ministries of Defense, Denmark, Finland, Norway and Sweden have coordinated a Nordic Stand-by Force available for peace-keeping duties by the United Nations. The five Nordic states jointly fund and manage development projects in Tanzania and Kenya as part of their development assistance policies. The national governments provide joint information services abroad and joint tourist and travel bureaus have been established in many European cities. When abroad, Scandinavians can be assisted by joint consular service; that is, in case the 'home country' of a travelling Scandinavian does not maintain a consulate in a particular location, assistance can be obtained from any Nordic state consulate. This arrangement has been formalized in the Helsinki Treaty on Cooperation.

In sum, the outcome of the parallel national action process has been the establishment of increasingly integrated Nordic societal conditions in most spheres of life. The Scandinavians have complete freedom of movement and transferability of all their social security rights in a region with nearly identical legal systems and mutually enforceable laws. Economic relations are characterized by recently intensifying Nordic economic integration within a larger Western European economic framework, but based on different national policy positions. Resources and skills are shared extensively in education and research where a new network of trans-Nordic institutions with supra-national administrations are emerging. Except for the high politics issue areas of national security and military alliance policies, the Scandinavian states have developed a highly integrated pattern of behaviour in international politics.

Summary and Conclusion

The central thesis addressed in this chapter is that there is a need to redirect the focus in regional integration studies from a concentration on political structural transformation leading to the replacement of separate states by a larger regional state to a focus on the process of changes in behavioural codes of conduct among existing states. The Scandinavian experiences have been treated as an illustrative, empirical model for such a redirection of focus.

The case of Scandinavian integration has been presented by a description and analysis of the governing conditions, the structure and process, and the outcomes of a process characterized as parallel national action. Treated in an historical perspective, the governing conditions consist of: 1) the rejection of the constitutional fusion approach and supra-national institutions; 2) the sanctity of maintaining the five autonomous states as the basis for regional integration; and 3) the exclusion from the integration process of the 'high politics' issue areas of national security and military alliance policies.

Scandinavian parallel national action is characterized by a consensus-building process in which an extensive integrative network is maintained and promoted by Nordic regional organisations facilitating interaction among interest groups, political parties, parliaments, political executives and civil administrations of the five national political systems. The outcomes of the parallel national action process have been an extensive equalization of societal conditions in legal, social and economic issue areas and the removal of barriers to interaction by the creation of an open flow of people, goods and services within the region. They have also involved a sharing and pooling of resources and skills in cultural, educational and scientific research issue areas leading to the establishment of new Nordic common administrative institutions. Finally, in the conduct of extra-regional relations, the five Nordic states have developed an integrated behavioural code of conduct involving coordinated policy positions in international institutions and joint behaviour in general international bargaining and negotiations.

Among the most significant limitations of the Scandinavian parallel national action approach to regional integration is the exclusion of security policies. It demonstrates the inability to increase the level of integration to a high politics issue area, and that, within the parallel national action framework, such shifts in levels of political integration are more susceptible to the expressed political will of the individual states than is assumed in both classical

307

functionalist and neo-functionalist integration theories. Viewed in a power politics perspective, the conflict among larger European states intruded into the Nordic region and prevented the states' previous parallel national action responses of joint neutrality policies from becoming part of the political integrative behaviour pattern which developed in the low politics issue areas. Similarly, the Nordic states have been unable to institutionalize regional economic integration in the form of an economic union because of the high degree of economic interdependence in a wider European economic network which characterize the individual Nordic states' economies and because of perceived incompatibilities between national security policies and formation of an economic union.[48]

Conclusion

The use of a case study approach to assess the general development of theoretical frameworks has its limitations. The caveat normally issued that a particular set of exeperiences may not be a sufficient basis from which to generalize must be heeded. The Nordic case has often been considered unique because of the high degree of cultural homogeneity among the Scandinavian peoples and the extensive similarity in their political systems and in their levels of economic development. In that perspective, it could be argued that the reason for the success of the parallel national action process is the very high degree of mutual confidence which already existed based on the commonality of attributes among the five political systems. In many respects, these arguments are quite persuasive, but their importance should not be exaggerated. While cultural diversity is greater among the European peoples in general than is the case in Scandinavian, the persistence of strong nationality identification among the Nordic peoples has been as important a factor in the development of separate, autonomous nation states in that region as it has been in the rest of Europe. Furthermore, socio-economic developments during the past thirty years have created a high degree of similarity of societal conditions in many of the political systems of the economically developed states. It is, therefore, not considered pretentious or unrealistic to draw on the Scandinavian experiences as a basis from which to suggest a new conceptual framework.

The Western European integration experiences since the end of the Second World War have been analyzed predominantly on the basis of the neo-functionalist analytical framework. It has been assumed that the establishment of regional institutions with supranational authority such as the European Coal and Steel Community, the European Economic Community and the European Atomic Energy Authority would be the initial steps in the process of forming a new regional state.

With thirty years' hindsight, the interpretive historian could reconstruct the neo-functional perspective of the need to form a larger European 'super state' to be a time-and-place-bound perception induced by Cold War conditions combined with the decolonization process experienced by some of the major Western European states. A change in these conditions such as gradual adjustment to non-imperial status by major European states in addition to detente between East and West in Europe suggest that the ideological commitment to form a Western European state was a transitory phenomenon. Recent developments suggest the emergence of a regional structure in Western Europe of a number of medium-sized nation states strongly legitimized by the various peoples on the basis of cultural identity, but involved in extensive integration processes in low politics issue areas while changing toward an integrative behavioural code of conduct among the states in high politics issue areas. These changes are indicated by the large number of nationally staffed advisory boards which have been added in the last ten years to the existing supranational institutions for the purpose of dealing with the economic union issue areas,[49] by the changing style of operation adopted by the Commission with emphasis on the tasks of coordinating interests and activities of the member states,[50] and by the recent formation of the European Council as a forum for consultation and deliberation among the member states' leading political executives, but placed outside the supranational institutional structure.

Conversely, the Scandinavian experiences indicate that what has been considered 'outcome indicators' of socio-economic integration within the European Communities have been achieved in Scandinavia without the use of supra-national institutions and the 'community method' of decision-making.

In a different regional context, the Eastern European experiences with cooperative and emerging integrative processes, analysed by Prof. Simai elsewhere in this volume, also suggest the applicability of the parallel national action framework with its focus on behavioural changes in code of conduct among actors in a firmly fixed structural setting of separate nation states.

Expansion, modification and change of focus in theoretical frameworks are attempts by scholars to adapt to the complexities of empirical events for which previous theories could not account. The trend in regional cooperation and integration suggests that the parallel national action framework, as illustrated by the Scandinavian experiences, might be highly relevant as a model by which to capture an expanding scope of social, economic and political integrative behaviour which are unaccounted for by the neo-functionalist theories with their focus on structural transformation. While the expectations of regional political community formation created by the latter theories lead to pessimistic conclusions of failure, the parallel national action framework could be used as an analytical tool by which to reveal less spectacular, but highly significant increases in cooperative and integrative behaviour patterns within the various regions of the global political system.

Notes

1. The connotation of the terms 'Scandinavia' and 'Nordic' has often been disputed among scholars specializing in the region. Historically, 'Scandinavia' covers the kingdoms of Denmark, Norway and Sweden while 'Nordic' covers the three kingdoms plus Finland and Iceland. In recent issues of major atlases all five states were identified as Scandinavian. In present-day usage within the region, 'Scandinavia' and 'Nordic' are used interchangeably to encompass all five states, a practice followed throughout the discussion in this chapter.

2. See Stanley V. Anderson, *The Nordic Council: A Study of Scandinavian Regionalism*, Seattle and London: The University of Washington Press, 1967. Amitai Etzioni treats Scandinavian cooperation in a broader perspective, but the focus is on the supranational institutional potential of the Nordic Council organizations, 'The Stable Union: The Nordic Associational Web', in *Political Unification: A Comparative Study of Leaders and Forces,* New York, Holt, Rinehart and Winston, 1965. A generally descriptive, historical account of Nordic cooperation is provided by Frantz Wendt, *The Nordic Council and Cooperation in Scandinavia*, Copenhagen, Munksgaard, 1959.

3. Amitai Etzioni, *op. cit.*, chapters 1–3.

4. For an interesting analysis of recent tendencies toward a reassertion of cultural community identity as a challenge to existing state authorities, see Seyom Brown, *New Forces in World Politics,* Washington D.C., The Brookings Institution, 1974, chapter 9.

5. The distinction between high and low politics refers to the differences in perception of salience various issue areas have for the maintenance of political autonomy by a nationality group. Joseph Nye characterizes high politics as emotion laden and low politics as utilitarian in *Peace in Parts*, Boston, Little, Brown and Co., 1971, p. 41. Leon Lindberg and Stuart Scheingold treat the differentiation more in terms of styles of decision-making in which, ' . . . High politics presumably involves bold and dramatic moves like threats, *faits accomplis*, emotional appeals, all-or-nothing demands. In contrast, economic or welfare aims go along with an incremental decision-making style, involving pragmatic and step-by-step strategies, bargaining and

310

exchange of concessions.' *Europe's Would-Be Polity*, Englewood Cliffs, New Jersey, Prentice-Hall, 1970, p. 123. Stanley Hoffmann uses the distinction as a fixed dichotomy in which national security and general foreign policy issue areas are considered high politics and economic relations are low politics, 'Discord in Community: The North Atlantic Area as a Partial International System', in F.O. Wilcox and H.F. Haviland, editors, *The Atlantic Community: Progress and Prospect*, New York, Praeger, 1963. In his analysis of external relations of the European Communities, Karl Kaiser has challenged Hoffmann's usage of the distinction as a fixed dichotomy and he rightfully admonishes scholars to treat it as a relative and varying spectrum because, '. . . The same issue may shift on the spectrum between "low" and "high" (a) according to specific circumstances, (b) within time and (c) between different countries.' 'The U.S. and the E.E.C. in the Atlantic System: The Problem of Theory', *Journal of Common Market Studies*, Vol. V, No. 4 (June 1967), p. 401. The distinction is treated loosely in this chapter to convey a difference in the salience accorded to national security and military alliance policies as well as issue areas directly challenging the maintenance of state sovereignty which are considered by the actors to be high politics compared to issue areas concerned with pragmatic everyday socio-economic relations which are considered low politics. There seems to be a growing shared perception of the difference in salience although we take Kaiser's point that high and low politics must be treated as variant conditions. In fact, similarities and differences in perceptions of salience of issue areas may actually be an indication and measurement of political integration.

6.   Charlotte Muret, 'The Swiss Pattern For A Federated Europe', Anthology, *International Political Communities*, Garden City, New York: Anchor Books, Doubleday and Co., 1966.

7.   The basic postulates of the classical functionalists are discussed by the founder of this school of thought, David Mitrany, in his *A Working Peace System*. Chicago: Quadrangle Books, 1966. Part I. The most recent review and assessment of the functionalist theories are found in A.J.R. Groom and Paul Taylor, editors, *Functionalism: Theory and Practice in International Relations*, London; University of London Press, 1975, and in the chapter on functionalism by Paul Taylor in this volume.

8.   The initial and major source of neo-functional theories are found in the writings of Ernst B. Haas whose many published works about integration should be consulted. Since *The Uniting of Europe* in the mid-fifties, Haas has continuously expanded and revised his theoretical framework. In an assessment of integration theory published in 1971 entitled 'The Study of Regional Integration: Reflections on the Joy and Anguish of Pretheorizing', (in Leon Lindberg and Stuart Scheingold, *Reginoal Integration: Theory and Research*, Cambridge, Mass., Harvard University Press, 1971), Haas remained quite preoccupied with the structural character-istics of 'the dependent variable' of the integration process: the insitutional aspects of political community formation. In a very recent paper, Ernst Haas has concluded that theories of regional integration are becoming obsolescent because the regions will increasingly become insufficient bases of problem solution due to growing global interdependence. The turbulence created in the broader global field makes the need for extra-regional ties more significant than broadening the scope or raising the level of integration within the regional framework. While integration is still defined in terms of 'institutionalized procedures devised by governments for coping with the condition of interdependence' (p. 210), the neo-functional dynamics

311

governing regional integration tend to succumb to 'disjointed incrementalism' and non-functional 'fragmented issue linkages'. Consult his 'Turbulent Fields and the Theory of Regional Integration' in *International Organization*, Vol. 30, No. 2, (Spring 1976), pp. 173–212. The implications of this thought-provoking paper for further development of the parallel national action framework will be incorporated in a review of integration theories in a forthcoming paper. For another recent review and assessment of integration theories, consult Reginald Harrison's, *Europe in Question: Theories of Regional Integration*, London, George Allen and Unwin, 1974 and Harrison's chapter in this volume. The reader should also consult the writings of such integration theorists as Philippe Schmitter, Leon Lindberg, Stuart Scheingold and Joseph Nye among others.

9. For example: 1) Leon Lindberg has changed his emphasis to viewing integration as a general process of collective decision-making among state actors (in 'Political Integration as a Multi-Dimensional Phenomenon Requiring Multivariate Measurement', Lindberg and Scheingold, *Regional Integration . . . op. cit.*); 2) In the 'Concordance System' developed by Donald Puchala as a new conceptual framework there are many attributes similar to the parallel national action framework presented here and he rejected outright the political structural emphasis of the neo-functionalists (in 'Of Blind Men, Elephants and International Integration', *Journal of Common Market Studies*, Vol. 10, No. 3 (March 1972)); 3) Joseph Nye's disaggregated conceptual framework incorporates the need to study policy integration as an important component in political integration processes. He observes that, ' . . . Our concern here is not with the institutions or methods used in making decisions, but with the extent to which a group of countries act as a group (by whatever means) in making domestic and foreign policy decisions.' *Peace in Parts, op. cit.*, p. 41.

10. These definitions fall within the sociological concepts of 'Gemeinschaft' and 'Gesellschaft' as developed by Toennies and Durkheim. Our definition of community bonds as the basis for nationality identification is analyzed in detail by Karl Deutsch in his work on nationalism; see especially his *Nationalism and Social Communication*, Cambridge, Massachusette: M.I.T. Press, 1966. The concept of 'ethnicity' used in Seyom Brown's analysis of substate actors challenging existing state authorities is an example of group action based on community bonds (*op. cit.*). The Western European international integration process was first analyzed according to the society-community conceptual distinction by Paul Taylor in 'The Concept of Community and the European Integration Process', *Journal of Common Market Studies*, Vol. 7, No. 2 (December 1968). This approach was further expanded upon by Ronn D. Kaiser in 'Toward the Copernican Phase of Regional Integration Theory', *Journal of Common Market Studies*, Vol. 10, No. 3 (March, 1972).

11. Herbert C. Kelman, 'Patterns of Personal Involvement in the National System: A Social-Psychological Analysis of Political Legitimacy', James N. Rosenau, editor, *International Politics and Foreign Policy*, New York, The Free Press, Second edition, 1969.

12. A third type would be a multi-state nation. The Federal Republic of Germany, the German Democratic Republic and Austria would be a case in point.

13. Reginald Harrison, *op. cit.*, pp. 235–237.

14. For a more elaborate historical analysis of Scandinavian relations, see Henning Neilsen, *Nordens Enhed Gennem Tiderne*, Copenhagen, Nyt Nordisk Forlag, Arnold Busck, 1938. For a more detailed discussion in

English, see Gunnar P. Nielsson, *Denmark and European Integration: A Small Country at the Crossroads*, Los Angeles, U.C.L.A. Unpublished Ph.D. Dissertation, 1966.

15. The Pan-Scandinavian Movement has been analyzed by Julius Calusen, *Sknadinavismen Historisk Fremstillet*, Copenhagen, Det Nordiske Forlag, 1900.
16. Lindberg and Scheingold, *Europe's Would-Be Policy, op. cit.*, pp. 41 and 123.
17. The Finno-Soviet relationship is analysed in John P. Vloyantes, *Silk Glove Hegemonv: Finnish-Soviet Relations, 1944–1974*, Kent, Ohio, The Kent State University Press, 1975.
18. A discussion of the Danish formulation of policy leading to NATO membership is found in Erling Bjoel, *Atomvaabene og Fremtiden*, Copenhagen, Det Danske Forlag, 1963.
19. The concept of a 'Benelux Procedure', which refers to the method used by governmental leaders from Belgium and the Netherlands in deciding to form a customs union, has been used throughout the post Second World War debate in Scandinavia to convey the basic distinguishing characteristics of the Continental European approach to regional integration which has been very different from the Scandinavian approach.
20. We have adopted the term 'political executive' instead of 'government' in order to differentiate between the activities and responsibilities of the high level, elected political elites which constitute the Cabinet in a parliamentary political system and the civil servants which constitute the permanent staff of the national administration.
21. Bo Anderson, 'The Nordic Organization Research Group', conference paper mimeographed in *Conference on Scandinavia and European Integration*. Edited by Clive Archer, University of Aberdeen, March 1973.
22. Frantz Wendt, *op. cit.* and *Nordisk Samarbejde Idag*, Copenhagen, Foreningen Norden Udgivelse, 1971.
23. Gunnar P. Nielsson, *op. cit.*, chapter VI.
24. *Ibid.*, chapter VII.
25. The Contact Man System is discussed within a more comprehensive context of transgovernmental integration in Scandinavia by C. Robert Dickerman in 'Transgovernmental Challenge and Response in Scandinavia and North America', *International Organization*, Volume 30, No. 2, (Spring 1976).
26. Ove Rainer, 'Det Raettliga omraadet', *Nordisk aembetsmannamoete i Storlien*, Stockholm, Nordiska Raadet, Nordisk Udredningsserie, 1969:9. My translation from page 13. For a brief discussion of the Nordic Contact Man System in English, see Herman Kling, Swedish Minister of Justice, 'Legislative Cooperation Between the Nordic Countries', in *Nordic Cooperation*. Stockholm: Nordiska Raadet, Nordisk Udredningsserie, 1965:9.
27. For a more detailed description and analysis of the Nordic Council, consult Stanley Anderson, *op. cit.* and Frantz Wendt, *op. cit.*
28. The Fagerholm Committee on reorganization of the Nordic Council published its report in English as *The Organization of Nordic Cooperation*, Stockholm, Nordiska Raadet, Nordisk Udredningsserie, 1970:13, and as part of the report on the Nordek proposal in *Expanded Nordic Economic Cooperation*, Stockholm, Nordiska Raadet, Nordisk Udredningsserie, 1969:17. The revised Helsinki Treaty has been published in English by the Nordic Council entitled *Treaty of Cooperation Between Denmark, Finland, Iceland, Norway and Sweden,* without publishing information. The reorganization is discussed in English by Emil Windsetmo, 'Revision of the

Helsinki Treaty of Cooperation and Recent Developments in Nordic Cooperation', *Nordic Cooperation in a European Perspective*, Stockholm, Nordiska Raadet, Nordisk Udredningsserie, 1972:1 and by Gustav Petren, 'The Institutions of Nordek', *Nordic Economic and Cultural Cooperation*, Stockholm, Nordiska Raadet, Nordisk Udredningsserie, 1969:21.

29. For a more detailed analysis of Nordic Council procedures, consult Stanley Anderson, *op. cit.*, chapter 4.

30. A complete overview of the status of Nordic Council Plenary Assembly's recommendations and the Presidium's formal statements between 1953 and 1961 is provided in *Nordiska raadets verksamhet, 1952–1961,* Stockholm, Nordiska Raadet, Nordisk Udredningsserie, 1962:8.

31. *Nordiska ministerraadets arbetsformer*, Stockholm, Nordiska Raadet, Nordisk Udredningsserie, 1971:5.

32. *Treaty Between Denmark, Finland, Iceland, Norway and Sweden Concerning Cultural Cooperation*, published by the Nordic Council without publishing information.

33. The full text of Article 38 is: 'The authorities in the Nordic countries may correspond directly with each other in matters other than those which by their nature or for other reasons should be dealt with through the agency of Ministries of Foreign Affairs.' *Treaty of Cooperation . . . op. cit.*, p. 9. A Norwegian official in the Ministry of Foreign Affairs described the development of diffusion of intra-Nordic interaction channels this way: 'What happened was roughly this: For a period of time after the war, almost all matters between Scandinavian countries went through the foreign offices and embassies. Then other entities began dealing directly, but consulting closely with the foreign office. Eventually they simply sent us drop copies of correspondence and memoranda. Finally that stopped, too.' Interview statement quoted by C. Robert Dickerman, *op. cit.*, p. 223.

34. Interview statement by Emil Windsetmo, quoted in *ibid*, p. 221.

35. Based on the inventory-overview of parallel national action provided in *Oeversikt oever lager tillkomna genom nordiskt samarbete*, Stockholm, Nordiska Raadet, Norkisk Udredningsserie, 1965:2.

36. The partial statistics on the flow of Nordic migrant workers is presented by Helge Seip, 'Social and Economic Problems in Connection With the Nordic Labor Market', *Nordic Economic and Social Cooperation*, Stockholm, Nordiska Raadet, Nordisk Udredningsserie, 1968:7, p. 47. The total Nordic Labor force statistics are taken from *Yearbook of Nordic Statistics*, Stockholm, Nordiska Raadet, Nordisk Udredningsserie, 1971:21, Table 11. (The total work force figure is the sum of the 1965 figures for Denmark, Sweden and Iceland and the 1960 figures for Norway and Finland plus seven percent which was the average increase in the other countries for the five year time span).

37. For a more detailed explanation of the Nordic Customs Union proposals in the 1950's, see Nielsson, *op. cit.*, chapters VII and X.

38. The Nordek plans are analyzed in Gunnar P. Nielsson, 'The Nordic and the Continental European Dimension in Scandinavian Integration: NORDEK as a Case Study', *Cooperation and Conflict*, No. 3/4, 1971.

39. Charles G. Nelson, 'European Integration: Trade Data and Measurement Problems', *International Organization*, Vol. 28, No. 3 (Summer 1974), p. 423.

40. Wilhelm Paues, 'Scandinavian and European Integration: Scandinavian Experiences in E.F.T.A.', mimeographed in *Conference On Scandinavia and European Integration, op. cit.*

41. Vloyantes, *op. cit.* and Nielsson, *op. cit.*

42. *E.F., Danmark og Skandinavien*, Copenhagen, European Communities Information Service, December 1974.
43. Mr. Roger Selbert, a Ph.D. student at the University of Southern California is presently researching that question as his dissertation topic which is entitled 'Compatible Two Sphere Integration: The Simultaneous Danish Participation in the European Communities and Scandinavian Cooperation'.
44. Nordisk aembetsmannamoete . . . , *op.cit.*, p. 15.
45. Per Haekkerup, 'Nordic Cooperation and the World Around Us', *Nordic Cooperation, op. cit.*. p. 29. Professor Nils Andren has concluded in his analysis of the subject that, ' . . . Joint consultation almost assumes the sanctity of an ethical principle in inter-Nordic relations.' 'Nordic Integration: Aspects and Problems', *Cooperation and Conflict*. No. 1, 1967, p. 11.
46. See Bruce Russett, *International Regions and the International System*, Chicago, Rand McNally, 1967. Chapter 4 contains the results of a factor analysis of similarity in U.N. voting behaviour on various issues.
47. For a detailed account of this experience, see the paper by the Nordic Chief Negotiator, Nils Montan, 'Nordic Cooperation in the Field of International Trade Policy', *Nordic Economic and Social Cooperation, op. cit.*
48. Martin Saeter, 'The Nordic Area and European Integration', *Cooperation and Conflict: Nordic Journal of International Politics*, 1/2 1975.
49. For a discussion of this institutional development, consult Roger Broad and R.J. Jarrett, *Community Europe Today*, London, Oswald Wolf, 1972.
50. In a recent study of the changing role of the Commission, Paul Taylor observed: 'The Commission of the European Communities – the main independent, active element in the Brussels institutions – has in effect renounced its claim to be a rival center of authority, a putative European government. It has accepted the role of *actor*, like any other in the European *Gesellschaft*, with the specific task of encouraging European arrangements and encouraging alliances to solve particular problems. In other words, it is no longer out to challenge national governments. In helping them to define their interests and to form alliances, it reinforces their right to exist.' 'The Politics of the European Communities: The Confederal Phase', *World Politics*, Vol. 27, No. 3, (April 1975), p. 347.

Selected Reading

1. Frantz Wendt, *The Nordic Council and Cooperation in Scandinavia*, Copenhagen, Munksgaard, 1959.
2. Stanley V. Anderson, *The Nordic Council: A Study of Scandinavian Regionalism*, Seattle and London, The University of Washington Press, 1967.
3. *Nordic Cooperation*, Nordisk Udredningsserie, 1965:9.
4. *Nordic Economic and Social Cooperation*, Nordisk Udredningsserie, 1968:9.
5. *Nordic Economic and Cultural Cooperation*, Nordisk Udredningsserie, 1969:21.
6. *The Organization of Nordic Cooperation*, Nordisk Udredningsserie, 1970:13.

7. *Nordic Cooperation in a European Perspective*, Nordisk Udrednings-serie, 1972:1, Nordisk Udredningsserie is published in Stockholm by the Nordic Council.
8. *Cooperation and Conflict: Nordic Journal of International Politics,* 1/2 1975. Special issue on elite attitudes and Nordic government policies concerning questions of integration and cooperation in Europe in general and in the Nordic area in particular.
9. Barbara Haskel, *The Scandinavian Option*, Oslo, Universitetsforlaget, 1976.

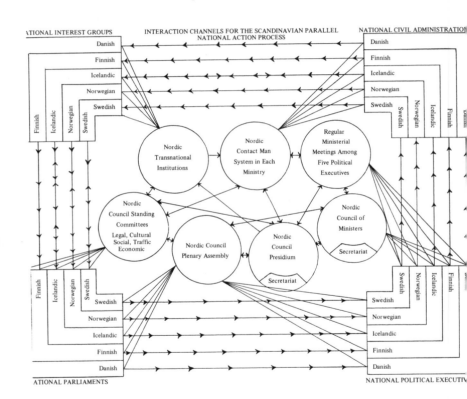

CHAPTER FOUTEEN

CONFEDERALISM: THE CASE OF THE EUROPEAN COMMUNITIES*

Paul Taylor

In this chapter the concept of Confederalism is used as an analogy to illuminate some of the main features of relations between member states of the European Communities in the 1970s.[1] There is a decentralized, though coordinated, system in which participating actors, including, particularly, governments, trade unions and business organisations, have a high level of interdependence with each other, but, nevertheless, preserve and even augment their autonomy. This pattern of inter-dependence coexisting with a continuing separateness of participating actors, which is summed up in the concept of Confederalism, is illustrated by reference to two interrelated themes. They are, first, the broadly defensive stance of the governments in their conducts of relations with the Brussels institutions; and second, the appearance of a system of political interaction which may be called a 'managed Gesellschaft'.

It is arguable that governments constructed the institutions of the European Community and defined their roles and their specific tasks in the Rome Treaty so as to make it easier for them to defend their interests as integration proceeded than it had been in the period 1950–1954. At the time of the negotiations in Brussels and in Rome, the Six realized that although they could agree in detail about tariff reductions, the creation of a Common Market, and the gradualist approach, there were many questions, for instance in agricultural policy, commercial policy, regional policy, and social policy, on which they could then only agree in outline. There was indeed an expectation that future compatibilities would allow detailed agreement, but there was no certainty that this would follow. It was agreed, therefore, that a mechanism would be created — namely, the Commission — which would draw up detailed proposals to which governments could respond at greater leisure.[2] The governments were in the position of being asked to agree to schemes which were put to them rather than initiating their own proposals: their role was a responsive or defensive one of catching the ball rather than throwing it. From the beginning, the institutions of the Communities made it easy for national governments to adopt a defensive stand if they so wished; they were designed to allow a relatively undramatic, stonewalling approach should the government's expectations of future compatibilities be unrealized. This defensive style is a characteristic and natural response of governments to the Communities and is in no way a departure from the intentions of the founders.

There are numerous examples of governments' dragging their feet in the development of the European Communities. It is not surprising, though, that, faced with a broadly uncooperative or defensive posture on the part of members, some governments became impatient and tried more desperate remedies. West Germany's procrastination over the arrangements for financing the Community's agricultural policy was one of the causes of France's partial withdrawal from the Communities in June 1965, at the onset of the crisis.[3] The Commission's proposals of March 1965 on institutional reform would probably have received the usual undramatic, defensive cold shoulder from the French had they not been linked with an issue about which the French Government felt strongly, and had agreement on this issue not already been considerably delayed in French eyes. The same kind of impatience was shown by West Germany before the Hague meeting of 1969. The occasional crisis is one of the dangers of the broadly defensive posture in governments which is encouraged by the Communities' institutional arrangements. One may conclude that a characteristic dynamic of integration in Europe is the reaching of a critical level of impatience with partners as a result of their failure to provide perceived benefits.[4]

The most powerful pressure toward the adoption of a defensive posture in the Confederal phase, however, probably derives from the very success of the integration process. Governments in the European Communities no longer preside over states whose various 'functional' tiers are largely coextensive. In many respects, states have been economically, legally, and politically penetrated by systems which

318

extend throughout the area of the European Communities and, often, beyond them. One result is that governments are now unable to take decisions which refer to their own territory without taking into account a range of influences, pressures, and sometimes rules which originate outside their own frontiers, and which they are unable to control. It has been calculated that in West Germany, 'about two-thirds of all questions of agricultural policy . . . can no longer be made in a purely national context, but rather must be made within the decision-making structure of the agricultural system of the European Communities.'[5] Upwards of 50 per cent of the external trade of members of the Communities is with other members. In member states, the law of the Communities has a status comparable with municipal law; in Britain, 'Parliament has identified an area within which it intends to refrain from exercising its own legislative power.'[6] Within the Communities, according to one commentator, are to be found about three thousand nongovernmental international organisations, including some powerful multinational companies – by far the largest concentration in the world.[7] It is hardly surprising that governments, when faced with these developments, have been pushed toward a more defensive posture.

Writing about relations between developed states in general, Edward Morse finds that 'It is often concluded that the increases in national cohesiveness that accompany modernization counteract international interdependence. Actually the reverse is true.' He elaborates, 'as the levels of interdependence within a state rise, the same order of trade has increased implications for domestic employment, fiscal, monetary, and welfare policies.'[8] Within the Communities, it may be added, the higher the level of trade with other members, the greater is the impact of variations in their trade upon national attempts to control, for example, employment levels, interest rates, and welfare standards. It may well follow that it is partly because of the development of higher levels of international interdependence that national cohesiveness increases; in reacting to increasing levels of international inter-dependence, governments seek to involve themselves in larger areas of national economic and social life. This reaction derives from their urge to defend themselves against international functional encroachment on their traditional domain.

A second theme which emerges from an examination of the Confederal phase of integration is that of the 'managed Gesellschaft'. The central features of this system are the undermining of the

319

hierarchy of actors and interests, both at the national and the European level and, as a corollary, the legitimization of an increasing range of interests which are fed into the political arena. The development of mechanisms for the management of relations between existing actors of more or less equal status, whose interests are generally seen as having more or less equal validity, is increasingly the condition for stability. It is not that all interests are in principle equally worthy or just, and that this is part of the essential condition of society, but rather, that they have come to be accepted as such, at least in part because of the integration process.

Popular loyalties have so far not focused upon the institutions of the Communities. At the same time, though, governments are no longer able to marshal popular support or tolerance in the way that was once possible.[9] In the mid 1970s governments in a number of West European states, such as France, Britain, and Italy, were uncertain and ailing. Changes in popular attitudes have helped to undermine the authority of governments. The Community method of decision making is one of the factors which has encouraged groups within the state to articulate their interests and to judge them as equally valid with those of governments. This undermining of the hierarchy of interests, as well as the fracturing of the earlier agreement about priorities among values and attitudes within the state, has contributed to the reduction of the status of governments in the Community's political system. Despite the increasing pervasiveness of government activity, the authority and status of governments seem to be declining.

Dissatisfaction with existing conditions within a particular state is reinforced by comparison with conditions in other states; claims — which may even challenge the authority of governments — are legitimized. The developments of May 1968 in France, and the success of the workers there in achieving unprecedented increases in wages, certainly sharpened the appetites of trade unionists in other European states and reinforced their determination to achieve a more equitable distribution of wealth. Expectations within the Communities, and the fact that transmission of demands is made easier by the extensive range of interdependencies and transnational links, have helped to undermine the hierarchy of interests within the states.

It is hard to escape the conclusion that international interdependencies make it more difficult for national governments to control their economies. As the Nine have a greater range of interdependencies with each other than with outsiders, it is argued that the

320

development of the European Communities has added to the difficulty. The importance of this development for the status of governments should be stressed: it means that they are now weakened in their command over the levers of economic power which was once one of the hallmarks of government. And this has happened precisely at a time when economic success — the ability to deliver the goods — has been the main test of political virtue. In this sense, they have been reduced in status. It means also that, in trying to compensate for the loss of mechanisms of control, governments are increasingly pushed toward what might be called government by alliance. They are increasingly faced with the need to form effective alliances or sets of alliances with other governments in order to achieve specific objectives. Furthermore, governments may enter into arrangements with other organised groups, such as trade unions, or business organisations, involving negotiations and concessions on their demands in return for help with the running of the economy. The 'social contract' in the UK is one example of this.

Two developments which affected the status of governments adversely have now been identified; they are each partly attributable, though not exclusively so, to membership in the European Communities. Membership has contributed to the weakening of the Gemeinschaft in the nation-state, has helped to undermine the hierarchy of values and attitudes, and has reduced the authority of governments. Membership has also exacerbated the problem of control over national economies and has disposed governments to seek alliances with other organized groups in an attempt to regain control. The weakening of agreed values in the state, the declining authority of governments and the reduction of the effectiveness of their mechanisms for control have encouraged organized groups to increase their demands on governments, and to view their own and the governments' interests as possessing an equal validity. The Community links have certainly contributed to these developments.

There is, however, no tendency for governments to be eliminated as actors from the European *Gesellschaft*. In fact, their right to remain as actors has, if anything, been reinforced by developments in the Communities over recent years. The absence of a *Gemeinschaft* at the European level means that there is no means of establishing the priority of any one set of interests and no way of deciding whether any actor should be eliminated from the system. It is accepted that satisfaction of any one interest depends upon the construction of appropriate alliances and power and influence between groups, including governments, rather than upon a government's ability to relate specific demands to a general interest.

It is essential to realize that — in accordance with the Confederal model — this is as true at the Communities level as at the national one. The Commission of the European Communities — the main independent, active element in the Brussels institutions — has in effect renounced its claim to be a rival centre of authority, a putative European government. It has accepted the role of actor, like any other in the European *Gesellschaft*, with the specific task of encouraging European arrangements and encouraging alliances to solve particular problems. In other words, it no longer sets out to challenge national governments. In helping them to define their interests and to form alliances, it reinforces their right to exist. The total effect has been an equalization of the hierarchy of actors both at the national and at the European level.

The range of initiatives taken by the governments of the Six at The Hague in December 1969 signalled the arrival of a new kind of politics between governments in the Communities. The Government of West Germany under the leadership of Willy Brandt showed signs of having abandoned the role of 'economic giant and political dwarf'. A range of factors such as the success of the *Ostopolitik* and the new approach towards *détente*, the abandonment of the Hallstein doctrine, and the energy and political standing of the German Chancellor contributed toward a new forcefulness in German diplomacy. The relative decline in France from the high plateau of economic and political power in 1967 under President de Gaulle made the resurgence of West Germany more striking. At the summit, it was the Chancellor rather than de Gaulle's successor, President Pompidou, who proved to be the dominant statesman.[10] The range of proposals for further integration which emerged from the Hague meeting was the first fruit of a phase of integration which, because of the German recovery, was marked by much more intensive diplomatic acitivity, at a higher level, than there had been in the Communities since 1958. The German interest and activity were instrumental in demonstrating that diplomacy and the convergence of diplomatic objectives were now the touchstone of success in the integration process. The Commission was faced with a new situation in which, paradoxically, the condition of further progress towards integration was the reassertion of the separate identity of the government actors and their engagement in a higher level of diplomacy — than had hitherto been the case. It could but respond to their new awareness of themselves and their interest in integration, and seek to adjust to the new intergovernmental machinery which they created.

The impact of the new phase of integration upon the Commission and its role in decision making in the Communities was clearly visible at the time of the enlargement of the Communities and the accession of three new members, including Britain, in January 1973. The Commission of Thirteen under President Ortoli was different in many respects from its predecessors. The membership of Britain in the Communities strengthened the idea of the informal representativeness of individual commissioners. It is certainly not suggested that any members of the Commission or their staff were in direct receipt of specific instructions, but member governments aimed to get their men into positions of responsibility for areas in which they are particularly interested. Since the advent of British membership, the notion that European commissioners should in some way strive for the definition of the pure form of European interest has weakened. It was no accident that responsibility for two areas in which the British government was particularly interested was allocated to British commissioners: George Thomson became responsible for regional questions, and Christopher Soames was placed in charge of relations between the Communities and the developed countries.

Because of their awareness of the importance of integration to their separate interests, governments have generally appointed men of high ability to the Commission. At the same time, it was inevitable that a phase of integration which stressed diplomacy and the rights of individual actors should spawn institutions which did not necessarily accrue to the centre of Brussels. The Commission had to make the task of coordinating the work of intergovernmental institutions a much more important part of its work: it set itself the task of *managing* the *Gesellschaft* rather than of obtaining higher levels of unity under more centralized institutions.

Thus, the Commission, in relation to developments at the European level, became in some ways more like governments at the national level. It found itself unable to sustain its claim of being a putative European government which would accede to an unusual authority and power as national governments lost some of their traditional functions within the state. Half-hearted (and unsuccessful) attempts have been made to amend the Treaty of Rome under the terms of Article 236, so that new areas could be brought within the framework of the Treaty, protecting the cohesiveness of the control institutions.[11] The Commission and governments became more like each other as actors, seeking alliances with other actors as one condition of success, and attempting to extend their presence in striving for proper coordination and management. Like national governments, the Commission also sought alliances with the so-called 'social partners' — trade union federations and the representatives of the national confederations of industry in Brussels. It may be that in addition to the pressures of the European Communities, there is a vast range of influences deriving from the processes of modernization and the development of the welfare state, which affected governments and the Commission alike, and which were conducive toward the same changes in their status as actors. Among these was the development of attitudes and values, in national leaders and in commissioners, which tend to be managerial and technocratic in style and disposed them to see the major test of their success in the growth of material standards. The experience and style of the European Communities certainly reinforced these attitudes.

These then are the elements of politics in the European Communities which are illuminated by the concept of Confederalism. It is apparent that the mixture of interdependencies and the assertion of independence by participating actors and the weakening both of claims to supranationalism, and of a revival of national autarky, are developments of the concept which are fully consistent with its character. They represent, however, a deepening and extension of the concept.

Notes

*   This chapter is a version of Paul Taylor, 'The Politics of the European Communities: The Confederal Phase', which originally appeared in *World Politics*, 27, no. 3 (April 1975), published by Princeton University Press, Reprinted by permission of the publisher.
1.   For a preliminary account of the Confederal phase, see Paul Taylor, 'The Common Market and the Forces of History', *Orbis*, XVI, Fall 1972, pp. 743—59.
2.   For an account of the powers of the Commission, see Roy Pryce, *The Politics of the European Community*, London, Butterworth, 1973, pp. 55—64.
3.   Nina Heathcote, 'The Crisis of European Supranationality', *Journal of Common Market Studies*, v, Devember 1966, pp. 140—71.
4.   See Leon N. Lindberg, 'Integration as a Source of Stress on the European Community Systems', *International Organization*, 20, 1966, pp. 254—272.
5.   Karl Kaiser, 'Transnational Politics: Toward a Theory of Multinational Politics', *International Organization*, xxv, Autumn 1971, p. 799.
6.   Geoffrey Howe, 'The European Communities Act 1972', *International Affairs*, Vol. 49, January 1973, p. 6.
7.   See Kjell Skjelsbaek, 'Transnational Associations and their Functions', in A.J.R. Groom and Paul Taylor, eds., *Functionalism and International Relations: Theory and Practice*, London, University of London Press, 1975.
8.   Edward L. Morse, 'The Transformation of Foreign Policies: Modernization,

Interdependence and Externalization', *World Politics*, xxii, April 1970, p. 389.

9. See G. Ionesan, *Centripetal Politics: Governments and New Centres of Power*, Hart-Davis, MacGibbon Ltd., London, 1975, for an interesting examination of an analogous theme.
10. See account in Use Kitzinger, *Diplomacy and Persuasion,* London, Thames and Hudson, 1973, pp. 68–72.
11. See President Ortoli's Introduction to the Sixth General Report of the Communities, Brussels, European Communities Information Service, February 1973, p. 4.

Selected Reading

1. G. Ionescu, *Centripetal Politics: Governments and the New Centres of Power*, Hart Davis, MacGibbon Ltd., London, 1975.
2. Donald Puchala, 'Of Blind Men, Elephants and International Integration', *Journal of Common Market Studio*, Vol. X, No. 3, (March 1972).
3. Leon N. Lindberg and Stuart A. Scheingold, *Europe's Would-Be Polity*, Englewood Cliffs, Prentice Hall, Inc., 1970.
4. Joseph S. Nye, Jr. and Robert O. Keohane 'Transnational Relations and World Politics: a Conclusion', *International Organization*, Vol. 25, No. 3, 1971, pp. 721–748.
5. Geoffrey L. Goodwin and Andrew Linklater, *New Dimensions of World Politics*, London, Croom Helm, 1975.
6. Paul Taylor, 'The Politics of the European Communities: the Confederal Phase', *World Politics*, 27, No. 3, April 1975.

CHAPTER FIFTEEN

FEDERALISM: THE CONCEPTUAL SETTING

George A. Codding, Jr.

The concept of federalism has had an important place in international organisation literature. Almost from the beginning of the modern nation state men have put their minds to the problems of expanding the territorial limits of their creation to include more and more territory and more and more people. The motives for this expansion have varied from the simple desire for more power, imperialism, to the desire to construct an edifice better equipped to meet the evolving needs of mankind. Among the latter are the advocates of the federalist approach to supranational political authority.

Although, as we shall see, there is an infinite variety in the details of the various federal plans for international integration, there are certain core elements. The most basic of these is the creation of a supranational government which will share power with member states. The amount of this power, which depends upon the functions to be given to the supranational government, is set forth in a basic treaty, a constitution, which cannot be changed easily by either level of government. As defined by Carl J. Friedrich: 'A federal system then is a particular kind of constitutional order. The function it is supposed to serve is to restrain the powers wielded by the inclusive community, *as well as* those of the communities included within it. It is . . . a kind of division or separation of powers, but applied on a spatial basis.'[1]

The process of integration is as simple as the concept itself. Through education and propaganda the political elites of the area to be federalized will be made to realize the need for the creation of a supranational federal system. Once the need is realized, the political leaders will sit down together to draft the constitution which will create the new supranational state and the necessary institutions which will permit it to carry out those tasks desired by the member states and which will tend to preserve the division of powers between the levels of government. The new world constitution would come into effect upon ratification by the member states.

There are a number of basic assumptions to this somewhat unsophisticated 'future world' model building which contain both the theory's strength and its weaknesses. The first is the assumption that the nation-state system, as it is presently constituted, is incapable of carrying out certain tasks which are crucial to the well-being of mankind, such as the control of international violence. The second is that man's creation, government, despite all of its imperfections, can be adapted for use as a supranational authority. Third, the protection of sectional differences, which is inherent in the federalist position, is both healthy and desirable. And fourth, the federalist approach relies heavily on man's rationality in that he will be able to perceive the need for a revolutionary change in his governance and that he will be willing to make that change. We will deal with these in more detail as we proceed.

Historical Setting and Schools of Thought

While the creation of federations of states for various purposes dates back to antiquity,[2] the concept of federalism is a fairly modern invention. Carl J. Friedrich, for instance, traces the beginning of federalist theory to Althusius in the 16th century.[3] Other important names in this early period include the theorists Grotius and Montesquieu and three of the first designers of a world federal government, Duc de Sully, William Penn, and Abbé de Saint-Pierre.[4] Most of these early schemes for a world federal government, it should be noted, were concerned mainly with the integration of the 'civilized' states of Europe.

The successful American experiment in federalism and its apologia, the *Federalist* papers, set off a spate of federalist theorizing which included some of the greatest names of the times, including Immanuel Kant, Jean-Jacques Rousseau, de Tocqueville, and Proudhon. The Swiss experience in federalism was not long in following and helped to reinforce the proponents of the federal solution.[5]

In this century, the period to which the bulk of this chapter is devoted, the Second World War, the events leading up to it, and its aftermath provided an impetus to federal world order modeling that has not as yet ebbed. Most of these plans were claimed by their proponents to be solutions to the problem of world peace. Among the more prominent of these plans are included the project of Ely Culbertson, the international bridge expert, which stressed the idea of an international police force; Emery Reves, who wrote *Anatomy of Peace*, where he preached that wars would be ended as soon as sovereignty was transferred to a larger unit; and Cord Meyer, who presented the first plan of the United World Federalists.[6] Of a different nature was the draft constitution of The Federal Republic of the World, inspired by the bombing of Hiroshima, and drafted by a group known as the Committee to Frame a World Constitution, under the leadership of Chancellor Hutchins of the University of Chicago.[7]

One of the most important names of the times was Clarence K. Streit, who argued that while world federation should be the ultimate goal, it was absolutely essential to start with a smaller group of nations with something in common and to build from there.[8] The impact of the federalist movement in the United States was so strong that by 1950 twenty-one states had passed resolutions favourable to a world federation of one type or another and hearings were being held on the subject in the Senate Committee on Foreign Relations.[8a]

Although the enthusiasm for the creation of a world federal government on a universal or large scale has tended to wane since the Senate Foreign Relations Committee held its hearings, the late 1950's did see the presentation of the comprehensive plan authored by Grenville Clark and Professor Louis B. Sohn, which has been revised on a number of occasions, and in 1972 the successor to the United World Federation, the World Association of World Federalists under the presidency of Norman Cousins, claimed national World Federalist Associations in thirty-three nations throughout the world.[9]

Post-Second World War institution building in Europe has provided the lodestone for integrationists, non-federal as well as federal. Among the major European groups are the European Federalist Movement, the successor to the European Union of Federalists founded in 1946, and the European Centre for Federalist Action (Centre d'action Europeene fédéraliste, or AEF), which dates from 1956 when it broke away from the other group. Among the names of prominent European federalists are Henri Brugmans, Rector of the College of Europe, Guy Heraud, Alexandre Marc, Denis de Rougemont, and Altiero Spinelli.[10] The European federalist movement that will be investigated in these pages has a slightly different orientation from the universalist or large-scale federalist movements already mentioned. The main thrust of these movements has been the creation of a supranational institution which would eventually eliminate the need for national armies and thus would tend to ensure international peace and order. This element is not a consideration in the European federalist movement, except perhaps for those who see it as a method of keeping Germany under control. The main considerations are economies of scale, the building of Europe into a democratic supranational institution of a size that would permit it to compete on an even footing with the superpowers in any field of national endeavour. In addition, although some see the proposed European federal government including eventually all of Europe, if it is mentioned at all, universalism is only a secondary aim.

The Federal Plan

The content of any particular federalist plan is limited only by the bounds of the imagination of the particular author, and there are many. Some plans are a page or two in length, some are several hundred pages. Nevertheless, there are two broad areas, at least in most of the older plans, which can be readily identified and grouped for comparative purposes — the extent of powers that should be granted to the supra-national authority and the structure of this authority.

Almost without exception, the universalists and quasi-universalists would grant the federal authority the powers necessary to maintain peace and security. For the minimalists, the powers would be restricted to this function. Cord Meyer believed that ' . . . only those functions of government that are determined to be indispensable to the prevention of war need to be transferred . . . while the member nations retain their independence of action in all other matters.'[11] Clark and Sohn in *World Peace Through World Law* echoed this sentiment: 'The powers of the world organisation should be restricted to matters directly related to the maintenance of peace. All other powers should be reserved to the nations and their peoples.'[12] These powers 'would *not* include such matters as regulation of international trade, immigration and the like, or any right to interfere in the domestic affairs of the nations . . . '[13] The purpose of this restriction, on the part of Clark and Sohn, at least, has nothing especially to do with any feeling that the central govern-ment should be limited to only those powers, but to the concern that if too much were attempted it might engender a crippling opposition to any supranational plans based upon the fear of interference in the domestic affairs of the nations and, in general, because agreement on anything further might well be beyond the powers of this generation of

329

mankind.[14]

The exact powers necessary to carry out this basic purpose would, for Clark and Sohn, include: 1) the power to enact and enforce laws and regulations relating to universal and complete national disarmament, including the control of nuclear energy and the use of outer space; 2) the power to enact and enforce laws and regulations to prevent actual or imminent breaches of international peace and any serious refusal to comply with the basic treaty; 3) the power to enact and enforce laws and regulations to prevent acts or omissions of individuals and private organisations which violate the basic treaty or which cause damage to the property of the supranational government or to any person in its service while engaged in official duties; and 4) the power to maintain a military force large enough to enforce universal and complete disarmament and for 'the prevention and removal of threats to the peace, for the suppression of acts of aggression and other breaches of the peace, and for ensuring compliance with this revised Charter and the laws and regulations enacted thereunder.'[15] Clark and Sohn would also confer the power to raise revenues and to make the jurisdiction of the judicial arm compulsory in certain disputes.

Clarence Streit would widen the scope of the powers of his original supranational government to include such things as the right to grant citizenship, the right to regulate interstate and foreign trade, to coin and issue money, and the right to govern communications.[16] Perhaps the most detailed of the plans is *A Constitution for the World* drafted by the Committee headed by Chancellor Hutchins (see footnote 7), which provides for: the regulation and operation of means of transportation and commerce which are of federal interest, 'laws concerning emigration and immigration and the movements of peoples; the granting of federal passports; the appropriation, under the right of eminent domain, of such private or public property as may be necessary for federal use' and administration of the federal capital district.[17] In justification of the wider powers, Elisabeth Borgese argues that 'war is not something separate that can be added to or subtracted from the total weave of the social, political, and economic life of peoples.'[18]

The powers that the European federalists would grant to their supranational authority differ from the others primarily because of the difference in its basic purpose. As a superpower among superpowers, it must be given authority over foreign affairs and defense policy, powers which would be non-existent in the other plans. The emphasis on economic problems in their model, the EEC, and the wider range of authority over economic and social problems in European states also has had an effect on European conceived proposals as contrasted to those which have come from American authors. Pinder and Pryce point out a number of issues which cut across national boundaries which must be regulated by the supranational authority, including modern industrial production, monetary stability, communications and multi-nationals. Underlying everything is the need for large-scale social and economic planning.[19]

An interrelated problem to which the federalists have addressed themselves is the structure of the proposed federal world authority. In general, the architects of federal world government have tended to borrow from the familiar. Saint-Simon, writing in 1814, advocated that a federated Europe be governed by a single parliament and a single king which would regulate all questions of common concern including colonial expansion and economic and social affairs of the component states.[20] American writers and those inspired by the American system tend to envisage an organisation similar to the American federal system. As stated by Clarence Streit: 'Those who would constitute unions can turn now to many time-tested successes. For reasons that will be seen when we study carefully the American Union I believe that we should turn particularly to the American Constitution and experience for guidance.'[21] Streit advocates a two-house legislature, on the American model, with one based on population and the other on member states. The latter, which would have the task of safeguarding the small democracies and decentralization, would be made up of two representatives for each member state.[22] The Streit proposal also provided for an independent Supreme Court. Streit abandoned the American presidency, however, for a five-man executive which would delegate its responsibilities to a Prime Minister and his cabinet.

Clark and Sohn's proposals, as well as a number of the early post-Second World War ones, including that of the United World Federalists, would build on the United Nations. Among the reasons given are that 'it seems logical and reasonable to utilize an existing organisation of such scope and experience,'[23] that the primary purpose of the UN is to prevent war, and that the creation of a new world organization adequately equipped to maintain peace would necessarily overshadow the present United Nations.[24] The Clark and Sohn proposal envisages the transformation of the General Assembly of the United Nations into a popularly elected body with final responsibility for disarmament and the maintenance of peace. In the new General Assembly states would be given voting power proportionate to their populations.[25] The present UN Security Council would be replaced by a seventeen-member Executive Council, elected by the General Assembly, which would act as the executive arm of the world government with broad powers to supervise and direct the disarmament process and other aspects of the system for the maintenance of peace. The new authority would have a revamped and strengthened International Court of Justice and Economic and Social Council. Innovations in the Clark and Sohn proposal include a World Peace Force of from 200,000 to 600,000 effectives and 600,000 to 1,200,000 reserves to police the disarmed world, and a revenue system made up of a specific portion of the taxes of the subordinate units. In the third edition of the plan Clark and Sohn added another new organ, the World Development Commission, with 'very large sums at its disposal' with the task of aiding 'the underdeveloped areas of the world to the extent necessary to remove the danger to world stability and peace caused by the immense economic disparity between those areas and the industrialized regions of the world.'[26]

With the Europeans, as would be expected, the institutions of the European Economic Community provide the foundation on which to build the federalist edifice. They have succeeded in bringing about a degree of economic integration between the member states and they have passed the test of time. What would be more logical than to give these institutions political as well as economic power?

John Pinder and Roy Pryce provide us with a multi-phased, long-term plan to accomplish this purpose. The main thrust of this proposal is to replace the nation-state dominated Council of Ministers as the final and unchallengeable source of decision-making by the Commission and Parliament. There is no strict time limit as regards the moving from one stage to the next, the only criteria being the progressive rein-forcement of the common institutions so that they would ultimately be capable of assuming the powers which at present are largely in the hands of national authorities.'[26a] In the first stage, the transitional period, arrangements would be made to institute a system of direct financing for the Community along with a new procedure for the approval of the annual budget in which the Commission and Parliament would have a major role. At this stage plans would also be made to introduce, again by stages, direct election of a substantial proportion of the members of the Parliament and to involve the Parliament in the legislative process. The Council would be required to transmit its decisions to the Parliament and Parliament would have to approve these decisions before they had the force of law, and Parliament would be given the power to amend the Council's proposals. In the second stage other existing Community institutions, such as the Economic and Social Committee and the Court of Justice, would be strengthened and a new institution would be created to represent regional authorities. In the final stage the direct election of all the remaining members of Parliament on a uniform system would be introduced as would be a new method for the selection of the Commission which would eliminate the present role of the European governments. One possibility would be a two-stage direct election on the French model, or election indirectly by an electoral college or by Parliament.[27] These two institutions would then assume the ultimate decision making power of the Community. The final result would be a federal government with three levels, Community, regional, and national, with an independent source of income and based on the democratic process.[28]

If there is disagreement among federalists as to the proper structure for the new federal world government, there is just as much disagreement as to the proper strategy to achieve it. Probably the foremost division is that between the universalists and those who would accept a federation in a smaller geographical area, either as an end in itself or as one piece of a puzzle to which other pieces will be added as circumstances dictate. Among the former are the World Federalists and Clark and Sohn. Inasmuch as universal disarmament is a prerequisite to world peace, one of the primary aims of the Clark and Sohn proposal, they are forced to argue that virtually the whole world must accept permanent membership. Anyway, since the Clark and Sohn plan would not come into effect until ratified by five-sixths of the world's population and must include each of the twelve largest nations, 'it is possible, and even probable, that there would actually be no nonmember nations whatsoever.'[29] However, in case there are states which refuse to join, they would in effect be under the authority of the world government because they will be bound to refrain from violence and to settle all their disputes by peaceful means.[30]

Clarence Streit is an example of those who would start with a less ambitious number of nation-states, a more homogeneous group. In one of his earlier books he advocated a federal union of the United States and the members of the British Commonwealth. In his 1940 book he proposed to start with 'the North Atlantic or founder democracies' which would include the United States, the British Commonwealth (specifically the United Kingdom, Canada, Australia, New Zealand, South Africa, and Ireland), France, Belgium, Netherlands, Switzerland, Denmark, Norway, Sweden, and Finland. These states

333

were selected because they include 'the world's greatest, oldest, most homogeneous and closely linked democracies, the peoples most experienced and successful in solving the problems at hand — the peaceful, reasonable establishment of effective interstate democratic world government.' This group did not have too great a linguistic diversity and above all: *'None of these democracies has been at war with any of the others since more than 100 years.'*[31] Later Streit changed his founders of the union to the fifteen-nation membership of NATO (this substituted Iceland, Luxemburg, West Germany, Greece, Italy, Portugal, and Turkey for Australia, Ireland, Finland, New Zealand, Sweden, Switzerland and South Africa.) This new combination of founder states was much less ideal than the original fifteen, but more practical in that they had already made some efforts in common. As the term 'founders' suggests, Mr. Streit had no exclusivest tendencies. The founding fifteen would actually be so strong and democratic, according to Streit, that the Union would be such a powerful attraction to other countries that one by one their citizens would turn their governments into democracies and enter the Union until there would be a single peaceful democratic world government.[32] Streit did not rule out the possibility that the Atlantic Union would provide an immense impulse toward federation in other regions of the world which some day would federate with each other and the Atlantic Union.

Europe provides a third approach, with federal theorizers and the federal movement directed primarily at creating a new federal state out of a number of European states and only secondarily or incidentally to serve as a nucleus for a larger federation. The aim, in fact, of some of the schemes is to create a federal union of Western European democracies which would permit it to remain independent of other major powers, including the United States.[33] Others, while starting with the Western European democracies, expect the new federal union eventually to include all of the states of Europe, both East and West.[34]

Perhaps the most important aspect of strategy is the method which is employed to influence governments to give up their power to the supranational federal government. Some are very simple and direct. Streit, for instance, sees an overwhelming pressure arising from the people. To obtain the Federal Union, 'the first thing those who want it should do is to say so . . . ' .[35] The supporters of the Federal Union need not wait on diplomats to obtain it for them; they 'need only turn to themselves and their neighbours . . . The first necessity then is

334

that Unionists wherever they are should make known their will for The Union and organise their neighborhood, and state and nation, and keep on uniting for The Union, and coordinating their work in all the democracies, until they form the majority needed to get The Union.'[36] Direct pressure on public authorities is important. The federalist 'need only write, telegraph, telephone his Representative, Senator, Deputy, Member of Parliament, Premier, President.'[37] Eventually these pressures will have the necessary effect. 'The raindrop on the window seems powerless, but the crudest mill-wheel moves if only enough raindrops take the same channel.'[38]

A more sophisticated approach is evident in the European branch of the federalist movement. In fact, according to one authority, the 'theoretical discussion of federalism as a strategy for bringing about political unification arises almost entirely in the context of contemporary European integration.'[39] This same authority divides the European federalists into the moderates and the radicals. The moderates, such as those represented by the AEF, believe in an incremental, evolutionary approach, and will take any opportunity offered to create political institutions. First the activity of the EEC and the Parliament, along with propaganda from the federalists, will draw the attention and the support of various groups in industry, commerce and agriculture to European unity. The second stage would be to bring about an agreement to elect the European Parliament by direct suffrage. The final stage would be the drafting of the federal treaty by the Parliament and its ratification by the member states. The federalists at all times would be involved in explaining, interpreting, and working to move the process from step to step.

The radicals in Europe, on the other hand, under the banner of the MFE (European Federal Movement), are for more drastic action. First the task is to create an intense international campaign of public persuasion to convince individuals as well as leaders and groups that the nation-state as it is known is obsolete and that it is up to the people to help create the alternative. Rally massive support for calling a constituent assembly which will have the limited task of drafting the federal treaty, which will then be submitted to governments for ratification. An interesting offshoot of the radicals identified by Harrison are those who feel that it would help, perhaps even be necessary, to have a crisis to exploit in addition to the necessary popular force. The main advantage claimed for the radical method is that it would bypass the states by making the constitution drafting a matter between parties with interests at stake and not governments.

335

The moderate method, it is claimed, would demand too much of the good will of governments by making them parties to the process of giving up their own power.[40]

Claims and Counterclaims

The advantage claimed by the federalists for a federal supranational political authority are numerous. Above all, the division of powers between different levels of government recognizes and accounts for the dual trend toward the need for worldwide solutions to worldwide problems and the contrary trend toward the need for local solutions for local problems. Some problems, such as interstate violence, obviously demand the highest level of action. According to the World Association of World Federalists, peace requires that the world community substitute the process of law for armed conflicts in settling disputes: 'We believe . . . that world federal government with powers adequate to establish and maintain laws and justice on the world level is the only practicable way to achieve a just and lasting peace.'[41] Clark and Sohn add development to world priorities that only a world federal government would be in a position to attack. Other problems demand purely national solutions, such as freedom to manage domestic affairs and to choose political, economic, and social institutions.[42] Only those close to the problem can provide effective and acceptable solutions.

It also provides a barrier to central despotism by guaranteeing autonomy of its sub-units and their participation in the federal government. The central government will have only that authority which is specifically granted in the constitution while the member states will retain all the rest, and this division of authority is protected by being stated clearly in the founding document which should be incapable of easy change and which is protected in its turn by the institutional framework. Further, and this is a corollary, the federal system is a guarantee of regional diversity, a characteristic which is inherently good. In addition, by keeping a considerable amount of decision-making at the local level one would be guaranteeing the participation of as many people as possible, the civic participation counselled by Rousseau.

The federalist approach is also claimed to have a number of tactical advantages. First, it will appeal to the weaker nation-states, those which will be more reluctant to enter into a supranational authority, both as regards the retention of local authority and the placing of restrictions on the power of the central authority.[43] It is in effect a method of achieving world order at a minimal cost to national identifies, another attraction to the states which are asked to give up some of their sovereignty. Second, it is an attractive plan. It is attractive because of its simplicity and the familiarity of the analogy from which it derives.[44] Finally, it is attractive because it is realistic. It does not rely on the back-door approach to integration that is advocated by the functionalists or the incidental approach of the neo-functionalists, but rather it relies on the direct approach which recognizes the importance of political will and political settlement.

The critics of the federalist position, and there are many, fall into two categories, those who question the intrinsic value of the federal form of government and those who question the merits of the direct political approach of the federalists to structural change. One of the more vocal of the critics is David Mitrany, the father of the functionalist approach to integration in which the final form of supranational government simply evolves from function. The heart of the 'federalist fallacy' according to Mitrany is the belief that a federal form of government is adequate for present-day needs. Mitrany and most other critics question the ability of any federal state to suppress internal armed conflict.[45] In addition, federal states are considered notorious for the difficulties they have encountered in the everyday performance of new tasks that have arisen since the Second World War, according to Mitrany, including such non-political tasks as banking, the building of highways, and the provision of health services.[46] The reason for this inability is a lack of flexibility which is a result of the federal compact, the heart of the federalist solution, the main purpose of which is precisely to delimit the competence of the various organs.[47] Problems are becoming larger and larger and governments, of necessity, are becoming omnipresent and almost omnipotent. The new supranational government cannot be restricted if it is to solve these problems. 'For any new federal experiment, if it is to be free to develop the modern attributes of a welfare society,' according to Mitrany, 'the working prototype is likely to be not the U.S. Constitution of 1787 but rather something nearer to the federal system of the U.S.S.R.'[48]

From a purely European context, the federalist solution is even more unacceptable to its critics. A supranational European government would have to have a free hand in both defense policy and foreign policy.

Federal states have had their right to act in the international arena challenged by their subordinate units, an unacceptable action in modern international politics. Even more serious, some federal states have been faced with the threat of secession and in one case there was a bloody civil war.[49] It is interesting to note that Pinder and Pryce, although federalists, when discussing the U.S. experiment in federalism, warn that 'it would be unwise for Europe to copy a system which itself is now considered by many to be outdated.'[50]

R.J. Harrison in his critique of the European federalist movement refutes the concept that federalism will remain a guarantee of local autonomy, individual freedom or even of democracy. 'Empirical studies have amply demonstrated,' according to Harrison, 'that the specification of powers in a formal constitution does not mean that there will be an absence of conflict over jurisdictions or that there will be no actual encroachment.'[51] He does concede, however, that a federal constitution and the machinery for its enforcement *tend* in the long run to preserve a balance between centrifugal and centripetal forces. As regards individual freedom, Harrison points to the studies of William H. Riker, who claims that it is not individual freedom that is protected in a federal state, but the special interests of capitalists, landlords, linguistic minorities, and racists.[52] Finally, as regards the argument that to leave meaningful decision-making to the local units encourages civic participation, Harrison points out that there is a much weaker turnout for state elections in the United States than there is for national elections, which has been attributed by some to fact that people are simply discouraged about the fact that 'state politics are more prone to corruption, more concerned with the spoils of office, more gerrymandered, administratively inefficient, weaker in quality of personnel, and more conservative than central government . . .'[53]

The second major areas of criticism deals with tactics. The opponents of the federalists consider the direct method of attaining supranational government of the federalists flies in the face of reality. 'Federalism continuously reminds politicians of what it is they are being asked to yield: political arrangements are necessary in order to get beyond existing political arrangements. The implication is that the question is so important that it cannot be left to existing politicians.'[54] Some even claim that the federal approach is so antagonistic to the power elites that even the advocacy of the idea itself is a hindrance to any political action.[55]

Neofederalism

The discussion up to this point may give the impression that all the international federalists have definite goals and definite sets of institutions to propose to the world at large. This was probably true to a great extent in the earlier post-Second World War years for most of the federalists, but more and more are turning away from the somewhat simplistic approach to a more pragmatic approach which has been described as neofederalism.[56] Basic to this approach, as we shall see, is a refusal to be tied down to any specifics, as regards to either the division of power or structure, much to the dismay of many of the critics of the more classical federal approach.

Carl J. Friedrich, for instance, has suggested that federalism is not necessarily only a union of states, but can also be a process 'by which a number of separate political organisations, be they states or any other kind of associations, enter into arrangements for doing various things jointly.'[57] Any action of this type is a part of a 'federalizing process'. Even in old federations there is never a constant relationship between unifying and diversifying forces, sometimes one being dominant and sometimes the other. In response, David Mitrany, points out that this 'is true of all government; and it is least true of federal government. A new union or association is not conceivable without some formal compact, whose main purpose is precisely to delimit the competence of the various organs.'[58] The very purpose of any such written compact, continues David Mitrany, 'is to introduce an element of fixity in the index of power; and no political system is so fixed as a federal constitution.'[59] Such tactical vagueness, according to Mitrany, destroys the meaning of federalism. Denis de Rougemont, long a leader in the European federalist movement, can also be described as a neofederalist. Addressing himself to the essential question of the division of powers between the various levels of government in the future European federal system, Mr. de Rougemont believes that the answer is so complex that it is beyond human reason. But, he does have a method by which the answer can be reached. The first step in the federalist analysis is to consider 'the nature of the task or of a particular function whose necessity has been agreed upon or recognized. As a second step, it estimates the optimum dimensions of the area of operation required, and does it in terms of the three following factors: the possibilities of *participation* (civic, intellectual, economic), *efficiency*, and *economy of means*. The third and final step, once the dimension of the problem and the corresponding unit (communal, regional, national, continental, or world-wide, according to the case) has been determined,' according to Mr. de Rougemont, is to designate the *level of authority* at which the *decisions* relative to the task will be taken.'[60] Mr. de Rougemont concedes that the number of combinations that this method would lead to would be staggering, but feels that this problem can be solved by the modern computer. 'For me,' he concludes, 'federalism is the autonomy of regions plus computers, in other words, respect for reality and for its infinite complexities finally made possible by modern technology.'[61]

The neofederalist approach has also invaded the international federalist movement. In a recent publication of the World Federalist Education Fund, Donald F. Keys explains the meaning of neofederalism and how it came to replace federalism for the world federalist movement. The early post-Second World War federalists were under the impression that all that was required was simply a structural change in the United Nations following the pattern set by the thirteen American colonies and the main doctrinal difference was that between those who would give a broad range of powers to the new federal United Nations government and who would grant it only minimal powers. A number of events occurred which chilled the federalist movement, including the Cold War, the nuclear arms race, and Vietnam, and caused it to reassess the function and goal of the federalist movement, The federalists found out what the functionalists had already found out, 'that the world community is in fact beginning to establish a series of global departments to deal with specific global tasks. Instead of the strictly vertical or hierarchical structure — which has been the presupposition and vision of early Federalists — we see a horizontal proliferation of organs to perform specialized functions.'[62] They also found that the nation-state was a harder obstacle to move than expected. 'There are no more illusions about the case of convincing governments to relinquish national sovereignty.'[63] The new strategy of the neofederalists, then, is no longer the frontal attack on national sovereignty but the backdoor strategy of the functionalists. In essence it is to reinforce these organs wherever they are found, both within and outside of the United Nations, in order to whittle away at national sovereignty and to create a firmer base on which to build the future world federal government. As a result, 'Federalists no longer have the luxury of seeking a neat and orderly solution to world government.'[64]

Functionalism and neo-Federalism are not the same thing, however, argues Donald F. Keys. The neo-federalists recognize that 'world institutions cannot stand on thin air but must be based upon "community".'[65] The traditional federalists, again according to Keys, have overlooked the cultural diversity in the world which is a serious obstacle to the necessary community of values and behaviour. The neo-federalist solution is to support a Planetary Citizenship Campaign, which 'attempts to accelerate the development of the world community-minded plasma that will support a fusion reaction of human convergence — a major 'consciousness-raising' exercise .'[66] In sum: 'The new federalism, or, if you like, neo-federalism, is no less idealistic than the old, but the time scales are different and the policies more pragmatic.'[67]

Whether or not the neofederalists are actually destroying the meaning of federalism by their new found pragmatism, or are merely taking on the colouration of their arch enemies the functionalists, is likely to remain a subject of discussion for some time to come among the theorists of international integration. The main problem, of course, is that there is little evidence that political integration is taking place in the world at large, or even within the confines of Europe, so there is no urgent need to solve this question or the numerous other problems that have been raised by the federalists and their critics. There is even the possibility that none of the present theories of integration have any real validity. This it seems is the thesis of some of the more recent writings of Ernst B. Haas.[68]

Nevertheless, the federalist goal remains a valid goal to the hoards of idealists who hope to transform an imperfect world into a better world. Men will continue to be attracted to it by its simplicity and the familiarity of the analogy. In Europe the European Economic Community and its institutions will continue to be considered as adaptable to federal ends and the mere presence of the EEC should keep the issue of European unity alive and with it the aspirations of the federalists. The statement by Ernst B. Haas, although directed specifically at the European experience, has a validity for all federalists: 'Federalist theories . . . retain relevance whenever a group of actors profess a commitment to the introduction of a specific set of objectives and plans which herald a new order and when a deep and abiding consensus on such a new order prevails for some time.'[69]

Notes

1. Carl J. Friedrich, *Man and His Government*, New York, McGraw-Hill Book Company, Inc., 1963, p. 597.
2. See Adda B. Bozeman, *Politics and Culture in International History*, Princeton, New Jersey, Princeton University Press, 1960, pp. 97–98.

3. See Carl J. Friedrich, *op. cit.*, p. 588.
4. *Ibid.*, pp. 587–590. See also, Louis René Beres, 'Examining the Logic of World Federal Government', *Publius*, Vol. 4, No. 3 (Summer 1974), pp. 77–79.
5. Friedrich, *op. cit.*, pp. 589–594. See also his *Trends of Federalism in Theory and Practice*. New York, Frederick A. Praeger, 1968, especially Chapter two.
6. See Ely Culbertson, *Total Peace: What Makes Wars and How to Organize Peace*, Garden City, N.Y., Doubleday, Doran & Company, Inc., 1943; Cord Meyer, Jr., *Peace or Anarchy*, Boston, Little, Brown and Company, 1947; and Emery Reves, *The Anatomy of Peace*, New York, Harper & Brothers Publishers, 1945.
7. See Center for the Study of Democratic Institutions, *A Constitution for the World*, New York, The Fund for the Republic, 1965, pp. 25–54.
8. See Clarence K. Streit, *Union Now With Britain*, New York, Harper & Brothers, 1941; and *Freedom's Frontier – Atlantic Union Now*, Washington, D.C., Freedom & Union Press, 1961.
8a. Norman Hill, *International Organization*, New York, Harper & Brothers Publishers, 1952, p. 585.
9. See Grenville Clark and Louis B. Sohn, *World Peace Through World Law*, 3rd ed. enlarged, Cambridge, Mass., Harvard University Press, 1966. And, World Association of World Federalists, 'The World Association of World Federalists', Ottawa, cira 1972.
10. Most of the information on the European federalist movement in this section comes from the excellent book *Europe in Question: Theories of Regional International Integration*, by Reginald J. Harrison, London, George Allen & Unwin Ltd., 1974.
11. Cord Meyer, Jr., *op. cit.*, p. 151.
12. Clark and Sohn, *op. cit.*, p. xvii.
13. *Ibid.*, p. xix.
14. *Ibid.*, p. xvii.
15. *Ibid.*, pp. 36–37. See also pp. 111–112.
16. Streit (1961), *op. cit.*, p. 242.
17. Center for the Study of Democratic Institutions, *op. cit.*, pp. 29 and 30.
18. *Ibid.*, p. 6.
19. Pinder and Pryce, *Europe after de Gaulle*, Middlesex, England, Penguin Books Ltd., 1969, pp. 16–19, 22–24, and 174.
20. See F. H. Hinsley, *Power and the Pursuit of Peace*, London, Cambridge University Press, 1967, p. 102.
21. Streit,(1961), *op. cit.*, p. 245.
22. *Ibid.*, p. 247–249.
23. Clark and Sohn, *op. cit.*, p. xlii.
24. *Ibid.*, p. xlii.
25. In the 1966 edition the states of the world were divided into six categories, the largest of which would have 30 representatives each and the smallest, one. *Ibid.*, p. xx.
26. *Ibid.*, p. xxxvii. For another example of a plan to build on the United Nations, see Everett Lee Millard, *Freedom in a Federal World*, 3rd ed., Dobbs Ferry, N.Y., Oceana Publications, Inc., 1964.
26a. Pinder and Pryce, *op. cit.*, p. 168.
27. *Ibid.*, pp. 166–177.
28. According to Harrison, 'The (European) federalists, as a movement, have addressed themselves in the seventies to the subordinate objective of providing popular authority for Community institutions and independent

financial resources, two of the most important attributes of political power'. Harrison, *op. cit.*, p. 59.

29. Clark and Sohn, *op. cit.*, p. xxvi.
30. *Ibid.*
31. Clarence K. Streit, (1961), *op. cit.*, p. 197.
32. *Ibid*, p. 199.
33. See for instance, Pinder and Pryce, *op. cit.*, chapters 7 and 8.
34. Denis de Rougemont, 'The Campaign of the European Congresses', *Government and Opposition*, Vol. 2, No. 3 (April–July, 1967), p. 349.
35. Streit (1961), *op. cit.*, p. 252.
36. *Ibid.*
37. *Ibid.*, p. 254.
38. *Ibid.*
39. Harrison, *op. cit.*, p. 46.
40. *Ibid.*, pp. 52.
41. World Association of World Federalists, 'Policy Statement', Washington, D.C., circa 1975 (mimeo.), p. 1.
42. See 'The World Association of World Federalists', published by The World Association of World Federalists, cinca 1974.
43. See Friedman, *Man and His Government*, op. cit., p. 597.
44. Charles Pentland is of the opinion that these two qualities are responsible for the fact that federalism continues to dominate the field of integration theory. See his 'Functionalism and Theories of International Political Integration', in A.J.R. Groom and P. Taylor (eds.), *Functionalism: Theory and Practice in International Relations*, London, University of London Press, 1975, p. 13.
45. See, for instance, Beres, *op. cit.*, pp. 84–87.
46. See David Mitrany, 'The Prospect of Integration: Federal of Functional?', in Groom and Taylor, *op. cit.*, p. 60.
47. *Ibid.*, p. 61.
48. *Ibid.*, p. 62.
49. *Ibid.*, p. 60.
50. Pinder and Pryce, *op. cit.*, p. 176.
51. Reginald J. Harrison, *op. cit.*, p. 66.
52. *Ibid.*, pp. 62–63.
53. *Ibid.*, p. 70.
54. Paul Taylor, 'Functionalism and Strategies for International Integration', in Groom and Taylor, *op. cit.*, p. 91.
55. David Mitrany, *A Working Peace System*, Chicago, Quadrangle Books, 1966, p. 170.
56. See Donald F. Keys, 'The New Federalists', *New Federalist Reprint Paper 1*, World Federalist Education Fund, Washington, D.C., Circa 1973, p. 7.
57. From papers presented at an Oxford meeting on Federation on September, 1963, and for the Sixth World Congress of the International Political Science Association in Geneva in September, 1964, as discussed in David Mitrany, *op. cit.*, pp. 60–61. See also Carl J. Friedrich, *Trends of Federalism in Theory and Practice*, *op. cit.*, p. 7.
58. Mitrany, *The Prospect of Integration, op.cit.*, p. 61.
59. *Ibid.* See also his *A Working Peace System, op. cit.*, p. 191.
60. Denis de Rougemont, 'Towards a New Definition of Federalism', *The Atlantic Community Quarterly*, Vol. 8, No. 2 (Summer 1970), p. 231.
61. *Ibid.*
62. Donald F. Keys, *op. cit.* See also Lawrence Abbott, *World Federalism: What? Why? How?*, Lawrence, Massachusetes, May 1976 (mime.), p. 27.

63. *Ibid.*, p. 12.
64. *Ibid.*, p. 7.
65. *Ibid.*, p. 12.
66. *Ibid.*, p. 13.
67. *Ibid.*, p. 1.
68. See, for instance, Ernst B. Haas, 'Turbulent Fields and the Theory of Regional Integration', *International Organization*, Vol. 30, No. 2 (Spring 1976), pp. 173–212.
69. *Ibid.*, p. 177.

Selected Reading

1. Carl J. Friedrich, *Trends of Federalism in Theory and Practice*, New York, Fredrick A. ???????????, 1968.
2. R.J. Harrison, *Europe in Question: Theories of Regional International Integration*, London, Allen & Unwin, 1974.
3. Arthur W. MacMahon (ed.), *Federalism, Mature and Emergent,* New York, 1955.
4. William H. Riker, *Federalism: Origin, Operations, Significance,* Boston, H.B. Brown, 1964.
5. A.H. Birch, 'Approaches to the Study of Federalism', *Political Studies*, Oxford, Vol. XIV, No. 1, Feb. 1966, pp. 15–33.
6. Clarence K. Streit, *Union Now with Britain*, New York, Harper Bros., 1941.

PART THREE

CHAPTER SIXTEEN

THEORIES OF INTERNATIONAL ORGANISATION: SOME NOTES ON THE LITERATURE*

A.J.R. Groom

While it is possible to identify broad approaches to theorising about international organisation and to group authors and institutions under particular rubrics, such a categorization is often unjust to noteworthy 'mavericks' or even to important 'schools' which do not fall easily into the general framework. As the framework for this volume evolved the '*lacunae*' became clearer. Besides the absence of a chapter on regionalism which immediately springs to mind (the reasons for which are given in the last chapter), transactionalism and transnationalism receive less than their due attention. The transactionalist and transnationalist approaches share with functionalism and networks the hallmarks of informality, diversity and flexibility. They are all concerned with the waxing and waning of systems of transactions and the facilitation of intensely responsive institutional arrangements. To a certain degree this *lacuna* is filled by reference below to some major contributions to the literature from these perspectives.

Other approaches are not so fortunate. This volume contains scant reference to process federalism or political gradualism as conceived by Dag Hammarskjold. Moreover, 'one world' or a 'shrinking world' are epithets often used to describe the contemporary world. They are not inaccurate: one world problems abound — population, food environment, development, even women — to name but a few and they have been recognised as such. The shrinking world is reflected in the prodigious movement and interdependence of goods, services, ideas and people. How can and should such developments best be conceptualised? This is hardly the subject for an annotated bibliographical essay which reflects more the state of the literature than its future direction. At present the literature is rather heavily weighted in favour of certain integration theories — in particular neofunctionalism, regionalism and federalism — to the neglect of other approaches such as anarchism, cooperation or harmonisation. Although this survey must perforce repeat the stress in the literature it does include some works on a wider range of modes of international organisation. Thus before concentrating on the literature on integration two caveats must be borne in mind: firstly, the typology which grew out of the compilation of this volume (chapter 5) is not always reflected in the chapters in this part although some reference is made to the relevant literature below and, secondly, any survey of literature reflects the past and can at best only presage the future.

Integration and disintegration are age-old concerns of politics, political science and, indeed, all social thought. For integration can be conceived in terms of a single dimension, such as the economy, groups of dimensions or the totality of relationships. It is relevant at all levels of analysis from two persons or a family to world society at large. Moreover, it can be seen as a state of affairs or as a process. In the former, criteria are set and integration has occurred when these requirements are met. Disintegration occurs when the criteria which were formally met are no longer fulfilled. The criteria themselves are usually specified by the observer or participant since there is no generally accepted essentialist definition of integration. Integration as a state of affairs is not incompatible with the notion of integration as a process. It is the process whereby units move between conditions of complete isolation and complete integration. Here the focus is upon the process of moving towards one or the other end of the spectrum rather than uniquely upon its integrative end. Thus integration involves movement towards or away from collective action based upon consensual values for the achievement of common goals in which the parties have long run expectations of mutually compatible and acceptable behaviour and in which the process is self-maintaining. Integration is ubiquitous in that no actor can exist in total isolation so that the process of integration and disintegration provides an organising theme at all levels of society and between all 'disciplines' of the social sciences.

Integration, as a state of affairs, has not traditionally been conceived as the dominant characteristic of world society. On the contrary world society and, in particular, inter-state relations are often described as being anarchic in nature — a situation which has been consecrated in the doctrine of sovereignty. Indeed, it is this very anarchy, and

348

especially the absence of a central governing body at the world level with a virtual monopoly of organised force ruling a constituency that has accepted a set of rights and duties in relation to that body, that was used to justify the study of International Relations being separated from that of Political Science. But the dichotomy is not that stark. Consensus is not always the dominant characteristic of domestic relations within states either in the developed or developing world. Nor is it entirely absent between states, as the work of many functional institutions attests, or within world society at large where the growth of 'one world' problems, such as population or the environment involving state and non-state actors of a variety of kinds striving to arrive at a consensus, is clearly evident.

Integration is not, however, the dominant characteristic of world society nor of inter-state relations. Profusion would perhaps be a better term: a profusion of systemic ties, whether power dominated or legitimised, in the widest variety of functional dimensions involving a range of actors at and between various levels and involving world, regional, local and territorial ties. This profusion, which offers an abundance of possibilities, is due to a number of factors of which the industrial and French revolutions are especially imporant. As was argued in Chapter One the industrial revolution brought the makings of a world economy thus leading to a tremendous growth in transactions whereas the French Revolution was the harbinger of the nation-state which gradually imposed controls on such transaction flows. This has given rise to a plethora of international institutions designed for the most part to facilitate the smooth flow of transactions across state boundaries, that is, to harmonise systemic demands with national and state affiliations and institutions. But this profusion of systemic ties and institutions does not make a whole. There is no grand design of the type so-beloved by the advocates of world government. Perhaps this is not a bad thing since the rate and the magnitude of change are such that the variety of possibilities of response makes it unlikely that their present range will contain an appropriate response to change. Although there seems to be an assumption in the liberal Western democratic value structure that integration is a 'good thing' contemporary world society also gives many examples where 'independence', 'devolution', 'non-alignment', 'neutralism' and the like are prized values. Moreover, it is not a question of all or nothing, integration or isolation, but a question of more integration in one sphere and not so much in another.

Studies of integration have been given a fillip by two factors in the postwar world — the example of the European Communities and the emancipation of the colonial world. The European Communities have attracted an inordinate amount of attention, particularly from scholars in the United States, perhaps to the neglect of other important forms of organisation in terms of practical integration such as parallel national action in Scandinavia. The emancipation of the colonial world has given prominence to the question of integration in two ways. Firstly, there is the issue of integration within states, such as Nigeria or Pakistan, and then that of integration between states, as in the West Indies or Africa, either generally or in particular dimensions. It is interesting to note that while federalism as a means of integration had a modicum of success in an earlier round of decolonialisation in the United States, Australia, Canada and South Africa, it has a dismal record both within and between states in the postwar era in both the developed and developing worlds. Nevertheless, interest is provoked by problems, by failure as much as by success.

a. General Works

There are a number of general works in the field of integration which cover several different approaches. Sometimes these are by a single author but often they are collections of original articles or more frequently collections of reprints. Three volumes are particularly recommended in this category. R.J. Harrison's *Europe in Question*[1] is an excellent survey of the functionalist, neofunctionalist and federalist literature in reference to the European experience. Despite its title it is essentially a theoretical work. An anthology[2] entitled *International Political Communities* has been widely used as a course text in the United States and although the selection of reprints is now dated it still comprises a judicious selection from the literature of the day. Jacob and Toscano's volume[3] is also older but wears its years well. It is particularly useful in that it does not restrict itself to international integration but also considers integration in cities and other fora.

There is a considerable additional literature that merits attention including Paul Taylor's introductory *International Co-operation Today*[4] and Amatai Etzioni's *Political Unification*[5]. The case studies in the latter are poorly done. De Vree[6] and Pentland[7] cover similar ground to that surveyed in Harrison. Hodges' *European Integration*[8] is a strong rival except that as a reader of reprints it is neither as coherent nor as up-to-date. Nevertheless, it is a worthwhile selection. Finally, no reader will regret taking Cobb and Elder[9] off the shelf or Ake[10] particularly since the latter offers an African perspective on the subject.

b. Functionalism

While it is usually a futile exercise to try to attribute to any one writer the development of theory which is regarded as seminal, David Mitrany's development of functionalism is an exception to this rule. His classic essay, *A Working Peace System*[11], the ideas of which were first published in the inter-war period, has had great influence over the years as well it might since it is a cogent and powerful statement proposing an alternative to power politics in international relations. Mitrany died in 1975 a few weeks after the publication of some old and new essays entitled *The Functional Theory of Politics*.[12] Mitrany continued writing until his death at the age of 87, some of his last contributions being among his best. A case in point is his justly celebrated article 'The Prospect of Integration: Federal or Functional' revised for Groom and Taylor's edited volume *Functionalism: Theory and Practice in International Organisation*.[13] This is a collection of otherwise original essays on the theoretical aspects of functionalism followed by some case studies. The views expressed range from the committed to the opposed together with the agnostic and the sceptical. There has been a revival of interest in functionalism in the last decade, one of the earlier expressions of which was a Bellagio conference.[14] A more recent attempt to relate the theory to developments in East-West relations in Europe can be found in an article in the *Journal of Common Market Studies*.[16] Most students of international organisation are introduced to the theory of functionalism by Inis Claude through the critique he offers in his much-read *Swords into Plowshares*.[16] Functionalism, as Claude has admitted, is a very seductive approach to the problem of international organisation. Nowhere can this be more clearly seen than in the neofunctionalist school which, despite denying the functionalist approach by being territorial and state-centric, nevertheless owes much to Mitrany's notions of a learning process giving rise to task expansion and spillover to create a working peace system.

c. Neofunctionalism

The 'guru' of the neofunctionalists is undoubtedly Ernst Haas. Much influenced by Mitrany, but with a pressing and meritorious drive to be more rigorous in his methodology, he has pioneered and led the American study of European integration.[17] In addition he has applied the same approach to the ILO.[18] More recently he has expressed doubts about the whole neofunctionalist enterprise[19, 20] but, whatever

the current assessment of the neofunctionalist paradigm — and it is
increasingly critical — the impetus given to the study of integration by
Ernst Haas must be handsomely acknowledged. Leon Lindberg and his
colleague Stuart Scheingold have followed in the footsteps of Haas;
Lindberg's study of the early years of the Common Market was a
major contribution to the literature.[21] His work with Scheingold was less
felicitous perhaps because of an obstupefying use of jargon and a rigorous
attempt at measurement which did not yield as much in precise
observation as it lost in a sense of substance. *Europe's Would-Be
Policy*[22] also makes use of Easton's conception of systems analysis.
A less normative use of systems thinking might have been more
explanatory of the Common Market's difficulties. However, this work
is a major contribution to the literature both from the substantive and
methodological points of view. A later volume edited by Lindberg and
Scheingold first appeared as a special issue of *International Organisation*
and then as a book. It contains essays which can be taken as
representative of the neo-funcationalist approach[23] and also a useful
introductory contribution by Donald Puchala on Karl Deutsch's transactionalist approach. The neofunctionalists wrote prolifically in the
journals of the field and their articles have a prominent place in the
readers and anthologies on integration.One other work that grew out
of Mitrany's initial impetus is Sewell's *Functionalism and World
Politics*.[24] Sewell put Mitrany into a testable form in a rather different
way from the Haas-Lindberg school and his case study was the World
Bank group rather than the European Communities.

d. Regionalism

Regionalism as a doctrine has been written into the security and
economic provisions of the UN Charter. It was viewed as a half-way
house between world government and the sovereign state, as a means
whereby states with interests in common that were non-universal could
work together and as a form of hegemonial control for great Powers.
Few if any of these hopes and fears have been realised but John
Burton has related the early philosophy to functionalism and the
degree to which such regional bodies are associative or disassociative.[25]
More recently theories of regionalism have concentrated on integration
in the neofunctionalist mode, but not always. The regionalist-neo-
functionalist literature has been reviewed above but Joseph Nye has
had a foot in both camps. His edited volume, *International Regionalism*[26]
reprints several papers in the neofunctionalist mode while his *Peace in
Parts*[28] is a sterling effort to analyse the role of regional institutions in

the handling of conflicts between members. This study and his later work with Haas and Butterworth is worthwhile both from the conceptual and empirical points of view. To a certain degree it is more concerned with the ideas about regionalism which permeate the UN Charter than later neofunctionalist interpretations. Cantori and Spiegel,[29] like Nye, have tried to give a firm empirical basis to the concept of regionalism as an analytical tool. That they have failed is perhaps more to do with the geographical basis of regionalism and its single factor explanation of behaviour than the particular shortcomings of their research. Russett, on the other hand, proceeded inductively[30] and was rapped over the knuckles by Young[31] for his pains. His findings, however, suggest that the notion of region is not a multidimensional concept. Hypotheses and findings abound in Thompson's very useful article which reviews the literature in the field.[32]

e. Federalism

There is a voluminous literature on federalism within states fuelled not least by the doctrine's being more or less assimilated to holy writ in the United States. However, the emphasis here is more on federation as a means to integration (or in the case of the UK perhaps eventually to disintegration) between state actors. Empirically federation has been tried and failed since 1945 yet the doctrine is a very powerful one. Sir Kenneth Wheare has had a hand in the design of several such constitu constitutions and his *Federal Government*[33] is a classic. In the United States Carl Friedrich occupies a similar role and his *Trends in Federalism in theory and practice*[34] sets out the issues as he sees them. Earle[35] and Franck[36] have compiled useful collections and Birch has provided students with an excellent crib in an article summarising the different approaches to the subject.[37]

f. Other Approaches and Miscellaneous Works

The conceptual literature on some of the other approaches is indeed sparse. Transactionalism is perhaps the best represented particularly by the excellent pioneering work of Karl Deutsch.[38,39] More recently Keohane and Nye have sponsored research on transnational integration some of which has appeared in various issues of their house journal *International Organization*[40] but not to the neglect of transgovernmental relations.[41] Transactionalism, transnationalism and networks are closely related and Anthony Judge has written several articles on the latter in his house journal *International Associations*[42] as well as contributing to the Groom and Taylor volume.[13] Of considerable relevance in this context is a thought-provoking UIA symposium.[43]

Herbert Spiro has tried to come to grips with the notion of interdependence in a symposium article[44] while April Carter's work on anarchism is a fine introduction[45] to that elusive subject. On collective goods there is an excellent introductory article by Russett and Sullivan[46] supplemented by one by Ruggie.[47] Finally, no bibliographical survey would be complete without that misguided classic on *World Government through World Law*[48]. In a different category is Michael Haas' bibliography[49] and besides consulting that, a perusal of the past issues of *International Organization* and the *Journal of Common Market Studies* is a prerequisite for any serious reading in the field of integration.

Notes

*   This chapter is developed from a contribution to C.R. Mitchell and A.J.R. Groom (eds.), *International Relations Theory: A Critical Bibliography*, London, Frances Pinter, 1978. For the most part this survey concentrates on monographs rather than articles.
1.   Harrison, R.J. *Europe in Question,* London, Allen and Unwin, 1974.
2.   *International Political Communities: An Anthology*, New York, Doubleday & Co., 1966.
3.   Jacob, P.E. and Toscano, J.V. *Integration of Political Communities*, Philadelphia, J.B. Lippincott Co., 1964.
4.   Taylor, Paul, *International Cooperation Today,* London, Elek, 1971.
5.   Etzioni, Amatai, *Political Unification*, New York, Holt, Rinehart and Winston, 1965.
6.   De Vree, J.K., *Political Integration*, Paris, Mouton, 1972.
7.   Pentland, Charles, *International Theory of European Integration*, London, Faber, 1973.
8.   Hodges, M. (ed.), *European Integration*, Harmondsworth, Penguin, 1972.
9.   Cobb, R.W. and Elder, C., *International Community,* New York, Holt, Rinehart and Winston, 1970.
10. Ake, Claude, *A Theory of Political Integration*, Homewood, Ill., The Dorsey Press, 1967.
11. Mitrany, David, *A Working Peace System*, Chicago, Quadrangle Books, 1966.
12. Mitrany, David, *The Functional Theory of Politics*, London, Martin Robertson, 1975.
13. Groom, A.J.R. and Taylor, P. (eds.), *Functionalism: Theory and Practice in International Relations*, London, University of London Press, 1975.
14. Groom, A.J.R. and Taylor, P. (rapporteurs), *Functionalism,* New York, Carnegie, 1969.
15. Groom, A.J.R., 'The Functionalist Approach and East/West Cooperation in Europe', *Journal of Common Market Studies*, XIII (nos. 1 & 2).
16. Claude, Inis, *Swords into Plowshares*, New York, Random House, 1956.
17. Haas, E.B., *The Uniting of Europe*, London, Stevens, 1958.
18. Haas, E.B., *Beyond the Nation-State,* Stanford, Stanford University Press,

1964.
19. Haas, E.B., *The Obsolescence of Regional Integration Theory*, Berkeley, Institute of International Studies, 1976.
20. Haas, E.B., 'Turbulent Fields and the Theory of Regional Integration', *International Organisation*, Spring 1976.
21. Lindberg, Leon, *The Political Dynamics of European Economic Integration*, Stanford, Stanford University Press, 1963.
22. Lindberg, L. and Scheingold, S., *Europe's Would-Be Polity*, Englewood Cliffs, N.J., Prentice Hall, 1970.
23. Lindberg, Leon, *Regional Integration*, Cambridge, Mass., Harvard University Press, 1971.
24. Sewell, J.P., *Functionalism and World Politics*, Princeton, Princeton University Press, 1966.
25. Burton, J.W., 'Regionalism, Functionalism and the U.N. Regional Arrangements for Security', in M. Waters (ed.), *The United Nations*, New York, Macmillan Co., 1967.
26. Nye, Joseph, *International Regionalism,* Boston, Little, Brown and Co., 1968.
27. Nye, Joseph, *Peace in Parts,* Boston, Little, Brown and Co., 1971.
28. Haas, E., Butterworth, R. and Nye, J., *Conflict Management in International Organizations,* Morristown, N.J., General Learning Press, 1972.
29. Cantori, Louis and Spiegel, Steven C., *The International Politics of Regions,* Englewood Cliffs, Prentice Hall, 1970.
30. Russett, Bruce, *International Regions and the International System*, Chicago, Rand McNally, 1967.
31. Young, Oran, 'Professor Russett: Industrious Tailor to a Naked Emperor', *World Politics*, April 1969.
32. Thompson, W.C., 'The Regional Subsystem', *International Studies Quarterly,* March 1973.
33. Wheare, Kenneth, *Federal Government*, Oxford, Oxford University Press, 1963 (4th ed.).
34. Friedrich, Carl, *Trends of Federalism in Theory and Practice*, New York, Praeger, 1968.
35. Earle, Valerie (ed.), *Federalism,* Itasca, Ill., Peacock, 1968.
36. Franck, Thomas M. (ed.), *Why Federalism Fails*, New York, New York University Press, 1968.
37. Birch, A.H. 'Approaches to the Study of Federalism', *Political Studies*, February, 1966.
38. Deutsch, Karl, *Nationalism and Social Communication*, Cambridge Mass., Harvard University Press, 1966.
39. Deutsch, Karl (et al), *Political Community and the North Atlantic Area,* Princeton, N.J., Princeton University Press, 1957.
40. *International Organization,* 'Transnational Relations and World Politics' (Special Issue), Summer 1971.
41. Keohane, Robert and Nye, J., 'Transgovernmental Relations and International Organisations', *World Politics*, October 1974.
42. Judge, A.J.N., 'Network: The Need for a New Concept', *International Associations*, No. 3, 1974.
43. *Open Society of the Future*, Brussels, Union of International Associations, 1973.
44. Spiro, H., 'Interdependence: A Third Option Between Sovereignty and Supranational Integration', in Ghita Ionescu (ed.), *Between Sovereignty and Integration*, London, Croom Helm, 1974.
45. Carter, April, *The Political Theory of Anarchism*, London, Routledge and Kegan Paul, 1971.

355

46. Russett, B. and Sullivan, J., 'Collective Goods and International Organization', *International Organization*, Autumn 1971.
47. Ruggie, J.G., 'Collective Goods and Future International Collaboration', *American Political Science Review*, September 1972.
48. Clark, G. and Sohn, L.B., *World Government Through World Law*, Cambridge, Mass., Harvard University Press, 1966.
49. Haas, Michael, *International Organization: An Interdisciplinary Bibliography*, Stanford, Hoover Institute, 1971.

CHAPTER SEVENTEEN

THE INTERPRETATION OF INTERNATIONAL INSTITUTIONS FROM A THIRD WORLD PERSPECTIVE

Y. Tandon

There is one view that both progressive and reactionary regimes in the third world hold in common, each in their own way, namely that underdevelopment is their main enemy and national liberation and development their main objective. International organisations play a role both in defining the enemies and in combating them. Beyond this there is a divergence, even a multiplicity of viewpoints, and the principal reason for the divergence lies in the character of the ruling classes which hold power in these countries, and the objective laws that determine economic development and class struggles in the third world within the global context.

The objective laws we do not yet fully understand. They will become clearer as the revolutionary struggles of the masses of the third world develops. It is impossible to contrive laws in abstraction from political practice. Not until the Paris Commune, for example, was Marx able to formulate the specific laws of proletarian struggle against the bourgeois state. The sum of this experience was further added to by the revolutionary struggles of the Russian workers, soldiers and peasants in 1905 and 1917, by the Chinese revolutionary victory in 1949, and by the more recent victories in Vietnam and Cambodia. By now, therefore, the masses of the third world have a wealth of accumulated experience from which to derive general laws of revolutionary struggle against imperialism and under-development.

Lessons are learnt from failures just as well as from victories. To give one example out of many, when Allende fell in Chile in September 1973, his death summarised also a valuable lesson for the masses of the third world.

Not all are gifted, of course, to derive correct lessons from past experience. Not all are able, because of their own class positions, to derive the correct lessons for the revolutionary struggle of the masses. But whatever is absorbed of these experiences, filtered through their own class perspectives, form the basis of the strategies of struggle adopted by the leaders of the third world. Whatever their strategy, it has to be tested in practice. Some of these strategies abstracted from an incorrect summing up of the experiences of the working classes, such as Allende's strategy of the parliamentary road to socialism and Che Guevara's strategy of instant armed peasant revolutions, have failed in practice; others, such as the strategy of the revolutionary masses of Vietnam and Cambodia have succeeded; and yet others too numerous to count, have become the bases for reformist strategies adopted by many a leader in the third world. All these get reflected, partially or wholly, in the work of international organisations.

There is one more general point that must be made in interpreting the role of international organisations from a third world perspective. Every new phase in the development of international organisation begins with a promise of a better world to come, and the role of international organisations in bringing about this world. At present, for instance, it is the promise of a 'New Economic Order'. Only at the end of the period, retrospectively, does one know what really happened. Only then does it become clear that the earlier promises were really ideological assertions which camouflaged the actual forces at work. Ideological blinkers obfuscate vision. These blinkers must be removed for a scientific inquiry into reality in its true nakedness. Let us given an example from the past.

We refer to the sixty-five years, 1880–1945, before the onset of our present era. Remove the ideological chaff of peace, collective security, the White Man's burden and trusteeship, and these years are revealed in their nakedness as years of intense inter-imperialist struggle for the control of the third world. Dig deeper into the forces at work below the superstructure of international organisations, and they reveal inexorable laws of motion of capitalism tending towards imperialism. At the root of it lay the declining rate of profit for increasingly centralised capital, which required cheap raw materials for lowering the industrial cost of production at home, as

358

well as markets for industrial products.[1] This conjuncture in the development of capital coincided with the final victory of local industrial bourgeoisies in France, Germany, the United States and Japan, which created the basis for competition with Britain which had industrialised earlier. Both the first and the second world wars were a logical outcome of this inter-imperialist rivalry.

And what of the role of international organisations? They had two related functions during this period. One was as a means of resolving the inter-imperialist contradictions both in Europe and outside. And the other was to plan for the collective exploitation of the third world countries. Competition and cooperation between imperialist countries formed the basis of these organisations.

Despite its ideological protestations, 'peace' and 'peaceful change' were never, in fact, the function of the League of Nations. Peace can only be the outcome of the final liberation of the peoples of the world from oppresion and exploitation. How could peace be the function of the League of Nations when Belgian imperialism, for instance, found it necessary to cut off the hands of unwilling peasants of the Congo for failing to grow rubber, or when all imperialist powers found it necessary collectively to impose the smoking of opium on the Chinese peasantry because that was the only international currency (gold being in short supply) with which to pay for the exploitation of the same Chinese people? How could peace be the function of the League of Nations at the very time when some imperialist countries such as Germany and Japan were preparing, in the 1930's, for a further redivision of the world, while other imperialist countries such as France and Britain were determined to reserve colonial exploitation exclusively for themselves?

As long as imperialism exists, with its inherently predatory character, talk of peace can only be the continuation of political struggle by other means. 'War', Lenin wrote, 'is the continuation of politics of peace, and peace is the continuation of politics of war.'[2] International organisations are forums not of peace but of the continuation of politics of war by other means.

It is only from this theoretical perspective that we can understand the positions that the League of Nations took on, for example, the imperialist conquest of Manchuria by Japan, and of Abyssinia by Italy. Manchuria and Abyssinia symbolised not the 'failure' of the League of Nations, as some bourgeois writers argue, in an effort to mystify the reality;[3] they were symbols, on the contrary, of its success as an instrument for the continuation of imperialist politics, legitimised as an exercise in maintaining the so-called 'balance of power'.[4]

This, then, was the sum of experience of the third world in relation to international organisations in the period 1880 to 1945. What has been its experience since then?

1945–1975: General Characteristics of the Period

Two significant developments characterise this whole period. One is the rising sceptre of American imperialism until it reached a point, in the late 1960's when, in the words of the Chairman of the United States Congress Foreign Relations Committee J.W. Fulbright. 'At the present much of the world is repelled by America and what America seems to stand for', followed by a beginning of the decline of United States power towards the end of this period. This was symbolised in United States dominance within international organisations during the first part of the period, leading eventually to its losing control over most of these organisations, excepting those such as the World Bank group, which are peculiarly tied to American capital.

The second major characteristic of this period is the dramatic rise of the national democratic revolutionary movements in the countries of the third world. The essential content of this movement is anti-imperialist, but it is peculiarly prone to dilution because of the specific class character of the regimes in power in these countries. We shall analyse this in greater detail later.

Some people mention nuclear weapons as the third major development of this period. There is no question, of course, that nuclear weapons have introduced a new element in the situation that had not existed before. But every epoch has its own mode of combat corresponding to its principal contradiction, and the principal contradiction in the present epoch that we are considering here is between imperialism on the one hand and the oppressed masses of the third world countries on the other. The latter do not have nuclear weapons at their command, and even if they had, their use cannot be suitable to a form of warfare where the peoples of the oppressed countries have an interest in saving the masses and not in exterminating them. In the present epoch, the struggling masses have found their own means of struggle, political and military, against which nuclear weapons are of very little practical use. In the present epoch nuclear weapons must indeed be regarded as paper tigers, or, to use Lenin's equally sound metaphor, they are a colossus with clay feet.

Within this overall period three transitional phases may be identified.

1946–1956: United States Imperialism and the Character of Third World Nationalism

This first transitional phase was characterised not by the 'cold war', at least as far as the third world is concerned, but by the gradual take-over of the imperialist mantle by the United States. The cold war, from a third world perspective, did not begin until about 1955–56, when the Soviet Union acquired the capacity to penetrate the third world. But to this we shall come later.

The assumption by the United States of imperialist leadership was done within the broader context of the transfer of power from Europe to America of which the Truman Doctrine was the political expression. Its ideological component had two distinct elements.

One, paradoxically, was anti-imperialist in form, though of course, its opposite in substance. As a nation born out of anti-colonial struggle itself, the American people held high the banner of national self-determination. But like the Cheshire cat whose smile persists after the body has disappeared, the image of the United States as an anti-colonialist country persisted even after its material base had gone. Behind the smile now lurked not a cat but a veritable tiger ready to pounce on the colonies of other imperialist Powers. The second ideological element in United States imperialism was the defence of the 'free world' against the alleged menace of communism. Given the post-war infirmity of the European imperial Powers, the 'free world' leadership naturally *fell into the hands of the United States*. With these twin ideological declarations, American power began to pry open the doors not only in the colonial countries but also in Europe itself to penetration by American capital.

The penetration of Europe by American capital is not of direct relevance to this paper, but its context must be born in mind when analysing the penetration of former colonies of Europe by American capital.[5]

As far as the Middle East is concerned, the process had begun much before the War. In the 1950's, Saudi Arabia had faced a severe financial crisis, and had sold oil concessions to Standard Oil for a mere pittance of £50,000. In 1958 oil exploration had begun. In 1943 the

United States Air Force began constructing the airfield at Dhahran from which today massive assaults are being launched against revolutionaries fighting in the mountains of Dhofar. However, before the Second World War, the United States owned only 13 per cent of the Middle East oil. By 1960 they owned 65 per cent, and the corresponding British share declined from 60 to 30 per cent.

In Asia, American capital had already conquered the Philippines during an earlier period. In 1945, just prior to the granting of formal independence to the Philippines, U.S. capital owned 30 per cent of the islands' sugar *centrales*, 70 per cent of electric power, 40 per cent of mining and 70 per cent of the total trade.[6] Between 1945 and 1949, the United States, through the instrumentality of the United Nations, eased the Dutch out of Indonesia and thus prepared the way for American capital.[7] Similarly, Indochina fell to American capital after the capitulation of the French in 1954. Viewed in terms of only 'aid', Vietnam received $1,216.5 million between 1955 and 1959; Thailand $240 million and Burma $96.4 million between 1951 and 1959.[8] India's independence yielded another rich harvest for American capital. For the First Five Year Plan, 1951—56, 71 per cent of India's foreign aid came from the United States,[9] the beginnings of India's massive foreign debt problem, a major problem shared with most other third world countries in recent years.*

In Latin America, the United States had already replaced British and Spanish hegemony during an earlier period. In Cuba, for instance, prior to the 1959 revolution, United States capital controlled 80 per cent of the utilities, 90 per cent of the mines, 90 per cent of the cattle ranches, almost 100 per cent of the oil refineries, 50 per cent of the railways, 40 per cent of the sugar industry, and 25 per cent of the bank balances.[10] But not all areas of the Latin America had been effectively penetrated. This was now done in the period following the Second World War. The ideology of anti-communism served well in this regard.

* We may ask here how 'aid' is imperialism. Imperialism, in actual fact, is that period in the development of capitalism in which the export of capital over the simple export of commodities becomes capitalism's specific characteristic. Roughly speaking, this period dates from the 1880's. Imperialist, or monopoly capital, it must be remembered, is exported not only to the colonies and neo-colonies, but also to other imperialist countries (US capital to Europe and Japan and vice versa, for example). What is significant, however, is that in the colonies and neo-colonies, monopoly capital completely subjugates local 'national' capital to the needs of imperialist accumulation; in other words, it fetters the independent development of 'national' capital. Later we shall examine the case of Brazil as an example.

In Africa, the penetration of American capital had not yet begun, except in Liberia and Libya. Africa was still left largely to the exploits of European imperialism. The nationalist movements there and the threat of communism had not seriously begun until much later, and therefore the situation did not yet provide American capital with the ideological leverages it needed to pry open the closed doors of European monopoly. This, however, was not long to come. By 1967 the United States was the second biggest foreign investor in practically every important African country such as Zaire, Nigeria, Ghana, Kenya, Zambia and the Ivory Coast.[11]

Within limits, Afro-Asian nationalism during this period provided a congenial opening to American penetration. When it went too far, as in the case of Mossadeq in Iran in 1951, the United States acted fast to neutralise it, or, as in the case of Vietnamese nationalism, to deal with it militarily. But where it was pitted against local reactionary feudal power as in Egypt; or against a moribund European imperial power, as the Dutch in Indonesia, and the British in India, without being excessively militant, the United States was an ally, both within and outside the United Nations.

The character of this particular brand of nationalism requires further analysis.

Nationalism, a bourgeois ideology in its historical origin, especially an ideology of the rising merchant class in Western Europe at the decline of feudalism,[12] retained its essentially bourgeois character in its contemporary expression in third world nationalism. An essential feature of bourgeois nationalism is fear of the masses, even though, whenever it has suited its historical interests, it has used the masses as cannon-fodder against its enemies, be they local feudal aristocracy or foreign imperialists. This is what has given bourgeois nationalism its dual character: it is revolutionary in its struggle against feudalism and imperialism, and it is reactionary in its struggle against the working masses. Which particular aspect comes to the fore depends on what particular enemy the bourgeoisie is fighting. Within this general law of class struggle, there are, of course, variations because of varying circumstances of time and space.

Excepting China and Vietnam and some of the more recent revolutionary movements such as in Combodia, Laos, South Yemen and Oman, and perhaps in Guinea — Bissau and Mozambique, where the anti-imperialist struggle was waged on a united front of different classes but led by a *proletarian* ideology, the struggle against colonialism in the rest of the third world has been inspired and led by the local *bourgeois or petty bourgeois* elements born within the womb of, and dependent on, imperialism itself. Its deeply reactionary aspect in relation to the working masses is becoming particularly apparent in our own time, i.e. in the 1960's and 1970's, but even during the earlier period it had shown its paranoic fear of the masses.

For example, within months of the Free Officers' Revolution in Egypt in 1952, a revolution that fed itself on the patriotic and democratic mass movement that was aroused by humiliating defeat in the Palestine War, the new petty bourgeois government moved ruthlessly to squash the workers' strike at Katr El- Dawaar, leading to death sentences meted out to a number of working class leaders. After that the government went out systematically to destroy a reactionary organisation, the Moslem Brotherhood, not because of its religious threat, but because of its genuinely mass base, which, under revolutionary circumstances, could indeed have posed a threat to the ruling classes.[13]

In India, to take another example, the most violent military action in the early years after independence was taken not against Pakistan in the war over Kashmir or Hyderabad, but in the suppression of the mass peasant Telangana movement. Even Kwame Nkrumah of Ghana, to take an example from a later period, the father of modern African nationalism, struck with one hand at colonialism and with another at the workers at Sekondi-Takoradi. Within a few years of coming to power, Nkrumah had broken the back of the independent trade union movement with whose support he had come to power, and like Nasser and Nehru before him, opened up his country to American capital.[14]

These three N's of the third world — Nehru, Nasser and Nkrumah — despite their dualism, that is, an anti-imperialist position premised upon an essentially anti-mass line, were representatives of the more progressive sections of the third world. At least they had opted for non-alignment, as opposed to those who did not even pretend to be populist governments and made quick defence pacts with the imperialist countries.

Non-alignment was the ideology that best synthesised the dual aspects of petty bourgeois nationalism. It expressed, on the one hand, the aspirations of the local bourgeois and petty bourgeois elements to wrest control of the economy from their imperial masters, and, on the other hand, it specifically dissociated itself from the world-wide proletarian struggle against capitalism and imperialism.[15] It wanted freedom from imperial control but without losing power to

364

the masses of workers and poor peasants. In the end, being a weak and dependent 'national' bourgeoisie, even those of India and Brazil, the two largest third world states, they were to lose in their struggle against imperialism. But to this we shall come later.

At the time, however, in the 1950's and early 1960's, this brand of petty bourgeois nationalism posed a veritable threat to the more reactionary regimes resting on an alliance between imperialism and local feudal forces. In the Middle East, for example, in Syria, Iraq, the Lebanon, Yemen, and Saudi Arabia, the local petty bourgeois elements sought help from Egypt in their struggle against their own compradorial, feudal ruling classes. Nasserism symbolised revolution. It symbolised Arab dignity, anti-imperialism and anti-Zionism. But the compradorial regimes, especially those of Jordan and Saudi Arabia, proved too strong to be overthrown. Nonetheless, the whole decade of the 1950's and the 1960's were marked by internal contradictions between Arab states arising out of this situation.

For national liberation movements guided by a proletarian ideology, such as those in China and Vietnam, international organisations were of no use. They knew that for their kind of struggle, and given the world balance of forces reflected in international organisations, they could only win their battle through self-reliance.

But the petty bourgeois nonaligned regimes thought differently. For them international organizations, especially the United Nations, represented an opportunity to parley with their erstwhile imperial masters at a presumed level of equality. More substantively, international organisations served as a means of bringing collective pressure to bear on imperialist regimes to make concessions, and in this they found, especially during the period 1956—62, a partial ally in the United States, an ally at least when European imperialism was at stake. We have already referred to the Indonesian case. Towards the end of this period the Suez crisis once again brought third world nationalism and European imperialism in a situation of violent confrontation, this time with the additional possibility of the Soviet Union exploiting the situation for its own purposes, and the United States had to use its political and economic leverage against its European allies to pull out of the situation. Aside from such concrete cases, the United Nations served as a forum for a generalised assault on the whole system of colonialism and racialism, including its specific variety in South Africa.

For the more reactionary third world regimes, however, it was not the United Nations but the regional mutual security organisations, such as the Organisation of American States (negotiated in 1948), the South East Asian Treaty Organisation (negotiated in 1954), and the Central Treaty Organisation (first negotiated as Baghdad Pact in 1955) which better served their purposes. In the UN itself they simply pursued a policy tail endism to United States imperialism.

This, then, summarises the third-world perspectives on international organisations during this period. Subjectively the petty bourgeois nationalist regimes, which made the loudest noise, saw in the international organisations a means of liberation from their colonial masters; objectively, of course, they were only creating conditions for other forms of imperialist penetration, especially under United States leadership.

1956–1967: The High Point of United States Imperialism and the Apostasy of Third World Nationalism

For the petty bourgeois third world nationalists, the two seminal events with which this period begins and ends summarise the character of this period perfectly. The period begins with the post-Suez euphoria, a sense of triumph. It ends with the third Arab-Israeli War, and in a sense of total depression. But before we analyse this further, let us first look at its gobal context.

For US imperialism, the turning point comes about half way through this period, that is, with the 1962 Cuban crisis. Before this, the American imperial thrust was nervous and hesitant. The Soviet Union had shown its hand during the Suez crisis. Khrushchev and Bulganin had just made a triumphant tour of India, and had begun to pour aid into India's public sector. In Latin America, the Cuban revolution of 1959 had opened up a new era and there too Soviet penetration had become a real possibility. The 'cold war' was beginning in earnest in the third world.

US imperialism became jittery as a result. Whereas formerly it would ally itself with progressive petty bourgeois elements in the third world against backward feudal forces, now it chose the most reactionary elements with which to join forces to maintain stability and 'international order'. Whereas formerly, it relied on the United Nations, now it increasingly began to have faith in its own imperial power only. Thus for instance, when a Nasserite coup occurred in Iraq in 1958, US marines and British paratroopers were hurriedly dispatched to the Lebanon and Jordan respectively, creating an awkward situation out of which they were baled out by a convenient face-saving

366

formula worked out in the United Nations.

In Latin America, instead of assisting reformist attempts of petty bourgeois elements to oust dictator Batista, and coming to terms with Castro, the United States showed militant hostility, and within two years, a reformist Castro had turned 'Communist'. Having brought 'communism' to it shores, the United States now tried to get rid of it. It unsuccessfully sponsored an attempt by reactionary Cuban refugees at counter-revolution, ousted Cuba out of the OAS and got the OAS to pass a resolution in 1962 declaring communism as 'incompatible with the inter-American system'. Further, as a counter against the spread of Castroism, it set up the 'Alliance for Progress' to hem the peoples of Latin America in the folds of American imperialism.

The Soviet Union, on the other hand, had become buoyant. Its relative success at penetrating the former redoubts of Western imperialism in the Middle East and Asia led it into the illusion that it could plant its military presence within the very heartland of imperial capital, in the form of missiles in Cuba. But this military adventurism soon turned into its opposite. Already paranoic about communism, the American imperial giant rose to its full height, almost in paroxysm, and threatened an all-out war, if necessary, to get the missiles out of Cuba. The Soviet Union quickly complied, much to the chagrin of the Cubans.

The Cuban missile episode prepared the basis for the so-called 'detente' between the Soviet Union and the United States. (So-called because 'detente' is in reality a modified form of intensified competition among the super-Powers.) It led to strategic rethinking on the part of both the adversaries. The United States moved away from the early strategy of 'massive retaliation' to that of 'flexible response'. The Soviet strategic doctrine had earlier shifted in the opposite direction, from a primary preoccupation with conventional land warfare to an emphasis on nuclear weapons and a missile defence system. But after the Cuban crisis, and as Brezhnev — Kosygin leadership grew stronger, it defined its policy as one of 'flexibility with caution'.[16] The Partial Test Ban Treaty signed in Moscow in August, 1963, both symbolised the new detente, and inaugurated a series of disarmament negotiations as another arena of their political struggle.

From the third world perspective, the significance of the detente was that the United States gained in self-confidence, and launched a colossal offensive to crush peoples' revolutions everywhere. In mid-1965, it introduced a massive number of troops into Vietnam, at a time when the Soviet Union was attempting to stop the Vietnamese from launching a war of liberation lest it should provoke the Americans to escalate the war which would force it to intervene militarily. Encouraged, the Americans started bombing targets in North Vietnam. At the same time, it started supplying reactionary regimes in Thailand, Cambodia, Laos, and Phillipines and in Latin America with massive arms and technical advice on 'counter-insurgency' tactics. It was the heyday for the CIA, and for the American military strategists. In April, 1965, the United States landed 30,000 marines in the Dominican Republic to crush an alleged attempted communist takeover. In the Middle East, a coup in 1962 overthrew the Imamate regime in North Yemen. Egypt and Saudi Arabia immediately aligned themselves on opposite sides of the civil war, and the United States intervened to back up the reactionary Saudi-Imani forces. In Africa, supplied with NATO arms, Portugal launched massive assaults on the liberation movements in Angola, Mozambique and Guinea-Bissau.

Against this global context we must now reveiw the situation of the third world, and what use they made of international organisations.

We have already referred earlier to the aspirations of the petty bourgeois regimes that came into power in most third world countries. These were to secure control of their economies from the hands of the erstwhile colonial masters, but without transferring state power to the masses of workers and peasants. The first thing to do, however, was to crush mass militancy. This was already done in the older third world countries in Asia and the Middle East. In the newer countries in Africa, independence was handed over on a platter to petty bourgeois regimes in most countries. Where, however, there was some amount of mass political activity, as partially in Kenya in the form of a peasant squatters' revolt against white settlers (the Mau Mau movement), and as more fully in Algeria, the mass participation was short-lived. After independence, the mass line was quickly discarded yielding place to a commandist style of petty bourgeois rule. Development was to be ordered from above, and participation by the masses was to be carefully controlled and orchestrated from the top by the bureaucratic apparatus of the state.

With this the stage was now set to negotiate with imperialism for economic and political concessions. The petty bourgeois regimes were prepared to allow imperialism to extract surplus- value from third world workers and peasants, but they now claimed a greater share for themselves. With the entry of the Soviet Union, their bargaining power had increased. Now one great Power could be played against another, giving a substantive meaning to non-alignment which hitherto was purely doctinaire. And with the entry into the United Nations of a large number of their members, an illusion of power was created. In the post Suez euphoria, these regimes thought that they now held the Western countries at ransom, and through moral exhortations and voting victories in the United Nations, they would be able to squeeze enough aid from them to carry out their development programmes, as well as continue with their general assault on colonialism and racialism.

Aid became the cornerstone of their development strategy. The world's poor were going to be freed from hunger within a decade, and their economies were to 'take off' on a self-sustaining economic growth on the wings of bountiful aid from western capitals, and marginally from the Soviet Union. Now, retrospectively, we know that something had gone wrong very seriously, for not only have these countries not 'taken off' after almost twenty years, but many of them are now suffering from severe famine (e.g. Sahel countries in Africa, Ethiopia, parts of Latin America, India and Bangladesh), and the countries are now faced with amassive problem of foreign debt and low commodity prices. What indeed had gone wrong?

It would take volumes to analyse the problem. But basically there were two factors that the petty bourgeois nationalist regimes did not, and, because of their class position could not, understand. They did not understand that development is not an economic category, it is not a technical matter to be promoted simply by importing capital and technical skills, but a political category, one that involves transforming the relations of production in such a way as to give the direct producers themselves a control over the means of production and all the superstructural apparatuses of the state. Secondly, they had no understanding of the nature of imperialism, nor of such international organisations as the World Bank and the International Monetary Fund. Let us illustrate.

Take Brazil, for example, the second largest third world country, after India. The main contradiction, once the workers and peasants were put in their places, was between American imperialism and the weak 'national' bourgeoisies which still hoped to use the power of the state to wrest control over the economy. This they had hoped to achieve through liberal bank credits and restrictions on the importation of goods which were undermining their infant enterprises. But once the foreign exchange reserves, which had accumulated as a result of the war-time boom, were depleted in wasteful importation of consumer goods and in an import substitution industrialisation strategy that uses more foreign exchange than it saves because of the need to import technology and skills, the successive Brazilian governments were caught up in recurrent foreign exchange crises. In return for dollars to overcome these crises, the I.M.F. imposed conditions. These were to impose credit restrictions, control inflation, freeze workers' wages, and open all doors to the inflow and outflow of foreign private capital. The World Bank has a term for this — 'stabilization programme'.

The first major foreign exchange crisis had occurred in 1952. In 1953, President Vargas committed suicide, leaving a note that he had been frustrated by 'a subterranean campaign of international groups joined with national groups'.[17] Successive governments under Kubitschek, Quadros and Goulart found themselves squeezed between the demands of the local bourgeoisies on the one hand and imperialist capital on the other. In early 1964, the IMF visited Brazil, and stressed the importance of the stabilization programme. President Goulart agreed, but in response to pressure from the local bourgeoisie, he later reneged.* On 1 April, he was overthrown, and a military rule was imposed. On 5th April, the *New York Times* reported that 'the ouster of the Goulart regime has made a financial rescue operation possible for Brazil' since Goulart had become 'an obstacle to negotiation'.[18] In January, the IMF moved in with new credits, and debt scheduling from American, European and Japanese creditors. Aid poured in enormous quantities between 1964 and 1968, and so did Ford, Chrysler, Anaconda, Union Carbide, Bethlehem Steel, Dow Chemicals, and others. Within months the enterprises of the local bourgeoisie began to fall like skittles one by one: in the two years, 1966—67, there were 1,500 bankruptcies in Sao Paulo alone, defeated by multinational corporations and in the absence of

* It must be remembered that the bourgeoisie in the neo-colonies have a dual character. They are progressive insofar as they attempt to struggle against imperialism, and reactionary insofar as they suppress the masses of the people in their own turn. Their subjective ambition is to secure economic autonomy from imperialism, but without arousing the masses. This ambition, however, is never fulfilled. They cannot go too far in either direction, for if they take a very strong anti-imperialist position but without directly involving the masses on their side, they are soon brought back to line by imperialism. On the other hand, if they mobilise the masses, there is the risk that they might lose power to them (as could have happened in Chile had Allende acceded to the demand of the workers for arms in order to wage an armed struggle against imperialism and its local puppets). Caught in this dilemma, the bourgeoisie and petty bourgeoisie are constantly vaccilating in their relations with imperialism on the one hand and the masses of the people on the other.

state protection.[19]

The same thing happened in the Phillippines once the 'decontrol programme' was imposed at the behest of the World Bank and the IMF in 1962. But it was only the inflow and outflow of foreign funds that were decontrolled, for one of the conditions of IMF assistance was the imposition of controls over bank credit to the local bourgeoisies. Within four years, Filipino-owned enterprises were driven en masse to bankruptcy, their place being now taken over by multinational corporations.[20] Such examples as that of Brazil and the Philippines can be multiplied.[21]

Thus, the bourgeois and petty bourgeois regimes of the third world were utopian in thinking that they could beat imperialism with aid from imperialism itself. Their voting victories in the United Nations remained purely illusory. They transferred their voting strength from the U.N. General Assembly to a more specialised agency, the United Nations Conference on Trade and Development (UNCTAD), but there too, besides identifying their problems, though in purely economistic terms, they have not been able to achieve any substantive transformation of their dependent relationship to imperialism. By the end of this period, they discovered that they were even more subordinated to imperialism than before. In the earlier period at least they had sizeable foreign exchange reserves (India, for example, had £1,138 million held as reserves in Britain, Egypt and the Sudan had £402 million, and Ghana at independence had over £200 million) [22] and there was still some optimism that the local bourgeoisie would be able to develop independently of imperialism. By the end of this period they knew even if they would not admit, that their independence had been undermined.

This then, is the period when the third world countries' attitude to international organisations begins to reflect a certain degree of ambiguity. The more progressive regimes continued with their anti-imperialist, anti-racialist rhetoric in the United Nations, but with much less conviction, and with considerably reduced optimism. Their progressiveness and euphoric swagger of the earlier period was blunted by the harsh realities of this period — compare Nehru, Nasser, Nkrumah or Soekarno with their successors. With empty national coffers they were now beholden to imperialism and international organisations to bale them out. As a result their progressiveness lost its luster and high moralism, and they increasingly became victims of imperialist pressures exerted through international economic organisations. In throwing out European colonialism by the front door, they had only let in a more powerful and more subtle imperialism through the back door. By the end of this period, antiAmericanism had become a powerful political factor of global importance.

At the same time, events in Cuba and the use made by the United States of regional international organisations, as well as the United Nations, to contain and blackmail Cuba began to show the true imperialist character of international organisations.

In Africa, the more progressive regimes which at first favoured the United Nations as the forum for resolving the crisis in the Congo in 1961, soon realised, after the mysterious death of the nationalist Lumumba, that the United Nations was not the body they had thought it was. Here too, the United States was able to neutralise, through the agency of the U.N., all the progressive elements in the situation, and had put into power a government which was for 'peace and order' and for letting American investments in. The Organisation of African Unity, born in 1963 with what looked like considerable promise, languished in the role of a minor pipsqueaker in accompaniment to the empty sound and fury of the United Nations. The Rhodesian crisis after 1964 demonstrated this side of the OAU only too clearly, and this was further confirmed when civil war broke out in Nigeria in 1967−68. Of course, in the face of the formidable forces of imperialism, it would be useless to blame a mere artifact such as the OAU. Nonetheless, despite its obvious impotence, the OAU, like its sister organisation the Arab League, but unlike their third sister the OAS, continued to remain identified, at the popular level, as essentially a force for the liberation of the masses of the third world from imperialism.

1967−1975: Bankruptcy of Petty Bourgeois Nationalism and the Rise of Mass Movements

Two parallel and opposite forces characterise this period. By the end of this period, most third world countries were in the gravest economic crises: a result essentially of their dependence on world capitalism and of the policies pursued by their petty bourgeois and compradorial leadership. On the other hand, in some areas in South East Asia, Africa and the Middle East, imperialism was forced to withdraw: a result of mass movements, led by a conscious proletarian strategy.

Capitalism has inherent tendencies to periodic crises. One of these hit the centres of capitalism by the end of this period. Production fell in most capitalist countries from anywhere between 20 and 40

372

per cent. For example, steel production in the United States fell to 7.6 million tons in July, 1975, which was a drop of 31 per cent compared to the corresponding figure the previous year; in Britain it fell also by 31 per cent; in France, West Germany, Italy, the Netherlands, Belgium and Luxembourg, it fell by 28.7 per cent, and in Japan by 12.6 per cent.[23] Unemployment in the United States stood at a figure of 8 million in October, 1975, with one out of every four black workers out of a job.[24] Added to this was the increase in the cost of industrial production, as a result partly of the high oil prices imposed by the Oil Producing and Exporting Countries (OPEC) from the end of 1973, and the resulting inflation and commodity crisis.

Under imperialism, however, capitalist countries can transfer some of the effects of their crises over to the colonies and neo-colonies which, as a result, suffered an even more acute crisis. Unemployment, inflation, foreign exchange crisis, and scarcity of even basic consumer goods such as sugar and cooking oil (in some places even salt) reached staggering levels in most third world countries. By 1973 many areas had begun to report severe famine.

Prices of raw materials which had temporarily shot up after the rise in oil prices fell again during 1974. According to the statistics compiled by the IMF, copper prices dropped by 57 per cent in 1975, lead by 24 per cent, zinc by 56 per cent, and coffee, banana, cotton and beef, all export commodities of the third world countries, dropped by similar percentages. By contrast, the prices of manufactured products went up steadily. According to the June, 1975 issue of the U.N. *Monthly Bulletin of Statistics*, the unit value index of the United States and other industrial countries, taking 1970 as 100, rose to 145 in the first quarter of 1974, and to 187 in the first quarter of 1975.

The result was that Chile, for example, was expected to earn in 1975 $800 million less for its copper exports, and Colombia $224 million less for its coffee exports. According to the estimates of the Inter-American Development Bank, the Latin American countries (excluding those exporting oil) incurred a trade deficit of $8,700 million in 1974, or 13.6 times as much as in 1973. By 1974, Latin American external debt totalled $30.000 million. This was the experience also of most African and Asian countries which were tied to the apron strings of Western capitalism, a tale of increasing trade deficits, mass unemployment, dwindling foreign reserves and mounting indebtedness.

The 'Development Decade' of the 1960's in the UN now gave way to the 'New Economic Order' of the 1970's. The strategy is basically

373

the same; the only difference is that the industrialised Western countries are even less able than they were in the earlier period to make substantial 'con essions', for they are themselves in crisis. The 'New Economic Order' is in reality the Old Economic Order, with a different rhetoric.

The initiative in the third world, however, has begun to pass out of the hands of the bourgeoisie and into the hands of a proletarian leadership and mass movements. In the Middle East the turning point was the June, 1967 War which ended in a crushing defeat for the Arabs. The preceding regime of peace was based on a tacit agreement between Egypt and Israel. Nasser was reluctant to break the peace. Under it he had consolidated the rule of the petty bourgeoisie, and had made modest economic progress. Domestic peace was maintained on the myth of a 'socialist' programme, legitimised with Soviet aid, and a firm state control over workers and peasants. His anti-Zionist rhetoric camouflaged the fact that he had pre-empted any initiative on the part of the Palestinians themselves. The fragile structure collapsed, however, when Israel called his bluff by calculated attacks on Syria and Jordan which forced Nasser's hand.[25]

The ensuing defeat laid bare the bankruptcy of Nasser's policies. After the war, the United Nations passed Resolution 242 as the basis for settlement, which once again, did not even refer to the Palestinians as an interested party. It was a confirmation of the old Nasserite policy of ignoring the Palestinians while recognising their shadow. The October, 1973 War somewhat reversed the earlier defeat, but still the Palestinians were ignored. Egypt made a separate peace with Israel, mediated by Kissinger, and surrendered supervisory powers to U.S. imperialism.

But it was 1967, not 1973, which was the turning point in the Middle East. It paved the way for an indpendent Palestine resistance movement. The first thing that happened after the defeat of Egypt in 1967 was the break-up of the Movement of Arab Nationalists (MAN), which was closely linked with Egypt. Out of MAN's broken pieces arose, besides the two Palestine liberation organisations — the Popular Front for the Liberation of Palestine, and the Popular Democratic Front for the Liberation of Palestine — the Popular Front for the Liberation of Oman and the Arab Gulf, and the National Liberation Front in South Yemen. The situation prevailing then was wrapped up most aptly by the Popular Front for the Liberation of Oman.

'The defeat of 5th June, 1967 has concretely proved the failure of the policies of the Arab regimes on both the ideological and strategic levels. Those policies have now become totally discredited in the eyes of the toiling masses . . . The military defeat initiated debate within the ranks of the revolutionary forces in the Arab world . . . Those forces submitted themselves to thorough self-criticism and some petty bourgeois organisations [meaning MAN] collapsed under the strain. This debate was bound to reach the Arab Gulf where the Dhofar revolution carried its own self criticism and decided to extend its activities to all the areas of the Gulf, emphasising that the victory of the revolution essentially depends on the level of self-consciousness achieved by the masses.'[26]

One consequence of this shift to mass action was less dependence on petty bourgeois Arab regimes and on international organisations. In both South Yemen and Oman, revolutionary action started from rural areas, and after years of struggle and Nasserite attempts to derevolutionize them, they have finally worked out the correct anti-imperialist strategy in our present epoch, that is one based on a broad class front but led by a correct proletarian leadership and ideology. South Yemen is now partially liberated; the British, and the local ruling classes consisting of the sultans and the Adenis bourgeoisie, have been driven out. In Oman and Dhofar, however, the struggle continues against the combined forces of British imperialism, Iran and Saudi Arabia.

As for Palestine, the struggle has moved to a higher stage. Although the PLO is split among many movements and tendencies, it has succeeded in revolutionising the Arab masses, and in gaining for itself international recognition, including its admission in the debates in the U.N.'s Security Council, and other international organisations, such as the ILO. But despite its entry into international organisations, the Palestine liberation movement is not dependent on them. Its strength and the degree to which it has succeeded in revolutionising the Arab masses can be witnessed in the 1975–76 crisis in the Lebanon.[27] Six years earlier, in September 1970, the Palestinians had suffered almost total annihilation at the hands of reactionary forces in the Jordan; but in 1976, in the Lebanon, the Palestinians were defended by the guns of the Lebanese masses themselves, even at the risk of causing a civil war.

In Latin America, the revolutionary struggle of the masses against imperialism has been bogged down in either Guevarist adventurism or Chile-type populist reformism. Guevarism came nearest to expressing the revolutionary passion of the masses, but it was devoid of correct Marxist thought. It placed the military, not politics, in command, and expected the guerrilla army to perform the tasks of political leadership. Allendism, on the other hand, placed excessive faith on the patriotic promises of the 'national' bourgeoisie, not realising its dual and contradictory character that we analysed earlier. In the event, when the masses, even in the absence of a mass organisation and a correct ideological leadership, began demanding arms to push the struggle against imperialism a stage further, the 'national' bourgeoisie panicked and turned to imperialism itself for protection against the masses. But the failures of these petty bourgeois populist revolutionary movements are not a total loss, for out of criticism and self-criticism, will arise a correct strategy.

It is, above all, in South East Asia that the masses were guided by a correct revolutionary strategy. The Vietnamese analysed their situation in the following terms:

'What characterises neo-colonialism is the fact that it is effected not through direct administration by the imperialists, but through a servile native regime representing the interests of the feudal landlord class and the comprador bourgeoisie with a "national democratic" cloak.'[28]

The peasants are thus exploited by both imperialism and feudalism. A correct revolutionary strategy therefore has to have both democratic and socialist content, and the leadership has to be in the hands not of the feudal landlords or the comprador bourgeoisie, but in the hands of the proletariat in alliance with the peasantry. The strategy for the revolution in Vietnam was laid down as early as 1930.

'Its [the Party's] *Political Theses* of 1930 pointed out that the Vietnamese revolution must go through two stages: first, the national democratic revolution; then, a direct passage to socialist revolution, bypassing the stage of capitalist development.'[29]

To this end, the Vietnamese formed a broadly — based anti-imperialist national front and in a protracted struggle lasting over forty years defeated French and American imperialism one after another. The Khmer Rouge in Cambodia, basing itself on the same general strategy, and profiting from the experience of the Vietnamese, were able to organise themselves to defeat United States imperialism within five years. On 15th April, 1975, Cambodia was liberated; a fortnight later, on May Day, South Vietnam too was liberated.

In Africa, in the former Portuguese colonies, the liberation movements began at first to try to seek a political solution through the United Nations, and later, when the U.N. looked like a dead end, to organise an armed struggle. Thus in Guinea-Bissau, the PAIGC, born in 1956, launched its first armed action in early 1963; in Mozambique armed action began in 1964; and in Angola in 1961. Armed action also began in South Africa in 1961, although it soon died down, and in Zimbabwe and Namibia in 1966. In all these the U.N. had made no progress at all, and no amount of sophistry can prove otherwise. When Guinea-Bissau, Mozambique and Angola ultimately gained their independence, it was an outcome essentially of revolution in Portugal itself. If the past is any guide to the future, then it would appear that revolutionary changes in Zimbabwe, Namibia and South Africa will also only come as a result of armed action. International organisations are too peripheral to be of much significance.

Conclusion

We are now in a position briefly to summarise the main argument of this paper. It is this that we need first to be clear about what we mean by the 'third world perspective' when examining international oranisations. This paper has identified three such perspectives. One perspective belongs to the bourgeois or petty bourgeois 'nationalist' governments which are in power in most of the third world countries. They are progressive to the extent that they are at least subjectively anti-imperialist; and they are reactionary to the extent that they would sooner make their peace with imperialism than surrender power to the masses of workers and peasants. For them international organisations are perfectly suited for the task of mobilising collective pressure on their imperialist mentors so that periodic political and economic concessions can be extracted from them to appease the masses and to secure a greater share of the surplus-value out of the labours of their working masses. But international organisations have, for them, now reached a point of diminishing returns, and they are fast losing the initiative to the masses themselves under proletarian leadership.

There is secondly the perspective of some of the really backward regimes in the third world, such as Jordand and Taiwan, which are not even subjectively progressive, and for whom international organisations are of marginal significance for they prefer to deal with imperialism directly. These, however, in the long run are a dying race.

There is thirdly the perspective of the masses of the third world.

These masses have been suppressed for far too long, but they are awakening and beginning to show real power when guided by a correct proletarian strategy. For them, and for as long as international organisations continue to reflect the existing balance of class forces in favour of imperialism, world 'order' and 'peaceful change', these organisations must necessarily be very peripheral to their struggles: Peace for them is a product of the end of oppression and exploitation; and development is the product of class struggle.

Notes

1. For an analysis of the Capitalist laws of motion, see K. Marx, *Capital,* especially, Volume III, Part III: on 'The law of the Tendency of the Rate of Profit to Fall'.
2. Lenin, V.I., *Collected Works,* Moscow, 1974, Volume XXIII, p. 192.
3. As an example of a typically idealistic (in a philosophical sense, i.e. as opposed to materialist) interpretation of the League of Nations see Claude, Inis L. Jr., *Swords into Plowshares*, New York, Random House, 1964.
4. Fulbright, J.W., 'The Great Society is a Sick Society', *New York Times*, 20th August, 1967. It might be argued that the League was irrelevant to the underlying issues rather than consciously ill-disposed to colonial peoples. But such an argument would misunderstand the *objective* function of international organisations, and abstract it from their political underpinning. Organisations cannot be viewed in this manner as if in isolation from their immediate environment. The Mandates System of the league, for instance, was not 'irrelevant' to the question of colonial exploitation. It provided the ideological rationale for the appropriation of the former German colonies by Britain, France, Belgium and South Africa against the background of the Bolshevik Revolution and Lenin's, followed by Woodrow Wilson's, call for national self-determination. Furthermore, if an organisation allows an act of blatant aggression to be committed with impunity, as the League did in the cases of Manchuria and Abyssinia, this is not evidence of the organisation's 'irrelevance', but a reflection of the nature of specific interests represented in the organisation (in this case, of imperialist interests).
5. The situation has now reached a point where, by most accounts, US capital controls 50 per cent of the automobile industry in Britain, 40 per cent of the oil industry in Germany, 40 per cent of the electric and electronic equipment industry in France, and nearly all the large-scale industries in Canada. See Magdoff, Harry, *The Age of Imperialism*, New York, Monthly Review Press, 1969.
6. Gardner, Lloyd C., *Economic Aspects of New Deal Diplomacy*, University of Wisconsin Press, 1964, p. 179.
7. For an excellent account of this, see Tayler, Alastair M., *Indonesian Independence and the United Nations*, London, Stevens, 1960.
8. Fifield, R.H., *Southeast Asia In United States Policy*, New York, Praeger, 1963, p. 267.
9. Bettelheim, Charles, *India Independent*, New York, Monthly Review, 1968, p. 287.
10. Green, Felix, *The Enemy*, New York, Random House, 1971, p. 139.
11. United Nations, *Multinational Corporations in World Development*, New York, United Nations, 1973, ST/ECA/190, Table 35.

12. For an excellent account of the rise of nationalism during this period, see Towney, R.H., *Religion and the Rise of Capitalism*, Harmondsworth, Penguin, 1972.
13. See Hussein, Mahmoud, *Class Conflict in Egypt: 1945–1970,* New York, Monthly Review, 1973.
14. Fitch, Bob and Oppenneiser, Mary, *Ghana: End of an Illusion,* New York, Monthly Review, 1966.
15. At the Bandaug Conference in 1955 which for the first time brought together African, Arab and Asian nationalists, only China and North Vietnam saw the struggle for national liberation as part of the larger world proletarian struggle against capitalism and imperialism. The other delegations came from Afghanistan, Burma, Cambodia, Ceylon, Egypt, Ethipoia, Gold Coast, India, Indonesia, Iran, Iraq, Jordan, Laos, Lebanon, Liberia, Nepal, Pakistan, the Philippines, Saudi Arabia, South Vietnam, Sudan, Syria, Thailand, Turkey and Yemen.
16. *World Armaments and Disarmament,* SIPRI Year Book, 1974. Uppsala Almquist and Wiksell, 1974, pp. 72–97.
17. For the text of the suicide note, see Gerassi, John, *The Great Fear in Latin America*, New York, Collier/Macmillan, 1971, p. 425.
18. The account and the quotations are taken from Payer, Cheryl, *The Debt Trap: IMF and the Third World*, Penguin, 1974, pp. 143–165.
19. For examples of actual takeovers by multinational corporations, see Galeano, Eduardo, *Open Viens of Latin America*, New York, Monthly Review, pp. 242–3.
20. Lichauco, Alejandro, 'Imperialism in the Philippines', *Monthly Review*, July-August, 1973, Volume 25, Number 3. Lichauco himself was one of the people affected by the takeover by multinational corporations. At the time that Gulf Oil purchased the controlling share in Filoil, Lichauco was president of the Philippine Petroleum Association and executive Vice-President of the Anglo-Philippine Oil and Mining Corporation.
21. For other examples, see Payer, *The Debt Trap*, Note 18 above.
22. Bell, Philip W., *The Sterling Area in the Post-War World*, Oxford, Clarendon Press, 1958, p. 261; and Fitch & Oppenheimer, *loc. cit.*, p. 92.
23. International Steel Institute, Brussels, Report dated 20 August, 1975.
24. *Guardian*, New York, 5 November, 1975.
25. For an account of how the war started, and U.N.'s role in the Middle East, see Tandon, Y., 'The UNEF, the Secretary-General and International Diplomacy in the Third Arab-Israeli War', *International Organization,* Spring, 1968.
26. Quoted in Halliday, Fred, *Arabia Without Sultans*, Harmondsworth, Penguin, 1974, p. 365.
27. This chapter was written in May 1976.
28. Le Duan, *The Vietnamese Revolution: Fundamental Problems Essential Tasks*, Hanoi, Foreign Languages Publishing House, 1973, p. 24.
29. *Ibid.*, p. 21.

Selected Reading

1. D.W. Nabudere, *The Political Economy of Imperialism*, London, Zed Press, 1977.
2. Samir Amin, *Unequal Development: Social Formation at the*

Periphery of the Capitalist System, New York, Monthly Review, 1974.

3. Cheryl Payer, *The Debt Trap*, Harmondsworth, Penguin, 1974.
4. Mahmoud Hussein, *Class Conflict in Egypt,* New York, Monthly Review, 1973.
5. Eduardo Galeano, *Open Veins of Latin America*, New York, Monthly Review, 1973.
6. I. Wallerstein, *The Modern World System*, New York, Academic Press, 1974.

CHAPTER EIGHTEEN

INTERNATIONAL ORGANISATION NETWORKS: A COMPLEMENTARY PERSPECTIVE

Anthony J.N. Judge

Introduction

This chapter first discusses briefly the extent to which an interorganisational perspective is currently used in connection with the theory or practice of international organisation. The distinction between 'network' and 'system' is then examined and the complementarity of the two perspectives in relation to a structure-process continuum is emphasized. An attempt is made to sketch out a network model of society and the challenge it poses for data collection. The availability of data on organisational and related networks is then discussed before reporting on one extensive data collection exercise which demonstrates the feasibility of the approach. Some directions for analysis, and the possibility for predicting various kinds of network growth, are then considered. Finally, the question of network design and various policy implications are examined.

The conventional approach to the analysis of organisations, and especially international organisations, has focussed on individual [1] These have either been studied in isolation as particular ~~d processes)~~ or exceptions to this statement. For example, Edward Miles has under-taken a number of studies of the complex of international organisations concerned with special issue areas (e.g. space, law of sea). However, he is more concerned with the particular case and less with the general problems of analyzing and describing such patterns of structural inter-action. There has also been much work on the analysis of transactions or exchanges across national boundaries and on the formation of coalitions between nation states. The former tends naturally to emphasize the flows rather than the pattern constituted by the set of flows. The latter is, of course, primarily concerned with the nation state as an actor, and the power blocs constituted by such coalitions, rather than their fine structure.

William Evan, in his introduction to a reader on inter-organisational relations,[2] makes the point that: 'One basic assumption, however, has unified researchers from diverse disciplines and vantage points, viz., that a significant amount of the variance of organisational phenomena can be accounted for by concentrating on intra-organisational variables. . . In recent years, one can detect a rising tide of discontent with the predominantly *intraorganisational* focus of organisational research. One expression of this discontent is as follows: 'Too much sociological theory and research has been based mainly on the model of a single organisation, and attention has been focused on its internal processes, by and large. Surely this dominant model is not sufficient to analyze newer and more complex organisational forms such as the interlocking networks of organisation in the civil service, the multi-campus state university, regional consortia of educational institutions, multi-outlet distributive organisations in business, and multi-plant industrial concerns. Having become rooted in its social and technological environment and more complex ways, organisations find themselves both constraining and being constrained by these environments in new ways. Yet investigators of formal organisations have barely begun to attack these new relationships.'

There has of course been no lack of studies of the 'international system' but these have tended to focus on aggregated quantitative data relating to geographical areas or individual nation states rather than to organisational 'fine structure' which is the vehicle for the international system. Where a network orientation has been specifically used, it has been applied to the network of relations between nation states as in the case of Doreian, Harary and Miller, Schofield or Vaughn.[3] Although Vaughn, in his analysis of the EEC, also includes enterprises and the Commission itself. Where individual organisations or groups of

382

organisations have been considered they tend either to have been studied in terms of their use as control mechanisms for the international system (e.g. the United Nations) or as being limited in their activities by features of that system. Again the richness and diversity of the interacting organisational forms has been ignored (for example, the variety of forms discussed in Chapter 2 of this volume).

Efforts to move towards a broader perspective have been made: by various people advised by Chadwick Alger, focusing on problem-area organisation networks; by Elise Boulding, in connection with womens organisations and religious groups;[4] and by Diana Crane, in extending her work on discipline-related networks of scientists and the invisible colleges to networks of international scientific and professional associations.[5] The author, partly in collaboration with Kjell Skjelsbaek, has explored possibilities of tracking evolving networks of international organisations.[6] This resulted recently in the establishment of a data base on networks of organisations, problems, treaties, disciplines, and the like, which was used to produce the *Yearbook of World Problems and Human Potential*.

Before considering the contribution of research on social networks or the distinction, if any, between 'system' and 'network', it is useful to note the emergence of the use of 'network' in the practice of international organisations.

'Network' in practice

It is no exaggeration to state that the number of interlinked international organisation units is such that no one has a clear overview or understanding of how the complex functions (if at all, as some would have it). This was first clearly stated in 1969 with respect to one international organisation system in the Capacity Study of the United Nations Development System under Sir Robert Jackson, who commented,

'For many years, I have looked for the "brain" which guides policies and operations of the UN development system. The search has been in vain. Here and there throughout the system there are offices and units collecting the information available, but there is no group (or "Brain Trust") which is constantly monitoring the present operation . . . ' (vol. I., p. 12).

Elsewhere it is noted in the Study that,

'In short, there are now simply too many separate, inconsistent, incomplete information systems relating to some facet of development cooperation activities, and these systems are undirected or uncoordinated by any central authority.' (vol. II., p. 223).

The situation remains the same in 1977. There is no unit within the UN system which records the existence of all other units in the system or has a mandate to do so. This shows how difficult it is to obtain an overview of the interlinkages in even one large organisational complex. The impression of complexity and the operational constraints imposed by it have led those working with or within such environments to use the term inter-organisational 'network' to describe their perception. The term is also used to describe any complex of organisations (UN or not) which may be relevant to a particular issue. As will emerge from the discussion of the relationship between 'network' and 'system' there is obviously a well-founded reluctance to speak of a 'system' under such circumstances. (Sir Robert Jackson even went as far as to refer to the UN development system as a 'non-system'.)

In such an environment, therefore, when a proposal is now made for the creation of some broad-purpose organisational instrument, there is a tendency to advocate the creation of a 'network' of some kind even at the intergovernmental level. This deliberately avoids introducing the kinds of systemic linkages which are perceived as having malfunctioned in previous exercises.

Consider the following examples:

1. *United Nations International System for Information on Science and Technology*. 'UNISIST is a continuing, flexible programme based on a joint Unesco-ICSU Study whose aims are to coordinate existing trends towards cooperation and to act as a catalyst for the necessary developments in scientific and technical information. The ultimate goal is the establishment of a flexible and loosely connected *network* of information services based on volunatry cooperation.' (UNISIST Newsletter, 1st January 1973, page 2.)

Studies by international organisations of their environments also lead increasingiy to documents which refer to the existence of 'networks' of one kind or another.

2. *Multinational Corporations in World Development*. 'While the terms "corporation", "firm" and "company" are generally used interchangeably, the term "enterprise" is sometimes preferred as clearly including a *network* of corporate and non-corporate entities in different countries joined together by ties of ownership '

'By contrast, most developed host countries belong to a *network* of

384

advanced economic, and even political, relationships which allow for more successful economic and political bargaining.' (ECOSOC report on *Multinational Corporations in World Development*, page 4.)

When employed in connection with multinational corporations, the term may be used with negative connotations. At the national level studies have been made to identify the networks constituted by 'interlocking directorates' which are viewed as undesirable.[7]

It should also be remembered that the term achieved widespread use with the development of espionage and, more recently, terrorist networks.

It is appropriate to note that a 1975 conference of the United Nations Institute for Training and Research, in identifying the main problems of using the potential of NGOs in social and economic development, included that of developing the network of NGOs and made suggestions for a 'network approach'.[8] In a 1976 review of the action of environmental NGOs, a similar point is made at length in a report to the United Nations Environment Programme.[9] The author has recently described 34 practical problems hindering the utilization of NGO networks.[10] Alvin Toffler, in testimony before a US Senate Committee in 1975, has also stressed the importance of a network focus.[11] The Alliance for Volunteerism, a consortium of 14 U.S. volunteer groups has recently launched a research project on interagency collaboration which will focus on the question of networks.

There appears to be an emerging awareness amongst practitioners that the concept of a network, network organisation and 'networking' are appropriate to the current rapidly changing conditions which constantly give rise to fresh problems and unforeseen requirements for action — requirements which cannot be rapidly and satisfactorily distributed to organisations working in isolation within rigidly defined programmes. Networks are perceived as permitting all the decentralization necessary to satisfy the need for autonomous organizational development and individual initiative. They also permit very rapid centralization, canalization, and focussing of resources the moment any complex problem (or natural disaster) emerges which requires the talents of an unforeseen configuration or constellation of organisations.

Social Networks

There has been a considerable amount of work on 'social networks' by which is meant primarily networks of individuals, usually analyzed in terms of the pattern of their relationships around one individual. Arnold Toynbee favours the conception of society as the set of such networks.

'Society is not a crowd or cluster or clump of human beings; it is a set of *networks* of relations among human beings. Every human being is linked with others in a number of networks which are not mutually exclusive and are also not coextensive with each other.'[12]

A very useful clarification is made by J. Clyde Mitchell as follows:

'When Radcliffe-Brown . . . defined social structure as "a *network* of actually existing social relationships" . . . he was using "network" in a metaphorical and not an analytical sense. His use of the word evoked an image of the inter-connections of social relationships but he did not go on to specify the properties of these interconnections which could be used to interpret social actions except at the abstract level of "structure". Perhaps more often than not the word "network" when used in sociological contexts is used in this metaphorical way . . . But the metaphorical use of the word, however common it is, should not prevent us from appreciating that it is possible to expand the metaphor into an analogy . . . and use the concept in more specific and defined ways.'[13]

But despite the amount of work done on social networks, very little of it deals with inter-organisational networks. When it does, it is either at the community level or between individuals in institutional structures. There does, however, seem to be a marked sensitivity on the part of scholars in this area to the implication that much work remains to be done on inter-organisational networks. Some believe that development of formal analytical procedures is far ahead of the ability to collect adequate data. Consequently there is resistance to the optimistic note sounded by scholars such as Francois Lorrain:

'The abstract notion of a network is undoubtedly called to play a role in the social sciences comparable to the role played in physics by the concept of euclidean space and its generalizations. But the poverty of concepts and methods stands in dramatic contrast to the immense conceptual and methodological richness available for the study of physical spaces. A whole reticular imagery remains to be developed. At this time a network is understood to contain simply nodes and links and little else.'[14] (Paraphrase and translation).

The formal analysis of social structure from a network viewpoint is therefore still in its early stages. In a review of the literature Scott Boorman notes that, to a large extent 'the most fundamental problem is still the pre-formal one of whether networks matter: or, to put the question more definitely, when do networks matter and what kinds of social networks are operative in given circumstances? One of the continuing problems with the network concept is that it is deceptively vivid as a metaphor and all too elusive in practice. . . The still unfinished task of the theory is to give more concrete instances where a network perspective really buys something for scientific sociology in addition to a largely new vocabulary and a set of appealing metaphors.'[15]

Since the study of social networks has focussed on individuals, it remains to be seen to what extent the weaknesses of the approach would also apply in the case of organisations, particularly since data on relationships between large numbers of organisations may be more easily collected and as such any analysis would tend to be more relevant to decision-making about the network and about particular organisations in it. It is not for nothing that one of the early studies in this area was funded by the US Office of Civil Defense.[16]

'System' versus 'Network'

The definition of 'system' (like that of 'structure') is the subject of continuing confusion. It is not surprising therefore that the implication that 'network' is in some way distinct from 'system' tends to give rise to vigorous debate. It is the mathematics-based pure and applied sciences which are most disturbed by the possibility of any distinction. Clearly, in purely formal mathematical terms, both system and network consist of an interconnected set of elements. But even when account is taken of the nature of those elements, the manner of their interconnection and the properties of the resultant whole, the distinctions between definitions of system and of network are confused especially where value-related questions are raised concerning the relative equitability of different social structures. The confusion and overlap is illustrated by the following definitions taken from the Yearbook,[17] of which the first two are for system and the last for network.

1. Any recognizable delimited aggregate of dynamic elements that are in some way interconnected and interdependent and that continue to operate together according to certain laws and in such a way as to produce some characteristic total effect. A system, in other words, is something that is concerned with some kind of activity and preserves a

kind of integration and unity; and a particular system can be recognized as distinct from other systems to which, however, it may be dynamically related. Systems may be complex, they may be made up of interdependent sub-systems, each of which, though less autonomous than the entire aggregate, is nevertheless fairly distinguishable in operation.

2. A regular interacting of an interdependent group of items forming a unified whole. A set of elements standing in interaction as expressed by a system of mathematical equations or an organization seen as a system of mutually dependent variables. A system may be characterized by: a particular relationship between elements which turns a mere collection of elements into something that may be called an assemblage; a pattern in the set of relationships which turns the assemblage into a systematically arranged assemblage; and a unified purpose which turns the systematically arranged assemblage into a system.

3. A group of elements which may be partially or completely interconnected. The connections (termed branches or arcs) can represent roads, power lines, airline routes, information flows, predator-prey relationships in an ecosystem, logical relationships, or the generalized channels through which commodities flow. The elements (termed points or nodes) can represent individuals, communities, power stations, airline terminals, water reservoirs, libraries, organisations, namely any point where a flow or relationship of some kind originates, or terminates. In a more general case, the elements or points in the network may themselves be subnetworks composed of combinations of other kinds of elements.

The characteristics of the network's elements and relationships can be described by values, which may or may not be quantitative. The values can be fixed or they can vary in some way with time. Thus the relationship between two points may not exist during a particular period of time (as in an electrical circuit), or several possible relationship paths may exist between two points (as in a telephone circuit). Different types of relationship may exist between the same two points.

The question of interest may be less the distinction between system and network, if any, and more the connotations of the terms in contexts associated with international and organisational activity. The question may then be why is there a preference for 'network' instead of 'system' under certain circumstances. Consider the distinctions in the case of a road system/network, a telephone system/network or a concept system/network before reflecting on the case of an inter-organisational system/network. Under what circumstances is there a negative connotation to either term?

The author recently presented to a meeting in Montreal the following suggestions as to how the distinction *tends to be made in practice.* Further points appear in the report of the debate.[18]

1. Systems tend to require more information for their description than networks, since flows must be described as well as structural relationships.

2. Systems are described primarily with quantitative information (which is both difficult and costly to obtain and has a short useful life), whereas networks may be described with non-quantitative structural information (which is more readily available at lower cost and has a longer useful life).

3. Systems tend to have a unique (or ultimate) controller regulating the state of the system as a whole, whereas networks tend to have a plurality of controllers (if any), with a relatively high degree of autonomy. (In other words, systems tend to be centralized in some sense, whereas networks tend to be decentralized or polycentric.)

4. Systems tend to be associated with imposed structures or patterns (even if limited to the choice of the system boundary), whereas networks tend to be associated with emergent structures or patterns.

5. Systems tend to have well-defined boundaries (even if they are open-systems) whereas the outer-limit (or fine detail) of a network is ill-defined and not of major significance to its description.

6. Systems tend to have well-defined, stable goals or functions, whereas networks, if they have any, may have ill-defined goals, a plurality of goals (possibly fairly incompatible), or may change goals relatively frequently.

7. Systems tend to have a more limited tolerance of changes to their environment, whereas networks tend to maintain a fair degree of invariance and coherence even in the event of highly turbulent transformations to their environment.

8. Societal system descriptions tend to be meaningful only at a macro-level to detached observers, whereas network descriptions retain their utility even when limited to the immediate environment of an involved participant at a particular node of the network.

9. Systems, and particularly their dynamics, tend to be difficult to represent, whereas complex networks can be represented with relative ease.

Complementarity of system and network perspectives

Rather than attempt to resolve the distinction between system and network, it may be useful to conceive of the two terms as being different but complementary conceptual approaches to a structure-process continuum.[19] When a system perspective is used, in practice the emphasis is on the properties and the characteristics of the whole conceived as a *set of interlinked processes* (over which a measure of centralized control is described). In the extreme case the set of processes can be viewed as energy field effects. The structure supporting the processes, if considered at all, is perceived and represented in terms of its gross features. When a network perspective is used, in practice the emphasis is on the properties and characteristics of the *continuous pattern of linkages* constituting the structure. The processes which may occur in the network, if considered at all, are perceived and represented in terms of the pathways through the network (the mapping of which constitutes the initial challenge). As the concern with processes builds up, the perspective shifts toward the system focus, whereas concern with detailed representation of the structure shifts the perspective towards the network focus. The system perspective therefore tends to be used when the structure is assumed to be relatively simple and conceptually well-defined but where the complexity of the processes poses a challenge to conceptualization and representation. The network perspective, conversely, is used when the processes are assumed to be relatively simple and well-defined but where the structural complexity poses a challenge to conceptualization and representation.

Expressed in these terms, the complementarity of the two perspectives highlights the problem of description, analysis and policy-formulation in relation to global society. A focus on the system process dynamics, as typified by the current approaches to world modelling, is obliged to eliminate structural (and especially fine structural) features to reach a level of aggregation which renders the analysis viable. A focus on the network of fine structure would presumably only be practicable if the complexity of process characteristics was highly simplified. Either filter can be employed, but both cannot yet be removed together and result in any practicable comprehensible investigation.

On the question of the importance of fine structure Donald Schon comments that,

'The map of organisations or agencies that make up the society is, as it were, a sort of clear overlay against a page underneath it which represents the reality of the society . . . There's basically no social problem such that one can identify and control within a single system all the elements required in order to attack that problem. The result is that one is thrown back on the knitting together of elements in *networks* which are not controlled and where the *network* functions and the *network* roles become critical.'[20]

In the introduction to the *Yearbook of World Problems and Human Potential 1976*, (see note 17) the author raises a related question:

'To what extent is the complexity of the problem system with which humanity is faced greater than that which its organisational and intellectual resources are capable of handling? Worse, is there a widespread unacknowledged preference for simplifying the representation of complex problem (and other) systems down to less than 10 elements so that they lend themselves to easy debate in public and in a policy-making environment (as might be suggested by some work of communication psychologist George Miller)? Are organisational and conceptual resources then marshalled and structured to match the problem system as simplified rather than to handle it in its more dangerous complexity, thus running the (unacknowledged) risk of leaving the problems uncontained and uncontainable by the resources available? Does this suggest a corollary to Ashby's Law of Requisite Variety which might read: 'That any attempt to control a psycho-social system with a control system of less complexity (i.e. of less variety) than that of the psycho-social system itself can only be made to succeed by suppressing or ignoring the variety (i.e. reducing the diversity) in the psycho-social system so that it is less than the relative simplicity of the control system?' Such suppression tends to breed violence, however.'

Some of these matters were recently explored during a panel on complexity as a constraint on social innovation during a meeting of the International Foundation for Social Innovation.[21] Such views suggest that it is of value to explore the possibility of representing aspects of global society as a network, especially the networks associated with international organisation.

Network model

There does not seem to be available any well-articulated conceptual model of the network structure of society. Such a model would be based upon the stable networks of interpersonal relationships whose existence is established by the many social network studies. It would include (a) the growth of such networks in terms of their present pattern as 'structural formula', (b) the multiplication of parallel networks distinguishing themselves by different priorities regarding the same field of concern, (c) the periodic changes in structure of the network in response to occasional changes in the state of the environment (e.g. activation of political networks at election time), and (d) the evolution of such networks, namely the emergence of new forms as a result of marked changes in the pattern of 'structural formula' (possibly determined by 'saturation' or 'maturation' thresholds). Within such a model it should be clear how changes in the network of interpersonal relationships are catalyzed by changes in (a) the network of concepts making up the body of knowledge, (b) the network of values in terms of which activities are undertaken, (c) the communication and information networks which facilitate contact and exchange and (d) the networks of treaties, laws and regulations which regulate or inhibit such contact and exchange. It should be clear how changes in relationship patterns are catalyzed by events such as isolated (or periodic) meetings which provide focal points through which new links are momentarily made and then possibly given permanence through the establishment of working relationships or even formal organisations. Such changes are provoked by changes in the perceived nature of the network of problems with which any particular zone of the interpersonal or inter-organisational network is confronted. Indeed there is considerable interaction between the various kinds of network noted above, leading to sympathetic structural changes, whether resulting in fragmentation or greater integration. (None of this is effectively registered by currently proposed social indicators.) Clearly new concepts, values or problems give rise to new meetings, new organizations, new information system and new regulations. These in turn catalyze the emergence of further concepts, values or perceived problems. There are many shifts and waves in the changing patterns of relationships. Many patterns are extremely short-lived and cannot constitute a basis for institutions of any permanence. Others survive for, and are exhausted by, a single meeting. Others give rise to information systems, possibly of rapidly diminishing significance. And of course some give rise to organisations through which particular networks of inter-personal relationships are activated and supported for long periods. The emergence of organisations in this way leads to the establishment of formal or informal networks of relationships between such bodies at the same level, with others at a 'lower' level (e.g. member organisations), or with others at a 'higher' level (e.g. bodies of which it is a member). Such networks themselves provide a framework through which new concepts, values or problems give rise to new meetings, new organisations, new information systems and new regulations. And the forms of the networks are themselves modified, to a greater or lesser extent, by such activity and by ongoing structural developments in the 'parallel' network of concepts, values or problems.

The structure of any of these networks is not only a matter for detached observation. Much energy is devoted by individuals and organisations associated with these networks to reordering them. Domains of influence are established around focal points: specific problems, values, and concepts are given territorial characteristics and stimulate appropriate behaviour. Portions of the network are ordered, bi-directional relationships are made uni-directional and focussed on particular nodes. Efforts are made to rationalize these changes by establishing hierarchical structures with well-defined boundaries, whether from existing networks or as a development within existing networks.

Just as hierarchies are created and embedded in networks, so there are networks which emerge and evolve within and between hierarchical structures. Very large hierarchical structures (e.g. the United Nations) are associated with very complex networks. Other hierarchical structures may be nested within such networks. A set of otherwise unrelated hierarchies may be tightly linked by networks (e.g. inter-locking corporation directorates, invisible colleges) which may extend between different kinds of hierarchies (e.g. old boy networks).

The model should also make clear how the variety of organizational forms and preoccupations is generated and interrelated within such networks (which would appear to be information analogues of the complex food webs which interrelate very diverse species in nature). In particular it would be valuable to clarify the functions of organisational variety of form and preoccupation and the advantages and disadvantages of reducing or increasing such variety. This would also help to determine the current significance of antiquated institutions and of the bodies created for fun or out of whimsy (e.g. the Association for the Promotion of Humour in International Affairs).

Do such bodies perform any useful function or would society function better if such organisational clutter was rapidly eliminated?

Data availability

Assuming that a model such as that sketched out above constituted a useful representation of one aspect of societal activity, the question is whether the relationships represented could be adequately captured in an information system. There is a considerable gap between the richness and diversity implied in the above model and in those depicting the international system as made up of some 150 states linked through an equal number of intergovernmental bodies and alliances into a handful of power blocs. An equivalent perspective is common at the national level within each nation state.

Clearly whilst it would be desirable to examine global society in terms of social networks of individuals, this does not seem to be practicable, although the implications of such networks should be borne in mind — particularly when considering the significance of census data on individuals abstracted from such networks. And although census data is available on individuals and on the commercial enterprises by which they are employed or from which they purchase products, none is readily available on the groups and associations in which they are active and through which their views are expressed and frequently molded. The importance of such information to government is illustrated by the fact that when it is collected such data tends to be maintained in central registries for official purposes often linked to national security and personnel vetting. Such data is also actively sought both by commercial groups eager to expose association members to particular products and services and by opinion forming bodies (e.g. the UN Office of Public Information) eager to orient association members to new values, issues and fund-donating opportunities. It is appropriate to note that data on national and local government units and their relationships is frequently also difficult to obtain in any systematic manner.

In the present circumstances it is perhaps fortunate that such national and subnational data is not more readily available, given the misuse to which it would tend to be subject. In fact, for purposes of initial research and general education, it would be much simpler, less costly and possibly more enlightening to simulate the growth and change of a variety of complex networks (and levels of networks) in a computer environment with suitable visual display facilities. A variety of conceptual and organisational entities and relationships could be 'grown' and analyzed under different conditions and subjected to different constraints. It would be relatively simple to work over extended time periods with a population of 10^4 or even 10^6 entities and an equivalent number of relationships which would otherwise constitute a formidable coding investment. It would be instructive to determine to what extent modules from the conventional system-oriented world models could be blended into such a framework. In relation to the formal analogue noted earlier, such a simulation might explore the following questions noted elsewhere by the author (see note 17):

'6. Can the relationships between problems (or between organiz-ations) be usefully conceived as analogous to the food webs and trophic levels within which animals are embedded? Does this help to suggest why different kinds of problems emerge as being of major importance at different times? How might the evolution of problems and problem systems be conceived in this light?
7. From what is the stability of a 'problem ecosystem' (as it might emerge from the previous point) derived? Is it useful to distinguish between degress of (negative) maturity of problem ecosystems and to attempt to determine the amount of energy required to maintain them? Is anything suggested for better understanding of problem systems by the fact that a highly diversified ecoysystem has the capacity for carrying a high amount of organization and information and requires relatively little energy to maintain it, whereas, conversely, the lower the maturity of the system, the less the energy required to disrupt it. Thus anything that keeps an ecosystem oscillating (or 'spastic'), retains it in a state of low maturity, whence the possible danger of simplistic reorganisation of organisational, conceptual, or value systems. Is the problem of understanding and organizing the maturation of natural ecosystems of a similar form to that of understanding and organising the disruption of problem ecosystems? '

Data collected

Partly in an attempt to explore the possible characteristics of a model such as that sketched above, a special programme was initiated in 1972 by the Union of International Associations (publishers of the *Yearbook of International Organizations*) jointly with Mankind 2000 (which initiated the series of International Futures Research Conferences). This programme resulted in 1976 in the publication of an experimental

13-section *Yearbook of World Problems and Human Potential*. Each of the sections is devoted to a particular kind of entity (whether international organisations, world problems, values, multilateral treaties, and the like.) Each section is structured on computer files as a series of entities linked together in networks. Entities in different sections are also linked in networks. A summary of the numbers of entities and relationships is given as Table I (see p. 403).

The kinds of relationships that could be registered in this way clearly depend on the nature of the entity-pair so linked. Formal relationships (e.g. membership, consultative status) were registered between organizations, but most relationships could only be established as related subjects (e.g. a treaty on 'child labour' and a world problem of 'child labour').

Some data collected for the 1977 edition of the *Yearbook of International Organizations* (a companion volume to the above publication) is useful as an indication of intraorganizational networks (relating to international organisations). This has been presented as Table 3 of Chapter 2 and summarizes the national member links to international bodies. Clearly it does not cover intra-secretariat links.

This project illustrates the possibility of tracking complex networks involving international organisations although it remains to be seen how best the data tapes can be analyzed and whether they can be effectively updated as is intended.

Directions for Analysis

Organisation is best depicted as a network. The mathematical theory of networks derives largely from certain branches of topology and abstract algebra. The theory of graphs is often presented as a kind of general theory of networks; however, other than in the area of operations research, it has not proved itself to be very useful in sociology. The theory rarely handles networks with several distinct types of relationship, each with its own configuration of links. It is precisely such networks which are of most interest in sociology. It also tends to exclude networks in which some of the points have links back to themselves, and it is often just such networks which are important in representing social structures.

A final disadvantage of the theory of graphs is that it only offers a fairly limited range of means of global analysis of networks. In such a situation it is not possible to provide more precise descriptions of networks as structures with particular characteristics, or as made up of sub-structures with particular characteristics. It is therefore difficult to distinguish clearly between networks of different types; especially since an adequate description depends upon structural rather than quantitative information. It is curious that none of the sciences appears to have developed a terminology to facilitate communication about irregular, complex, multi-dimensional structures.

Conventional analysis of networks provides information on such characteristics as number of nodes, number of links, centrality of a node and interconnectedness of a group of entities. Such characteristics give very little information on the structural features, patterning or irregularities of a network.

The term network generally implies the presence of

(a)   relationships between a particular node and some more central node (i.e. 'vertical' relationships);

(b)   relationships between a node and less central nodes (i.e. a network of more than one level);

(c)   relationships between nodes having a similar relationship to a more central node (i.e. 'horizontal' relationships);

and possibly also:

(d)   relationships between a particular node and more central nodes *other* than the one noted in (a) (i.e. a network with several centres);

(e)   relationships between a particular node and nodes more central than those noted in (a) and (d) (i.e. a network with links across levels, or 'jumping' levels);

and possibly also:

(f)   direct relationships between the most central node(s) and the least central node(s);

(g)   relationships such that the node which is the least central under one set of conditions may be the most central node (in the extreme case) under another set of conditions.

Clearly networks vary a great deal in their possession of one or more of these characteristics. The first three are typical of most formal organisations (organisations as networks), although (c) is less frequent or raises problems, in organisations of a more bureaucratic style. An organisational hierarchy, having characteristics (a) and (b), may therefore be considered as an ordered network. The degree of ordering is decreased or diluted (at least in one sense) with the presence of the other characteristics.

To the extent that the last four characteristics are embodied in networks, and particularly the last two, there is a tendency for the networks to become less formal and more difficult to document. This does not of course necessarily imply a decrease in their functional significance in society — it may even imply an increase.

The degree of centralization raises a difficulty in that some may prefer not to apply the term network in situations where centralization is high, particularly where this implies ultimate control by a single centre. Others, however, may consider that situations of (very) low or 'variable' centralization are not of immediate interest, whether or not they can be adequately studied.

The problem in determining directions for analysis is that so little of the considerable body of literature on social networks has been explored in terms of its relevance to the study of inter-organisational networks, and few of the scholars interested in social networks have any interest in inter-organisational networks except as networks of individuals. It is appropriate to note that Johan Galtung has recently suggested that 'structural analysis is indispensable at any level of society analysis, from inter-personal to inter-national'. He advocates the use of this approach for the development of a needed range of social indicators, particularly of relevance to development.[22]

Predictive possibilities

The data available and the manner of its organisation suggest interesting possibilities for predicting:
- the *growth* of networks, namely the extension of an existing network of a given pattern or 'structural formula'
- the *multiplication* of networks, namely the emergence of parallel networks with a different slant or mode of activity in relation to a common subject domain
- the *evolution* of networks, namely the emergence of new forms with the occurrence of marked changes in the pattern or 'structural formula'
- *impact-effects* within and between networks.

Such prediction is not confined to networks of organisations and is in fact dependent upon examination of the interactions between networks of organisations, occupations, disciplines, problem-areas, and the like. Growth or evolution of any of these networks will tend to provoke corresponding growth or evolution in the others with which it interacts.

1. *Network growth*

It is possible to make use of existing *ordered subject domains*, applied against semi-ordered domains of organisations, problems, disciplines or occupations, to detect subjects which have a significant probability of being expressed in organisations, problems or like phenomena.

The simplest and most common example of an ordered subject domain is a hierarchically organised thesaurus (e.g. the Universal Decimal Classification system). Specialized thesauri have, for example, been developed to order occupations,[23] commodities,[24] economic sectors,[25] and diseases.[26]

A simple procedure (perhaps overly simple in the light of further investigation, but an advance on the current state of affairs) that can be adopted, is to check off in any such hierarchy the nodes for which corresponding organisations, problems, or the like exist. Then, by inspection, it is possible to note unchecked nodes which are apparently 'late' in being activated in terms of any such correspondence. This may best be clarified by the following diagram:

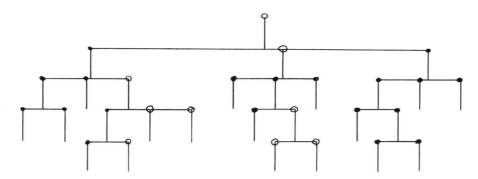

The solid circles indicate checked nodes for which a corresponding organisation, problem, or appropriate phenomena exists, whereas the unfilled circles indicate the lack of any such correspondence (or lack of adequate data). The degree to which any particular branch is 'filled' may be considered to exert a 'probability pressure' on the change in the status of those remaining unfilled. This approach at least raises the question as to why a particular correspondence has not been found. This may be very useful, in the case of organisations for example, to identify domains in which a formal organisation has not been created because an organisational substitute has been found satisfactory (e.g. a periodic meeting, a journal, a treaty). The possibilities of this approach emerged in the collection of information on world problems. Where these were related to commodities, economic sectors, diseases, or occupations, gaps in any hierarchy of problems immediately became apparent and raised useful questions.

399

Clearly there are possibilities for refining this technique by exploring matches between several hierarchies simultaneously. Matching the disciplines against the (ILO) catalogue of professional occupations brings out underdeveloped features of the latter which may suggest areas of emergence of organisations, problems, and treaties. This approach is not limited to matches between hierarchies. It may also, and possibly more realistically and usefully, be applied by using computers to detect degrees of correspondence between any isomorphic structures. This would of course be more appropriate in the case of those networks which cannot be usefully assumed to be hierarchically ordered. In this way it could well prove possible to explore the manner and speed at which networks of organisations are likely to develop specialized branches to break down some subject domain — possibly to a point of saturation at which a paradigm shift becomes necessary.

Where parts of the network are tied to geographical regions (e.g. Scandinavia, Europe, Caribbean), the presence or absence of particular regional components could be used in a similar way to predict the emergence of others. For example, European professional regional organisations are likely to emerge before equivalent African or Asian bodies. It might be possible to estimate the degrees of lag for certain categories between different regions. (This would of course be dependent on the national and sub-national networks.)

2. *Multiplication of networks*

In attempting to predict the emergence of organisations it is of course not possible to limit attention to the simple breakdown of subject fields. Even a superficial check of the range of international organisations shows that a particular subject may be the focus of an organisation with slants or modes such as

- study of/research on
- in support of
- media information about
- specialized documentation on
- funds for
- providers/producers of
- users/consumers of
- affected by
- professionals of
- workers in

Each of these modifiers, and the list is neither complete nor systematic, may give rise to parallel networks interwoven to different degrees.

400

Presumably at some stage it will be possible to clarify the possible scope for organisation formation by combining a series of factors of this kind.

3. Evolution of networks

In the absence of any analyses and comparisons of organizational networks which could be used to distinguish types of networks, or structural formulae for networks, it is only possible to suggest that networks may be subject to structural shifts after periods of growth. (Some indications may possibly be gleaned from the literature describing transport and communication networks within and between urban centres.)

When a network has grown, in terms of a given formula, it appears to reach a point of strain, in relation to the demands placed upon it, at which some new structural formula becomes desirable. (From a strictly formal point of view, the need for such changes and their nature is evident in the evolution and morphogenesis of biological forms.) It is through such structural transformations that new varieties of organisational network emerge. This is perhaps most clearly seen in the emergence and increasing complexity during the twentieth century of inter-corporate networks, whether in terms of financial control (e.g. holding companies, inter-locking directorates) or movement of products (between corporations producing or using goods and services). It is less clearly documented in the case of the academic environment. Other possible models of interest might be developed from efforts to define the emergence of conceptual relationships between disciplines – particularly since it is probable that this would influence the interrelationships between the corresponding professional or scientific associations (cf. Jantsch,[27] Wahlin,[28] Kedrov[29]).

4. Impact-effects within and between networks

The structure of the international system of bodies which have mutual effects on one another may be described as a network of organisations and associations. Some of the bodies in the network may directly effect some of the problems in the problem complex which may also be described as a network.

In considering how impact occurs and is transferred (i) between organisations, (ii) on to problems, (iii) between problems, and (iv) from problems onto organisations, a series of possibilities of increasing structural complexity may be borne in mind. To illustrate this series, consider the structures illustrated in Table 1. A particular element transferring impact-effects may do so as follows:

1. Directly onto the target structure (i.e. no branching, 1 element).
2. Via a series of intermediary elements (i.e. no branching, more than 1 element).
3. Via two branches, both going direct to the target structure (this case could possibly be combined with the first).
4. Via two branches, one going direct to the target structure and the second via one intermediate element.
5. Via two branches, both with more than one intermediate element.
6. Via two branches, each with one element connected to that in the other branch.

The situation is complicated by the fact that most of the above structures contain branches, implying a *divergence* of impact. But clearly if the impacts were transferred from the branches, rather than to them, there would be *convergence* of impact through the structures:

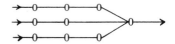

This therefore gives a second series of structures for transferring impact. Structures from each series may be combined:

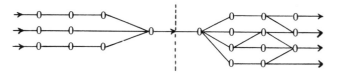

The structures may be combined in branching or converging series, and even with loops back to an earlier structure — thus constituting networks of varying degrees of complexity. (Note that normally a structural element can not be considered an 'absolute originator' of impact nor an 'absolute sink' for impact.)

Up to this point the elements making up the structures have been considered as made up entirely of organisations or entirely of problems. But impact can be transferred between organisation and problem structures as noted above. In other words the structures considered above can be either organisations or problems, and they can transfer impact to organisations or problems (in similar structures).

This leads to mixed impact-transferring structural sequences of the

TABLE 1: IMPACT STRUCTURES OF INCREASING COMPLEXITY

Units	Impact links	Link branches	Branch linkage	Structure (+)
1	1	(1)	0	
$1 + m\ (\geqslant 1)$	$1 + n\ (\geqslant 1)$	(1)	0	
1	2	2	0	
$1 + m\ (\geqslant 1) + m^1(\geqslant 0)$	$2 + n\ (\geqslant 1) + n^1(\geqslant 0)$	2	0	
$3 + m\ (\geqslant 0)$	$\geqslant 4$	2	1	
> 3	> 4	2	$\geqslant 1$	
1	3	3	0	
$\geqslant 4$	$\geqslant 3$	3	0	
$\geqslant 4$	> 3	> 3	$\geqslant 1$	
1	4	4	0	
$\geqslant 5$	> 4		0	
$\geqslant 5$	> 4	> 4	$\geqslant 1$	
1	p	p	0	
$\geqslant (p + 1)$	$\geqslant p$	$\geqslant p$	0	
$\geqslant (p + 1)$	$> p$	$> p$	$\geqslant 1$	

(+) Note that impact is understood as being transferred from left to right through these structures (i.e. divergently in most cases), but there exists an equivalent (mirror-image) sequence in which impact would be effectively transferred from right to left (i.e. convergently). Structures from the two sequences can be combined or linked together, provided that they match.

following types:

1. Organisation to Organisation
    1.1   to Organisation
                1.1.1   to Organisation   (OOOO)
                1.1.2   to Problem   (OOOP)
    1.2   to Problem
                1.2.1   to Organisation   (OOPO)
                1.2.2   to Problem   (OOPP)

2. Organisation to Problem
    2.1   to Organisation
                2.1.1   to Organisation   (OPOO)
                2.1.2   to Problem   (OPOP)
    2.2   to Problem
                2.2.1   to Organisation   (OPPO)
                2.2.2   to Problem   (OPPP)

3. Problem   to Organisation
    3.1   to Organisation
                3.1.1   to Organisation   (POOO)
                3.1.2   to Problem   (POOP)
    3.2   to Problem
                3.2.1   to Organisation   (POPO)
                3.2.2   to Problem   (POPP)

4. Problem   to Problem
    4.1   to Organisation
                4.1.1   to Organisation   (PPOO)
                4.1.2   to Problem   (PPOP)
    4.2   to Problem
                4.2.1   to Organisation   (PPPO)
                4.2.2   to Problem   (PPPP)

Clearly these sequences can be further extended to cover more complex patterns of interaction between organisation and problem networks. It should be stressed that the organisation structure, for example, in any of the above sequences (e.g. PPOP) may itself be a complex sequence of structures as discussed earlier. To the extent that it is advisable to distinguish between intergovernmental organisations and international associations (i.e. nongovernmental structures), the organisation structures must be split into two types (e.g. O and O^1).

This approach would probably demand that the problems be also split into at least two groups, those recognised by intergovernmental organisations and those recognized by international associations (e.g. P and P^1).

Combining these together would result in description of impact chains of such forms as $OPO^1 OPOP^1$, etc. Whether or not this split (namely O and O^1 and P and P^1) is made, the real situation is probably much more complex because of the network characteristics which would give impact networks such as

$$\longrightarrow OPOOP$$
$$O$$
$$P$$
$$\longrightarrow PPOOPOOPOPPOO \longrightarrow$$
$$O \quad P$$
$$PPOOOOPO \longrightarrow$$

Such situations are somewhat more complex than those addressed by conventional studies of impact such as whether organisation A makes an impact on B. Clearly organisation A may not make an impact directly on B, but it may do so on C and D (perhaps via many intermediate bodies or problems) which then may make an impact on B.

The social sciences are some way from being able to describe such sequences and track impacts through them. It is even uncertain that there would be any consensus that such an approach is relevant to current preoccupations which depend upon simplication of complex situations to render them communicable within the political arena.

At some stage it may be possible to track the movement of impact through such structural sequences in terms of how different structural components amplify, dampen or store and release impact under different conditions. The meaning of 'impact' may well be as elusive as that of 'electricity', to whose movement through circuitry the above situations bear some resemblance. The question of the distinction between positive and negative impact would also have to be considered.

Network design

a. *Interorganisational design*

There is little available knowledge on interorganisational design for the obvious reason that whenever there is any organisational initiative, there is a natural tendency to design a single organisation, however large and cumbersome, and little incentive to explore the possibility of interorganisational networks with a minimum, if any, of centralised

405

control. As William Evan notes in an editorial comment introducing a chapter of readings on designing and managing interorganisational systems: 'Given the state of the art in research on interorganisational relations, it may seem both premature and hazardous to concern oneself with normative questions of designing and redesigning inter-organisational systems.' (See note 2.) The three articles he includes as illustrations of potentially useful approaches make the point that much remains to be done. One deals with strategies for resolving interorganizational conflict, the second focuses on the Antitrust Division of the US Department of Justice, and the third examines the role of computer-based communications systems in effecting interorganisational linkages (in a product marketing context). None gets to grips with the actual design of organisation networks. There have however been a number of studies of decision-making in an inter-organisational environment.[34]

b. *Matrix organisation*

This approach, developed and implemented by NASA for the moon project, is a major step toward network design but in itself is inadequate because it has a single-purpose structure in which the purpose is formulated by one body and is thus more like a 'system'. Within the matrix structure, each participating body, whether controlled by NASA or not, is considered to be at the intersection of influences from other parts of the structure and itself in turn influences several others. It is a system which tends to diminish the visibility of authority and to emphasize consensus as an operative mode. Operating decisions are part of the give and take of specialized units struggling for a share of the system's total resources.

c. *Potential association*

The insights derived from use of a network model as a way of structuring perceptions concerning society can be used to move towards the development of an alternative style of organisation. In testimony before the Committee on Foreign Relations of the United States Senate, Alvin Toffler outlined this possibility in the case of international NGOs, in response to a question on how to organize a wide variety of interest groups into a coherent network:

'One of the reasons I argue the case for much more attention to the NGO's is that the NGO's form the potential for any number of temporary, mission-oriented consortia that could be brought together,

whether they are environmental organisations or scientific organisations or organisations concerned with community development of
food or whatever the issues are. It is possible to put together
temporary consortia to deal with specific problems.

Now in order for that to work you have to have some coordination
or management. But what I am describing need not be a pyramid.

Now, here is one way to verbalize the alternative·organisational
structure. Think of the pyramid. Then think of a thin frame, a very
thin frame which is essentially coordinative, which is a thin layer of
management and direction, with a whole series of essentially
temporary organisational clusters of modules that have relatively
short life spans, and among which people float quite freely. They
move from one module to another rather than being frozen in a
single bureaucratic niche. If we pump some funds into the non-
governmental sector, we might help to create precisely this thin
coordinative system at the top. We would then have a basis for a
very large, very diverse, very flexible, ad-hocratic organisation a
that could operate in the international field.' (See note 11.)

Nor does Toffler limit this technique to NGOs:

' . . . we need to think in terms of the creation not of a single
center, or a single world government that will some day govern the
nations of the world, but rather in terms of a self-regulatory *network*
of transnational institutions, multiple institutions, a polycentric
system. Such a transnational *network* can provide a higher degree of
stability for the planet than the centralized model based on a single
international governmental organisation . . . we must first recognize
that the U.N. is only a tiny piece of a swiftly emerging transnational
mosaic or *network* of institutions which are part of the new
super-industrial system. This *network* consists of thousands of
organisations and millions of individuals around the world in
continually shifting relationships with one another.' (See note 11.)

Elsewhere the author has discussed the concept of a 'potential
association'[30] as an innovative response to the new operational requirements necessitated by the approach suggested by Toffler. Such an
association would, as such, not have 'members' in the conventional
sense of a defined set of individuals or units of organisation subscribing
in common to a particular set of views. The emphasis would be
switched to objectifying the tenuous concept of a group of bodies

which *could* link together in different transient patterns under appropriate conditions. The need to centre attention on existing organisations (with their tendency to self-perpetuation and to constituting obstacles to social change) is diminished in favour of recognition of the range of *potential patterns* into which the component entities in the potential pool could 'gel' in response to new conditions. A meaningful and dynamic social framework for conventional, 'permanent' organisations is thereby supplied. Thus whilst society may, with the use of an approach of this type, form a highly ordered (low entropy) complex at any given time — satisfying short term, stability requirements — the high probability of switching later to completely different high order patterns supplies the 'randomness' (high entropy) condition essential to the facilitation of social change and development in response to new conditions. In this connection Johan Galtung's view of the importance of high entropy for world peace is noteworthy:

'Thus the general formula is: Increase the world entropy, i.e. increase the disorder, the messiness, the randomness, the un-predictability — avoid the clear-cut, the simplistic blue-print, the highly predictable, the excessive order. . . Expressed in one formula, this seems to capture much of what today passes as peace thinking, particularly of the associative variety.'[31]

In other words we have a means of ensuring high social stability at each point in time with low predictability over time, or alternatively, and paradoxically, we can think of it as a potentially (i.e. unrealizable) highly ordered situation over time which 'contains' a sequence of very disordered situations. An advantage of this is that people and power groups have somewhat greater difficulty in taking up feudalistic roles in potential structures (if in fact it is possible to do so).

d. *Organisational tensegrity*

There is an unexpected formal analogy between some architectural design constraints and aspects of organisation and network design. Architecture is no longer restricted to simple arches and domes which derive their stability by allowing structural weight to impinge on the compressive continuity of bearing members and protecting the result by occasional tensional reinforcement — an approach which bears considerable resemblance to the conventional hierarchical organisation. Instead of thinking in terms of weight and support, the space enclosed may be conceived as a system of equilibrated omnidirectional stresses.

Such a structure is not supported by the lowest level. It is pulled outward into sphericity by inherent tensional forces which its geometry also serves to restrain. Gravitation is largely irrelevant.

Many parallels can be explored with the organisational development from hierarchies to networks and away from oppressive structures. The value of this is that considerable thought has already been given to the nature, construction and stabilizing forces within the resultant architectural geodesic and tensegrity structures.[32] It may well be that this will provide the necessary clues on how to design some useful organisational networks for those cases where the hierarchical form is no longer appropriate.

Policy Implications

1. *Facilitation of network processes*

It is clear that intra- and inter-organisational networks are growing, multiplying and evolving in response to perceived social problems and possibilities for action. These changes are in large part unplanned (and unfinanced) from any central point and appear to be self-correcting in that 'excessive' development is compensated by the emergence of counteracting networks. Little attention is given to facilitating this growth so that in some cases it may be considered dangerously 'spastic'. Despite this the network of organisations (international, national, and local) of every kind and with every pre-occupation, represents a major unexplored resource. The (synergistic) potential of this network, if its processes were facilitated, is unknown.

Possibilities for facilitating these processes include:
- facilitative (as opposed to obstructive) legislation
- subsidized postal and telephone communications
- creation of facilitative environments where organisations and people can meet and interact informally to catalyze, wherever possible, the emergence of action programmes or formal collaboration
- creation of information systems and devices to facilitate the development of new contacts in response to new issues (e.g. social action 'yellow pages', network maps, on-line intellectual communities, community interaction software packages)
- examination of the significance of the number and reticulation of organisations in a society as a social indicator, both in terms of development and quality of life.

2. *Network organisational strategy*

The elements of the strategic problem at this time include:

- a vast and largely uncomprehended network of perceived problems and problem systems, on which no single body has (or possibly could have) adequate information.
- a vast and fragmented network of conceptual tools and knowledge resources which is not (and possibly could not be) comprehended by any single body.
- a vast and largely uncomprehended network of agencies, organisations, groups and active individuals spanning every conceivable human interest on which no body has (or possibly could or should have) adequate information.

These networks, and others, are not static structures. They are changing rapidly in response to pressures and opportunities perceived in very different parts of the social system. As such they, and component sub-networks, are not controlled or controllable by any single body, if only because the complexity cannot be handled by any single body or group of bodies.

The strategic problem therefore is how to ensure that the appropriate organisational resources emerge, and are adequately supported, in response to emerging pressures and opportunities. But it would seem that this must be achieved *without* organising and planning such organised response — for to the extent that any part of the network is so organised, other parts will develop (and probably should develop) which will favour and implement alternative (and partially conflicting) approaches.

The challenge is therefore to develop the meaning and constraints of what may be termed a network strategy. This is an approach which facilitates or catalyzes (rather than organises) the emergence, growth, development, adaptation and galvanization of organisational networks in response to problem networks, in the light of the values perceived at each particular part of the social system.

3. *Network vocabulary*

Whether amongst academics, policy-makers, administrators, or other practitioners, the frequency with which 'network' is now used is not matched by any increasing facility in distinguishing between types of network. Because clear and simple concepts are lacking, together with the appropriate terms, discussion of such social complexity can only be accomplished, if at all, by the use of extremely cumbersome and lengthy phrases which tend to create more confusion than they eliminate. A vocabulary is required which is adapted to complexity. In the absence of such a vocabulary, debate tends to avoid discussion of issues which emerge from such complexity and concentrates on issues which can be adequately expressed via the existing vocabulary. This creates the illusion that the issues which can be discussed are the most important because of the visibility accorded them by the vocabulary at hand.

There is therefore a real challenge to the social sciences to identify concepts associated with complexity and to locate adequate terms with which to label them. Johan Galtung, has for example, offered suggestions for 'a simple vocabulary, with a minimum of terms as well as for some graphic symbols that can be used to depict various structures, from family relations to international conflict formations, across levels of social organisation.'[22] The author has also suggested a series of terms as an illustration of the possibilities.[33] The development of such a *network vocabulary* would provide a powerful means for objectifying and de-mystifying the complexity of the organisational, problem and conceptual networks by which we are surrounded and within which most of our activity is embedded.

Notes

1. Brian C. Aldrich, 'Relations between organizations, a critical review of the literature', *International Associations*, 24, January 1972, pp. 26–29. Michael Aiken and Gerald Hage, 'Organizational interdependence and intraorganizational structure', *American Sociological Review*, 33, 1968, 6, pp. 912–930. Herman Turk, 'Interorganizational networks in urban society; initial perspective and comparative research', *American Sociological Review*, 35, February 1970, pp. 1–19. Roland L. Warren, 'The interorganizational field as a focus for investigation', *Administrative Science Quarterly*, 12, December 1967, pp. 396–419. M.F. Tuite, M. Radnor and R.K. Chisholm (eds.), *Interorganizational Decision Making*, Chicago, Aldine-Atherton, 1972. E. Litwak and L.F. Hylton, 'Interorganizational analysis, a hypothesis on coordinating agencies', *Administrative Science Quarterly*, 6, March 1962, pp. 397–420. E. Litwak with J. Rothman, 'Towards the theory and practice of coordination between formal organizations', in W.R. Rosengren and M. Lefton (eds.), *Organizations and Clients*, Columbus, Charles E. Merrill, 1970, pp. 137–186. P.E. White and G.J. Vlasak (eds.), *Inter-Organizational Research in Health*, Conference proceedings, National Center for Health Services Research and Development, US Department of Health, Education and Welfare, 1970.
2. William Evan (ed.), *Inter-organizational Relations; selected readings*, London, Penguin, 1976.
3. R. Patrick Doreian, 'Interaction under conditions of crisis; applications of graph theory to international relations', *Peace Research Society: Papers*, XI, Budapest Conference, 1968, pp. 89–107. F. Harary and H. Miller, 'A graph theoretic approach to the analysis of international relations', *Journal of*

Conflict Resolution, 1970, 14, pp. 57–63. Norman J. Schofield, 'A topological model of international relations', (Paper presented at the 8th European Conference of the Peace Research Society (International), London 1971). William M. Vaughn, 'Network analysis of regional subsystems: some applications to the EEC'. (Unpublished paper, St. Thomas University, New Brunswick, 1972.

4. Elise Boulding, 'Network capabilities of transnational religious associations', *International Associations,* 26, 1974, 2, pp. 91–93. Elise Boulding, 'Female alternatives to hierarchical systems, past and present', *International Associations,* 27, 1975, 6–7, pp. 340–346.

5. Diana Crane, 'Transnational networks in basic science', *International Organization,* 25, 3, Summer 1971, pp. 585–601. Diana Crane, *Invisible Colleges; diffusion of knowledge in scientific communities,* Chicago, University of Chicago Press, 1972. Diana Crane, 'The international system as a network; factors affecting the political and social impact of international scientific and professional associations'. (Paper presented at a conference on international scientific and professional associations and the international system, Philadelphia, 1976.)

6. A.J.N. Judge, 'The visualization of the organizational network', *International Associations,* 22, May 1970, pp. 265–268; 'Information systems and interorganizational space', *Annals of the American Academy of Political and Social Science,* 393, January 1971, pp. 47–64; 'The world network of organizations', *International Associations,* 24, January 1972, pp. 18–24; 'Nature of organization in transnational networks', *Journal of Voluntary Action Research,* 1, 3, Summer 1972 (abridged version of paper presented to the convention of the International Studies Association, Dallas, 1972). A.J.N. Judge and Kjell Skelsbaek, 'Bibliography of documents on transnational association networks', in *Yearbook of International Organizations,* Brussels, Union of International Associations, 1974, pp. S 55–73; 'Transnational association networks; selected list of research topics on international nongovernmental organizations', *International Associations,* 24, October 1972, pp. 481–485. A.J. N. Judge, 'Inter-organizational relationships; in search of a new style', in *The Open Society; report of a seminar to reflect on the network of international associations,* Brussels, Union of International Associations, 1973, pp. 115–132.

7. J. Sonquist and T. Koenig, 'Interlocking directorates in top US corporations; a graph theory approach', *Insurgent Sociologist,* 5, 1975, Spring, pp. 196–229. R.J. Mokken and F.N. Stokman, *Invloedsstrukturen van Politieke en Ekonomisch Elites in Nederland,* Amsterdam, Institute of Political Science, Department of Research Methodology, 1971.

8. 'The potential of NGOs in social and economic development; report of a UNITAR Conference, July 1975', *International Associations,* 28, 1976, 2, pp. 95–100.

9. *The potential for environmental action 1976; report to the United Nations Environment Programme,* Nairobi, NGO Environment Liaison Centre, 1976, pp. 40–48 (UNEP Project RB–0303–75–01).

10. A.J.N. Judge, 'Practical problems in using the potential of INGO networks', in *The Future of Transnational Associations; in the perspective of a new world order,* Brussels, Union of International Associations, 1977, (Document 22).

11. Alvin Toffler, 'The USA, the UN, and transnational network', (Extracts from testimony before the Committee on Foreign Relations, 94th Congress 1975), *International Associations,* 27, 1975, 12, pp. 593–599.

12. Arnold Toynbee, *Aspects of Psycho-history: Main Currents in Modern*

Thought, New York, Center for Integrative Education, 1972.
13. J. Clyde Mitchell, *Social Networks in Urban Situations*, Manchester University Press, 1969, p. 2.
14. François Lorrain, *Reseaux sociaux et classifications sociales*, Paris, Hermann, 1975.
15. Scott Boorman, *Outline and Bibliography of Approaches to the Formal Study of Social Networks*, Harvard University, Department of Sociology, 1973 (Fels Discussion Paper, no. 87). H.C. White, *Do Networks Matter?*, Harvard University, Department of Sociology, 1972, p. 35.
16. George Beal et al, *System Linkages among Womens Organizations*, Iowa State University, Department of Sociology and Anthropology, 1967.
17. *Yearbook of World Problems and Human Potential*, Brussels, Union of International Associations and Mankind 2000, 1976.
18. Organizational systems versus network organization, *Transnational Associations*, 29, 1977, 9 and 10.
19. Gerald Holton, 'The roots of complementarity', *Daedalus*, Fall 1970, pp. 1015–1054.
20. Donald Schon, 'What we can know about social change', *The Listener*, 1970.
21. A.J.N. Judge, 'Complexity; its constraints on social innovation', *Transnational Associations*, 29, 1977, 4, pp. 120–125; 5 pp.
22. Johan Galtung, *Structural analysis; vocabulary, graphs and structures as indicators,* Oslo, University of Oslo, 1976 (World Indicators Program, no. 12).
23. International Labour Office, *International Standard Classification of Occupations*, Geneva, ILO, 1969.
24. United Nations, *Standard International Trade Classification*, New York, United Nations, 1961 (and updates).
25. United Nations, *International Standard Industrial Classification of All Economic Activities,* New York, United Nations, 1968 (and updates).
26. World Health Organization, *International Classification of Disease*, Geneva, WHO, 1967.
27. Erich Jantsch, 'Towards interdisciplinarity and transdisciplinarity in education and innovation', *Interdisciplinarity*, Paris, OECD, 1972, pp. 97–121.
28. Ejnar Wahlin, 'A common classification for Swedish research projects', *International Classification*, 1, 1974, 1, pp.21–26.
29. B.M. Kedrov, 'Concerning the synthesis of the sciences', *International Classification*, 1, 1974, 1, pp. 3–11.
30. A.J.N. Judge, 'Wanted: new types of social entity', *International Associations*, 23, March 1971, pp. 148–152 (The role of the potential assocation), pp. 154, 170 (Matrix organization and organizational networks).
31. Johan Galtung, 'Entropy and the general theory of peace', in *Proceedings of the International Peace Research Association*, Assen, Van Gorcum, 1968.
32. R. Buckminster Fuller, *Synergetics; explorations in the geometry of thinking,* New York, Macmillan, 1975.
33. A.J.N. Judge, 'Network-related concepts; a vocabulary adapted to social complexity and social process', in *Les Problèmes du Langage dans la Société Internationale*, Bruxelles, Union des Associations Internationales, 1975, pp. 218–221 (Report of a symposium held in Paris, 1974).
34. M.F. Tuite, M. Radnor and R.K. Chisholm (eds.), *Interorganizational Decision Making*, Chicago, Aldine-Atherton, 1972.

413

CHAPTER NINETEEN

UTILISING THE SYSTEM: A NON-GOVERNMENTAL PERSPECTIVE

Abdul S. Minty

This is a brief account of how the Anti-Apartheid Movement, a non-governmental organisation based in Britain and specifically committed to working for an end to apartheid and colonialism in Southern Africa, works both nationally and internationally in order to secure support for its objectives. It is an example of how a pressure group can use the network of IGOs, INGOs and NGOs to further its purposes and of how other actors respond to such pressures.

To understand its present role and influence it is important to trace the history: it was established in June, 1959 in response to the call of the late Chief Albert Lutuli, President of the African National Congress of South Africa (ANC), and other anti-apartheid leaders who appealed for an international boycott of South African goods and the total isolation of the apartheid regime. The Boycott Movement, as it was then known, was founded as an independent organisation in Britain sponsored by public figures drawn from all walks of life, including the Labour and Liberal Parties, trade unions, churches and the arts. The campaign concentrated on winning support for a consumer boycott and rested on the proposition that international economic and other links with South Africa help to sustain the apartheid regime and should be ended.

Individuals who were opposed to apartheid could engage in personal action by refusing to buy South African products and thus demonstrate their support for the oppressed African, Indian and Coloured people of South Africa. The Boycott Movement did not suggest that a consumer boycott alone could bring the apartheid regime to its knees. For economic measures to make an impact of that kind it needed all Members of the United Nations to adopt a programme of economic sanctions which would need to be implemented strictly by South Africa's major trading partners.

As a result of the controversy surrounding the boycott campaign the issue of apartheid was discussed and debated much more widely than ever before in Britain. The South African Foreign Minister was among the first to argue that the boycott would hurt the African people most and this was also claimed by business and other groups in Britain which had a vested interest in South Africa. However, the Boycott Movement found that its campaign developed rapidly and, in order to focus national action in a concentrated period, decided to organise a one-month intensive campaign during March 1960. On February 28th it was launched at a mass rally of over 20,000 people in Trafalgar Square which was addressed by leading public figures including the leader of the Labour Party, Hugh Gaitskell.

In virtually every town and city throughout Britain there existed a voluntary group to promote the Movement's campaign. The broad national support expressed for the campaign caused serious concern in Pretoria about the potential danger of a growing international boycott movement against apartheid. The fact that there existed so much opposition to South Africa in Britain, its biggest trading partner and largest overseas investor as well as long-standing ally, was particularly serious. Various pro-South African organisations were set up in Britain to counteract the Boycott Movement and existing business organisations in London also began to issue propaganda in defence of South Africa.

Once the British campaign got under way new groups were established in several Scandinavian and other western ~~~~~~~ ~~~~~~~~ ~~

home to millions of people all over the world. It provoked deep international anger and spontaneous demonstrations took place outside
several South African embassies. In Britain the demonstrations continued
for three days and nights and the Embassy decided to keep its doors
locked and the outer metal gates bolted.

The House of Commons expressed its sympathy with the bereaved in
South Africa and similar motions were adopted in other parliaments as
well as at the United Nations. Apartheid could no longer be considered
as a matter 'essentially within the domestic jurisdiction' of South
Africa by the major western governments which had held that view until
then. It is important to recall that 1960 also marked the era of African
decolonisation and the Sharpeville shootings took place in the context
of a wider African revolution.

The massacre and the subsequent reign of terror and brutality
unleashed by the Pretoria regime against its opponents led to the
Boycott Movement changing its name to the Anti-Apartheid Movement:
it was essential to work more systematically and on a comprehensive
scale with a long term perspective because of the seriousness of the
problem. Among the first issues to be taken up by AAM was the supply
of British military equipment to South Africa. The Sharpeville photo-
graphs had clearly shown that British-made Saracen armoured cars
had been used to attack the crowds. Special leaflets calling for an arms
embargo against South Africa were printed. These were distributed at
the Aldermaston march of the Campaign for Nuclear Disarmament in
April 1960, as well as at other similar public events throughout the
year. As the arms embargo campaign developed the Conservative
Government decided to ban the export of weapons designed for
internal use. This was a minor victory but the campaign had to be
intensified to secure a complete embargo on all weapons exports to
South Africa.

The Arms Embargo

Britain was South Africa's major arms supplier and closest military ally.
There was a defence pact between the two countries in the form of the
1955 Simonstown Naval Agreement which specifically provided for
the supply of British naval equipment to the Pretoria regime. Any
campaign which was aimed at reversing this policy and securing an
arms embargo would have to overcome enormous pressures and
problems. It was clear that nothing much could be achieved from
within the Conservative Party which was in large measure sympathetic
to South Africa. Support had to be secured from within the Labour

416

movement in order to influence a future Labour Government, as well as winning much needed public support. The Liberal Party was sympathetic to the African cause as were several church leaders. Thus, the campaign was directed at winning broad public support expressed through resolutions, petitions, meetings and the like. After a long period of consistent campaigning the Liberal and Labour Parties committed themselves to the embargo in early 1963. At a mass AAM rally in Trafalgar Square on 17 March, 1963, the newly elected leader of the Labour Party, Harold Wilson, committed a future Labour Government to the arms embargo but he urged that since the matter was urgent the Conservative Government should 'Act now and stop this bloody traffic in the weapons of oppression'.

AAM had already submitted detailed information to all Members of the United Nations about the need for an international arms embargo. At the same time the matter was taken up bilaterally with those governments which were selling weapons to South Africa.

An interesting and lengthy correspondence developed with the United States of America. AAM made representations via the Embassy in London and soon received a substantive response from the State Department in Washington which drew attention to South Africa's role in the last war and pointed out that it formed part of the western world and was strongly anti-communist. These were some of the reasons why the USA considered it essential to sell military equipment to South Africa. AAM replied to each of the points in detail and concluded by asking whether Washington wished to have South Africa as an ally against communism despite the racist and fascist nature of the Pretoria regime — and if this was the case then the United States of America ought to say so clearly so that the world would know the position. Some weeks later, in the summer of 1963, the State Department informed AAM that it would operate an arms embargo against South Africa as from January 1964 but that all outstanding contracts would be honoured.

On 7th August, 1963, the UN Security Council adopted a resolution which called upon all States to 'cease forthwith the sale and shipment of arms, ammunition of all types and military vehicles to South Africa.' (Resolution 181). Britain and France abstained in the vote and explained that they would not supply South Africa with arms for internal suppression. The decision of the Security Council came about as a result of a number of factors. The most important was that it followed the first Summit Conference of Independent African States which had taken an uncompromisingly strong stand on apartheid.

Secondly, the United Nations Special Committee Against Apartheid, which had been established by the General Assembly that year (following a proposal made by AAM to the United Nations) had just published a report on the rapid build-up of military and police forces in South Africa.

AAM had established close working relations with the UN Special Committee since its inception and was able to co-operate closely on all issues. From time to time AAM would make proposals to the Committee which related to suggestions regarding future United Nations policy on Southern Africa as well as proposals about the working of the Special Committee. For example, almost at the very beginning of the establishment of the Special Committee AAM urged that the Committee should take on an active role by making direct representations to those governments and organisations which were involved in collaborating with South Africa in one way or another. Today the Committee makes direct representations to Governments and also to international and national organisations including sports bodies, trade unions, student groups, church organisations and the like. The Special Committee also organises special seminars on South Africa to which representatives of AAM have been invited together with other similar organisations and these opportunities are also utilised to make specific proposals as well as to raise special issues of international importance such as the arms embargo and the question of investment and trade links with South Africa. Whenever AAM officials have visited New York they have been granted official hearings by the Special Committee and there are also further meetings held with specific sub-committees of the Special Committee. The Chairman of the Special Committee plays a vital role in the work of the Committee and regular contact is maintained with him or her. So far all the Chairmen have been African Ambassadors and their commitment to the anti-apartheid cause is a major factor in making the work of the Committee effective.

As a result of the close relations developed between AAM and various African States, both bilaterally and via the work of the Special Committee and other UN organs dealing with Southern Africa as well as contact made at Commonwealth and other conferences, it has been possible to channel relevant information with policy proposals both to the Organisation of African Unity and the United Nations. It is difficult to assess the precise role and influence of AAM in securing certain decisions but there is no doubt about the valuable contribution made by the information provided by AAM to international organisations and governments. By specialising on a particular question it is possible to secure changes in policy once the information collected is made available in the proper quarters. Such information provided by AAM was received with interest by those governments and organisations which supported the policy and work of the Movement. But governments which were unsympathetic could not altogether ignore AAM because of the wider influence it was able to generate both within Britain and internationally in Africa, Asia and the United Nations.

In Britain, the Labour Party was returned to office in October 1964. Prime Minister Wilson soon announced that a complete embargo would be implemented against South Africa although the Buccaneer aircraft already ordered and awaiting delivery would be supplied. But no new orders would be accepted. As a result France gradually became South Africa's main arms supplier and close military co-operation developed between the two countries. French public opinion was not as well informed about South Africa as British opinion. There were also fewer historical links between the two countries. Various organisations and individuals involved in public action over the Algerian war had stopped being active and it proved difficult to establish an effective anti-apartheid movement. France was also not subject to as much pressure as Britain from its ex-colonies in Africa. Meanwhile South Africa began to establish its own armaments industry with foreign assistance, mainly from its traditional trading partners.

The arms embargo soon became more difficult and complicated to monitor and enforce. The problem was serious because the decisions taken by the traditional arms suppliers did not come about as a result of any deep motivation: it was much more a response to national and international pressure. For example, spare parts for equipment already supplied were not prohibited by the United States of America or Britain; military patents for the production of equipment in South Africa were not banned; international armaments firms began to establish subsidiaries in South Africa without any discouragement or control by their governments. Thus multinationals which had been prevented from exporting arms to South Africa began to set up plants inside South Africa to make them locally. They were circumventing the international arms embargo and when the governments concerned were approached they refused to take action to interfere with this process on the grounds that they did not support a policy of interfering with normal economic relations with South Africa. South African military officials continued to visit high level western military institutions for research and training. It is difficult to organise mass national campaigns on technical questions particularly when the

Government is in fact operating a partial arms embargo.

All the loopholes in the international arms embargo were drawn to the attention of the United Nations regularly both through its committees and via Member States. AAM enjoyed close relations with various Commonwealth Governments and the Commonwealth Conferences provided additional opportunities for raising the question of the arms embargo. At each Conference AAM submitted a memorandum to all Governments and it usually drew attention to the operation of the arms embargo and made proposals for its strict implementation. Many governments in turn approached AAM for specific details about South Africa's defence policy and related matters which would then form the basis of their statements and proposals. This form of cooperation usually continued after the Conferences.

Between 1963 and 1964 the Security Council adopted three resolutions on the arms embargo but the matter was not discussed in the Council again until 1970 following the return of a Conservative Government to power in Britain. The Labour Government had implemented a partial arms embargo during the period 1964—70. The Conservative Party, under the leadership of Edward Heath, put considerable importance on reversing this policy so that South Africa could purchase British equipment for external defence. In May 1970, a month before the British General Election was due, AAM had an opportunity to give evidence to the UN Special Committee on Apartheid in New York. Attention was drawn to Sir Alec Douglas-Home's visit to South Africa in 1968 when he discussed with South African leaders a plan to put the Cape sea route under the protective wing of NATO. AAM expressed its alarm at recent speeches and statements by Conservative leaders which 'not only cover the relaxation of the arms embargo but envisage the extension of the Simonstown Agreement and possible arrangements with NATO to help defend South Africa's so-called interest in the Indian and Atlantic Oceans'. The AAM went on to state that 'it is timely for the Security Council to once again consider the issue of South Africa and the arms embargo and to cover the following loopholes in the embargo'. Among the loopholes mentioned were: military patents, other military know-how and blue-prints, overseas investments in the South African domestic armaments industry, skilled technicians from western countries taking up employment in the domestic armaments industry, the provision of military and police training for South African personnel in other countries, and finally, an end to nuclear co-operation between certain western countries and South Africa.[1]

Following the return to power of a Conservative Government in Britain the Security Council met and adopted Resolution 282 on 23rd July, 1970. The Security Council called upon all States to strengthen the arms embargo:

'(a) By implementing fully the arms embargo against South Africa unconditionally and without reservations whatsoever;
 (b) By withholding supply of all vehicles and equipment for use of the armed forces and paramilitary organisations of South Africa;
 (c) By ceasing supply of spare parts for all vehicles and military equipment used by the armed forces and paramilitary organizations of South Africa;
 (d) By revoking all licences and military patents granted to the South African Government or to South African companies for the manufacture of arms and ammunition, aircraft and naval craft or other military vehicles and by refraining from further granting such licences and patents;
 (e) By prohibiting investment in, or technical assistance for, the manufacture of arms and ammunition, aircraft, naval craft, or other military vehicles;
 (f) By ceasing provision of military training for members of the South African armed forces and all other forms of military co-operation with South Africa.'

Since the Resolution was comprehensive and clear it was inevitable that France, Britain and the United States abstained in the vote.

By this time the situation in Southern Africa had become much more critical for Portugal and South Africa since the armed struggle in the Portuguese colonies was making dramatic progress. Powerful forces in the major western countries were now supporting South Africa's demand that the western powers relax the arms embargo and develop even closer relations with South Africa in order to defend western interests in the region. This tendency caused considerable alarm in Africa and the Organisation of African Unity decided, in 1970, to send a special mission headed by its Chairman, President Kenneth Kaunda of Zambia, to several western capitals. At an earlier meeting of the OAU Council of Ministers in February–March, 1970 a resolution adopted on apartheid stated that 'any form of military and other co-operation with (the) minority regimes constitutes a hostile act against all African States and their peoples'.

The OAU meeting with Prime Minister Heath in October 1970 was tense and it was followed by a visit to Washington which proved to be virtually abortive as a result of an apparent misunderstanding about the timing of a meeting with President Nixon — which in fact did not take place. The meetings in Bonn and Paris were apparently conducted in a much more pleasant atmosphere despite the seriousness of the issue.

The Commonwealth

British relations with African countries were seriously strained as a result of the determination of the Heath Government to resume the sale of arms to South Africa. AAM intensified its national activities and a mass rally was called in Trafalgar Square on 25th October, 1970. Special messages of support were received from all over the world including one from the Indian Prime Minister, Mrs. Gandhi. With the forthcoming Commonwealth Conference in Singapore due in January, 1971, AAM issued a simple Declaration which stated: 'I am totally opposed to the sale of arms to apartheid South Africa.' This Declaration was issued at the end of November in the form of a petition to be presented to the Commonwealth Conference and within seven weeks over 100,000 British people had signed the statement and returned it to AAM. On 7th January they were taken to Singapore by a representative of the Movement to be handed over to the Chairman of the Commonwealth Conference, Premier Lee Kwan Yew.

It is not the normal practice of the Commonwealth to accept petitions and representations critical of Member States. However, the Declaration did not mention any country by name and simply expressed opposition to all arms sales to South Africa. Since the arms embargo was a legitimate issue of international concern it was possible to engage in the campaign in this form and attempt to present the petitions. There was widespread opposition among the Afro/Asian and Caribbean Members of the Commonwealth to Britain's proposed arms sales. Before the Singapore Conference AAM had undertaken a series of visits to most Commonwealth diplomatic missions in London for consultations. It would have been politically difficult for the petitions not to be officially received and the Foreign Minister of Singapore accepted them on behalf of the Chairman of the Conference. This was the first case of its kind in the history of the Commonwealth.

The AAM Declaration was supported officially by the Labour and Liberal Parties, the British Council of Churches, the Trade Union Congress, the United Nations Association and a wide variety of other non-governmental organisations as well as 100 Anglican bishops. Earlier the Archbishop of Canterbury had himself written to Prime Minister Heath expressing his 'disquiet'.

Because of the uncompromising position taken by the Heath Government there was the real likelihood that the Commonwealth itself would not survive after the Singapore meeting. This danger led to even greater support for the arms Declaration and a special AAM public meeting held in London on 18th January, timed to coincide with the eve of the arms discussion at Singapore, sent a cable to Prime Minister Heath urging him to heed British and Commonwealth opinion and abandon arms sales to South Africa.

Several African and Asian countries had already stated that a British decision to reverse the embargo could lead to the end of the Commonwealth and Canadian Prime Minister Trudeau stated on the eve of the conference that a chain reaction could carry Canada with it. At the Conference, when the item was reached, Heads of Delegations dispensed with their advisers and assistants and discussed the issue of two full days.

Finally it was announced that an eight nation study group would be established to investigate the security of the maritime trade routes in the South Atlantic and the Indian Oceans. This was a compromise whereby Britain was expected to do nothing until the group had presented its report. However, within weeks the British Government announced that it would supply South Africa with seven Wasp helicopters due to its legal obligations under the Simonstown Agreement. Nigeria immediately withdrew from the study group as did several other members and the group never met.

The Commonwealth crisis showed how much tension could be generated on the question of arms sales to South Africa. The experience at the Commonwealth Conference in Singapore and at other international governmental conferences is that if specific issues relating to Southern Africa are to be raised it is important to be able to provide precise and reliable information. Governments often do not have much of the available information at hand. Information also has to be interpreted and presented in a meaningful way so that Government leaders who are always hard pressed for time are not required to read through unnecessary detail.

The fact that AAM was able to mobilise widespread support inside Britain for an end to arms sales made it possible for it to make representations to other governments on this subject with added credibility. Also, the level of domestic opposition in Britain to arms sales made it easier for certain Commonwealth leaders to take up the issue with increased vigour. The relationship between domestic pressure and international action has been very direct on the arms issue as with other campaigns of a similar nature. It is a two-way process in that that adverse reaction of Commonwealth leaders to the original intention of the Heath Government to sell arms itself helped to strengthen the domestic campaign within Britain.

It can well be asked whether all this activity is useful since the Heath Government in fact supplied seven Wasp helicopters despite domestic and international pressure — and the Commonwealth remained intact. There is no doubt that the campaigns on the subject of arms sales helped to focus attention on South Africa and demonstrated the considerable opposition to apartheid which existed in Britain and the Commonwealth. Secondly, it is likely that had there been no controversy surrounding the policy of the Conservative Government in 1970 it would probably have sold even more arms to South Africa and developed closer military ties with the Pretoria regime. That was certainly its declared intention, announced by Premier Heath upon winning the general election in May 1970.

The role of the Commonwealth in relation to Southern Africa has often been underrated. There is also a widespread view that the Commonwealth is merely the last vestige of the British Empire and that it is not an effective intergovernmental organisation. But judgement as to its usefulness depends almost entirely upon what expectations there are of such an informal organisation. It is unique in that virtually all its Conferences are in fact attended by most Heads of Governments so that it is in effect a special international Summit Meeting. The United Nations and the Organisation of African Unity are both very important organisations in relation to Southern Africa but the Commonwealth provides a special opportunity to exert direct influence on Britain and other countries in relation to developments in Southern Africa.

It is instructive to examine the record of the Commonwealth in relation to Southern Africa. Soon after Sharpeville, in 1961, a Commonwealth Conference took place in London. Prior to that AAM lobbied all Members over several months to seek support for the exclusion of South Africa from the Commonwealth. Within Britain support for this policy was obtained by AAM from the Labour and Liberal Parties as well as several major trade unions. When the Conference opened there was a 72 hour vigil (to mark the 72 killed at Sharpeville and Langa) organised by AAM and leading public figures joined the demonstration. It achieved considerable publicity and several Heads of Governments agreed to meet representatives of AAM. The South African Prime Minister, who attended the Conference, insisted that the Commonwealth should not discuss South Africa's domestic policies but since the majority of Commonwealth Members would not accept this position there was deadlock. Britain was not in favour of embarrassing South Africa and tried to suggest some compromise but the Afro-Asian Governments would not retract their position AAM wanted the apartheid issue discussed by the Commonwealth and also urged that South Africa be excluded from it. This created a very difficult situation for the Commonwealth which had never excluded a Member before. On the eve of the Conference, when all Commonwealth leaders had arrived in London, *The Observer* newspaper carried a long article by Dr. Julius Nyerere of Tanganyika. In it he stated that if South Africa was still a Member of the Commonwealth when Tanganyika achieved independence at the end of 1961 then his country would not apply for membership of the Commonwealth. This sealed the issue and it became highly probable that South Africa could no longer remain in the Commonwealth. Thus, when it declared itself a Republic in May 1961 the Pretoria regime did not bother to apply for membership. This was the first major blow to South Africa's external relations. Since then, the question of apartheid has been discussed at virtually every Commonwealth Conference either directly or indirectly over issues such as Rhodesia.

Following the seizure of independence by the Smith regime in Salisbury in November 1965 every Commonwealth Conference has given priority to that problem. The British Government made several attempts to reach a settlement with Ian Smith and the fact that no sell-out was possible is in all probability largely due to Commonwealth pressures. The Commonwealth connection has been used very astutely by African, Asian and Caribbean Heads of Governments to impress upon Britain the danger of handing over power to a minority regime without taking adequate account of the majority African population. AAM has been able to lobby all Commonwealth Conferences since 1960 since most of them in the early years took place in London. Later when they were held in Singapore, Ottawa and Jamaica respectively it was possible to send a representative to those countries. The Jamaica Conference in April, 1975 took the unprecedented step of inviting representatives of the African people of Rhodesia to take part in its proceedings when discussing that subject.

These developments signify the fundamental transformation of the British Commonwealth into the Commonwealth where Britain and the older members no longer enjoy dominant influence.

The Arms Embargo during the 1970's

The Conservative Government did not supply any other items of major combat equipment to South Africa besides the Wasp helicopters. However the loopholes remained and nothing was done to strengthen the embargo.

Meanwhile the Labour Party in opposition had adopted a much stronger policy on Southern Africa and the election manifesto contained a pledge to implement the arms embargo against South Africa. In 1974 Labour was returned to power once again and it successfully increased its majority in the House of Commons in a further election in October. Within days of its victory the Royal Navy was participating in joint naval exercises with the South African navy. This was the second such exercise that year and both with a Labour Party in power. AAM organised a national protest campaign and obtained considerable support from within the Parliamentary Labour Party as well as the National Executive of the Labour Party. There was sharp domestic and international controversy and the Foreign Secretary, James Callaghan, responded to the protests by promising to review the Simonstown Agreement. By the end of 1974 it was announced that Britain had decided to terminate the Simonstown Agreement. This was a considerable victory for the anti-apartheid lobby but whilst it ruled out future joint exercises between the two navies it did not mean that British warships would not call at South African ports. Upon returning to power in 1974 the Labour Government also announced that it would implement the arms embargo strictly. This policy was warmly welcomed at the Kingston Commonwealth Conference in April, 1975.

At the end of 1975 an employee of Marconi Ltd. made public his decision not to work on a defence contract for South Africa which was for the supply of a tropospheric communications system. AAM investigations revealed that contracts of this type could be placed since the relevant regulations in the Export of Goods (Control) Order 1970 permitted it. The Order provides that certain goods listed in Schedule 1 are prohibited for export but may be sent to any 'port or destination in the Commonwealth, the Republic of Ireland, the Republic of South Africa or the United States of America'. It is remarkable that South Africa is accorded a special status which is apparently denied to most western European countries including members of NATO. It was difficult to organise a major campaign on this issue because of the claim by Marconi and the Government that the equipment was in fact for civilian use even though ordered by the South African Armaments Board. If there had been a Commonwealth conference taking place shortly or some other major meeting with British and African leaders it is likely that the Labour Government would have banned the export of this equipment. As it is the initial pressures of AAM led to the Government placing the tropospheric system under licensing control in April, 1976. This meant that it could no longer be exported without Government approval. In October that year it was granted a licence on the basis that it was not an item which fell within the British arms embargo. Since then AAM representations to the Government about possible similar contracts in the future have produced the response that the Government would not disclose such confidential information but that AAM should be assured that the arms embargo will be implemented. The problem arises not so much because the Government opposes the embargo as a matter of policy but because of the way in which it interprets and implements that embargo. In 1976 it also became known that a firm in the Channel Islands had supplied South Africa with engines for its Centurian tanks. This was a clear breach of the embargo and Prime Minister Wilson condemned it. There was a prosecution and the firm concerned was fined by the court. These are only some examples of violations of the arms embargo.

Examples such as these have to be followed up and although campaigns result in considerable success it is not always possible to stop all the deals. What is crucial is that the matter should be kept under constant surveillance with prompt action. In matters of defence it is often difficult to obtain all the information yet AAM had been able to reveal a large number of loopholes in the British embargo during 1970.

A Mandatory Embargo

There have been two recent attempts in the Security Council to adopt a resolution making the arms embargo against South Africa mandatory under Chapter VII of the UN Charter. They were both tabled in debates about Namibia. The first was in June 1975 and the second in October 1976 — on both occasions the three permanent western members, Britain, France and the United States of America, used the Triple Veto. They hold the view that the situation in Namibia and South Africa's illegal occupation of that territory do not amount to a threat to international peace within the meaning of Chapter VII of the

Charter. It is difficult to accept that if Smith's UDI in 1965 was considered by Britain to amount to a threat to world peace, then the increasingly dangerous situation in Namibia in 1976 is less of a threat. Of course the problem can best be understood in the context of the 'no confrontation with South Africa' policy of the major western governments.

In conclusion, it needs to be pointed out that the AAM is essentially a British organisation and none of its six full-time staff concentrates on international work alone. AAM is financed by its members and donations from supporters including grants made sometimes by organisations such as the World Council of Churches. The Movement relies heavily on volunteer assistance and it is therefore remarkable that it has been able to work consistently on Southern African issues since its inception in 1959. AAM is a membership organisation based in Britain. It has a National Committee composed of members elected by the Annual Conference of members and representatives of various organisations (numbering over sixty at present) including representatives of African liberation movements, British trade unions, churches, student groups and representatives of over 40 local AAM committees throughout Britain. The National Committee is the policy making body of AAM and it elects the officers and an Executive Committee which meets monthly and is responsible for the day to day work of the Movement. The National Committee meets quarterly.

Although this account concentrates almost exclusively on the arms campaign AAM also works on a large number of other issues. For example, for two years prior to the Olympic Conference in Baden-Baden, Germany in 1963, AAM made representations to all Olympic bodies throughout the world and sent a representative to Germany to work for South Africa's exclusion from the Olympics. South Africa was suspended in 1963. This was the first major victory in the field of sport. Later similar action was taken by the international football organisation, FIFA. Once the process was started it was taken up in virtually all fields of sport. In cases such as cricket and rugby where the international organisations were much more sympathetic to South Africa, national demonstrations involving thousands of people in Britain, Australia, New Zealand and Ireland led to their eventual exclusion or put a stop to their overseas tours.

The AAM has also worked closely with non-governmental organisations such as Amnesty International. In this case it tries to ensure that they have all the relevant information about political prisoners in Southern Africa and also to consider and organise joint action wherever possible. The World Council of Churches is another organisation with which close relations are maintained so that its Programme to Combat Racism is more effective. AAM officials take part in some WCC conferences and send information regularly to its office in Geneva.

From time to time when appropriate contact is also made with the UN specialised agencies such as the WHO, ILO, UNESCO, or FAO on specific issues relating to Southern Africa. Letters containing proposals are sent to the respective Director-Generals or suggestions are channelled through the UN Special Committee Against Apartheid.

If international work is done on a comprehensive scale to cover all organisations which may be relevant to Southern Africa it could take up enormous resources and time. It is impossible to do that for a small voluntary non-governmental organisation. The approach is much more to work on specific *issues* which are considered to be important and then to follow them up both nationally and internationally at various levels.

The AAM is not simply a lobby organisation which makes representations to governments and organisations. It is basically a public campaigning organisation committed to supporting the African freedom struggle in Southern Africa and aims to win the widest possible solidarity with that struggle. By working for international disengagement from South Africa and furthering the boycott move-ment it acts in support of the oppressed majority in Southern Africa — it is by no means an easy task to accomplish in those western countries which have long historical, economic, cultural and political ties with the white population of South Africa. The international economic stake in the apartheid system is substantial and it tends automatically to act in defence of the status quo in South Africa. Ultimately, freedom in Southern Africa will only be achieved by the oppressed people themselves but international action in support of that struggle can make it a little less difficult.

Notes

1. For full text see UN Unit on APARTHEID, Notes and Documents, No. 17/70 May 1970, pp. 1—8. The UN Special Committee Against Apartheid and the UN Unit publish documents and reports which cover the work of various NGOs. The British AAM publishes its own monthly *Anti-Apartheid News*.

CHAPTER TWENTY

INTERNATIONAL ORGANISATION IN WORLD SOCIETY
A.J.R. Groom

The previous chapters of this part of the book have been eclectic. This chapter will follow the same pattern and suggest some implications for international organisation of the emergence of a tantalisingly incomplete yet suggestive conceptual framework. The development of International Relations as an academic discipline will be related to the study of international organisation and institutions. In particular, the 'world society', 'cobweb model', 'transnational', 'non-state-centric conceptual framework', as variously it has been called, will be examined and this will raise issues concerning the level and unit of analysis, the unity of the social sciences, theories of decision-making and change and the categorisation of substantive questions. There follows a consideration of these issues in the light of the different approaches to international organisation which form the central section and *raison d'être* of this volume. Finally, a brief mention is made of some modes of institutionalisation which are not analysed elsewhere in this volume.

International Relations and International Organisation
The study of International Organisation, which forms part of the broader field of International Relations, was initially created as an academic subject by diplomatic historians and international lawyers. It is not surprising that they employed their previous conceptual frameworks and methodology in studying the new field. Thus the study of international organisation and institutions was, for a long time, characterised by a legal analysis of constitutional documents and an historical narrative of

the activities of the major institutions. The analytical framework of the latter was the traditional power politics approach of the diplomatic historian with an occasional exhortary dash of legalism or idealism. States, however, were seen as clearly the major actors and IGOs the principal source of their activities in the institutional world. Thus the study of institutions was chiefly of the 'high politics' activities of bodies such as the League of Nations rather than functional IGOs such as the Universal Postal Union or INGOs such as the International Committee of the Red Cross. This is hardly surprising since International Relations too developed as a discipline concerned with the analysis of 'high politics' relationships such as diplomatic, political, colonial, security and, occasionally, economic relations between states. The state was the unit of analysis and power politics was the question of substantive interest. Indeed, this was so virtually by definition. 'International Relations' struggled to free itself as a separate discipline from 'Political Science' on the grounds that relations between individuals, groups and the government within a polity were normally within the framework of a generally accepted consensus which legitimised a central authority and so gave it both the means and the duty to lay down and to enforce law and order whereas between states there was dissensus, anarchy and no central authority. In particular, since international society had as its members sovereign and equal states there could be no central authority unless it was created by states. Moreover, since there was no central authority there could be no monopoly of organised force. In short, there were no means of deciding upon and enforcing law and order comparable to the institutions of domestic society. Furthermore, law and order could not be maintained through consensus because inter-state relations were characterised by power politics. Thus there was a fundamental difference between intra- and inter-state relations sufficient to justify a disciplinary boundary. Gradually, however, the view began to be voiced that such dissensus and anarchy in inter-state relations need not be so and, in fact, are not entirely so and, what is more, should not be so.[1] The progressive rationalists to whom reference was made in a previous chapter and their successors argued that it need not be so, empirical research documented the extent to which it was not so in reality and the idealists argued that things should therefore be changed.

Academic interest then widened from a concern with traditional 'high politics' to the analysis of all manner of inter-state relations, that is, it concerned itself with inter-state relations in all domains and not just in 'high politics' and with non-power relations as well as with power politics. In part this was because power politics can characterise the decision-making process in any functional dimension and thereby make it a potential high politics question and in part it reflected the view that to understand power politics it was also necessary to study legitimised politics and the factors likely to give rise to the change of one into the other. Moreover, legitimised relationships began to be considered, by some at least, as significant in themselves, both quantitatively and qualitatively, since they provided the very stuff of international behaviour in its everyday form. If the goal was to understand the totality of inter-state relations then there was no justification in ignoring normal behaviour. Power politics were not forgotten, but they only constituted part of the whole, albeit a highly important part, if only because of its consequences. The notion of the state as the basic unit of analysis was, however, common to both those who restricted themselves to power political relationships and to those whose horizons extended to non-power relationships or legitimised politics.

This broadening of approach and the change of emphasis that the study of both power and legitimised relations between states entailed are of considerable significance for the importance given to international institutions. In inter-state power politics international institutions are essentially a convenient form through which the great Powers can express, and perhaps implement, their will. The institutional framework does not influence that will to any significant extent nor is there any derogation of great Power sovereignty. Functional organisations are considered of little moment since they have no great relevance for traditional high politics and, in any case, the state remains an effective gatekeeper for their activities. Moreover, international organisation at the high politics level is not dependent on institutions such as the United Nations since the great Powers are able to handle their relationships informally or through traditional diplomatic channels and, of course, they can make their writ run in their own spheres of influence by time-honoured methods. However, it is a different question when the subject matter is broadened to include non-power relations, for then institutions play a greater and more independent role. International secretariats, for example, can enhance their role beyond administrative tasks and contribute significantly to the decision-making process for their various spheres of activity. Sovereignty may be eroded through task expansion and spillover and may give rise to a network of intergovernmental functional systems with their attendant organisations, such as WHO, owing as much to the functional imperative as to the political will of governments. The everyday aspects of international integration in a variety of functional dimensions are now seen as a central interest and so are their mode of organisation and institutional forms. Nevertheless, the basic unit of analysis is still the state, since its high politics role and gatekeeping function remain important.

The domain of legitimised politics has no obvious boundary since 'low politics' activities may exist independently of the state and operate trans-nationally. Thus the state as the unit of analysis came to be questioned and not only in matters of low politics. Non-state actors, be they national liberation movements such as the Palestinians, multinational corporations such as Lockheed, or a body such as the World Council of Churches, may play a role in high politics that state actors can neither control nor ignore. Significantly, one of the examples cited is itself formally constituted as an international institution. The level of analysis problem thus became more acutre and reflected itself in doubts concern-in the appropriateness of the state as the unit of analysis.

These changes in the study of International Relations — the interest in legitimised relationships and the questioning of the state as the inevitable unit of analysis — occurred at the same time as behaviouralism was making its mark in all the social sciences, thereby giving an element of unity to social science. Behaviouralism is much more than a fetish for quantification for its own sake. While rigour in observation and analysis are the hallmarks of the behavioural approach it is also characterised by a degree of conceptual innovation. The attempt to be strict in the application of scientific method united those of the behavioural per-suasion in different social sciences and the cross-fertilisation of hypotheses and methodologies — together with the migration of researchers and students between the different disciplines — promoted an awareness of the unifying elements in social science as a whole. Initially behaviouralists gave a great deal of attention to the individual as actor (they were reacting to the formal study of formal institutions). But the realisation that individuals are role enactors, and that role variables themselves are subject to structural constraints all of which are related to a particular input at a particular time, caused the pendulum to swing back so that the behavioural implications of formal and informal institutions were given greater attention. Since these considerations were evident in most of the social sciences 'behaviouralism' provided an element in common which facilitated unity. In International Relations it led some scholars to dispense with the state-as-actor model and concentrate upon decision-making at the micro-level. Others experimented with notions of 'world society' encompassing high and low politics, varied levels of analysis and a new unit of analysis — system. Of course, the state-as-actor remained of great interest, but its axiomatic use as a unit of analysis was questioned. Moreover, the realisation grew that not only were there a great many actors other than states, but that these actors were also engaged in the same type of activities as state authorities both structurally, in that the processes of decision-making were comparable, and also substantively as, for example, in the field of development. Thus International Relations became much more problem oriented rather than unit, that is, state oriented and this change in orientation led scholars to trespass into other fields since problems such as conflict or development cannot easily be confined to any one of the social sciences. 'World society', 'cobweb model', 'transnationalism', 'non-state centric model', have all been used to describe this phenomenon. An outline of the 'world society' approach and an examination of some of its implications for international institutions and organisations is the next task.

The 'World Society' approach in comparison with the traditional approach

What is meant by 'world society'? It most emphatically does not mean a world government on the model of governments in domestic society. However, a wide variety of interpretations can be found and in some cases the only element in common is a sense of dissatisfaction with the traditional state-centric model of International Relations. The interpretation of 'world society' which follows is, therefore, in no sense based on a consensus.[2] The essential elements of the approach can be brought out by contrasting it with the traditional approach in such fundamental aspects as the level of analysis problem.[3] The problem arises from the observation that the same phenomena have differing significances when considered from various levels of analysis. For example, war has been attributed to the nature of man, to the domestic form of states and to the anarchic inter-state system to give but three hypotheses drawn from different levels of analysis. The student of International Relations traditionally would concern himself with analysing the phenomenon of war — one of his central preoccupations — in its manifestation in the sphere of inter-state relations. He might also consider the proposition that states with particular forms of government, say liberal democracy, are more or less prone to be involved in particular types of war, but not without a sense of guilt from trespassing on the preserve of the political scientist. Yet, what if, as some assert, war has its origin in the nature of man? Surely in such circumstances the appropriate level of analysis would be the individual, although there would be ramifications of findings at this level for other levels of analysis. If this theory of the cause of war is correct then the study of war would be severely handicapped for those who took the state as the unit of analysis and restricted themselves to the inter-state system. Even if this hypothesis of the cause of war is not espoused it is clear that many phenomena of great importance at the interstate level are intimately linked to other levels of analysis. The world society approach, while acknowledging that changing levels of analysis implies the necessity of estabishing rules for the transfer of findings from one level to another, asserts that social phenomena cannot be studied in their entirety unless there is a willingness to change levels of analysis, to look at several different levels at the same time and to conceive of relationships across levels. The phenomenon of war and, more generally, of conflict, encompasses many different levels of analysis. The same holds for many of the other phenomena which are of interest to the International Relations scholar. In such cases there is likely to be no one level of anlysis fixed in advance that is appropriate and, equally, by implication, there can be no determination *a priori* of any one unit of analysis. By confining an analysis to the inter-state level it is possible to adopt the state as unit of analysis, but if substantive issues involve changing the levels of analysis and, in addition, if there are many non-state actors, such as the Churches or multinational corporations, active and important on the world scene then the appropriate unit of analysis is no longer restricted to the state, although the state is still an actor. How does this affect the study of international organisation and institutions and what is the appropriate unit of analysis?

In the traditional approach to the study of International Relations international organisation and institutions are seen as being the creation of states designed to further the interests of states both collectively and individually. IGOs have therefore been given the most attention by practitioners and academics alike. However, some IGOs make provision for a consultative role for non-state actors and institutions as, for example, in Article 71 of the UN Charter, and there is a notable and isolated deviation from the usual strict division between IGOs and INGOs in the tripartite structure of the ILO. Nevertheless, INGOs are usually ignored since, although they operate internationally, they are not state actors and therefore fall between the national and inter-state levels of analysis. The study of international organisation and institutions is therefore lop-sided. The world society approach should correct this since it is not tied to the state as a unit of analysis.

In the world society approach the unit of analysis is a system, that is, a set of patterned interactions. The observer, given his interests, seeks to identify the actors related to this field of enquiry and to map and analyse the transactions between these actors. If the observer is a general systems theorist he will assume that all life is organised on systems lines, whether it is so perceived or not, and that such systems exhibit specific properties. His task will then be to give an empirical definition of these objective systems of behaviour and to reveal their inherent properties. On the other hand, if he is a systems analyst he will merely be concerned with the organisation of data around a construct of system in the hope that it will further his purpose. In this case he is giving meaning to data rather than revealing a pre-existing law.[4] Such a system of transactions may include the widest diversity of actors from the Security Council of the United Nations to the organiser of a gang of mercenaries.

If, however, academic interests are followed without heed to the level of analysis or the hierarchical standing of the actors and if, as a result of breaking away from the confines of the traditional approach concerns are now more varied, are there any boundaries to the study of world society? The answer to this question is 'no' twice over: 'no' in the sense that all the social sciences are involved, not in an interdisciplinary way in which an economist, for example, would offer his contribution as a member of that discipline, but in an adisciplinary way in which the economic aspect of a particular problem would be investigated to the extent to which it is thought by the researcher to be relevant to the questions being asked; the answer is equally 'no' in that there is *a priori* no level of analysis that can be excluded. In the world society approach social science, and indeed science, once again finds the unity that it lost during the nineteenth century. Methodologically unity comes from behaviouralism and conceptually it is brought about through systems thinking.[5] The image of the world is not necessarily and axiomatically hierarchical, with a hierarchy based on power and with states the dominant actors as in the traditional approach. Rather it is conceptualised as a cobweb of systems of transactions from all manner of functional dimensions, with a diversity of actors, and a variety of types of relationships from the conflictual to the legitimised, both within and between systems, some of which may indeed be hierarchically organised.

In such a conceptualisation the study of international organisation and institutions clearly has a different significance from that of the traditional approach. Any set of patterned interactions implies an element of organisation, otherwise the pattern could not be sustained.

However, it is the institutional forms that differ most in the world society approach: these forms include not only IGOs and INGOs but BINGOs and a host of other NGOs. In short, the study of international institutions as part of the discipline of International Relations transforms itself into the study of the purpose, performance and effect of institutional forms associated with an actual or putative system of transactions. It is not merely the study of the necessarily minor role international institutions play in facilitating and influencing, modestly, inter-state power politics as in the UN Security Council or the rather more significant forum and service roles of the Specialised Agencies.[6] The arguments justifying the study of such institutions have been given elsewhere and they are equally applicable in the world society model, although the range and diversity of institutional forms in the latter is daunting. But there is more to it than this. International institutions are, like any other institution, mediators of change. Some facilitate change, while others do not. Since change is a seemingly inevitable part of the human lot and its processes are fraught with significance then the impact of institutional forms on these processes of change is a fundamental aspect of social science. The world society approach brings this out. For example, it is becoming evident at many levels of social organisation, whether it be large schools, the military-industrial complex or the UN network of organisations, that some institutional forms give rise to the pursuit of institutional values at the expense of the original purpose for which the institution was established or of wider human values. This may in its turn create frustration and give rise to conflict in a clash between human and institutional values. Organisational needs generated by a system of transactions come first, but they can be thwarted by the subsequent growth of independent institutional values as when the Palestinians, for example, were shut out of the decision-making process in the Middle East conflict, in part because they did not constitute a state. Only after a tragic wave of 'terrorism' were they allowed a greater degree of participation. Too often institutions do not fulfill the needs for which they were created. By concentrating on systems of transactions the world society approach alerts us to such problems not only at the inter-state level but in many and varying contexts. Institutions are not only the instruments for the imposition of law and order, as they were conceived in the early days of the study of International Relations, they are also the meeting point of present values and emerging future needs. The extent to which means are found to adjust present values to changing future needs determines the likelihood and degree of conflict and institutions may have either a supportive or aggravating role in this process. This problem is universal and although the world society approach suggests that its conception should not be subject to boundaries of level of analysis or discipline the world society approach, and with it the study of organisation and institutions, is not without its sub-divisions.

The bases of the world society concept

The elements of the world society concept can be classified in two ways: the first group are essentially structural or to do with processes while the second are concerned with substantive issues. The notion of system is crucial in that any social scientist must assume that there is some degree of regularity in human behaviour. Without such regularity there can be no learning from the past, no meaningful analysis of the present other than an idiosyncratic description and no possibility of using probabilistic theory for the purposes of planning and prediction. Without regularity in behavioural patterns we can only chronicle 'one damn thing after another'. However, if we assume a degree of regularity or patterns of behaviour then the notion of system is useful in enabling their identification. Regularity, behavioural patterns, systems of transactions all imply a degree of organisation, structure and attendent institutional forms. The idea of systems needs, that is, what is required for the system and its institutional forms to survive, is a helpful analytical device but it has the danger of survival being imputed as a goal. In the world society approach there is no such commitment and systems needs are merely measuring rods to estimate the likelihood of or to state the requirements for survival or pattern maintenance; they are not a statement of desiderata. Throughout the approach there is an awareness of change and consequently this gives rise to an analysis of unit response to the environment and particularly of the extent to which role moulds behaviour. The interaction of role, structure and unit with an imput is seen in terms of a cybernetic process.

At the level of organisation there is a simple model or life cycle which consists of a patterned interaction of input, process, output and feedback. It is the model Karl Deutsch has used in his seminal *The Nerves of Government*.[7] It implies that any system, if it is to exhibit any pattern and therefore organisation, even if it changes over time, must be able to react to the environment, to integrate its sub-units and to have self-knowledge in order to be able to set goals. Such goals need be neither homeostatic, that is pattern-maintaining as with the structural-functionalists, nor teleological, as with the Marxists, but rather they are open-ended and changing as patterns are established, evolve, fade away or collapse. The institutional fulfillment of these functions is, however, anything but simple and it can perhaps best be related to the focii of the world society approach. How then does the world society approach break down into constituent parts?

The world society approach discards discipline, methodology and level of analysis as the fundamental organising notions for the social sciences. The sub-divisions of social science are, in this view, related to the hypotheses being subjected to empirical examination. The hypothesis itself suggests those empirical data which are appropriate. The identification of the parties involved and the specification of their relationships is crucial as an organising factor and fraught with difficulty in its implementation, for there is the danger of finding only more or less what the operationalisation of the hypothesis permits. If a bad choice is made then there is little that can be done other than starting again. It is even difficult to ascertain when a bad choice has been made since there are no objective criteria for judgement. Hence feedback is crucial for if it indicates that the hypothesis being examined or the methodology being utilised, in other words the whole project, does not appear to be very useful or is being improperly conducted then there are grounds for reconsideration. This is a formidable challenge for apart from the human and practical investment in a project there is a tendency to find conditions which fulfill hypotheses rather than those which falsify them. Negative feedback or dissonance is not easily perceived and is still less readily acted upon. Nevertheless, the hypothesis does provide a guide to which parts of world society are central to the research and which are not. It is not necessary to study everything about everything, but only that which seems relevant to the hypothesis. In this way students of world society will be drawn through their inclinations (or paymasters) to particular aspects and these interest areas, although closely related, provide general focii for the study of world society analogous to those of discipline, methodology or level.

Decision-making is common to all aspects of social science. Social science is about behaviour and behaviour implies choice, that is, decision-making. Politics, too, is about decision-making, that is, the formulation and articulation of demands, the consideration of alternative ways of responding to demands, the response itself and the assessment of feedback: it is about the setting of goals, the allocation of means and the assessment of the consequences of the means-ends relationship, in short, it is about values. Thus politics exists in every relationship, for example, between husband and wife, members of the Mothers Union or the UN Security Council. A central area of concern in social science is therefore the nature of politics or the decision-making process whatever the formal standing of the actors. Any transaction can be situated on a spectrum which runs from power politics to legitimised politics. Power politics occur when the behaviour of an actor is decided by criteria which are not acceptable to it or in situations in which it is impeded by structural factors from knowledge of possibilities that would otherwise be open to it (structural violence), while legitimised politics is a situation in which the behaviour of an actor is determined by criteria fully acceptable to it and in which it has 'perfect knowledge'. Clearly these are ideal types neither of which exist in practice: they are merely the end points of a spectrum which are never reached. The manner in which and the reasons why a relationship moves between the poles of the spectrum giving a mix of power and legitimacy is fundamental to an understanding of behaviour in any systemic setting.

The focus on decision-making points to a second factor common to all the social sciences — response to change — since the need for decision-making arises precisely because of change. Change is endemic in world society and it occurs because stimuli vary both endogenously and exogenously at all levels and in every facet of the social and natural environment. No individual or group has the same experience and this gives rise to differing stimuli since one man's reaction is another man's stimulus and the process thus becomes self-perpetuating. Politics is about response to change: in power politics the burden of adjustment is thrust upon the environment (including other actors), in legitimised politics adjustment takes place, while collapse is always possible either through the choice of inappropriate policies, insufficient means, insufficient knowledge or the failure to recognise the change in the environment.[8] Since change is endemic and decision-making (that is politics) is universal the scope of the study of world society is hardly limited even if the decision-making process in response to change does point to its essence. Rather we must look to notions of authority, legitimacy, participation, conflict, integration, development, security and identity as nodal points around which the study of world society can be organised.

This list is arbitrary but it seems to reflect some of the present major concerns of those who are adopting a world society approach. The list will vary over time in response to the changing environment although this particular list does appear to cover some basic long term questions which, even though they may not be eternal, are more than a passing fancy. These nodal points are neither a complete list nor are they always clearly differentiated one from the other. A brief mention of each may give a flavour of the world society framework sufficient to consider some of its implications for institutionalisation.

Authority appears to be under strain throughout world society. Authority can be either ascribed, achieved or legitimised. Only in the latter case, that is, when it is legitimised, is it acceptable. Legally ordained hierarchical authority — whether ascribed, traditional, achieved or bureaucratic — without sociological legitimisation by the other actors in the system soon degenerates into coercion or structural violence. Yet legitimised authority is proving harder to establish. Actors want the benefits of organisation but they are loath to accept differentiation, whether between child and parent, student and professor, male and female, management and labour or developing and developed countries. Differentiation seems to be acceptable only when it proves to be both efficient and just and when there is a full sense of participation despite the differentiation. The authority problem is thus ultimately concerned with notions of legitimacy and participation.[9] But it is not only a question of reactions to unacceptable forms and processes of differentiation, the authority structures also serve as a scape goat for the frustrations of alienation and stress. Individuals are being called upon to play a wide variety of roles and to change them with great frequency. *Gesellschaften* may be meritocratic, rational, efficient and responsive to change, but they lack the security, both psychological and sociological, of *Gemeinschaften*. These thoughts have, of course, considerable ramifications for the study of institutions. Authority structures are of necessity institutionalised, either informally or formally, so that if they are to avoid the revolt against authority they must seek to enhance the sense of participation of those connected with their endeavours and they must develop their *'Gemeinschaft'* qualities. Mitrany has addressed this question:

'The problem, broadly speaking, is to find an arrangement which would show a measurable and acceptable relation between authority and responsibility, which would exclude no participant arbitrarily from a share in authority, while bringing that share into relation not to sheer power but to the weight of responsibility carried by the several members. The issue is not wholly avoided in a functional organisation but it is sufficiently mitigated to be no longer numbly obstructive, because any transfer of authority would be limited in scope and degree to the purpose in hand . . . Instead of the legal

441

fiction of equality there would thus be an evident and factual inequality in certain spheres, springing from real differences in capacity and interest with regard to some specific function but also limited to that function. It would neither trespass upon fundamental principles nor offend against sentiments of national differences. The position of inferiority would be factual and partial and it would be changeable.'[10]

Another nodal point in the study of world society is conflict. Conflict is endemic in the sense that separate decision-making centres will, if only on a random basis, produce outputs that are incompatible. Conflict, in common parlance, occurs when there are no mutually acceptable means for dealing with such random or, indeed, intended incompatibilities and a 'real' conflict relationship therefore develops. Conflict can occur between any two decision-making centres whether individuals, states, an individual and a state and the like. Clearly the nature of the actor will be important since individuals cannot usually pursue their conflicts with armed forces and states can, but there will be much in common. For example, a parent deterring a child faces structural similarities with one state deterring another state in so far as there is a structural relationship in both instances between whatever is at stake, the sanction being threatened and the probability of the application of the sanction with such ensuing problems as credibility and communication.[11] Role behaviour by leaders in different sorts of conflicts such as communal conflict or industrial disputes are other examples of situations which have elements in common and the relevance of institutional factors can also readily be seen in alliances.

Integration studies provide another central theme. Integration involves a degree of collective action, based upon a value consensus, for the achievement of common goals in which the parties have long run expectations of mutually compatible and acceptable behaviour and in which the process is self-maintaining. Clearly in all integration (and disintegration) processes there is an organisational and institutional aspect whether it be between private individuals, citizens of a town or states. Integration is ubiquitous in that no actor can live in isolation so that the process of integration and disintegration provides an organising theme at all levels of society and between all 'disciplines' of the social sciences. A similar trend that has more recently come to the fore is that of development and not merely in the context of the so-called developing countries or at the community level since it also concerns the promotion of human values even at the expense of institutional values. However, it is in regard to developing countries that contemporary IGOs and INGOs have played a major role to the extent that 'developmentalism' has become a significant ideological justification for their work.[12]

A time-honoured quest is that for security. It can take two forms: the most usual interpretation is to consider security as being a situation in which an actor can, in the worst case of attack imaginable, still ensure its survival in an acceptable way. This type of security predicates threat and seeks to parry it. In so doing it has a proclivity to be self-defeating since, on the basis of worst case analysis, one man's preparations to ensure security may be seen as a threat by another man. The second form of security comes not through separation but through association.[13] In an associative security system the parties are mutually, effectively, but not necessarily equally, balanced in their dependences to the degree that an actor can ill-afford to ignore the interests of others, for to do so would put its own interests at peril. Ideally each actor would have a valued and valuable role to play in the systems of transactions of its choice and thus it would have little incentive, because of mutual dependences, to cut off its nose to spite its face. When they are successful such systems of security go unnoticed since they are not defined as such even though, in effect, they provide security.

Security through association is linked to a further focal point in the study of world society — that of the search for identity. Increasing awareness of ethnic or communal characteristics is a feature of our age. It reflects a quest for identity. Ethnic and communal awareness can, but need not, give rise to antagonism. Being different has no inherent connotation of 'better' or 'worse', although it is often construed to mean not just 'better for us' but 'better' in a seemingly objective sense. The latter situation usually arises in response to a perceived rejection. Without a sense of identity there is likely to be no notion of self or no self-respect. However, a sense of identity arises from a meaningful relationship with others. If such a relationship does not exist or has been destroyed then deviant behaviour can be expected whether in the case of adolescents or the Japan of the inter-war period. In such circumstances differences take on the appearance of 'better' or 'worse'. Mutual dependencies, if they are legitimised, thus create a much valued sense of identity as well as a sense of security. Institutional forms that are both open and participatory are also a supportive feature for the expression of identity and therefore a means of facilitating non-deviant behaviour.

Exclusive institutions have the opposite and deleterious effect.

In considering these nodal points in the world society approach it is at once evident that to abandon a self-imposed restriction to inter-state relations and disciplinary boundaries is to create new perspectives. They are as different as looking at Mt. Blanc from an airliner and looking at it from the shores of Lake Geneva or from Chamonix. The same mountain appears to be different from each perspective. The world society approach has the same effect. No longer is the mountain of social science viewed from the perspective of Economics, Psychology or International Relations, but it is considered in an adisciplinary manner concentrating on problems such as development, security or authority. Moreover, while due attention must be paid to the validity of transferring findings from one context to another, the appropriate question concerns the relevant unit of analysis or system rather than the level of analysis to which the research will be linked.

Implications for international organisation and institutions
In viewing these new perspectives some passing remarks have been offered on their implications for international organisation and institutions. This is a topic that must now more fully occupy the attention. How do the approaches analysed in the central section of this volume reflect these developments in the study of world society? Co-operation is clearly an approach to be used where states are the main actors or gatekeepers. It is a method which protects sovereignty. To a lesser degree this is also true of association since, apart from interim arrangements, the intention is that those areas not covered by the association agreement shall remain exclusively within the province of the associate or the IGO concerned. This is, for example, the case of Finland and EFTA. The federal approach, where the rigidity of the constitutional division of competences and its territorial basis reinforces 'states' right', is not dissimilar. It might be thought that parallel national action would serve a like purpose, but this is not so since it is closer to harmonisation or co-ordination. Parallel action also enhances participation to the extent that national governments, bureaucracies, parties and pressure groups can play an integral part in promoting or rejecting the activity being contemplated. The state is still a gatekeeper, as with harmonisation and co-ordination, but there is a freedom to join or not on each issue and transnational groups political, bureaucratic and private can organise on pan-regional lines thus to a certain extent by-passing the state structure. Neo-functionalism could be seen as a step further in the de-thronment of

the state, but neofunctionalism is really federalism by instalments. Competences are transferred function by function to a 'supranational' body which will eventually become a new state. After parallel national action the next step towards a theory of organisation most ressembling the world society approach is the notion of a 'commonwealth' in which there are extensive arrangements for managing relations between the various actors in the system. Governments are not challenged directly but other actors apart from states play roles which can ultimately constrain governments. The same may be said *a fortiori* of functionalism. The functionalist approach is to by-pass state structures by making form follow function. It is thus very much in line with the world society approach, although it was, of course, developed before it. Even more apposite from the world society point of view are networks. Anthony Judge uses the notion of network to describe a psycho-social system engendered by and giving rise to flows of transactions between nodes and the 'evolution of the network itself over time in response to new challenges and opportunities'.[14] This could also be a description of the systems thinking that lies in the heart of the world society approach.

At this point one of the advantages of the world society approach bears reiteration. The world society approach does not replace the traditional conceptual frameworks of International Relations with a new conceptual framework. Rather, it supplements them and in seeking to incorporate them into a broader framework its aspirations are holistic. It is not that inter-state power politics have been abolished, but merely that they are part of a greater social fabric which they influence and by which they are influenced. Forms of international organisation and institutions more appropriate to the traditional model are an integral part of world society and a valid subject for research. But networks must not be neglected either, since the world society conceptual framework indicates that they too may be important.

Other modes of institutionalisation

The analysis of conceptual approaches to international organisation and institutions in this volume is far from complete. This final section recognises some of these omissions by referring to some of the other approaches to be found in the literature such as interdependence, anarchism, collective goods and regionalism. The notion of interdependence is something more than a placebo enunciated by politicians at Heads of Government meetings (and particularly those connected with the non-socialist world's economic difficulties). It can also be used as an analytical tool to describe a relationship. Factors to be considered include bilateral, multilateral, direct or indirect inter-dependence; the volume, intensity and complexity of the relationship; the degree to which it is tight, loose, overlapping or separate; its substance, procedures and structures.[15] Questions can also be asked regarding the degree to which interdependence masks imperialism. The concept of interdependence can be applied either in the traditional state-centric model or in a world society framework. It can, moreover, be an instrument of power politics or of legitimised politics. Unfortunately the generality of its application limits its usefulness since the categories into which it can be divided do not differentiate phenomena sufficiently clearly to be useful and there is a tendency to relate everything to everything else thereby frustrating the purpose of analysis. In these circumstances concepts such as parallel national action or commonwealth may be more useful tools of analysis.

Anarchism is a proposal for organisation without institutions. It has more than a little in common with functionalism and networks in that, while relationships are not eschewed and some element of organisation is therefore inevitable, the institutional encumbrances are kept to a minimum. Contemporary anarchistic thought does not appear to encompass world society. Rather it is concerned with the micro level and presumes that the whole is more-of-the-same — a simple aggregation of parts — linked where and when necessary by *ad hoc* arrangements on a basis of the most absolute freedom.[16] Nevertheless, anarchism, along with networks and functionalism, does accord with the world society concepts of an emphasis on systemic transactions, changing levels of analysis and great responsiveness to demands for change. Its weakness lies in its lack of intellectual rigour, the absence of a macro theory of anarchism and, therefore, its lack of practicality since while communes can flourish successfully on anarchistic lines on the fringes of society they are frequently dependent on the existence of that society for their ability to survive and flourish.

Anarchists despise private property because of the effect its possession has on society and the individual and they therefore encourage the free use of assets. However, to a certain degree we are all anarchists in the sense that collective goods exist at all levels of organisation. Russett and Sullivan have outlined cogently the theory of collective goods in the context of international organisation.[17] There are some assets from which it is not feasible to exclude particular actors and others for which the enjoyment by one actor does not lead to the diminution of satisfaction or opportunity for others. Examples of this are free medical care in the U.K. for everyone in Britain regardless of nationality or any other qualification and the provision of security for all in a defence unit. A collective good is thus a public good and 'increasingly even the nation-state can no longer provide desired benefits because of the ever-greater collective goods properties between nations'.[18] Since there appears to be a growth in the number, variety and importance of collective goods due in part to the 'shrinking world', a parallel need for organisation and institutions to facilitate this growth is evident. The functionalist mode of organisation accords well with this and it fits equally well into the world society framework.

Collective goods are an aspect of the 'one-world' problems that have become a feature of the work of international institutions in the seventies. Population, food, the environment, the oceans, outer space — even women — have all been examples. Although the problems may be 'one-world' problems, they do not, however, affect the relevant actors in world society equally, nor are there any 'one-world' answers readily apparent. These problems provide an admirable test for the relevance of the models considered in this chapter and for the conceptual approaches to international organisation and institutions which are the subject of this book. It may well be that some 'one-world' problems will have several answers of a regional character, for example, a law of the North Sea and adjacent areas, which will give a new fillip to one major approach that has not been considered in this volume, namely, regionalism.

Regionalism as a theory of organisation came to the fore with the UN Charter. Indeed, the Charter is imbued with it not only in the chapter (VIII) specifically devoted to the approach but also in the chapters devoted to security and to economic questions. The motivations for this were mixed, especially on the part of the veto-Powers. For example, regionalism encompasses the Monroe Doctrine, which had been specifically sanctified in the League of Nations Covenant. But there were other motivations. The UN was intended to be virtually universal in membership, but its members did not always have universal interests. It was felt, therefore, that it would be sensible to allow regional consideration of questions of less than universal interest, at least initially, provided that this was done in accordance with the principles of the Charter. The assumption was that member sates in the same geographical region would share interests, have the knowledge appropriate for the consideration of the questions under discussion and an element of goodwill towards their neighbours. Empiric ally, of course, these assumptions are not well-founded. Equally it was hoped that such bodies would give the small states an opportunity to make

447

their views felt, but this might (and did) prove illusory as in the cases of the OAS, which was dominated by the United States, and the Arab League which was set up at British prompting in order to facilitate the British hegemonial role in the Middle East. There were also those who advocated regional institutions as a step towards world government. While it was admittedly unrealistic to attempt to destroy the state-system and establish a world government in the immediate future, it was the hope of advocates of world government that regionalism would prove to be the precursor of universalism and that success at the regional level would be a prelude to success at the world level and give rise to a world government.

As the regional institutions of the postwar period were set up they began to fall into two categories — the associative and the dis-associative.[19] Associative institutions are open to all in the region and to any outsiders who can lay a reasonable claim to a functional interest in the region. For example, the USA, as a non-European Power but an occupying Power in Germany, joined the Economic Commission for Europe and Switzerland, a non-member of the UN, also became a *de facto* and then a *de jure* member. However, some regional bodies do not seek to accommodate all states within the geographical region in their work. Indeed, they act as a vehicle for co-ordinating action against other states in the geographical region, as for example, in the cases of the OAU and the RSA, the Arab League and Israel, the Council of Europe and the socialist and dictatorial countries and the OAS and Cuba where Cuba was actually expelled mainly at the behest of the United States when the Castro regime adopted a Marxist orientation. In this case a regional body, rather than facilitating accommodation, promoted confrontation. It is not the only example for institutions such as NATO are no more than alliances directed against non-member states. However, one aspect is common to all these bodies: they are all inter-governmental and have in practice not succeeded in creating supranational institutions that have stood the test of time. They are thus state-centric and can therefore be readily accommodated under the rubrics of co-operation, harmonization, coordination or, at the most, parallel national action or commonwealth.

In the last two decades regionalism has taken on two further diverse aspects. Beginning with the European Economic Community several attempts have been made to bring about regional integration on neo-functionalist lines. The basis is still a geographical region but the goal is no longer inter-governmental co-operation, rather it is supra-national integration, possibly in a federal mould, using the tactic of functional instalments. However, such developments, whether in Europe, Latin America or Africa, do not depend for their success or failure exclusively or even mainly on geographical propinquity and so they can be more appropriately classified under the neo-functionalist rubric.

The second new element in regionalism has arisen from the collapse of the colonial empires. Regional institutions were often created to fulfill the functional role that the institutions of Empire had formerly served. Where the colonial Powers had treated several territories as one for a particular purpose the newly-independent governments often considered it useful to continue the arrangements through a regional body. The East African Common Services Organisation is a case in point. In addition, while proud of their independence and wishing to savour it fully, the new governments were also willing to acknowledge a symbolic feeing of regional solidarity which had been difficult to express under colonial hegemony but which, nevertheless, had constituted a moral, ideological and sometimes practical support during the move towards independence. This is particularly true of pan-African and pan-Arab bodies which, in some cases, have developed an instrumental as well as symbolic role.

Although the region has been a fashionable mode of institutionalisation since the Second World War, conceptually such institutions can more properly be categorised in ways other than by region. So far no definition of a region has been given although the literature abounds in such definitions.[20] It is abusing the commonsense meaning of the term to envisage it in any other way than primarily as a geographical entity. If the theory is to be of interest to the student of international organisation and institutions its advocates must be able to demonstrate that geographical variables are a prime influence on behaviour. Clearly geographical variables are often of some influence but there seems to be little empirical evidence in the literature to suggest that they should be made the great organising factor. There appear to be no multi-dimensional geographical regions: indeed, region may only be a useful organising concept within a particular functional dimension such as health, where geographical variables play an important role. Perhaps practitioners and scholars alike are the victims of images built up from childhood of the maps of the continents of the world that so often adorn the classroom wall. But geographical propinquity can mislead: could any two groups be closer in a wide variety of dimensions yet geographically so distant as Britain and New Zealand? Regional institutions are, nevertheless, focal points of behaviour and therefore grist to the mill, but regionalism appears to be a barren doctrine and

449

the phenomena that it seeks to describe can better be studied using other conceptual frameworks.

There is no intention in this volume generally to make value judgements concerning various modes of organisation. In many cases there is no one royal road to the good life; each must find his own way. However, in the contemporary world organisational forms that maximise participation and flexibility seem to be valued, to thrive and to prosper, while those that protect institutional values rather than respond to felt needs all too often become the cause of conflict or wither on the vine. But there is no empirical evidence that can justify dogmatism. In a society which is experiencing rapid change in almost every field of endeavour simple prudence suggests that everything possible should be done to promote variety in the conceptualisation of organisation and its institutional forms. Since the direction of change is uncertain the suitability of one or another concept or form cannot be vouchsafed. However, by casting the mind as widely as possible a better response to the challenges of change may be found. If this volume has contributed in the smallest way to that purpose it will have achieved its goal.

Notes

1. More recently the usual assumption of intra-state consensus has come to be doubted too.
2. See J.W. Burton, A.J.R. Groom, C.R. Mitchell and A.V.S. de Reuck, *The Study of World Society*, Pittsburgh, International Studies Assocation, Occasional Paper No. 1 for a more detailed analysis.
3. See Kenneth N. Waltz, *Man, the State and War*, London, Columbia University Press, 1959, and J. David Singer, 'The Level-of-Analysis Problem in International Relations' in Klaus Knorr and Sidney Verba (eds.), *The International System: Theoretical Essays*, Princeton, Princeton University Press, 1961.
4. See Burton et al, *op. cit.*, pp. 57 et seq., and for a discussion of operationalisation, see A.J.R. Groom, 'Conflict Analysis and the Arab-Israeli Conflict' in James Barber, Josephine Negro and Michael Smith (eds.), *Politics between states: conflict and cooperation*, Milton Keynes, Open University Press, 1975.
5. Thomas Kuhn has shown us how and why these changes occur and Karl Deutsch has summarised the actual changes. See Thomas S. Kuhn, *The Strucutre of Scientific Revolutions*, London, University of Chicago Press, 1970, 2nd edition enlarged and Karl W. Deutsch, *The Nerves of Government*, London, Collier-Macmillan, 1963 and especially Part One.
6. See R.W. Cox and H.K. Jacobson et al, *The Anatomy of Influence*, London, Yale University Press, 1973.
7. Deutsch, *op. cit.*
8. See Deutsch, *op. cit.*, pp. 221−2 in which he spells out these factors as (i) loss of power, i.e. resources vis-à-vis the environment, (ii) loss of intake,

i.e. contact with the environment, (iii) loss of steering capacity, i.e. of control and ability to modify behaviour, (iv) loss of depth of memory and quality of memory, (v) loss of capacity for partial inner arrangement, i.e. rigidity, (vi) loss of capacity for fundamental rearrangement of inner structure.

9. Participation is conceived as a situation in which an actor deems itself to be playing an appropriate role in a decision-making process on terms that are acceptable to it in systems of transactions chosen by it.
10. David Mitrany, *A Working Peace System*, Chicago, Quadrangle, 1966, pp. 64–5.
11. See A.J.R. Groom, *Strategy in the Modern World*, forthcoming.
12. See R.W. Cox and H.K. Jacobson, *op. cit.*, pp. 404, 425.
13. See A.J.R. Groom, 'Security by Association: Western Europe, The Arab World and the Super Powers', *Contemporary Review*, August 1975.
14. Anthony Judge, 'Network: The Need for a New Concept', *International Associations*, No. 3, 1974, p. 170.
15. This list is taken from Herbert J. Spiro, 'Interdependence: A Third Option between Sovereignty and Supranational Integration' in Ghita Ionescu (ed.), *Between Sovereignty and Integration*, London, Croom Helm, 1974, p. 148.
16. See April Carter, *The Political Theory of Anarchism*, London, Routledge and Kegan Paul, 1971.
17. This paragraph is based on Bruce M. Russett and John D. Sullivan, 'Collective Goods and International Organization' in Edwin H. Fedder (ed.), *The United Nations: Problems and Prospects*, St. Louis, University of Missouri Centre of International Studies, 1971.
18. *Ibid.*, p. 95.
19. See J.W. Burton, 'Regionalism, Functionalism and the United Nations', *Australian Outlook*, Vol. 15, 1961.
20. See for example, W.R. Thompson, 'Regional Subsystem: A Conceptual and a Propositional Inventory', *International Studies Quarterly*, March 1973.

Selected Reading

1. J.W. Burton, *World Society*, London, Cambridge University Press, 1972.
2. J.W. Burton, A.J.R. Groom, C.R. Mitchell and A.V.S. de Reuck, *The Study of World Society: A London Perspective*, Pittsburgh, International Studies Association Occasional Paper No. 1, 1974.
3. Joseph S. Nye and Robert O. Keohane (eds.), 'Transnational Relations and World Politics', *International Organisation*, Summer, 1971, Special Issue.
4. James N. Rosenau (ed.), *Linkage Politics*, London, Collier-Macmillan, 1969.

BIOGRAPHICAL NOTES

George Codding is Professor of Political Science at the University of Colorado. He has held office in several academic associations in the USA and has acted as consultant to the ITU and to UNESCO. He has written many articles and his monographs include: *The International Tele-communication Union* (reissued in 1972 by Arno Press), *The Universal Postal Union* (New York University Press, 1964), *The Federal Government of Switzerland* (George Allen & Unwin) and *Governing the Commune of Veyrier*.

Leon Gordenker is Professor of Politics and Faculty Associate of the Center of International Studies at Princeton University. His most recent book is *International Aid and National Decisions* (Princeton, Princeton University Press, 1976).

A.J.R. Groom has taught International Relations at University College London since 1965 where he is also associated with the Centre for the Analysis of Conflict. His *British Thinking About Nuclear Weapons* was published by Frances Pinter in 1974 and he has edited several other volumes and contributed articles to journals and symposia in several countries including *World Politics, International Affairs, Political Studies, Journal of Common Market Studies, Round Table, British Journal of International Studies* and Swiss, Yugoslav, Canadian and Austrian journals. His interests include theory of international relations, strategy and conflict as well as international organisation.

R.J. Harrison was educated in England and the United States. He taught International Politics at Victoria University of Wellington from 1957–67, and was a well-known broadcaster and television commentator on international affairs in New Zealand. Following a developing interest in European integration, he returned to England in 1967 and is now Senior Lecturer at Lancaster University, teaching European government, Community politics and integration theory. His articles and reviews on integration have appeared in *Political Science, Politique Etrangère, Revue du Marché Commun, Political Studies* and the *Journal of Common Market Studies*. His recent book, *Europe in Question* (Allen & Unwin, 1974) is an exposition and critique of contemporary theories of regional integration and his *Comparative Politics of Advanced Industrial Societies* is to appear in 1978.

A.J.N. Judge has an academic background in Chemical Engineering (London) and Management (Capetown). Since 1962 he has been connected with the Union of International Associations in Brussels where he is now Assistant Secretary General. He has written numerous articles and reports on the inter-relationship between the network of international organisations and the design of the information systems on which they depend. He is closely associated with the UIA's *Yearbook of International Organisations* and *Yearbook of World Problems*.

John N. Kinnas studied Political Science in Athens and International Relations at University College London, where he received his Ph.D. His academic interests centre on international organisation and the analysis of foreign policy on which he has published monographs in Greek and contributed extensively to Greek learned journals.

Abdul S. Minty is a South African. He came to Britain in 1958 to continue with his studies. He is a founder member of the Anti-Apartheid Movement in London and is its Honorary Secretary. He has represented AAM at various international conferences and addressed various United Nations Committees. He has been invited to give evidence to the United Nations Security Council on three occasions as an individual expert. From 1970 Abdul S. Minty has been a Research fellow of the Richardson Institute for Conflict and Peace Research and has been working on South Africa's Foreign and Defence Policies. He has written various articles and reports on South Africa's defence policies and is the author of *South Africa's Defence Strategy*, (London, AAM, 1969) and *Apartheid: A Threat to Peace*, (London, Anti-Apartheid Movement, 1976).

Stuart Mungall is a graduate student in the Department of Government, Manchester University. He received his B.A. degree from Lancaster University. His special interests are European Integration and the problems of Post-Industrial Societies.

Gunnar P. Nielsson is Assistant Professor in International Relations at the University of Southern California in Los Angeles. Born in Denmark, he received all his university education in the United States, doing post-graduate work as a Woodrow Wilson Fellow at the University of California at Berkeley (M.A.) and the University of California at Los Angeles (Ph.D.). He was the Director of the University of Southern California's post-graduate International Relations Program in the United

Kingdom for six years. His special interest is in international relations theory, organisation, integration and European international politics.

P.R. Saunders graduated from the University of California, Irvine, and is a doctoral candidate in politics at Princeton University. He has been a Fellow of the University Consortium for World Order Studies and is John Parker Compton Fellow in the Center of International Studies at Princeton.

Mihály Simai graduated at the University of Economics, Budapest, Hungary in 1952. M.A. in Economics, 1957. Ph.D. in Economics, 1962. Doctor of Economic Sciences (given by the Hungarian Academy of Sciences), 1971. Elected as a Correspondent Member of the Hungarian Academy of Sciences, 1976. Past positions include: Advisor to the Hungarian Bank of Investments, 1958–1964. Member of the U.N. Staff (Economic Affairs), 1964–68. He is now Professor of International Economics (since 1969) and Deputy Director of the Institute of World Economics (since 1973). He has been Editor of the periodical *Valosag* (Reality) since 1969. His books include: *Towards the Third Milleneum* (Budapest, 1971, 1976), *U.S. Before the 200th Anniversary* (Budapest, 1975), *Planning and the Plan Implementation in the Developing Countries* (Budapest, 1974), *Foreign Trade and Central Planning* (Joint Editor, Cambridge, U.K., 1971), *Encyclopedia on the Developing Countries* (Joint Editor, Budapest, 1974). He has been President of the World Federation of U.N. Associations, a member of the Governing Board of the International Peace Institute in Vienna, and has occupied senior positions in a number of national academic associations.

Yashpal Tandon, presently Professor of Political Science and International Relations at the University of Dar es Salaam, took his degrees at the London School of Economics. He taught at Makerere University, Uganda, from 1964 to 1972, during which time he also served as Executive Director of the Carnegie Endowment Institute in Diplomacy (1965–69) and as Executive Director of the Makerere Institute of Social Research (1971–72). He also taught at the London School of Economics (1972–73) and was a Senior Research Fellow at Columbia University, New York (1967–68). He is the author of several articles on international relations and the political economy of Africa and has edited *Readings on African International Relations* (1972, 1974) and *Technical Assistance Administration in East Africa* (1974). He is the Chief Editor of *Utafiti*, the journal of the Faculty of

Arts and Social Science at Dar es Salaam, and on the Editorial Board of several other journals.

Paul Taylor has written extensively on international relations theory, particularly integration theory, and on the European Communities. His articles have appeared in numerous journals, in Britain and in the U.S.A., including *World Politics, Political Studies,* the *Journal of Common Market Studies* and *Orbis,* He is also the author of *International Cooperation Today* (Elek, 1971) and Co-Editor, with A.J.R. Groom of *Functionalism: Theory and Practice in International Relations* (University of London Press, 1975). He has taught International Relations at the London School of Economics since 1966.

INDEX